ROME AND PERSIA IN LATE ANTIQUITY

The foundation of the Sasanian Empire in AD 224 established a formidable new power on the Roman Empire's Eastern frontier, and relations over the next four centuries proved turbulent. This book provides a chronological narrative of their relationship, supported by a substantial collection of translated sources illustrating important themes and structural patterns. The political goals of the two sides, their military confrontations and their diplomatic solutions are discussed, as well as the common interests between the two powers. Special attention is given to the situation of Arabia and Armenia, to economic aspects, the protection of the frontiers, the religious life in both empires and the channels of communication between East and West. In its wide chronological scope, the study explores the role played by the Sasanians in the history of the ancient Near East. The book will prove invaluable for students and non-specialists interested in late antiquity and early Byzantium, and it will be equally useful for specialists on these subjects.

BEATE DIGNAS is Fellow and Tutor in Ancient History at Somerville College, Oxford. Her recent publications include *Economy of the Sacred in Hellenistic and Roman Asia Minor* (2002) and she has edited a forthcoming book *Practitioners of the Divine: Greek Priests and Religious Officials from Homer to Heliodorus*.

ENGELBERT WINTER is Professor of Ancient History at the University of Münster. He has participated in numerous field surveys and excavations in Turkey and published many books and articles on Roman–Persian relations and the history and culture of Asia Minor.

ROME AND PERSIA IN LATE ANTIQUITY

Neighbours and Rivals

BEATE DIGNAS AND ENGELBERT WINTER

CAMBRIDGE
UNIVERSITY PRESS

CAMBRIDGE UNIVERSITY PRESS
Cambridge, New York, Melbourne, Madrid, Cape Town, Singapore, São Paulo

Cambridge University Press
The Edinburgh Building, Cambridge CB2 8RU, UK

Published in the United States of America by Cambridge University Press, New York

www.cambridge.org
Information on this title: www.cambridge.org/9780521614078

Originally published in German as *Rom und das Perserreich: Zwei Weltmächte zwischen Konfrontation und Koexistenz* by Akademie Verlag GmBH, Berlin 2001, and © Akademie Verlag 2001

First published in English by Cambridge University Press 2007 as
Rome and Persia in Late Antiquity: Neighbours and Rivals

English edition © Cambridge University Press 2007

Printed in the United Kingdom at the University Press, Cambridge

A catalogue record for this publication is available from the British Library

ISBN   978-0-521-84925-8 hardback
ISBN   978-0-521-61407-8 paperback

Contents

Figures

Maps

Preface

In 2001 our *Rom und das Perserreich. Zwei Weltmächte zwischen Konfrontation und Koexistenz* was published by the Akademie Verlag, Berlin. Naturally, comments made by friends and colleagues as well as academic reviews encouraged us to think further about the issues of our book and also about its place among textbooks and scholarly works. We are hoping that *Rome and Persia in Late Antiquity: Neighbours and Rivals*, a revised and expanded translation, is an adequate response to the many suggestions we have received since 2001, among these the observation that our book did not have a counterpart in the English language that would correspond to its scope and format.

Even more than the German volume, the present study of Roman–Sasanian relations has been guided by our attempt to focus on the interests and independent policies of the eastern power. In reaction to the conventional and still prevalent eurocentric perspective of many scholarly works we emphasise the Eastern textual and visual testimonies. We have done so with the help of Ph. Huyse (Paris), who translated crucial passages from the trilingual Šāpūr Inscription (the Parthian text) as well as the inscriptions of the Zoroastrian priest Kartēr (Middle Persian) into English for us. Petra Sijpesteijn (Oxford) helped us with the translation of excerpts from Arabic texts and David Taylor (Oxford) with the Syriac texts. Thank you!

We have expanded our study by including a new chapter on the role of Armenia (**26**). Here, we are grateful to Tim Greenwood (St Andrew's), who not only translated the Armenian passages but also gave patient advice on the interpretation of the material. Moreover, the new book has chapters on Sasanian warfare (II.2) and on the relationship between rulers (II.8). We have also paid more attention to aspects of diplomacy and religion during the late phase of Roman–Sasanian relations.

It has been a pleasure to work with Cambridge University Press. We would like to thank Michael Sharp for accepting the book for publication, and Sarah Parker and Elizabeth Davey for their support and guidance during all stages of the production. Last but not least, Linda Woodward's copy-editing has been thorough, extremely helpful and efficient.

Oxford/Münster

BEATE DIGNAS
AND ENGELBERT WINTER

Abbreviations

AA	*Archäologischer Anzeiger*
AAG. Ph.-h. Kl.	*Abhandlungen der Akademie der Wissenschaften zu Göttingen*
AAntHung	*Acta Antiqua Academiae Scientiarum Hungaricae*
AAAS	*Les annales archéologiques arabs syriennes*
AAWW	*Anzeiger der Österreichischen Akademie der Wissenschaften in Wien. Philologisch-historische Klasse*
AchHist	*Achaemenid History*
ActIr	*Acta Iranica*
AHB	*The Ancient History Bulletin*
AJA	*American Journal of Archaeology*
AJPh	*American Journal of Philology*
AMI	*Archäologische Mitteilungen aus Iran*
AnalBolland	*Analecta Bollandiana*
AncSoc	*Ancient Society*
ANRW	*Aufstieg und Niedergang der Römischen Welt*
AnTard	*Antiquité Tardive*
ArOr	*Archív Orientální*
AW	*Antike Welt*
BASOR	*Bulletin of the American Schools of Oriental Research*
BCHI	*Bastan Chenasi va Honar-e Iran. Revue d'archéologie d'art iraniens*
BHAC	*Bonner Historia Augusta Colloquium*
BJb	*Bonner Jahrbücher*
BMGS	*Byzantine and Modern Greek Studies*
BSAC	*Bulletin de la Société d'Archéologie Copte*
BSO(A)S	*Bulletin of the School of Oriental (from vol. 10 ff. and African) Studies*

ByzF	Byzantinische Forschungen. Internationale Zeitschrift für Byzantinistik
ByzZ	Byzantinische Zeitschrift
CAH	The Cambridge Ancient History, Volumes I–XIV
CFHB	Corpus Fontium Historiae Byzantinae
CHI	The Cambridge History of Iran, Volumes I–VIII
CHR	Catholic Historical Review
CIL	Corpus Inscriptionum Latinarum
CP	Classical Philology
CQ	Classical Quarterly
CSCO	Corpus Scriptorum Christianorum Orientalium
CSHB	Corpus Scriptorum Historiae Byzantinae
DNP	Der Neue Pauly
DOP	Dumbarton Oaks Papers
EA	Epigraphica Anatolica. Zeitschrift für Epigraphik und historische Geographie Anatoliens
EHR	English Historical Review
EI	Encyclopaedia of Islam
EncIr	Encyclopaedia Iranica
EOS	Atti del Colloquio Internazionale AIEGL su Epigrafia e Ordine Senatorio: Roma, 14–20 maggio 1981
E&W	East and West
G&R	Greece and Rome
GRBS	Greek, Roman and Byzantine Studies
HAW	Handbuch der Altertumswissenschaften
HdO	Handbuch der Orientalistik
IF	Indogermanische Forschungen
IrAnt	Iranica Antiqua
JA	Journal Asiatique
JbAC	Jahrbuch für Antike und Christentum
JDAI	Jahrbuch des Deutschen Archäologischen Instituts
JHS	Journal of Hellenic Studies
JNES	Journal of Near Eastern Studies
JNG	Jahrbuch für Numismatik und Geldgeschichte
JRA	Journal of Roman Archaeology
JRAS	Journal of the Royal Asiatic Society
JRS	Journal of Roman Studies
JSAI	Jerusalem Studies in Arabic and Islam
LMA	Lexikon des Mittelalters
MBAH	Münstersche Beiträge zur antiken Handelsgeschichte

MH	*Museum Helveticum*
NC	*Numismatic Chronicle*
NZ	*Numismatische Zeitschrift*
OCP	*Orientalia Christiana Periodica*
OLP	*Orientalia Lovaniensia Periodica*
OrChr	*Oriens Christianus*
PLRE	*Prosopography of the Later Roman Empire*
PSAS	*Proceedings of the Seminar for Arabian Studies*
QC	*Quaderni catanesi di studi classici e medievali*
RAC	*Reallexikon für Antike und Christentum. Sachwörterbuch zur Auseinandersetzung des Christentums mit der antiken Welt*
RE	*Pauly-Wissowa Realencyclopädie der classischen Altertumswissenschaft*
REA	*Revue des Études Anciennes*
REB	*Revue des Études Byzantines*
REtArm	*Revue des Études Arméniennes*
RevBibl	*Revue Biblique*
RGG	K. Galling, *Die Religion in Geschichte und Gegenwart. Handwörterbuch für Theologie und Religionswissenschaft.* 7 vols., 1957–65.
RhM	*Rheinisches Museum für Philologie*
RIC	H. Mattingly, *The Roman Imperial Coinage.* 10 vols., 1923–94.
RIDA	*Revue internationale des droits de l'antiquité*
RstorAnt	*Rivista storica dell'antichità*
SBAW	*Sitzungsberichte der Bayerischen Akademie der Wissenschaften*
ŠKZ	*Inscription of Šāpūr I at the Ka'ba-i Zardušt in Naqš-ī Rustam*
StIr	*Studia Iranica*
TALANTA	*Talanta. Proceedings of the Dutch Archaeological and Historical Society*
TAPhA	*Transactions and Proceedings of the American Philological Association*
TAVO	*Tübinger Atlas des Vorderen Orients*
TravMem	*Travaux et mémoires. Centre de recherche d'histoire et civilisation byzantine*

WJA	*Würzburger Jahrbücher für die Altertumswissenschaft*
YCS	*Yale Classical Studies*
ZDMG	*Zeitschrift der Deutschen Morgenländischen Gesellschaft*
ZKG	*Zeitschrift für Kirchengeschichte*
ZPE	*Zeitschrift für Papyrologie und Epigraphik*

Introduction: West and East, friend and foe, counterpart and mirror image . . .

Relations between Romans and Persians in late antiquity were bound to be turbulent, to say the least. We are looking at those who conquered the possessions of the heirs of Alexander the Great versus those who claimed to be the heirs of the Achaemenid Empire, which was conquered by Alexander the Great. 'Heritage' and its claims often foreshadow war, in this case centuries of warfare that lasted throughout the existence of the relationship between the two powers, i.e. the third to the seventh century AD. On both sides war was accompanied by complex attempts to justify their respective goals, in both active and reactive ways. Rome's claim for world domination was accompanied by a sense of mission and pride in Western civilisation; it was met by Eastern myths and oracles prophesying the downfall of the Western power.[1] Our sources reflect strong Roman ambitions to become a guarantor of peace and order.[2] Simultaneously, they reflect long-standing prejudices with regard to the Eastern power's different customs, religious structures, languages and forms of government. As a consequence, a wide gap separated the two cultures and negative attitudes that stemmed from existing political, military and economic rivalries were constantly reinforced. In the company of most ancient – and often Western – observers, it is tempting to associate our theme with an 'everlasting' conflict between West and East, between a 'civilised' Roman world and a barbarian enemy, and hence to describe the struggle between the two super powers as a clash of fundamentally alien cultures.[3]

This approach is a phenomenon that applies not only to antiquity but also to the present day, possibly more than ever before. The world of the

---

[1] See e.g. *Or. Sib.* 3. 350–5; on these examples of the Sibylline oracles, which originated in a Jewish context from the second half of the first century onwards, see Gauger 1998: 440–51; for references on the intellectual context of this source see ibid. 543–4; cf. also Potter 1990; Fuchs 1964.

[2] Winter 1998: 46–65.

[3] On the evolution and tradition of the term *barbaros* see Speyer 1992: 811–95; Hall 1989 and on the latter Metzler 1992/3: 215–23; on the tendency towards Eurocentrism in classical scholarship see Hauser 2001b: 83–104.

I

'Oriental' appears alien to those of us who represent the 'Occident' and its tradition. However, in the face of progressing technology, new forms of communication and an increasing globalisation in the social, political, cultural and economic realms, the necessity and willingness to welcome the 'other' has taken on new dimensions. The attempt to understand the character and characteristics of a different culture has to include the ability to relieve tensions in a peaceful way, by way of dialogue and negotiation, explanation and reflection. This cannot happen unless the relations between West and East are based on a foundation that shows respect for the history of the East and does not shape this history according to Western needs. By adopting this wider perspective, i.e. by looking beyond a Graeco-Roman antiquity, we avoid an approach that makes us juxtapose supposedly relevant and irrelevant, central and peripheral cultures.

These prerogatives bear on a study that focuses on the relations between Rome and the Sasanian Empire founded in 224. Deliberately, the following chapters do not only convey information regarding Roman–Sasanian contacts and conflicts but also examine the role the Sasanians played in the history of the eastern part of the ancient world. The nature of our source material favours an emphasis on Roman history and often leads us to notice historical developments in other regions only insofar as they bear on Roman interests. However, apart from the fact that from the third century onwards the history of Rome was mainly shaped by the relations with its Eastern neighbour it is necessary to address social and political developments outside the Roman sphere of influence in their own right. Moreover, it is not justified to limit one's focus on armed conflicts and to assume that an Eastern perspective on Roman–Sasanian relations did not exist beyond aspects of military strategy, or that it cannot be assessed.[4] Rome and Persia interacted consistently and shared many points of interest with regard to trade, the protection of the frontiers, cultural and religious policies. These frequent and intensive contacts characterised the relations between the two throughout the period. On multiple levels the Sasanians pursued active goals in their dealings with the West, which forced the Romans to be extremely vigilant and evoked strategic as well as political reactive measures on their side. Ironically, pointing to Persian ambitions and ideologies of domination may also be perceived as a eurocentric perspective, assigning one-sided aggression to the East. This is certainly not intended but it is rather the case that the Roman ideological background is

---

[4] See e.g. Wirth 1980/1: 306–7.

much better known to the reader. It is the goal of this book to illuminate the much less-known Persian position and thereby to enable the reader to contrast and compare in a more balanced way. The tradition of a 'pro-Roman' historical scholarship with all its ideological nuances and consequences has to be challenged and dismissed.[5] Aware that we are examining a period and topic that are not only under-studied but also loaded with sensitive actuality, we address both the 'unaware' as well as the 'too-aware' reader.

The scope of this study does not allow for a general analysis of or comparison between the two powers. Excellent works for background and further reading have been written, of which we suggest but a few. A. H. M. Jones' and A. Cameron's surveys of the later Roman Empire,[6] P. Brown's *The World of Late Antiquity*[7] and now S. Mitchell's *A History of the Later Roman Empire AD 284–641. The Transformation of the Ancient World* [8] provide the best outline of the whole period. The essays in the guide to *Late Antiquity* edited by G. Bowersock, P. Brown and O. Grabar[9] inform the interested reader on topics that are of much relevance for our context. The alphabetically listed entries in the second part of the same volume can be used as a reference work for specific terms and themes, people, places and institutions – much more exhaustive and detailed than the brief glossary at the end of this volume. For the period between 180 and 395, D. Potter's *The Roman Empire at Bay*[10] assesses the Roman situation well, focusing both on the structures of government and the Persian challenge in particular. For background reading on the history of Byzantium, the works of W. Treadgold[11] are highly recommended. On the Sasanian side the works by Wiesehöfer and Frye are outstanding introductions.[12] The Sasanian source material is well presented in Wiesehöfer, Yarshater 1983b and Howard-Johnston 1995b. In his excellent contribution to Cameron's *Byzantine and Early Islamic Near East*[13] J. Howard-Johnston compares the structures of both empires (with a closer focus on the Sasanian background).[14] The proceedings of an international colloquium on the relations between the Sasanian Empire and the Mediterranean World have now been published and include many important contributions.[15] For good discussions of the Roman East the

---

[5] J. Wiesehöfer's work represents this new approach in an exemplary way; see now his pointed analysis of the 'traditional Romanocentrism' in Gruen 2005: 105–20.

[6] Jones 1964; Cameron 1993a.   [7] 1971.   [8] 2006.   [9] 1999.   [10] 2004.

[11] 1997 and 2001.   [12] Above all Wiesehöfer 2001; Frye 1984.   [13] 1995.

[14] 1995b: 157–226; the chapter also provides an excellent overview of the Sasanian source material. See now also Howard-Johnston 2006.

[15] Wiesehöfer and Huyse 2006.

reader may also be referred to the works by Millar, Ball and Humphrey, as well as the relevant volumes of the *CAH* and the *CHI*.[16]

With regard to its theme, scope and focus on the source material, our book is closest to H. Dodgeon and S. Lieu's *The Roman Eastern Frontier and the Persian Wars AD 226–363. A Documentary History*[17] and its successor by G. Greatrex and S. Lieu (*Part II. AD 363–630*).[18] As it distinguishes itself from these superb sourcebooks in many ways, it complements and is complemented by them. The present volume intends to be neither a comprehensive sourcebook nor an analytical study of Sasanian Iran. We believe that the exemplary character of carefully selected passages and historical commentary make the material accessible to a wider readership and allow the readers to survey the relations between the two empires over a long period of time. Our detailed introductory and explicatory comments to each passage aim to assist an undergraduate and non-specialist audience, who, as we believe, are often not familiar with the majority of the quoted authors and texts, nor with the historical context. However, we are hoping that specialists on the subject also find the volume usable and readable from 'cover to cover'.

'The Fascinating Enemy' is the title of A. Nünnerich-Asmus' editorial preface in a recent issue of the *Antike Welt*[19] that focuses on 'Persia and Rome'. The expression captures the rich texture of Roman–Sasanian relations. An examination of not only the textual but also the visual evidence explains how the fascination with and competitive nature of the 'other' created a 'likeness' that influenced the relationship as much as one-sided concepts of cultural superiority. The many illustrations in our volume serve to illuminate the multi-layered character of self-representation and cultural exchange. The triumphal reliefs on both sides, to give but one example, are very similar in nature; although they are meant to convey a stark contrast between the respective victorious rulers and their enemies, they utilise the same techniques and share crucial symbols. As both pieces of art and means of political propaganda, these material sources form an essential part of our subject. The large number of maps are included to assist the reader with an immediate understanding of the events. They also remind us that

---

[16] Millar 1993 and 2006, with an emphasis on the Graeco-Roman presence in the East; Ball 2000, with its focus on the importance of Eastern influence reacting in part to Millar; Humphrey 1995–9; on the Roman East see also Alcock 1997.
[17] 1991.   [18] 2002.   [19] Heft 1/2006: 1.

Romans and Sasanians were neighbours and rivals whose competition for supremacy affected not only two peoples but all those within and between the two empires. In addition, maps and their shifting geographical centres are a means to manifest that modern scholarship is moving away from eurocentric views.

The following study consists of two main parts. The first part begins with a brief survey of Roman–Parthian relations in order to set the stage for questions of continuity and change. After that, the chronological narrative sets out the development of the relationship between Rome and the Sasanians from the third to the seventh century. As episodes of peace and war characterised the relations, above all the military conflicts between the two empires are analysed and form the core of the narrative. The longer, second part presents a wide range of source material, which is placed in its context and illustrates patterns and structural premises. Throughout the book, cross-references link both parts. 'Sources and Contexts' starts with assessing the political goals of the two sides, which, if they amounted to a programmatic foreign policy, would have determined relations from the beginning (II 1). In order to set the stage for the discussion of the military confrontations (II 3), a short discussion of Sasanian warfare precedes this chapter (II 2). 'Diplomatic solutions' (II 4) are expressed in the numerous peace treaties that concluded the many wars fought between Rome and Persia from the third to the seventh century. However, Part II also points to the close diplomatic relations between West and East that existed at all times, and to the numerous contacts that emerged through common interests between the two powers. Chapter II 5 focuses on the special role of Arabia. After that, Armenia, an area that was of particular interest to both sides, trade and economy, and the protection of the frontiers are examined (II 6). The religious life in both empires and the role played by Christianity and Zoroastrianism in their political and ideological confrontation form another important theme (II 7). Surprisingly, the rulers of both empires did not perceive each other as 'alien counterparts' but formed personal relationships characterised by mutual respect and even affection. In this context the 'legitimacy of kingship' was closely linked with the notion of a 'family of kings', two concepts that are discussed in chapter II 8. Apart from wars, all these factors shaped and intensified relations tremendously throughout the course of late antiquity. The final chapter discusses the disposition and actual channels that facilitated an exchange of information between East and West (II 9), a process that was far from one-sided and included multiple agents and every aspect of life.

More than once the Byzantine author and diplomat Peter the Patrician will be quoted in this study. In his view, 'It is obvious for all mankind that the Roman and the Persian Empires are just like two lamps; and it is necessary that, like eyes, the one is brightened by the light of the other and that they do not angrily strive for each other's destruction.' Wishful thinking, one may say, if one looks at the almost continuous sequence of wars fought between Rome and Persia, and at the actual downfall of both empires. For us, however, it may be an inspiration.

In order to express the phonetic value of the languages involved, we are using a few diacritical or phonetic signs when transliterating Persian, Arabic, Syriac or Armenian names, titles and places.

With regard to the Persian material, the most frequent transliterations are č for a pronunciation 'ch' (as in *chill*), ğ for 'j' (as in *jeans*) and š for 'sh' (as in *shell*). 'X' (which is rendered as 'ch' in many other modern works) should be pronounced in the same way as the 'ch' in Scottish *loch*. S is sharp as in *loss*, whereas z has a pronunciation as in *size*. ʿ renders an explosive glottal sound, whereas ʾ implies a glottal sound that stops the flow of air. It is extremely difficult to spell names, titles and places in a consistent way as Latin, Greek or modern familiar forms of some names and places exist which do not correspond to the general phonetic transliterations of the original languages. In these cases we have used the more familiar version at the expense of consistency. This also applies to Greek names, places and terms, which, unless their Latinised (such as Ephesus or Heraclius) or Anglicised (Constantinople or Maurice) forms or versions are more familiar, are transliterated on the basis of the Greek sounds and endings. The translations of the sources follow the original text as close as possible but also try to be readable and understandable.

PART I

Narrative

Rome and Iran to the beginning of the third century AD

Around the middle of the third century BC the kingdom of the Parthians emerged in the Eastern parts of the Seleucid kingdom. Originally the nomadic tribe resided in the area between the Caspian and the Aral Seas.[1] Around 250 BC Arsaces I, who was to become the first Parthian king (247–217 BC) and who became the first representative of the 'dynasty of the Arsacids', led the Parnians, as they were called, into the province of Parthava, which was situated east of the Caspian Sea and was part of Seleucid Iran.[2] Although at first this campaign amounted to no more than one of the frequent insurrections against an unstable Seleucid rule in one of the Eastern provinces, after a few setbacks the Arsacid kings managed to take firm hold of these areas. When the Parthians embarked on their Western expansion during the second century BC, the Seleucid kingdom, which was among other things confronted with the new world power of Rome in the West, was not able to stop them.[3] During the reign of the most significant Parthian king, Mithradates II (124/3–88/7 BC), the Arsacids succeeded in extending their rule into Armenia and Mesopotamia.[4] This was the beginning of an 'international role' for the Parthian kingdom, a phase that also entailed contacts with Rome.[5] Favoured by the decline of the Hellenistic kingdoms and driven by an immense desire for expansion during the first two centuries BC, the Romans extended their rule not only into Asia Minor but throughout the entire Eastern Mediterranean world.[6]

[1] For the history, culture and sources of the Parthian Empire see Schippmann 1980; Bivar 1983b: 21–99; Wolski 1993; Wiesehöfer 1996: 115–49, 1998a and 2001: 163–204; Frye 2000: 17–22; Wolski 2003.

[2] For the beginning of Parthian rule, the foundation of the Arsacid Empire and the chronology of events see Brodersen 1986: 378–81; Boyce 1994: 241–51; Olbrycht 1998: 51–76 and 2003: 69–103; Drijvers 1998: 279–93 and 1999: 193–206; Lerner 1999.

[3] Wolski 1969: 188–254 and Dobbins 1974: 63–79.   [4] Arnaud 1987: 129–46.

[5] For Parthian–Roman relations in general see Ziegler 1964; Keaveney 1982: 412–28; Dabrowa 1983; Campbell 1993: 213–40; Millar 1996: 127–47; Kennedy 1996a: 67–90; Isaac 1992: 19–53; Butcher 2003: 32–78.

[6] On the expansion of Roman rule in the eastern Mediterranean see Gruen 1984 and Sherwin-White 1984; also Millar 1996: 19–53.

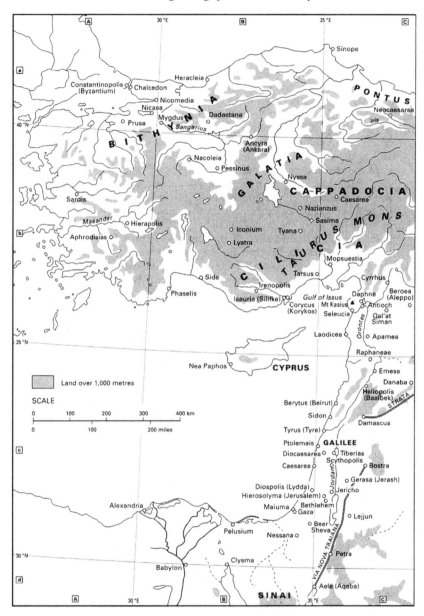

Map 1: Asia Minor and the Roman Eastern provinces

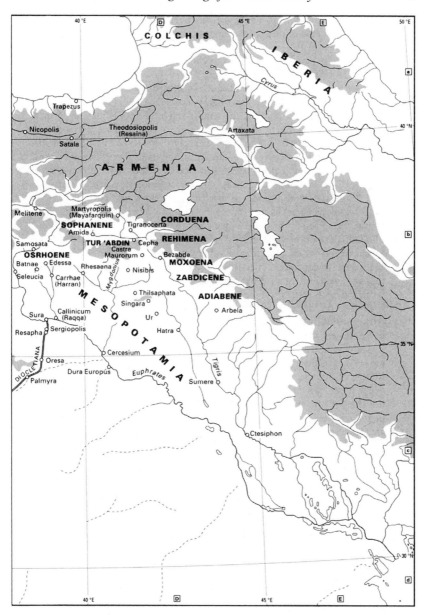

Map 1: (*cont.*)

Since 64 BC, when Pompey had established the province of Syria,[7] Rome had been the immediate neighbour of the Parthian kingdom. But already before that official contacts existed; in 96 BC Sulla received the Parthian ambassador Orobazos on the western banks of the river Euphrates. As Roman power was increasing dramatically in the East, the Parthians sought peaceful relations and wanted to come to a settlement that guaranteed mutual respect. During the meeting, the two empires established *amicitia* between them.[8] Plutarch's account of the protocol is revealing.[9] Sulla sat in the centre and presided over the proceedings. He obviously claimed an exceptional role. Also present was the Cappadocian king Ariobarzanes, a man who favoured and was dependent on Rome and who – just like Orobazos – sat next to Sulla. It becomes clear that the Parthian ambassador was placed on the same level with him and the Parthian kingdom thus viewed as a second-rank power. It was probably for good reasons that Orobazos was executed after his return.[10]

Roman foreign policy in the following years confirmed Western feelings of superiority. Although in 69 and 66 BC a *foedus* was concluded with the Parthians, which saw the Euphrates as the Western frontier of the Parthian kingdom, Roman diplomatic activities reflect strategic interests rather than the effort to come to a settlement with an equal partner. After the *foedus* of 66 BC had been concluded, Pompey's behaviour made it clear that Rome was not going to tolerate any rival.[11] When Roman soldiers broke the agreement and crossed the Euphrates, the Parthian king Phraates III warned Pompey to respect the river as the boundary but the latter declared that he would give way to military force only.[12] Rome did not feel obliged to comply with legal norms but was convinced of its political, military and cultural superiority over the East.

When Crassus launched another attack on Mesopotamia in 54 BC, the Parthian kingdom was well prepared. In 53 BC Rome suffered a major defeat at Carrhae. The Roman standards fell into Parthian hands and Crassus was killed.[13] The outcome of this battle is significant for subsequent Roman–Parthian relations because it influenced Rome's policy in the East considerably. Whereas the Romans had treated the Parthians with arrogance before, after the defeat they reversed their attitude and rather overestimated the opponent's military force; Rome sought revenge.[14]

---

[7] On Pompey's settlement see Freeman 1994: 143–70; on Syria in general see Kennedy 1996b: 703–36.
[8] Sherwin-White 1977: 173–83; Keaveney 1981: 196–212.
[9] Plut. *Sull.* 5.4–5.   [10] Karras-Klapproth 1988: 101–2.
[11] Keaveney 1982: 412–28; Hillman 1996: 380–99.   [12] Cass. Dio xxxvii.6.1–2.
[13] Plut. *Crass.* 18–33; Cass. Dio xl.16–27; Marshall 1976; Shahbazi 1992: 9–13; Tucci 1992.
[14] Timpe 1962: 104–29.

Caesar's plans for a Parthian War[15] and the intense preparations prior to Antony's Parthian campaign[16] confirm Rome's respect for the military force of the Parthian kingdom. However, the Romans were still not willing to acknowledge their opponent in the East as an equal power. In the late republican period Roman foreign policy strove to create a Rome that was, as Cicero puts it, 'lord over kings, victor and ruler over all nations' (*dominus regum, victor atque imperator omnium gentium*).[17] The claim for world domination prevented the *imperium Romanum* and other states from coexisting as equal partners bound by principles of international law. However, Augustus' policy in the East paved the way for a new attitude. In order to come to an official agreement concerning the political relations between the two powers, the Parthians had to return the Roman standards they had captured at Carrhae; they agreed to do so in 20 BC when Rome demonstrated its military strength in the East.[18] It is not surprising that in Roman eyes the *foedus* concluded between Augustus and Phraates IV (38–3/2 BC) was a great success.[19] Given that public opinion in Rome was all in favour of war, it was even more important that the *princeps* decided to restore the Roman–Parthian *amicitia* and to conclude a *foedus* in 20 BC according to which the Romans respected the Euphrates as the frontier between the two powers.[20] The treaty acknowledged the fact that Rome was, in the long term, not in a position to control vast territories beyond the Euphrates. Augustus pursued a policy 'within the existing borders of the empire' (*intra terminos imperii*)[21] although official propaganda continued to emphasise an 'empire without borders' (*imperium sine fine*).[22] However, by refraining from further expansion in the East Rome acknowledged the military strength of the Parthian kingdom. Authors of the early imperial period talk about the Parthian kingdom and the Roman empire as *maxima imperia*[23] and as 'the two greatest rules under the sun',[24] and the Augustan historian Pompeius Trogus saw the world as divided between Romans and Parthians;[25] there is no doubt that such statements reflect emerging rules of an international community of which the Parthian kingdom was a part. On an

---

[15] Malitz 1984: 21–59.

[16] Craven 1920; Bengtson 1974; Schieber 1979: 105–24; Hersh 1980: 41–5.

[17] Cic. *Dom.* 90.   [18] Timpe 1975: 155–69.

[19] On the significance of returning the standards see Zanker 1987: 188–96; in this context see also Schneider 1998: 95–147.

[20] Strabo XVI.1.28; on Strabo's representation of the Parthians see Bosi 1994: 109–222; Drijvers 1998: 279–93.

[21] Tac. *Ann.* I.11.   [22] Verg. *Aen.* 1.279.   [23] Tac. *Ann.* II.56.

[24] Ios. *AJ* XVIII.46; on the representation of the Parthians in Josephus see Rajak 1998: 309–24.

[25] Iust. XLI.1.1; on this passage see also Van Wickevoort Crommelin 1998: 261; on the Parthians in Pompeius Trogus see Alonso-Nunez 1988–9: 125–55.

ideological level, however, Rome's claim for world domination remained intact.[26] Many comments made by poets of the Augustan period, who represented the opinion of the nobility in the city of Rome, reflect the view that no state or people could be equal to the *imperium Romanum*.[27]

Augustus initiated a policy that refrained from conquests beyond the Euphrates and acknowledged the Parthians as a second world power equal to Rome. Although Nero (54–68) fought a Parthian War over Armenia, the Arsacid ruler Tiridates was eventually crowned by Nero as king of Armenia in a great Roman spectacle,[28] and we may say that Augustus' policy of cooperation laid the foundation for a more or less uninterrupted peace between the two powers throughout the first century AD. The fact that in AD 66 the so-called 'Armenian question' found a solution must have strengthened relations even further (**26**).[29] Local conflicts, Rome's fortification of the frontier along the Euphrates and in the Caucasus and a tightened Roman rule in the Eastern provinces did their part to see relations deteriorate but did not immediately lead to new armed confrontations on the Eastern frontier of the Roman Empire.[30] Rome, however, improved its military position significantly during this period.[31]

At the beginning of the second century the emperor Trajan (98–117) intended to conquer the Parthian kingdom and thereby turned the dream of Roman world domination into political reality.[32] Our ancient sources do not reveal the precise reasons for the emperor's Parthian campaign. It looks as if ideas of world domination and military glory[33] were equally important as strategic considerations regarding a stronger Roman frontier beyond the Euphrates. Trajan rejected Parthian efforts to come to a peaceful settlement.

Contemporary observers criticised the emperor's actions prior to the military confrontations[34] and accused him of turning his back on a Roman policy in the East that had prevailed since Augustus, namely a policy that acknowledged the sovereignty of the Parthian kingdom as a political factor within a community of states that abided by the same international laws.[35]

---

[26] On the image of the Parthians in the West see Sonnabend 1986.

[27] For references see Wissemann 1982.

[28] Anderson 1934: 743–80; Ziegler 1964: 67–78; Wagner 1985: 31–42.

[29] Wolski 1983a: 269–77; for the period after 34/5 see also Schottky 1991: 81–7; for the position of Armenia between the two great powers in general see Garsoïan 1997a: 63–94 and 1985: 95–116.

[30] For developments within the Parthian kingdom during the first century see Dabrowa 1981: 187–204; Schottky 1991: 61–135; Ash 1999: 114–35.

[31] For the fortification of the Roman–Parthian frontier along the Euphrates from Augustus to the Flavian emperors see Dabrowa 1980: 382–8; Wagner 1985: 19–57; Bosworth 1976: 63–78; Mitchell 1993: 118–42.

[32] On Trajan's political goals see Eadie 1985: 407–23.

[33] Cf. esp. Cass. Dio LXVIII.17.1.   [34] E.g. Front. 15.   [35] Cf. Ziegler 1964: 102.

In spite of Trajan's great military successes, his Parthian War (114–17) ended with a fiasco.[36] Late in Trajan's reign revolts took place in the conquered territories, and the new provinces of Armenia, Mesopotamia and Assyria were eventually lost. Trajan's successor Hadrian (117–38) returned to the Augustan policy of 'sustaining the empire within its borders' (*coercendi intra terminos*)[37] and restored the *amicitia* with the Parthian kingdom on the basis of the *status quo* that had existed before the war.[38] In its outline, this policy was not even changed by the successful Parthian Wars of L. Verus (161–9) and Septimius Severus (193–211), who – after Trajan's offensive – advanced a second and third time as far as the Parthian capital Seleucia-Ktēsiphōn.[39] Rome withdrew after these successes. Its declared goals were different from those of the beginning of the second century and no longer extended to the subjugation of the Parthian kingdom. But whereas the Eastern power had retained its political sovereignty, Rome's military successes improved its strategic position along the Eastern frontier considerably, in particular by moving the frontiers forward to the Chaboras-Singara line, which created a boundary within Mesopotamia, and finally establishing the province of Mesopotamia during the reign of Septimius Severus.[40] Roman control over upper Mesopotamia represented a permanent and immediate threat to the Mesopotamian heartland of the Parthian kingdom. This was the end of a policy that firmly recognised the Euphrates as the border between Romans and Parthians.

At the beginning of the third century AD Caracalla (211–17) launched yet another attack against the Parthians.[41] In contrast to his predecessors, he seems to have pursued the conquest of the Parthian kingdom. Apparently, his plans amounted to world domination and were guided by the idea that he would become a successor of Alexander the Great – he was certainly not prepared to acknowledge Parthian sovereignty. Caracalla's attempts to create a *casus belli* for a 'justified war' illustrate this position no less than his actions during the Parthian campaign when he desecrated the graves of local rulers in the Adiabēnē.[42] In contrast, ancient authors mention Caracalla's plans to marry the daughter of the Parthian king Artabanos IV.

[36] Lepper 1948; Eadie 1985: 407–23; Lightfoot 1990: 115–26; Wylie 1990: 37–43.
[37] See note 21 above.
[38] Birley 1956: 25–33 and Birley 1998: 66–76.
[39] Birley 1987: 140–7; 1988: 201–4; Rubin 1975: 419–41; Speidel 1985: 321–6; Potter 1991: 277–90; Millar 1996: 80–99 and 111–26.
[40] On the fortification of the Roman Eastern frontier along the Tigris and Chaboras under the Severan emperors see Kennedy 1987: 57–66; Wagner 1985: 63–7; 1983: 103–30; Millar 1996: 127–41.
[41] Heichelheim 1944: 113–15.　　[42] Cass. Dio LXXIX.1.1–2.

The king's refusal led to war.[43] Caracalla's request was certainly unrealistic and the Roman emperor may have anticipated the refusal in his political calculations. Nevertheless, Herodian's account of the situation is revealing.[44] It mentions a Roman embassy dispatched to propose the marriage to the Parthian king. The ambassadors claimed that if the empires of the Romans and the Parthians, which in their words were the greatest of the world, were no longer separated by a river and frontier but formed a single empire, no opposition would arise because the other barbarian nations would be an easy prey to these. Although we have to be cautious when using Herodian as a historical source, his ideas reflect contemporary views and throw light on the relations between the two single great powers at the beginning of the third century.[45]

Caracalla's war of aggression is therefore surprising. In order to explain his political goals, in particular the dream of succeeding Alexander the Great,[46] we have to take into account the character and personality of this Roman emperor. After Caracalla's assassination, his successor Macrinus (217–18) immediately announced that his predecessor had done wrong by the Parthians and restored peace. In 218, after a battle fought at Nisibis during which both sides suffered heavy losses, a treaty was signed. According to Herodian, the Roman emperor Macrinus was delighted about having won the Iranian opponent as a reliable friend.[47]

Be that as it may, until its downfall the Parthian kingdom was and remained an openly acknowledged serious opponent, who required constant Roman vigilance.[48] Internal developments in Iran made it impossible to intensify Roman–Parthian relations and to strengthen emerging signs of an international law. In 224 the rise of the Sasanians, fostered, to be sure, by the confrontations and tensions between Parthians and Romans during the first two decades of the third century, led to the fall of Arsacid rule.

Modern scholars long underestimated the Arsacid dynasty and regarded Parthian–Roman relations solely from the Roman perspective. Inevitably, scholars did not acknowledge an 'active' Western policy on the part of the Arsacids. Above all the many works of G. Wolski[49] have opened the discussion to new views, and the era of the Parthian kings within the

---

[43] The historicity of Caracalla's plans is controversial; see Ziegler 1964: 132–4.

[44] Herodian IV.10.2–4.   [45] Ziegler 1964: 133–40.

[46] On Caracalla's *imitatio Alexandri* see Cass. Dio LXXVIII.7.1–4; Herodian IV.8.1–3.

[47] Herodian V.1.4.

[48] There has been a lively scholarly discussion regarding the goals and character of Rome's military and strategic policy along the Eastern frontier of the empire. Cf. Luttwak 1976; MacMullen 1976; Isaac 1989: 231–4; 1992 and Zyromski 1998.

[49] Wolski 1966: 65–89; 1976: 195–214; 1985: 163–73; 1983b: 137–49.

history of Iran as a whole has gained significance – in particular with regard to the study of the Achaemenids and the Sasanians. Relations with Rome were in fact a major structural element in the history of the Parthian kingdom. Wolski is right in emphasising that the 'Iranicism' of the Arsacids played an important role in their conflict with Rome. The recollection of the significant Achaemenid past[50] encouraged the Arsacids to stand up to the Roman Empire, an aspect that widens the scope of Arsacid policies tremendously.[51] A prime example is the following: according to the Roman historian Tacitus, the Parthian king Artabanos II (10/11–38) threatened the Roman emperor Tiberius (14–37) by referring to the old Persian and Macedonian conquests and by boasting that he would gain possession of what Cyrus and later Alexander had ruled.[52] By comparing the first Arsacid ruler with the first Achaemenid ruler Cyrus (559–530 BC) the third-century author Justin also underlines this claim.[53] The Parthians thus continued Achaemenid traditions and can be counted among the 'first pioneers of Iranicism'.[54]

K. H. Ziegler hesitates to label Arsacid foreign policy 'programmatic'[55] because there was no Arsacid ideology equivalent to the Roman idea of world domination. He argues that Parthian goals never amounted to the destruction of the Roman Empire and that even the claims made by Artabanos II in Tacitus' account aimed at territorial gains that were modest in comparison with later Sasanian claims.[56] It is crucial for an assessment of Roman–Sasanian relations to examine whether the Sasanians took up goals of the Arsacid rulers and continued their Western policy or developed plans that went beyond any foreign policy pursued by the Parthians. Given that the late phase of Parthian–Roman relations was characterised by mutual respect and appreciation – certainly beyond a *modus vivendi*[57] and with options for a formalised relationship on the basis of an international law,[58] one also has to ask if and to what extent the rising Sasanian Empire was prepared to use the opportunity and to further develop existing relations.

---

[50] Metzler 1982: 130–7.
[51] On the goals of Arsacid foreign policy and on Arsacid military strength see Kennedy 1996a: 67–90.
[52] Tac. *Ann.* VI.37. Cf. Wiesehöfer 1986b: 177–85; Ehrhardt 1998: 299 with further references.
[53] Iust. XLI.5.5.   [54] Wolski 1983b: 147.   [55] Dabrowa 1984: 153.
[56] Ziegler 1964: 86; cf. also Zyromski 1998: 11.
[57] Wirth 1980/1: 324.   [58] Ziegler 1964: 140.

CHAPTER 2

Rome and the Sasanian Empire:
A chronological survey

2.1 THE THIRD CENTURY: THE ORIGINS OF
SASANIAN INTERESTS IN THE WEST

The rise of the Sasanian dynasty, the revolt of Ardašīr I (224–40) against the Arsacids, the fall of Parthian rule and the foundation of the Neo-Persian Sasanian Empire (map 2)[1] – together, these were not only a turning point within the history of Iran[2] but also a benchmark regarding Iran's relations with Rome. Although Ardašīr's hostile attitude against Rome was at first a mere continuation of Parthian sentiments, within a few years of his reign the king established, consolidated and centralised his rule[3] to the extent that his ambitions threatened wide areas of the eastern half of the Roman Empire. The West knew that Ardašīr's claims would go beyond the borders of the Parthian kingdom and that he would ask for more than declarations of loyalty from the many client kings within his empire; it was clear that he would claim all the territories that had once belonged to his Achaemenid ancestors. Rome therefore considered the Sasanian dynasty as a serious opponent right from the beginning of their relations (**1**).[4]

As soon as Ardašīr had established his rule he turned towards the West. According to the contemporary historian Herodian, Ardašīr I responded to a letter from the Roman emperor Severus Alexander (222–35), in which the emperor warned him to respect peace and reminded him of the great victories of Augustus, Trajan and Septimius Severus,[5] by asking Rome to

---

[1] For a chronology of the early Sasanian rulers and the beginnings of Sasanian history see Altheim-Stiehl 1982: 152–9; Sundermann 1990: 295–9; Richter-Bernburg 1993: 71–80.

[2] For the history of the Sasanian Empire see Morony 1997: 70–83; Christensen 1944; Widengren 1971: 711–82; Frye 1983a: 116–80; 1984: 287–339; Schippmann 1990: 10–79; Wiesehöfer 2001: 151–221; see Shahbazi 1990: 588–99 for a survey of the multi-faceted relations between Iran and the West.

[3] With regard to the activities of the first Sasanian king see Wiesehöfer 1986a: 371–6.

[4] On 'Achaemenid echoes' see Frye 1983c: 247–52 and Roaf 1998: 1–7.

[5] Herodian VI.2.4–5.

18

withdraw altogether from Syria and Asia Minor.[6] Between 230 and 232 Ardašīr invaded Roman territory but was stopped in 233 by a counter-attack of Severus Alexander, who had successfully reorganised Rome's desolate Eastern frontier units. The Sasanians withdrew from the areas they had conquered and the *status quo ante bellum* was restored. Although this first military confrontation was not a victory for either Persians or Romans, the fact that a Persian advance had been prevented was viewed as a major triumph in the West (**4**).

Soon the Sasanians invaded again. When in 235 the assassination of Severus Alexander caused political unrest in the Roman Empire, Ardašīr I once more turned to the West. In 235 and 236 he apparently gained control of a number of fortresses in Roman Mesopotamia, among these the important cities of Nisibis and Carrhae.[7] Ardašīr not only attempted to conquer Roman frontier areas, but he also advanced into southern Mesopotamia, the western coastal regions of the Persian Gulf and eastern Arabia.[8] Above all he must have been interested in trade with India and therefore tried to control seafaring in the Persian Gulf. It looks as if Ardašīr actually gained control over the northern part of the eastern coast of the Arabian Peninsula. His activities along the Persian Gulf, which primarily illustrate economic and strategic motives, affected Roman economic interests. Immediately after the fall of the Arsacid dynasty Ardašīr had occupied Spasinu Charax on the Šatt al-ʿArab and thereby threatened the trading metropolis and Roman colony of Palmyra, which was located in the Syrian Desert, and engaged in trade with Indian luxury goods along the Persian Gulf; in consequence also Roman interests in trade in the region were threatened. This situation could not but affect relations between the two powers (**23**).

Moreover, both powers contended for the well-fortified caravan city of Hatra, which had turned into one of the most important Arabian centres during the course of the second century; because of its location in northern Mesopotamia, the city functioned as a junction for caravan routes and a stop on the route from Nisibis to Ktēsiphōn (**22**). Herodian describes Hatra as an impregnable fortress.[9] The 'city of the sun-god' with its many shrines was also an important destination for pilgrims and derived further wealth from this.

---

[6] Ibid. VI.2.5–6; VI.4.4–5; Potter 1990: 372–5 suggests that Ardašīr's goals were more modest, namely to establish or secure control over the former client kingdoms such as Hatra and Armenia, which had fallen under Roman rule.

[7] Wiesehöfer 1982: 437–47; Kettenhofen 1982: 21–2 and 1995a: 159–77.

[8] Widengren 1971: 754–5; Whitehouse and Williamson 1973: 29–49; Frye 1983b: 167–70; Winter 1988: 72–9; Potts 1990: 228–41 and 1997: 89–107.

[9] Herodian III.9.4.

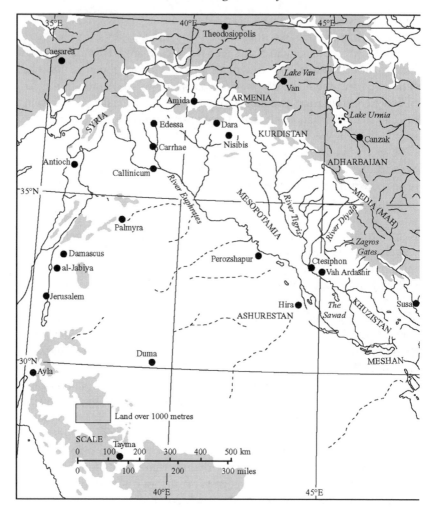

Map 2: Sasanian Iran

When Ardašīr I had taken over Parthian territories he had also made
an unsuccessful attempt at capturing Hatra. Losing a fortress of immense
strategic importance for securing middle Mesopotamia to Rome threatened
the Persian Western frontier considerably. Only towards the end of Ardašīr's
reign the Sasanians managed to capture Hatra after a two-year siege and
probably by treason.[10] Scholars date the fall of Hatra to some time between

---

[10] Tabarī, tr. Nöldeke 33–40; Bosworth 31–7 (827–30).

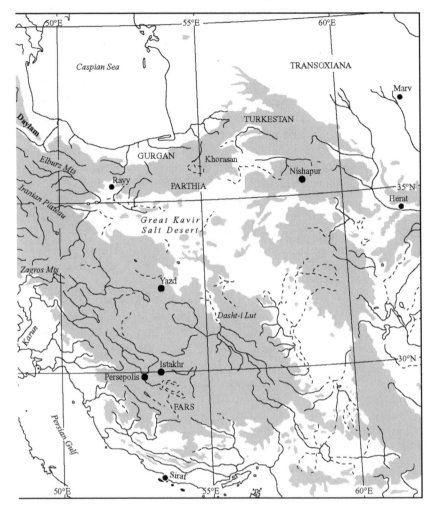

Map 2: (*cont.*)

April 12 and September 30 of the year 240.[11] It was a blow to Rome because controlling Hatra put the Persians in a much better strategic position in northern Mesopotamia. The already strained diplomatic relations between Rome and Persia took a turn for the worse when Ardašīr I died. From a Western perspective the conquest of Hatra was the cause of the new war

---

[11] The conquest of Hatra is closely linked to the beginning of the reign of Šāpūr I; see **22** with further references.

that broke out during the reign of Ardašīr's son and successor Šāpūr I (240–72).[12]

In the spring of 243 the Roman emperor Gordian III (238–44) set off with his army from the Syrian metropolis Antioch on the Orontes, crossed the Euphrates and won back the cities of Carrhae and Nisibis, which had been occupied by the Sasanians.[13] Under the command of the Prefect of the Guard Timesitheus the Romans defeated the Persians at Rhesaina and then advanced into the Sasanian province of Āsūrestān.[14] They probably intended to get as far as the Sasanian capital Ktēsiphōn[15] but at the beginning of the year 244 Šāpūr I scored a decisive victory against the Roman army at Mišīk. Gordian III died in battle (**5**). His successor Philip the Arab (244–9)[16] concluded a peace with Šāpūr and withdrew. Although Rome had to pay large sums of money and lost influence in Armenia the Roman emperor boasted about the peace (**16**).

The peace of 244 lasted for only a few years. Šāpūr claimed that Rome was to be blamed for new confrontations because it had done wrong by Armenia.[17] When the Arsacid king of Armenia had become the victim of Persian intrigues his son Tiridates, who was not yet of age, went over to Rome (**26**). Šāpūr saw the regulations of the *foedus* of 244 violated and used the opportunity to take over Armenia.[18] In 252 he eliminated the Arsacid royal house and turned Armenia into a Sasanian province under the command of his son Hormizd.[19] This development brought significant strategic advantages for the Sasanians, and this not only with regard to the looming conflicts with Rome but also with regard to their military and economic interests in the Caucasus region.

From 252 on Šāpūr was once more at war with Rome.[20] He boasted of a spectacular victory at Barbalissos over a Roman army of 60,000 men.[21] Afterwards the Persians invaded the Roman province of Syria. They captured Hierapolis, Antioch on the Orontes and further Syrian cities and

---

[12] Schippmann 1990: 19.   [13] On Gordian's Persian expedition see Kettenhofen 1983: 151–71.

[14] Amm. xxiii.5.17.   [15] SHA *Gord.* 27.6.

[16] On this emperor and his rule see de Blois 1978–9: 11–43 and Körner 2002.

[17] ŠKZ § 9 (p. 294 ed. Back).

[18] For the possible causes of the Sasanian expedition against Armenia and the course of events see Chaumont 1976: 169–76 and below (**26**) with further references.

[19] For an examination of Šāpūr's intervention in Armenia see Schottky 1994: 223–35, esp. 231–2; see again **26** below.

[20] It is difficult to establish a chronology of the various Sasanian expeditions between 253 and 256; see Kettenhofen 1982: 50–96; Schippmann 1990: 21–3; Potter 1990: 189–96 and 290–7; Strobel 1993: 220–56.

[21] ŠKZ § 9 (p. 295 ed. Back).

also made an advance into Cappadocia.[22] Exceptionally important was the destruction of the caravan city Dura-Europos in the central Mesopotamian steppe.[23] After the fall of Hatra, the Romans had now lost a further important trading base in the region. In the second half of 253, however, the Persians suffered a first setback when one of their columns was stopped at Emesa and defeated, possibly by the Palmyrene Odaenathus (died in 267). In the following years this man figured prominently in Persian–Roman confrontations. When Šāpūr I rejected his offer of an alliance, Odaenathus asked Rome instead and soon after his support became crucial for the Roman position in the East (**23**).

At first Šāpūr I used the internal difficulties Rome faced during this period for further offensives.[24] In 260 the Persians defeated the emperor and his personal army. At Edessa they captured high Roman officials and Valerian himself.[25] Within all of Sasanian history this was one of the greatest triumphs over their Western opponent. Over and over again Šāpūr I boasted of this triumph (**5**). According to his own words, the king exploited Valerian's defeat at Edessa by taking thirty-seven cities in the Roman provinces of Syria, Cilicia and Cappadocia.[26] Apparently he also occupied the Syrian metropolis Antioch on the Orontes. Among the numerous Roman prisoners were many engineers, scholars and artists, who were deported and resettled in the modern provinces of Fārs and Hūzistān. Many of them found a new home in cities founded by Šāpūr I. These men contributed to a spread of Western 'know-how' to areas beyond the rivers Euphrates and Tigris and thus enhanced the infrastructure of the Sasanian Empire (**36**).

Numerous Christians, and among these priests and Church officials, also entered Persia and established organised congregations.[27] These were not bothered by Šāpūr I because the king hoped that by tolerating Christians, whose fellow believers in the Roman Empire were persecuted at the time of the deportations, he would gain an advantage in his conflict with Rome. However, the quick spread of Christianity in the Sasanian Empire endangered the position of the Zoroastrian priesthood, whose claims to power

---

[22] The individual dates are uncertain. An advance between 253 and 255 is as likely as one in 255/6.

[23] MacDonald 1986: 45–68; Millar 1996: 445–71 and 1998b; Pollard 2004: 119–44.

[24] Strobel 1993: 243–4.

[25] On the Roman–Sasanian confrontations of the year 260 and on the capture of Valerian see Kettenhofen 1982: 97–126.

[26] *ŠKZ* §§ 10–17 (pp. 295–306 ed. Back); regarding the number of cities conquered by Šāpūr I see Maricq and Honigmann 1953: 144.

[27] For the religious life in the Sasanian Empire see the respective entries in *CHI* III.2 1983: 819–1024; for the position of Christianity see Atiya 1991; Wiesehöfer 2001: 199–216; see also chapter 7 below.

became more and more visible towards the end of Šāpūr I's reign, and in particular after his death. Although the Christian population displayed loyalty towards the king in many instances, as a guardian and protector of Zoroastrianism he was ultimately not allowed to tolerate Christianity (30). Here we see clear parallels to the developments in the Roman Empire where reasons of state were also responsible for persecutions of the Christians.

Šāpūr I's long-standing policy of religious tolerance favoured especially the rise of Mani, the founder of Manichaeanism,[28] a religion that was for a short time a religious alternative to Zoroastrianism, but at the end of his life the king turned to Zoroastrianism.[29] In his Great Inscription Šāpūr proclaimed that he owed his political successes entirely to the goodwill of Ahura Mazda (30). At the beginning of the fourth century Constantine the Great displayed a similar attitude with regard to the Christian God after his victories over Maxentius and Licinius.[30] Both rulers propagated their close relationship with a supreme god in a way that illustrates structural similarities between their ideas of kingship. On the Eastern side, one is reminded of the Sasanian reliefs that capture the 'King of kings' receiving the ring, symbol of his divine rule, that is Ahura Mazda handing over his power to the secular ruler; on the Western side, what comes to mind are the many images that underline the close link between emperor and God and show the emperor as the executor of divine plans in the world.[31] Further parallels to the religious situation in Persia can be observed with regard to the motives, goals and consequences of Constantine's religious policy. As the Sasanian kings supported Zoroastrianism a long time before the conversion of Constantine, religious developments in Persia must have been significant for the events in the West.[32]

It is striking how much Šāpūr I's aggressive policy against Rome reinforced the claims made by the founder of the Sasanian dynasty, Ardašīr I, namely to rule the territories that had once made up the Achaemenid Empire (2). During his reign, Sasanian interests in the West reached a high point for the first time and Rome had to apply all its energies in order to

[28] On Mānī and the religion named after him see MacKenzie 1979: 500–31; Hutter 1988; Lieu 1992 and 1994.

[29] On Zoroastrianism in the Sasanian Period see Zaehner 1975 and 1961; Duchesne-Guillemin 1983: 866–908 and Boyce 1984a: 101–43 and 1984b.

[30] See Brandt 1998: 32–7 and 128–46 for references.

[31] One famous example is the silver medallion from Ticinum, which probably dates to the year 315; see Brandt 1998: 135–7.

[32] Paul 1983: 108–12.

deal with the threat. Although Šāpūr I suffered setbacks towards the end of his rule, West and East always remembered that he had defeated the Romans several times, that Gordian III had met his death in the battle of Mišīk and that Valerian had been captured.

The activities of Odaenathus of Palmyra rather than Roman offensives deserve credit for the fact that the territories and cities conquered by Šāpūr I remained in Persian hands only for a short period of time. On behalf of the Romans Odaenathus promoted Western interests against Sasanian claims. Šāpūr I's earlier rejection of Odaenathus' offer to ally himself with Persia backfired. The Roman emperor Gallienus (260–8) invested the Palmyrene king with almost unlimited power, and from the second half of the year 260 onwards the Sasanians suffered several defeats at his hands. From 264 onwards the Eastern frontier of the Roman Empire was quiet.[33]

When Odaenathus was assassinated in the spring of 267 Šāpūr I was finally liberated from a dangerous opponent. With Odaenathus' help Palmyra – which was favoured by its geographical location in the first place – had developed into a powerful buffer state between Rome and Persia. Odaenathus' successor Zenobia (267–72) took advantage of the so-called crisis of the Roman Empire[34] and fostered an unparalleled rise of Palmyrene power. Eventually, the creation of a Palmyrene kingdom that was independent from Rome was not tolerable. In the year 272 the Roman emperor Aurelian (270–5) attacked Palmyra and captured Zenobia, who was paraded through Rome in the emperor's triumph (**23**).

The Sasanians did not intervene in the confrontations between Rome and Palmyra, possibly because the short reigns of Hormizd I (272–3) and Bahrām I did not allow for any bold initiatives in foreign affairs. Removing Palmyrene power from the political map certainly strengthened the Roman position. Aurelian adopted the titles *Parthicus* and *Persicus maximus*[35] and thereby emphasised his military achievements in the East. The Roman emperor Probus (276–82) travelled to the East twice; these visits included diplomatic contacts with the Persian opponent but no armed conflict. A Roman offensive was planned for the year 283 but was abandoned when the emperor was assassinated.[36]

---

[33] De Blois 1975: 7–23.
[34] On this 'crisis' see Potter 1990; Bleckmann 1992; Strobel 1993; with further references Witschel 1999; Strobel 2001: 239–78.
[35] *CIL* III 7586 (= *ILS* 8925); VI 1112; VIII 9040; XII 5549 and 5561; XIII 8973 (= *ILS* 581); see also Kettenhofen 1986: 138–46.
[36] SHA *Prob.* 17.4; 20.1; for the year 279 the title *Persikos megistos* is attested; cf. *P. Oxy.* XIV 1713; for Probus' activities in the East see Crees 1965: 110–11 and 124–5; Kreucher 2003: 82–3 and 179–86.

His successor Carus (282–3) was proclaimed emperor with the explicit goal of destroying the Persian Empire.[37] This may be literary fiction but Carus translated into action a long-planned military offensive against the Sasanians. The Roman army invaded Mesopotamia and did not meet any Persian resistance.[38] Internal unrest during the reign of Bahrām II (276–93) may have favoured the successful advance and capture of Ktēsiphōn.[39] This was the only time ever that the Romans captured the Persian capital, which to some extent made up for the humiliation Rome had suffered in 260. Not surprisingly, Carus also adopted the titles *Persicus maximus* and *Parthicus* in order to display his success over the Eastern rival.[40]

Carus' sudden death prevented Rome from further advances. In the *Historia Augusta* we read that he was struck by lightning while in his camp at the Tigris. No Roman emperor was destined to advance beyond Ktēsiphōn.[41] According to the words of this so-called 'Ktēsiphōn oracle' Carus died because he did not abide by an oracular prophecy that anybody who tried to conquer the Persian capital would be punished. Rome's cautious dealings with Persia were thus expressed not only in political terms but also as a motif in the realm of myth and fiction. Carus' successor, Numerianus (283–4), withdrew his army immediately and without even negotiating for a peace.[42] The campaign thus had no consequences for the Sasanians. Rome was not able to use the prestigious victory over Bahrām II and did not gain any territory in the long term. The latent state of war and the unsettled situation along the frontiers that had existed already before Carus' Persian campaign continued.[43]

Too many unresolved issues prevented a formal peace or agreement regarding the frontiers, and this did not change until the Roman emperor Diocletian (284–305) consolidated his rule and returned to the East in 286. Immediately, he started to reorganise Roman rule and the defence system along the frontier, a development which caused Sasanian concern. In the year 287 Bahrām II sent ambassadors to Diocletian in order to negotiate for a peace treaty.[44] Apparently the negotiations were successful and a peace was concluded without any territory changing hands. Diocletian was satisfied that the Sasanian king respected the existing Eastern frontier and in

[37] Anonymus post Dionem, frg. 12 (*FHG* IV 198).
[38] SHA *Car.* 8.1; Aur. Vict. *Caes.* 38.2–3; Eutr. IX.18.1; Fest. 24.
[39] SHA *Car.* 8.1; *Pan. Lat.* XI (III) 17.2 (p. 268, rec. Mynors).
[40] *CIL* VIII 12522 (= *ILS* 600); *IGRR* I 1144.
[41] SHA *Car.* 9.1; in this context see Kerler 1970: 263–4.   [42] Aur. Vict. *Caes.* 38.6.
[43] For the Persian campaign of the emperor Carus see Winter 1988: 130–7.
[44] *Pan. Lat.* X (II) 7.5; 9.2.

288 returned to the Western parts of his empire in order to intervene in the conflict with the Alamanni.[45]

Bahrām II's readiness to come to a friendly understanding with Rome indicates that the Sasanian king was preoccupied with domestic affairs.[46] His brother Hormizd was rebelling against the legitimate ruler with the help of Eastern peoples such as the Saka and the Kūšān,[47] and the Zoroastrian priest Kartēr was exerting more and more influence in the empire. The latter, who had been a political factor already during the reign of Šāpūr I, was now at the zenith of his power and had great influence over Bahrām II.[48] The king backed Kartēr in pursuing a repressive policy that aimed at the elimination of all non-Zoroastrian religions in Persia (**29**).[49] Measures by which Bahrām increased the powers of the Zoroastrian priesthood reflect the king's efforts to unify his kingdom as well as to strengthen his own position.[50] This period saw the origins of the union between the Sasanian monarchy and the Zoroastrian religion that would become so significant for the history of the Sasanian Empire (**28**). The priest Kartēr expanded his power enormously and became the leading exponent of a movement[51] that gained more and more independence from the monarchy. Reflecting the king's weak position, this development is probably the reason why Bahrām yielded to Diocletian and was eager to come to an agreement with the emperor. From now onwards religious affairs became a significant and growing factor in the relations between the two great powers.

Both sides respected the agreement of 288 while their energies were applied elsewhere. Already in 290 Diocletian once more headed East. In the following period he took numerous measures in order to strengthen the Roman position along the Eastern frontier.[52] Above all, he intervened in Armenian matters by restoring Tiridates III to the throne in 290, thereby increasing Roman influence in this strategically important region.[53] Although Tiridates' realm of influence was limited to Western (Lesser) Armenia, Diocletian used the opportunity to win an important ally for the imminent conflict with Persia (**26**). The difficult situation

---

[45] On the Roman–Sasanian peace treaty of 288 see Winter 1988: 137–51.

[46] On the king's struggle to legitimise his rule see Winter 1988: 138–41.

[47] *Pan. Lat.* x (11) 7.5; 9.2; on the Saka see Bosi 1994: 109–22; Narain 1987: 27–31 and 1990: 151–76; on the Kūšān see the glossary, and below p. 93 with n. 107.

[48] For Kartēr and his rise to power see Sprengling 1940a: 197–228; Chaumont 1960: 339–80; Hinz 1971: 485–99.

[49] Brock 1978: 167–81.   [50] Decret 1979: 130–1.   [51] Metzler 1982: 144.

[52] The title *Persicus maximus* of the year 290 (*CIL* III 5810) emphasises Diocletian's successes in the East; cf. Enßlin 1942.

[53] Chaumont 1969: 93–111; Kettenhofen 1995c: esp. 48–55 and 144–68; see also p. 128 with n. 47 below.

mentioned above forced Bahrām II to watch the activities of the Roman
emperor without taking any action.

Since the capture of Valerian in the year 260 the balance of power
between West and East had changed. The Sasanian Empire, which from
its foundation in 224 had pursued an aggressive policy against its Western neighbour and had inflicted major defeats on Rome, suffered setbacks
that were the result not only of its own internal situation but also of a
recovering Roman Empire from the beginning of the 270s. In particular
Diocletian's sensible and far sighted reforms[54] helped to get over the so-
called crisis of the Roman Empire, and this had to affect the relations with
the Eastern neighbour. Only when Persia's internal struggle for power[55]
ended in favour of king Narsē (293–302) was the Eastern power in the
position to revert to the policy of expansion pursued by the early Sasanian
kings.[56]

In 296 Narsē used the first opportunity for a military offensive against
Rome and invaded the Roman part of Armenia. He benefited from the fact
that the Romans had to deal with a revolt against their rule in Egypt. In
297 Diocletian was determined to end the political unrest and issued an
edict against the Manichaeans, whose religion was one of those persecuted
by the Zoroastrian priest Kartēr in the Sasanian Empire but who from a
Western perspective were perceived as followers of a Persian religion.[57] It is
not clear, however, if the so-called 'Edict against the Manichaeans' of 297
(**31**), which formed part of a general policy of religious restoration pursued
by Diocletian and his fellow emperors,[58] should be seen in the context of
the new Persian war. However, it is remarkable that persecutions of the
Manichaeans ceased in Persia after 297 in order that their support could be
used in the battle against Rome.[59]

In the year 297 the armies of Narsē and Galerius ([293] 305–11), who
had been made Caesar by Diocletian because of his military successes,
clashed between Kallinikos and Carrhae; the Romans were utterly defeated.
Ammianus Marcellinus tells us that Diocletian hurried to the scene and that
Galerius, clad in purple, marched for nearly a mile before the carriage of
the enraged emperor. Possibly, Diocletian humiliated Galerius in this way

---

[54] Brandt 1998: 19–26.

[55] On the quarrels over the succession to the throne after the death of Bahrām II in 293 see Tanabe
1991: 7–39.

[56] For a different interpretation see Wiesehöfer 1993: 373 n. 54, who argues that Narsē's attack was a
preventive measure and not part of an expansionist Western policy.

[57] On the revolt in Egypt and the role of the Manichaeans as 'agents of the Persians' see Seston 1939:
227–34.

[58] Strobel 1993: 337–8 and Brandt 1998: 25–6.   [59] Frye 1983a: 131.

in order to provoke his thirst for revenge.[60] And indeed, in 298 Galerius defeated Narsē at Satala in Armenia.[61] There are many attestations of this particular Roman triumph against its Eastern rival (6).

The new success against Persia made Rome forget the setbacks of the third century, in particular the capture of Valerian by Šāpūr I in 260. The reign of Diocletian instilled in the West a level of confidence regarding victory and peace that had been lost throughout the third century. Rome's successes reminded it of its former glory and accordingly were much emphasised in Western historiography. In the *Historia Augusta* Diocletian is called the 'father of a golden age' (*aurei parens saeculi*).[62] Aurelius Victor refers to him as a father who had acted on behalf of his people.[63] Even Eusebius of Caesarea mentions the fortune and wealth of the reign of Diocletian in his ecclesiastical history.[64] According to the emperor Julian (361–3) Diocletian, the 'ruler of the entire world', instilled such fear into his enemy that the Sasanian king had to accept his conditions for peace.[65] The panegyric literature praises the victory over Persia by emphasising that this empire was the only power in a position to diminish Rome's glory.[66] In its preamble, the *Prices Edict* of the year 301, which is preserved on stone, mentions that the most fortunate stability and peace had been restored in the Roman Empire, if only with great difficulty.[67] Coins that show the legend *pax aeterna* and *securitas orbis* were part of an imperial propaganda but also expressed how much the Romans hoped that they had returned to their former glory.[68] Diocletian was the man whom the state needed (*vir rei publicae necessarius*).[69]

In the light of his crushing defeat at Satala Narsē wanted to end the conflict as quickly as possible, in particular as he could otherwise expect Galerius to advance further into Sasanian territory. It was to his advantage that Galerius and Diocletian could not agree on a strategy.[70] Whereas Galerius intended to pursue Narsē, who had taken flight, and take possession of the Persian heartland, Diocletian saw the aims of the war fulfilled with the victory at Satala. He did not want to embark on new and uncertain

---

[60] So Klein 1997: 278.
[61] Enßlin 1936: 102–10; 1942: 40–5; for the chronology of the events see Barnes 1982: 54–5 and 63.
[62] SHA *Heliogab.* 35.4.   [63] Aur. Vict. *Caes.* 39.8.   [64] Eus. *HE* VIII.13.9.
[65] Iul. *Or.* 1. 18a–b.   [66] *Pan. Lat.* VIII (v) 10.4.
[67] *Edictum Diocletiani et collegarum de pretiis rerum venalium*, praef.; for an English translation of the preamble and an early list of the prices see Grazer in Frank 1940: 157–74 (= Lewis and Reinhold 1955 II: 464–72); for new fragments of the text see Crawford and Reynolds 1977: 125–51 and 1979: 163–210; S. Corcoran is preparing a translation of all fragments; see also Brandt 1998: 78–86.
[68] Cf. e.g. references in *RIC* VI 1967: 145.   [69] SHA *Car.* 10.1.
[70] Aur. Vict. *Caes.* 39.36; see also Kolb 1987a: 85.

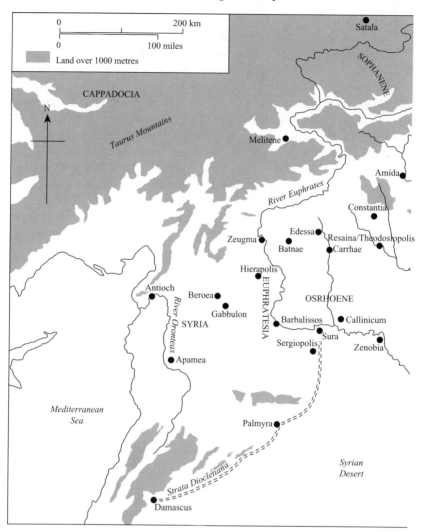

Map 3: Northern Mesopotamia and adjacent regions

military campaigns that could put at risk what had been accomplished so far. In the end, Diocletian prevailed in the negotiations at Nisibis. A peace treaty was concluded and put an end to the last of the Roman–Sasanian Wars of the third century. Although the *foedus* of 298 put the Sasanians at a major disadvantage (**17**), Rome intended to respect the sovereignty of the defeated Sasanian ruler.[71]

---

[71] Chrysos 1976: 11–17.

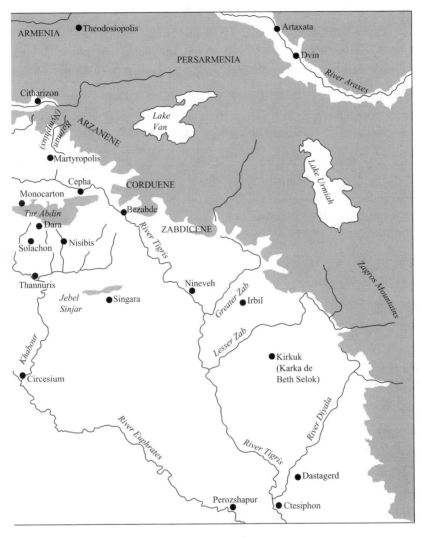

Map 3: (*cont.*)

There is no doubt that the peace treaty of 298 made the Roman Eastern frontier more secure. During the first Tetrarchy the so-called *Strata Diocletiana* from Damascus via Palmyra to Sura[72] was built and fortified with numerous forts (map 3), and a security zone with military roads, fortresses and watch towers created between Hauran in Southern Syria and the Sinai.

[72] See Eadie 1996: 72–82; Konrad 1999: 392–410.

The latter was later called 'Palestinian' or 'Arabian Limes'.[73] Given how important Persia was for Roman foreign trade (**28**), Diocletian had worked towards a settlement in which economic and strategic components complemented each other. It was his goal to reconcile questions of security with the control over the trade with the East, which was so important for Rome.[74] The treaty established the Mesopotamian city of Nisibis as central to the trade between the two empires (**17**), and this role would continue in the future. From now on economic and strategic factors were also important in the diplomatic relations between both empires (**27–28**). Although there were still unsolved problems to do with the spread of information through diplomats, defectors and spies (**35**), for the time being the peace treaty of Nisibis formed the beginning of a peaceful period between Rome and Persia that would last for forty years – an exceptionally long period of peace in the history of Roman–Sasanian relations.

2.2 THE FOURTH CENTURY: THE CONFLICT ESCALATES UNDER ŠĀPŪR II (309–79)

Very little is known about the successors of the Sasanian king Narsē, Hormizd II (302–9) and Adanarsē (309). They did not play a decisive role in Roman–Sasanian relations. It looks as if Hormizd II embarked on an unsuccessful Western campaign, possibly in order to take revenge for his father Narsē's humiliating defeat, which he had witnessed.[75] A small note found in the so-called *Chronicle of Arbela*, a Syriac–Nestorian source of the sixth or seventh century whose authenticity and reliability are controversial among scholars, should be mentioned in this context.[76] The chronicle claims that Hormizd initiated his Western campaign in order to avenge the Roman persecutions of Christians that took place during the reigns of Diocletian and Galerius.[77] Hormizd II indeed showed tolerance to the Christians, who were a persecuted minority in both the Roman Empire and the Sasanian kingdom. His Western advance, however, did not bear an impact on the peace of 298.

This peace between Romans and Persians ended during the reign of Šāpūr II (309–79), who renewed the aggressive Western policy of the early Sasanian kings. Šāpūr II intended to recover not only those territories

---

[73] On the development of this part of the Roman frontier see Graf 1978: 1–26; Kennedy 1982; Bowersock 1983: 76–157; Isaac 1992: 118–34.

[74] Seston 1946: 176–7.   [75] Wiesehöfer 1989: 68–71.   [76] See ibid. 68–9 n. 7.

[77] *Chr. Arb.* 11 p. 67, 9–11 (tr. Kawerau); cf. Assfalg 1966: 19–36; on the significance of this source see Kettenhofen 1995b: 287–319.

that had been lost in 298 but also all of Mesopotamia and Armenia. It is possible that the king followed a far-reaching and programmatic foreign policy which included the restoration of the former Achaemenid Empire as far as the Strymon river (**2**).[78] Although Persia struggled with a period of political unrest after the death of Hormizd II, Rome kept to the agreement of 298 and thus missed a good opportunity for a military attack. Šāpūr II was still a child when he took over the throne but soon managed to consolidate his reign – the longest and one of the most renowned reigns of all Sasanian kings. The year 338 was an important turning-point because at this time hostilities with Rome started again. Changes in religious affairs that had occurred within the Roman Empire dramatically affected the relationship between the two great powers. The reign of Constantine the Great (306–37) ushered in the turning-point known as the 'Constantinian Revolution'.[79] Since his victory over Maxentius (306–12) at the Milvian Bridge in the year 312 Constantine had been convinced that the well-being of the Roman Empire depended on its protection by the Christian God. From 312 onwards non-Christian religions were therefore repressed and the Christianisation of the Roman Empire took place at a much accelerated pace. The fact that Constantine turned to Christianity and furthered this religion in state and society encouraged the Christians in Persia to bond even more than before with their fellow-believers in the Roman Empire.[80] The more Constantine felt responsible for the well-being also of the Persian Christians, the more they became the natural allies of the Western arch enemy in the eyes of Šāpūr II. It is therefore not surprising that when the military confrontations between the two great powers resumed long-lasting and severe persecutions of the Christians in Persia began. Numerous acts of martyrs reflect the suffering of the Christians in this period and illustrate the political character of the persecutions (**31**). When Constantine the Great died on 22 May 337 in the middle of his preparations for the Persian War, Šāpūr II used the opportunity to conquer Armenia, which had been Christianised since the beginning of the fourth century. The attack formed a prelude to numerous armed confrontations between Rome and Persia.[81] These lasted to the death of Constantius II (337–61), who ruled over the Eastern half of the *imperium Romanum* after the death of Constantine. Neither of the two sides gained any major advantages during this period (**7**).

---

[78] For the Roman–Persian relations under Šāpūr II in general see Barceló 1981: 73–104 and Hunt 1998: 11–14, 39–43 and 73–7.

[79] See Brandt 1998: 32–4 and Girardet 1998.   [80] Blum 1980: 26–7.

[81] Blockley 1989: 465–90; on Constantius' objectives see Warmington 1977: 509–20.

When the Caesar Julian (361–3), who agitated in the West, refused to reinforce Constantius' army against the Sasanians, the emperor was in a difficult situation. When, moreover, in the spring of 360 Julian was proclaimed *Augustus* by his army in Paris, Constantius was forced to intervene against him in the West but died on his way in Cilicia on 3 November 361. Towards the beginning of the year 363 his successor to the throne, Julian, renewed the Roman offensive in the East in order to deal with the situation along the Eastern frontier of the Roman Empire once and for all. His advance far into Sasanian territory was successful at first but ended in catastrophe. The emperor was wounded in battle and died on 26 June 363 (**8**). In great haste a new emperor, Jovian (363–4), was proclaimed, who had to conclude a peace with Šāpūr II immediately. Jovian was in a hopeless situation and his main concern would have been to lead his army safely back to Roman territory; he therefore had no choice but to agree to the peace terms dictated by Šāpūr II, namely to surrender the conquests made by Diocletian, to give up Nisibis and Singara and to withdraw from Armenia (**18**). The hope for a lasting peace was not fulfilled. Šāpūr II felt bound by the treaty of 363 only as long as Jovian was alive. When the Roman emperor died in the following year he went back to his aggressive policy against Rome. In 371 he embarked on a campaign against Armenia (**8**), which led to nothing less than the division of Armenia between the Romans and the Sasanians. When Šāpūr II died in 379 Persia was more powerful than ever before. The king had been one of the greatest rulers on the Sasanian throne and was admired even by authors biased against him, such as Ammianus Marcellinus.[82] Apart from the continuing quarrels over Armenia,[83] the tensions between the two great empires ceased towards the end of the fourth century;[84] apparently the two sides moved closer together because both had a lively interest in guarding the Caucasian frontier and in sharing the cost of its defence (**27**).

2.3 THE FIFTH CENTURY: DÉTENTE AT THE ROMAN EASTERN FRONTIER

While the fourth century was characterised by the long reign of Šāpūr II and his aggressive Western policy and hence marked by numerous armed

---

[82] Schippmann 1990: 36–7.

[83] For a history of Armenia in the fourth century see Baynes 1910: 625–43; Garsoïan 1967: 297–320; ead. 1971: 342–52; Hewsen 1978/9: 99–126; for the partition of Armenia during the reign of Šāpūr III (383–8) see the references on p. 185 n. 56.

[84] For an analysis of Roman–Persian relations under Theodosius I see Gutmann 1991: 226–32.

confrontations between the two powers, the fifth century shows an easing of tension between West and East.[85] The Christians in Persia also fared better after the death of the 'great persecutor'.[86] Especially the reign of Yazdgard I (399–420) displays a sympathetic attitude towards the Christians (**32**). The king was determined to retain peace with the Romans. In 408/9 the two sides came to an agreement that regulated the trade between West and East and served the interests of both sides (**28**). The sources further illustrate good relations at the beginning of this century by telling us that the emperor Arcadius (383–408) asked Yazdgard I to become the guardian of his infant son Theodosius after his death (**9**). However, refraining from an expansive foreign policy against Byzantium and sympathising with the Christians made Yazdgard I the target of accusations by the bellicose Persian nobility as well as the Zoroastrian priesthood. Towards the end of Yazdgard's reign the Christians were persecuted again (**32**) and many Persian Christians escaped to the West. Yazdgard's successor, Bahrām V Gōr (420–39), demanded that Theodosius II (408–50) extradite them. When the latter refused, the Sasanian king continued the persecutions initiated by his predecessor. Moreover, in the year 421 Bahrām V started a war with Byzantium. As neither of the two sides achieved any noteworthy successes, the war did not last for very long and a peace was concluded just one year later (**19**).[87]

In the following period armed confrontations were only occasional and of short duration.[88] This is somewhat surprising if one considers how aggressive Sasanian attitudes towards Rome had been during the third and fourth centuries; the Roman Empire was in a difficult situation after the death of Theodosius the Great in the year 395 and during the course of the fifth century numerous peoples exerted pressure on virtually all borders of the *imperium Romanum*.[89]

Undoubtedly, developments in the religious sphere in the Roman Empire played a significant role in this context because in the past the situation of the Persian Christians had repeatedly provoked tensions between the great powers. The growing Christological differences within Christianity,[90]

---

[85] On the Byzantine–Sasanian relations in the fifth century see Synelli 1986: 47–73; Rubin 1986: 677–95 and Whitby 1988: 202–9.

[86] On the situation of the Persian Christians in the fifth century see Macomber 1968: 174–87.

[87] On the Roman–Persian relations in the first half of the fifth century see Lee 1987: 188–91; Schrier 1992: 75–86; Blockley 1992: 52–67; Greatrex 1993: 1–14.

[88] For an account of the confrontations between Theodosius II and Yazdgard II see Thompson 1950: 58–75.

[89] For a survey of the situation in the East from Theodosius I to Anastasius see Blockley 1992: 39–96.

[90] On these see Spuler 1961: 174–9; on the emergence of two separate Churches in the East see Heiler 1971: 303–403.

however, meant that in the fifth century the Christians in Persia were increasingly favoured and tolerated. After the Councils of Ephesus (431) and Chalcedon (451)[91] numerous followers of Nestorius' doctrine of Christ's dual nature fled to Persia and became crucial supporters of the Sasanian dynasty.[92] In contrast to the Christians, who were attached to the see at Antioch, the Nestorians were not seen as potential spies but rather as allies in the battle against Byzantium. At the same time the Byzantine emperor's claim to be the sole legitimate representative of the Christian Church was rejected.[93] As a consequence religious persecutions ceased. In the year 484 Barsaumā, a fanatical follower of Nestorianism, used his influence to the effect that the synod of Bēt Lāpāt,[94] supported by the Sasanian ruler Pērōz (459–84), imposed the Nestorian religion on all Christian communities in Persia.[95] Within a short period of time the Nestorian Church established a close net of dioceses throughout the empire and Nestorianism became something like a second 'state church' besides Zoroastrianism.[96]

Be this as it may, the lack of Persian pressure on the Western frontier may also be explained by the continuing conflicts with the Hephthalites, which forced the Sasanians to exert all their energies on the Eastern frontier (**10**).[97] The Hephthalites were among the peoples who had advanced from Dsungara to Central Asia and now ruled Sogdia, Bactria, the Western side of the Tarim Basin and Northwest India.[98] The Sasanian kings Yazdgard II and Pērōz I in particular had to cope with the attacks of these peoples, who were also called the 'White Huns'. Yazdgard II was even forced to move his residence to the East for a few years in order to take better action against the Hephthalites. When Pērōz I died in his battle against the Hephthalites Persian foreign policy entered a phase of complete inertia.

There were no new confrontations with the Romans, although the Western power repeatedly tried to gain from the problems faced by its Eastern opponent. Emperor Leo I (457–74) refused the payments for the defence of the Caucasus passes that had been agreed upon by both powers in 441 and served the interests of both sides (**27**). However, Procopius states that Zeno (474–5/476–91) sent the *magister officiorum* Eusebios as ambassador to the Sasanian king Pērōz I so that he would accompany the king

[91] On the councils of the fourth and fifth centuries see Young 1983.
[92] On Nestorianism see Stewart 1928.   [93] Hage 1973: 182–7.   [94] Morony 1990: 187–8.
[95] Gero 1981; on Barsaumā as mediator between East and West see Brock 1992; Brock 1996: 69–85 and Teixidor 1995: 499–510.
[96] For the consequences of this development on the unity of the Church in the West see Haussig 1959: 34–56.
[97] A survey of the history of Eastern Iran in the Sasanian period may be found in Bivar 1983a: 209–17.
[98] Zeimal 1993: 232–62.

on his campaign against the Hephthalites.[99] Other instances also confirm solidarity between the emperor and the 'King of kings'.

The period after the death of Pērōz I in 484 symbolised Persian weakness also in internal affairs because the Sasanian monarchy had to give in to the increasing claims for power made by the nobility. The successor of Pērōz I, Balāš (484–8), reigned for only a few years before he was deposed. A more and more powerful nobility handed the throne to Kavādh I (488–97/499–531). Within Persia, important events took place during the reign of this ruler, namely the so-called 'Mazdakite revolt' and the renewal and consolidation of the Sasanian monarchy (**11**). These events eventually led to renewed confrontations with the Romans.

2.4 THE SIXTH CENTURY: THE SASANIANS RENEW THEIR EXPANSIONIST POLICY IN THE WEST

When Kavādh I regained the Sasanian throne in the year 499[100] the focus of Persia's foreign policy shifted back to the West. A return to the aggressive Western policy of the Sasanian rulers of the third and fourth centuries triggered numerous armed confrontations.

In the year 502 the Sasanian king was in need of funds in order to pay the Hephthalites, who were now his allies. He approached the Byzantine emperor Anastasius I (491–518). When the emperor declined and instead demanded that the Sasanians return Nisibis, Kavādh used the opportunity to wage war against Byzantium.[101] In this war, which lasted for several years, Sasanian troops had the upper hand on many occasions and in 503 were able to take the strategically important city of Amida. In the year 505/6 the fighting ceased. Renewed confrontations with the Hephthalites finally forced the Persians to seek terms for peace and they agreed to give up Amida and further territories that they had conquered in return for a high sum. The subsequent peace was concluded for a period of seven years but actually lasted for over twenty years.[102]

Although the following years did not see any further armed conflicts, the Romans in particular engaged in activities that had long lasting consequences.[103] In light of the previous war Anastasius realised that the Roman fortifications along the frontier were insufficient and could not prevent Persian advances. In the following years he therefore built new fortresses close to the frontier.[104] In Armenia he undertook extensive work to fortify

---

[99] Proc. *BP* 1.3.8.   [100] Ibid. 1.6.1–18.   [101] Lyd. *Mag.* III.51–3; Ios. Styl. 7.11–12; Proc. *BP* 1.7.1–2.
[102] Proc. *BP* 1.9.1–25.   [103] Greatrex 1998: 120–2.   [104] Whitby 1986a: 717–35.

Theodosio(u)polis. Across from the Persian fortress at Nisibis he founded
the city Dārā-Anastasioupolis,[105] which provoked tensions with the Sasanians who claimed that the location of the city, only twenty-eight *stadia* from
the shared border, was a breach of the existing regulations. While open
confrontations did not take place during Anastasius' reign, the Persian War
was rekindled during the reign of his successor, Justin I (518–27).[106] One
main reason for this war was certainly the fact that both sides contended
for the important border regions Lazika and Ibēria as well as the Caspian
Gates. Kavādh I, who wanted to secure his son Xusrō's succession to the
throne, tried to come to a peaceful understanding with Byzantium but
failed (**12**).

After that the relations between the two powers deteriorated. The unan-
swered questions regarding Lazika and Ibēria once more shifted to the
foreground and were responsible for the war that broke out probably in
526, not long before the death of Justin I.[107] Kavādh I died in 531, and at this
point Romans and Persians were engaged in open war. In spite of several
successes neither of the two parties was able to gain an advantage, with
the result that a peace treaty was concluded in 532.[108] The Romans agreed
to submit large payments for the maintenance of the fortifications in the
Caucasus as well as the protection of this unstable region, and also to move
the base of the *dux Mesopotamiae* away from Dārā to Constantia.[109] The
Persians gave up significant places in Lazika, a region that was as important as it was disputed between the two empires. Although Procopius talks
about the conclusion of an 'Eternal Peace'[110] in the context of the treaty of
532, both powers were at war again shortly after.

After the long but turbulent reign of Kavādh I Persia flourished under
Xusrō I (531–79). This king received the title 'Anōšarvān' (= 'immortal
soul') and was praised above all for his cultural achievements. Even his
political opponents displayed respect to him, and during this period a
strong Western interest may be observed in developments in Persia (**37**).
The political relations with the Romans, however, did not remain unspoilt
for long. Both sides used the peaceful phase after 532 in order to consolidate
their own position of power and to carry out domestic reforms. Just as
Justinian I (527–65) achieved great successes in both internal and foreign
affairs,[111] Xusrō I reorganised Persian society and introduced reforms of the

---

[105] Proc. *BP* 1.10.1–19.   [106] For this Persian War see Vasiliev 1950: 254–74.
[107] Proc. *BP* 1.12.1–24.
[108] For the peace of 532 see ibid. 1.22.1–19; Rubin 1960: 291–7 and Greatrex 1998: 213–21.
[109] Proc. *BP* 1.22.3–5 and 16–18; Blockley 1985a: 70–1.   [110] Proc. *BP* 1.22.3.
[111] For a critical evaluation of Justinian's activities see Rubin 1960–95; Evans 1996; Meier 2003.

tax system as well as the military, which increased Sasanian strike power significantly.[112]

The period after the so-called 'eternal Peace' of 532 was therefore not really a détente because both great powers watched each other with suspicion. The great successes of Justinian I alarmed Xusrō I. Procopius tells us that the Sasanian king soon regretted having concluded the peace thereby facilitating his opponent's tremendous expansion of power.[113] Towards the end of the 30s the situation was so tense that war was almost inevitable. In most modern accounts Xusrō I is presented as the aggressor.[114] There were diplomatic activities preliminary to the war but these were geared towards improving their respective positions within a delicate international balance of power (**13** and **35**). A dispute over border-land between two Arab tribes, the Lahmids and Ghassanids, was used to justify the outbreak of new hostilities (**25**).[115]

From the spring of 540 Romans and Persians were once more at war. Initially, Xusrō I scored a prestigious victory when he attacked and took Antioch on the Orontes (**13**).[116] The inhabitants of the Syrian metropolis were deported to Persia (**36**). Justinian had not been able to stop the forceful Sasanian attack. As the majority of the Roman units were engaged in the West and not available to confront the Persian army, the emperor had to enter into negotiations (**35**). Both sides agreed to a truce under the following terms: Xusrō had to withdraw whereas the Romans were obliged to make not only a single payment but also an annual tributary payment of 500 pounds of gold.[117] Justinian accepted the terms because this was the only way for him to conclude his activities in Italy successfully.

Xusrō I withdrew his army very slowly to make sure that he would receive the stipulated payments. A formal peace treaty would not be concluded before the tribute had been handed over. The king moved his army to the gates of Chalcis, on which he imposed a ransom, and then crossed the

---

[112] On Xusrō I's reforms see Grignaschi 1971: 87–147; Gnoli 1985: 265–70; Rubin 1995: 227–97 and Howard-Johnston 1995b: 211–26.

[113] Proc. *BP* 1.26.2.

[114] The most elaborate account of Justinian's Persian Wars may be found in Rubin 1960: 279–84; see also Higgins 1941: 279–315; Blockley 1985a: 62–74.

[115] Already during the second half of the third century Rome and Persia had begun to entrust the defence of their frontiers to powerful Arab leaders (**24**). In the sixth century the allied Saracens, who fought both on the Sasanian and the Roman side, played a decisive role in the development of the armed confrontations between West and East (**25**); see in general Shahîd 1984; 1988 and 1995; Ball 2000: 30–105.

[116] Downey 1953: 340–8 and 1963: 247–53; Liebeschütz 1977: 487–99 and Börm 2006: 301–28; on the Byzantine–Sasanian confrontations between 540 and 544 see Trombley 2005: 392–6.

[117] Proc. *BP* 11.10.24; on tributary and subsidiary payments as a common element of late antique diplomacy see Isaac 1995: 129–32.

Euphrates at Barbalissos to extract money from several other cities.[118] The
Sasanians also besieged the city of Dārā in breach of the truce, but without
success.[119] In the light of these activities Justinian did not feel bound to the
agreements any more.[120] A peace was never concluded.

The following year saw further military conflicts. This time the theatre
of war was the region of Lazika, which had been the object of dispute
earlier during the reign of Kavādh I.[121] When the Lazi made an appeal
to Xusrō I to intervene against the quartering and rule of Roman troops
within their territory the king promised to protect them from the Romans
whom Justinian had sent to fight Xusrō.[122] With a strong force the Persians
conquered Petra, a fortress situated on the Eastern coast of the Black Sea.[123]
In the meantime the Roman general Belisarius, who had been recalled from
Italy and whom Justinian had sent against Xusrō in the spring of 541, arrived
in Mesopotamia. During the following years the battles in Armenia[124] and
Mesopotamia were fought with changing luck and neither of the two parties
scored a lasting success. Xusrō was hoping, however, that an advance into
Mesopotamia in the year 544 would bring a breakthrough. In particular, he
decided to conquer Edessa in order to get hold of the Roman possessions
beyond the Euphrates.[125] However, the siege of the city, which Procopius
describes at length, was not as successful as the king had hoped and the
Sasanians withdrew in return for a ransom payment.[126]

Both sides were now at the point where they recognised that the annual
wars, which were more or less nothing but raids, neither achieved territorial
gains nor served either side in the long term. They entered negotiations
for a peace. While Justinian had an overall peace within the entire East in
mind, Xusrō I was only prepared for an armistice. He did not want to give
up the dominant position he enjoyed in Lazika at the time. In the spring
of 545 Justinian I gave in and had to agree to considerable payments.[127]

The armistice was concluded for five years but only four years later the
confrontations resumed.[128] Until 556 the Sasanians suffered several major
defeats and were pushed back to the borders of Ibēria and the Persian part
of Armenia. Almost all of Lazika was once more under Roman control.[129]

---

[118] Proc. BP II.12.1–34.   [119] Ibid. II.13.16–27.   [120] Ibid. II.13.27–8.
[121] See Braund 1994: 287–314, esp. 292–6.   [122] Proc. BP II.15.1–31.   [123] Ibid. II.17.3–28.
[124] For the history of Armenia in the period see Adontz 1970.
[125] On the history and culture of Edessa, one of the most important cities in Northern Mesopotamia,
      see Drijvers 1977: 863–96 and 1980; Segal 1970; on Roman Edessa see Ross 2001.
[126] Proc. BP II.26.5–46 and 27.1–46.   [127] Ibid. II.28.6–11.
[128] For the sequence of events see Stein 1949: 503–16.
[129] The contemporary author Agathias gives us a detailed account of the armed confrontations regarding
      Lazika and the other Caucasian territories in the third and fourth books of his Histories; see also
      Stein 1949: 510–16.

In 551 a new armistice, which did not apply to Lazika, had been concluded for five years and was ending now. Xusrō wanted to conclude a peace and sent envoys to Justinian. In 557 both sides agreed upon a general armistice, which included Lazika. Until a final peace treaty had been signed each would remain in possession of the territories they were occupying.[130]

It is not clear why it took another five years before a formal peace was concluded, as both sides were interested in a permanent settlement. Justinian was threatened by the Huns at the borders of his empire, and Xusrō faced new and powerful enemies in the East.[131] It is likely that neither of the two sides wanted to initiate negotiations for a peace in order not to appear in the weaker position. Both powers acted defensively, watched the opponent suspiciously from a distance and tried to hide their own intentions.[132] Finally in autumn of 562 a formal peace (**20**) ended the second great Roman–Sasanian War of the sixth century.

In the following period the focus of Persia's foreign policy shifted to the East and to the Arabian Peninsula. Between 546 and 562 the powerful empire of the Western Turks had formed in the Sasanian East.[133] After the fall of the Hephthalite Huns in 557 these became a natural enemy of the Sasanians, especially when they allied themselves with the Romans and established contractual contacts with Justin II (565–78).[134] This alliance together with the Persian advance all the way into Yemen (**14**) led to new tensions shortly after the *foedus* of 562 had been concluded. Xusrō I Anōšarvān was still king when in the spring of 572 another long lasting war between Romans and Persians broke out (**14**).[135]

While Roman units attempted but failed to take Nisibis[136] the Sasanians captured the Roman fortress of Dārā and invaded and raided large areas of Syria.[137] In the following years both sides suffered heavy losses. Justin II was not getting any advantage out of the war and his empire was threatened by the Avars in the North and the Langobards in Italy; Tiberius, whom Justin had appointed to be his co-regent when he became severely ill in 574, therefore decided to come to terms with Xusrō I.[138] The parties agreed

---

[130] Agath. IV.30.8–10.   [131] Widengren 1952: 69–94; Golden 1992; Sinor 1990a: 285–316.

[132] Agath. IV.23.1.   [133] Sinor 1990a: 285–316; Golden 1992; Christian 1998.

[134] For Justin's attempt to engage the Sasanians in a war with two fronts see Frye 1983a: 158–9.

[135] On this third great war in the sixth century see Bury 1966: 95–126; Whitby 1988: 250–75; Cowe 1991: 265–76; Isaac 1995: 125–55.

[136] On the struggle for Nisibis see also Lee 1993a: 569–85 and Whitby 2000: 266–8.

[137] For these developments see Szádeczky-Kardoss 1979: 113–18; on the situation in Syria see Liebeschuetz 1977: 487–99.

[138] On the peace efforts during this period see Winter 1994: 605–6.

on a one-year armistice, which was later extended (575–8). As Armenia was excluded from the regulations, warfare continued. Diplomatic efforts did not bear fruit. As a consequence Xusrō eventually invaded Mesopotamia even before the armistice had expired. In spite of initial Persian successes in Armenia and in the Roman part of Mesopotamia[139] the Romans were able to repel the Sasanian king, who finally sought peace. Before ambassadors could be exchanged Xusrō I Anōšarvān died. His son and successor Hormizd IV (579–90) made demands that – as Tiberius' envoys claimed – the Romans could not possibly meet. The state of war continued and lasted throughout the reign of Hormizd IV, even after on the Roman side Maurice (582–602) had become emperor.[140]

Apart from the war in Mesopotamia Hormizd IV had to deal with the Turks in the East, the Chazars[141] in the North and Arab tribes in the South. In particular the Western Turks became increasingly dangerous, similar to the Hephthalites during the fifth century.[142] With great efforts and entirely owing to the military genius of the Sasanian general Bahrām Čōbīn the Western Turks were defeated and became tributary allies in 588/9.[143] Next Bahrām Čōbīn was sent to the Southern regions of the Caucasus so that he could fight the war against Byzantium from there. Although initially he was victorious, he suffered a great defeat in the plains of Azerbaijan.[144] Hormizd IV accused him of cowardice and decided to dismiss him.[145] His decision was to have far-reaching consequences for the course of Sasanian history and Persian–Roman relations.

Bahrām Čōbīn and his troops reacted with a rebellion and were soon supported by the Sasanian army in Mesopotamia.[146] Persia was in such turmoil that Hormizd IV was taken captive and blinded; in the spring of 590 his son Xusrō II Parvēz (590–628) was proclaimed king.[147] His attempts to reach an agreement with the rebels were to no avail and he fled from the general,[148] who ascended the Sasanian throne on 9 March 590 and became King Bahrām VI Čōbīn.[149] The latter had already sent envoys to Maurice

[139] Honigmann 1935: 22–3.   [140] Higgins 1939: 55–70 and Whitby 1988: 250–75 and 276–304.
[141] On the Chazars see Golden 1990: 256–84.   [142] See Frye 1983a: 156 and Bivar 1983a: 215.
[143] Tabarī, tr. Nöldeke, pp. 270–5; Bosworth 301–5 (992–4); on Bahrām Čōbīn see Shahbazi 1989: 519–22; for the confrontations with the Turks see Goubert 1951: 121–3.
[144] Theoph. Simoc. III.7; for a detailed analysis of this battle see Goubert 1951: 123–5.
[145] Ibid. III.8.1.   [146] Ibid. IV.1–2.
[147] For the chronology of events see Higgins 1939: 51–2; 1955: 97; in general see also Whitby 1988: 292–7.
[148] Theoph. Simoc. IV.10.1–11; cf. Frendo 1989: 77–88; on Xusrō II's escape into Roman territory see Goubert 1949: 81–98.
[149] Theoph. Simoc. IV.12.6; on the date of the crowning see Schreiner 1985: 300–1 n. 573–4 and Whitby 1988: 296.

asking the emperor not to ally himself with Xusrō. Bahrām promised that
if the emperor remained neutral he would hand over Nisibis and all of
Mesopotamia as far as the river Tigris.[150] Xusrō II Parvēz in turn offered
Maurice Dārā, Martyropolis, part of Armenia and remission of the annual
tributary payments.[151] In Constantinople the opinions on what should be
done were divided. The Senate demanded that Maurice give priority to
the interests of his own empire, that is, to let Persia fall into a state of
anarchy.[152] However, Maurice decided to support the legitimate claims of
Xusrō II Parvēz and to restore him to the throne.[153] In this way Maurice
abandoned the basic principle of Western policy not to intervene in internal
matters of the Sasanian Empire.[154] For the first time Roman and Persian
units fought side by side. In the spring of 591 Xusrō II embarked on an
advance against Bahrām VI Čōbīn. With Roman help he managed to defeat
the rebel.[155] The latter escaped to the Western Turks but was assassinated
a year later.[156] Xusrō II Parvēz was restored to the throne in 591[157] and
the same year brought about a peace treaty,[158] which ended the third great
Roman–Persian War of the sixth century.

The following paragraphs summarise the relations during this century:
at the beginning of the sixth century we observe a turning-point in the
relations between the empires. By renewing royal power, dealing with the
Mazdakite movement and introducing social reforms Xusrō I Anōšarvān
enabled the Sasanians, who possessed immense financial resources, to inflict
serious harm on their western neighbour. Although for a short period of
time the reign of Justinian I revived the former glory of the Roman Empire,

---

[150] Theoph. Simoc. IV.14.8; Theoph. *Chron.* A. M. 6080 (p. 265, 24–6, ed. de Boor).

[151] Theoph. Simoc. IV.13.24.

[152] There is silence on this conflict in the Greek sources but the oriental literature provides us with
stories embellished in the typical way; cf. e.g. the national epos Šahnāma by the Persian poet Firdausi
(died in 1020), a history of Persia from the beginning to Sasanian times (select Engl. tr. Levy 1996;
German tr. Mohl vol. 7: 101–23); according to Theoph Sim. IV.14.1 and Tabarī (tr. Nöldeke 283–4;
Bosworth 311–12 [999]) Xusrō II received military support from Byzantium without any delay.
Xusrō in fact had to wait several months for the requested aid; cf. Higgins 1941: 310 n. 88; on the
discussion in Constantinople regarding Roman involvement in the Sasanian succession see also
Goubert 1951: 143. See also ch. 8 n. 22.

[153] See also Frendo 1992a: 59–68 and Riedlberger 1998: 161–75.

[154] On the emperor's motives see Winter 1989a: 84–8.

[155] On the cooperation between Roman and Sasanian units and the decisive victory over Bahrām VI
Čōbīn at Gandzak see Theoph. Sim. V.11–2; on the date of the battle see Higgins 1939: 53–4 and
Schreiner 1985: 314–15 n. 744.

[156] See Christensen 1944: 445.

[157] Euagr. *HE* VI.19; Chr. pasch. a. 591; for an English translation with introduction see Whitby 2000.

[158] On this peace treaty see Goubert 1951: 167–70; on the frontier line after 591 see Honigmann 1935:
28–37.

the emperor expended Roman power and consumed resources during his numerous military campaigns.

During the sixth century the confrontation between Romans and Persians took place on a worldwide scale.[159] Not only the border areas but also the Avars, Turks, Chazars and Arabs were included in the struggle. Moreover, Roman activities in the Western empire as well as growing Sasanian difficulties in the East had an impact on the fighting between the two. Only when Maurice and Xusrō II joined forces towards the end of the century did tensions cease, and an agreement was reached. Corresponding to the good personal relationship between Maurice and Xusrō II Parvēz, who saw himself as the son of the Byzantine emperor,[160] the relations between the two sides remained friendly. However, this phase is not well documented. Xusrō II probably used the time in order to consolidate his rule, to revive the economy and to fill the royal treasury. When confrontations resumed at the beginning of the seventh century the Persians once more proved to be strong and very serious opponents for the Romans.

2.5 THE SEVENTH CENTURY: MIGHT AND DECLINE OF SASANIAN POWER

After Maurice's downfall and assassination by the rebel Phocas (602–10) in 602 the good relationship between Persians and Romans changed abruptly. Theodosius, supposedly Maurice's son, approached Xusrō II for help. The king was prepared to avenge Maurice's murder; he received Theodosius with open arms at his court and proclaimed him the legitimate ruler of the Byzantine Empire.[161] When he also imprisoned the envoys sent by Phocas to announce his take-over of the Byzantine throne, the two powers re-entered the state of war. Initially, Xusrō II must have perceived this situation not as fighting a war against the Romans but rather as dealing with a tyrant. The parallels with the events of 590/1 are obvious. According to the Byzantine historian Theophylact Simocatta, in the king's eyes Phocas' usurpation of the throne was a justified reason for war.[162] This war represents the last great Roman–Sasanian confrontation, which – after the pinnacle of

---

[159] Higgins 1941: 279–315.
[160] Theoph. Simoc. v.3.11; Theoph. *Chron.* A. M. 6081 (p. 266, 13, ed. de Boor) and Tabarī, tr. Nöldeke, 275; Bosworth 305 (994).
[161] Tabarī, tr. Nöldeke 290; Bosworth 317 (1002).
[162] Theoph. Simoc. VIII.15.7; however, the historian also remarks that the king used the events in Byzantium as a pretext in order to open war against the West once more; cf. Garsoïan 1983: 578.

Persian power – led to the fall of the Sasanian Empire and which brought on dramatic changes that involved the entire Middle East.[163]

At first Xusrō II was determined to exploit the desolate situation within the Byzantine Empire and to expand the borders of his kingdom. Certainly favoured by the rebellion of the powerful Roman general Narsēs[164] the Persian army began an almost unstoppable advance to the West. Within five years the entire Eastern part of the Byzantine Empire fell into Persian hands (**15**).[165] The difficult situation within the Byzantine Empire, which continued after Phocas' downfall in 610, forms the background to a letter written by the Senate of Constantinople to Xusrō II in the year 615. In this letter the 'King of kings' is asked to recognise the new emperor Heraclius (610–41)[166] as his 'legitimate child'. In turn, the emperor would honour him as a father deserved.[167] This is not the only example of a Byzantine emperor willing to pay a childlike respect to a foreign ruler.[168] At this point, however, Xusrō II was no longer prepared to abandon his plans of an expansion in the West. When Alexandria fell and Egypt was lost in the year 619[169] the Romans were altogether in a hopeless situation. In contrast, Persia was at the height of its power.

But the Romans recovered quickly. Internal developments helped the emperor to consolidate his position as well as to strengthen the empire's military force.[170] Moreover, after the fall of Jerusalem in 614[171] the Church supported Heraclius by offering its riches to help in his war against the Persians. Heraclius agreed to make high payments to the Avars and thereby managed to conclude a temporary peace (620) with them. His success marked a turning-point that eventually led to the final defeat and fall of the Sasanian kingdom.

On the day after Easter 622 Heraclius and his army left Constantinople in order to re-conquer the lost territories.[172] At the beginning of the year 623 the two armies clashed for the first time. The Persian general Šahrbarāz suffered a crushing defeat. As a consequence, Asia Minor was liberated from Sasanian rule. The victory boosted the morale of the Roman troops and had the Avars not broken the peace agreement they would have advanced even

---

[163] The most comprehensive account can be found in Stratos 1968: 103–17; cf. also Frendo 1995: 209–14.
[164] See Stratos 1968: 59–60.
[165] See Foss 1975: 721–47; Morony 1987: 87–95; Russell 2001: 41–71; Foss 2003: 149–70.
[166] On this emperor see Reining and Stolte 2002; Kaegi 2003.   [167] Chr. Pasch. a. 615.
[168] See Dölger 1964: 61 n. 63.   [169] See ch. 3 n. 219 below for references.
[170] Ostrogorsky 1963: 77–91; Stratos 1968: 257–82; Garsoïan 1983: 588–92.
[171] Clermont-Ganneau 1898: 36–54 and Wheeler 1991: 69–85.
[172] Oikonomidès 1976: 1–9.

further.[173] Be that as it may, it did not take Heraclius long to offer higher payments and buy the neutrality of the Avars once more. In the spring of 323 he began a new offensive via Cappadocia into Armenia, where he took Dvīn and other cities and also moved further south against Gandzak. Here he destroyed an important Zoroastrian sanctuary that had been founded by the first Sasanian ruler Ardašīr I (224–40), apparently in order to take revenge for the preceding raid of Jerusalem. The years 624 and 625 saw numerous confrontations between the two opponents in which the Romans were victorious for the greater part. However, as Heraclius could not score a decisive victory he withdrew to Cilicia in 625.[174]

In the following year Xusrō decided to attack Heraclius' army in Cilicia and to march against Constantinople in order to gain a sudden decisive advantage. Šahrbarāz crossed Asia Minor and advanced as far as Calchedon. The situation became even more threatening when, shortly after, the ruler of the Avars, the *Khagan*, also pressed against Constantinople with a large force and besieged the city from two sides.[175] However, the Avars suffered a major defeat by sea on 10 August 626 and immediately withdrew so that the Sasanian plan of a united front against Byzantium failed and with it the whole Persian offensive. Šahrbarāz returned from Calchedon to Syria. At this point the last great Roman offensive began.

While the capital was under threat, Heraclius stayed away from Constantinople so that he would not be surrounded. In Lazika he built up a new, powerful army and established contacts with the Chazars, a Turkish people located between the Sea of Azov and the Caspian Sea. This alliance between Romans and Chazars was to become both a threat to Persia and a characteristic of a new Roman Eastern policy.[176] In the summer of 627 Romans and Chazars fought successfully against the Sasanians in the southern Caucasus region and conquered Tiflis in Sasanian eastern Georgia. Then Heraclius decided to invade Sasanian territory.[177] At the ruins of Niniveh the Roman troops clashed with a Persian army that Xusrō II had sent against them in order to stop Heraclius' advance. When in December of 627 a battle was fought the Persians suffered a crushing defeat, which decided the war in favour of Byzantium. Heraclius moved on to find Xusrō II in his favourite residence at Dastagird. The Sasanian

---

[173] On the Avars see Samolin 1957–8: 62–5; Pohl 1988; Daim et al. 1996.
[174] Zuckerman 2002: 122–55.
[175] Barišić 1954: 371–95; Stratos 1967: 370–6; Howard-Johnston 1995a: 131–42.
[176] On Heraclius' stay in the Caucasus region and his diplomatic contacts with the Chazars see Stratos 1968: 197–203.
[177] For a detailed account see Kaegi 2002: 156–91.

king escaped to Ktēsiphōn whereas Heraclius took Dastagird and set up his camp for the winter at the river Narbas. He did not attempt to attack Ktēsiphōn because of its strong fortifications.[178]

Internal developments in Persia rather than military confrontation ended the struggle.[179] Xusrō II summoned all his generals in order to search for those who could be held responsible for the defeat at Niniveh. Provoked by fear, the generals revolted against Xusrō II Parvēz (590–628) and appointed his son Kavādh II Šērōē as the new ruler. They were supported by the nobility, whom Xusrō II had alienated more and more during his long reign. Moreover, his subjects had lost respect for the king when he took flight from Heraclius. All these factors contributed to Xusrō's downfall. On 25 February 628 Kavādh II Šērōē was proclaimed king and soon after his father was imprisoned and executed.

With regard to its external affairs, Persia was now in an entirely defensive position. Kavādh II and Heraclius concluded a peace (**21**) according to which the Persians were to give up the Roman territories of Armenia and the western part of Mesopotamia in the same year, Syria, Palestine and Egypt in the following year. The return and restoration of the Holy Cross in March of 628[180] symbolised the final victory of the West over the East and established a motif that would become notorious in the religious wars of later ages.

When Kavādh II Šērōē died during the first year of his reign (628) the Sasanian Empire started to disintegrate internally.[181] Kavādh's son and successor Ardašīr III (628–30) was still under age, and so Šahrbarāz, who had been a powerful general during the reign of Xusrō II, sought power. He killed Ardašīr and proclaimed himself king (630). Apparently Heraclius supported his activities by putting soldiers at his disposal.[182] The emperor's behaviour thus forms a stark contrast with Maurice's earlier reaction to Bahrām Čōbīn's claims against Xusrō II Parvēz. Heraclius was not interested in a legitimate succession but in exploiting Persia's internal difficulties, that is to make sure that his opponent would be weakened for as long as possible. Along with this attitude the direct relations between Romans and Persians ended because in both empires internal matters shifted to the foreground. As far as external matters are concerned, both were soon confronted with the onslaught of the Muslim conquerors.[183]

---

[178] Minorsky 1943–6: 243–65.
[179] For the events in the Sasanian Empire see Christensen 1944: 497–509 and Frye 1983a: 170–2.
[180] Cf. Baynes 1912: 287–99. [181] On this process see Schippmann 1990: 72–7.
[182] Nöldeke 1883: 31. [183] Cf. Fiey 1987: 96–103.

After a rule of only forty days Šahrbarāz was also killed. In the following period military leaders and members of the Sasanian dynasty contended for power. After Šahrbarāz' death the following held the Sasanian throne for short periods of time: Xusrō III, Bōrān,[184] Āzarmēduxt, Hormizd V, Xusrō IV, Pērōz II, and Tarruxzādh-Xusrō (= Xusrō V). The constant struggles did not end until Yazdgard III (632–51) was crowned as the last legitimate heir to the Sasanian throne. Yazdgard's determination to restore former glory is manifest in the fact that his coronation took place in Istakhr, the home of the Sasanian dynasty.[185] From Istakhr the king went to Ktēsiphōn and appointed Rustam supreme commander of his army. However, the long wars against Byzantium had exhausted the empire so that it could no longer develop great power.

In the meantime changes in the Arabian Peninsula affected the entire political and strategic situation in the Near and Middle East.[186] In the year 622 the prophet Muhammad founded a state in Madīna that would unite all Arabs under his own religious and secular rule. Muhammad intended to end tribal and religious fragmentation as well as Arab dependence on the great powers. Under the banner of Islam the prophet successfully put these goals into practice before he died in the year 632. His successors initiated a massive expansionist policy that combined religious fanaticism with an aggressive desire for conquest. The ensuing Arab offensive and their continuous triumphant progress were certainly facilitated by the weakness of the Romans and Persians, who had dominated the events in the Middle East for centuries.

After some fighting along the borders in 636 a major battle took place at Qādisīya close to Hīra, which was the old capital of the former Lahmid state, where the Arabs inflicted a crushing defeat on the Sasanians.[187] Shortly after the Arab conquerors captured Seleucia, crossed the Tigris, invaded Ktēsiphōn and advanced further into the interior.[188] In 642 for a last time a large Persian army answered their attack at Nihāvand but without success. The defeat accelerated the downfall of the kingdom. Although the Arabs had to continue fighting for some time before they had subjugated all areas within the Sasanian Empire, they faced merely local conflicts with individual independent rulers. Yazdgard III's reign continued void of glory.

---

[184] With observations on late Sasanian imperial ideology see Daryaee 1999: 77–82.
[185] Bivar and Boyce 1998: 643–6; Wiesehöfer 1998c: 1145–6.
[186] Endreß 1997; on the prophet Muhammad see Bobzin 2000.
[187] On this battle and the subsequent events see the detailed account by Spuler 1952: 8–21; cf. also 'Abd al-Husain Zarrīnkūb 1975: 1–33 and Hinds 1984: 39–53.
[188] Hinds 1984; 39–53; Daryaee 2002: 3–18.

Constantly in flight and in search for allies who would assist him against the Arab invaders he finally came to Merv where he was assassinated in 651. The death of this last member of the Sasanian dynasty marks the official end of the history of the Sasanian Empire, which in fact had already ceased to exist after the battle at Nihāvand.[189]

Although the Romans celebrated a triumphant success when the Holy Cross was restored in Jerusalem in March 628,[190] the continuous struggle with Persia had taken its toll. Soon after the Romans had re-conquered Syria, Palestine and Egypt, these territories were lost once more, this time to the Arabs. After a significant battle at the river Yarmūk in August 636 Syria fell into Arab hands.[191] The conquerors had already taken Damascus in 635, and in 637 Jerusalem fell. After the Persian defeat at Qādisīya the Arabs occupied the Roman possessions in Mesopotamia in order to attack Armenia from there. In 639 they finally attacked Egypt, which was conquered by 646. The most important Eastern provinces of the Byzantine Empire had thus fallen under Arab rule.[192] The Arab conquest reveals yet once more the historical significance of the struggle between the Romans and Persians for hegemony in the Near and Middle East: no doubt the exhausting confrontations between West and East had fostered the Islamic expansion.[193]

---

[189] See Tyler-Smith 2000: 135–70.
[190] Grumel 1967: 139–49; Whitby 1998: 247–73; on the date of this restoration see Speck 2000: 167–79.
[191] On the battle see Kaegi 1992: 112–46; on Syria during this period see Foss 1997: 189–269.
[192] Stratos 1972: 40–62; Donner 1981 and 1995: 337–60; Kaegi 1992.
[193] Zakynthinos 1979: 64–5; Kaegi 1992.

PART II
Sources and contexts

Political goals

In order to understand the intense and multi-faceted relations between Romans and Persians during the course of late antiquity – and in particular the many military confrontations that continued into the seventh century – one has to address the overall political goals of the two great powers. These goals are therefore the starting point of the second part of our survey, in which we present and analyse the source material.

Whereas Roman generals of the Late Republic already boasted that as Alexander's successors they had extended the borders of the Roman Empire to the ends of the earth[1] and scholars agree on Rome's claim to world domination,[2] namely to rule an *imperium sine fine* ('an empire without borders')[3] or 'an empire that extended from sun rise to sun set',[4] there is no corresponding consensus among scholars with regard to the goals that drove Sasanian foreign policy. The following examination therefore focuses on the Sasanian claims and the ideological background of the Sasanian foreign policy vis à vis Rome. This should not, however, evoke the impression that the Sasanians acted as aggressors and the Romans as defenders of threatened possessions or territories, which, obviously, the latter had conquered in long, violent wars from an unwilling population. On the contrary, the reader should be aware that such a 'eurocentric' view, which has been prevalent for many decades in the scholarly literature, is not justified in any way.[5]

1: Territorial claims of the Sasanians against Rome

The contemporary sources presented in this chapter indicate that immediately after AD 224 the Sasanians refused to acknowledge Rome's supremacy in the Near and Middle East. The enormous Persian capacity for expansion

---

[1] Diod. xl.4.   [2] Cf. Badian 1971; Raaflaub 1996: 273–314.
[3] Verg. *Aen.* 1.279; cf. also p. 13 n. 22 above.   [4] Horace *Carm.* IV.15.14–15.
[5] On the scholarly discussion see van de Mierop 1997: 285–306 and (with references) Hauser 2001a: 1233–43.

during the course of the third century was based on and reinforced by the euphoric successful foundation of the Sasanian Empire and moreover facilitated by the deep 'crisis' Rome faced during this period, a crisis that forced the Western power into a defensive position and led to the primary goal of preserving its own possessions. However, as soon as the political, economic and social problems of the Roman Empire receded, the Romans similarly exploited phases of instability within the Sasanian Empire and embarked on numerous military offensives against the territories held by their Eastern opponent in order to underline their claim to world domination, which continued to exist up to the fall of the Roman Empire. Evidently, the imperial prestige on both sides significantly fostered the emergence of conflicts between the two powers.

Herodian VI.2.1–2

(1) For thirteen years he [sc. Severus Alexander] reigned in this way, and so far as it was up to him, irreproachably. In the fourteenth year,[6] however, he was suddenly sent reports by the governors in Syria and Mesopotamia informing him of the following: the Persian king Ardašīr [I][7] had defeated the Parthians and had dissolved their rule in the East. He had put to death Artabanos,[8] who used to be called Great King and had worn two diadems.[9] Moreover, Ardašīr had conquered all of the barbaric areas around and was forcing them to pay tribute. He was still not satisfied and was not staying within the borderline of the river Tigris but crossing its banks and thus the borders of the Roman Empire. He was overrunning Mesopotamia and threatening Syria. (2) He was determined to re-conquer for Persia the whole territory across from Europe and cut off by the Aegean Sea and the Sea of Marmara, which as a whole is called Asia, because he viewed this as his inheritance, arguing that the whole area, as far as Ionia and Caria, had been administered by Persian satraps from the time of Cyrus, who was the first to transfer power from the Medes to the Persians, to the time of Darius, the last of the Persian kings, whose power the Macedonian Alexander destroyed. He claimed that it was now his task to renew this empire for the Persians just as they had possessed it in the past.

Herodian composed his history of the Roman Empire, which covers the time period between 180 and 238, in the third century. Although the author, who wrote in the Greek language, favoured the rhetorical and literary

---

[6] The number of years is historically not correct. It should be the tenth year of the reign of Severus Alexander (= 232), whose *dies imperii* was 13 March 222.

[7] Herodian calls the first Sasanian king Ardašīr I (224–40) by his Greek name 'Artaxerxes'; for reasons of consistency the translations of the sources use the conventional names of the respective rulers.

[8] This is the last Arsacid ruler Artabanos IV (213–24).

[9] On the iconography of this Parthian ruler with 'two diadems' see Gall 1980: 241–50.

aspects of his work over historical accuracy,[10] the above passage attests to important political changes within Iran. The successful revolt of the Sasanian Ardašīr I (224–40) against the ruling dynasty of the Arsacids led to the fall of the Parthian kingdom and became the foundation of the Neo-Persian Sasanian Empire. The consequences of this development for the Romans are evident. The Roman emperor received reports from the East that speak not only of an immediate threat for the Eastern frontier as well as Mesopotamia and Syria but also of Sasanian territorial claims that affected all of Asia Minor. Herodian explains these aspirations by referring to Ardašīr's argument that all territories east of Europe and the Aegean Sea had once been part of the Achaemenid Empire founded by Cyrus the Great, the ancestor of the Sasanians. Ardašīr thus presents his claims as an inherited right and his political goals as legitimate.

Cassius Dio, who wrote a history of Rome that ended with the events of the year 229, also points to the dangers arising for Rome when power in Iran changed hands. This contemporary author is in general judged to be a more reliable source, but in accordance with Herodian he states that Ardašīr was planning to re-conquer everything the Persians had once ruled, all the way to the Aegean Sea.[11] This also corresponds to the Sasanian tradition, which is now lost but has been passed on through Muslim scholars. The Arab historian Tabarī, who lived in the ninth/tenth century, is the main representative of this learned tradition.[12] He reports that Ardašīr started an uprising in order to avenge the blood of the last Achaemenid ruler Darius III, who had been defeated by Alexander the Great. Tabarī moreover reveals that Ardašīr intended to return power to the legitimate family and to restore it as it had existed during the reigns of his ancestors,[13] who had lived before the 'vassal' kings.[14]

Succession to the former Persian kings included, so Ardašīr believed, ruling the territories they had ruled. Although knowledge regarding the

---

[10] See Müller 1996; on Herodian as a historical source for the third century see Alföldy 1974: 89-111; Zimmermann 1999a and 1999b: 119–43.

[11] Cass. Dio LXXX.4.1.; cf. Bering-Staschewski 1981: 112–13; on the relation between Herodian and Cassius Dio see also Alföldy 1971: 360–6.

[12] Tabarī, tr. Nöldeke 2–3; Bosworth 3–4 (813–14); on Tabarī and his work see Sezgin 1967: 323–8; Springberg-Hinsen 1989: 32–4; see also the relevant chapters on the Arab authors al-Mas'ūdī (**29**) and Ibn Miskawayh (**29** and **37**).

[13] The Neo-Persian 'letter of Tansar', which probably goes back to the late Sasanian period but refers to the reign of Ardašīr states that the king did not want to give peace before he had avenged Darius against the successors of Alexander (letter of Tansar, p. 42; tr. Boyce 65; cf. Fowden 1993: 29–30; in n. 72 Fowden points to Mas'ūdī naming 'Ardashir as restorer of the Achaemenid achievement and principal forerunner of Muhammad's Islamic Empire'.

[14] This is a reference to Parthian rule; on the 'vassal kings' see the glossary.

Achaemenid dynasty must have been sparse during the Sasanian period, the fact that the Western and Eastern traditions agree speaks for itself. Apparently, immediately after the foundation of the empire in 224 the Sasanians demanded possession of all of Mesopotamia, Syria, Asia Minor, Armenia and Egypt as well as control over Arabia and the Red Sea. These goals conflicted with the claims made by the Roman emperor, who saw himself as successor to Alexander the Great and wanted 'to rule the world'; they deepened the antagonism between the Western and the Eastern power and led to numerous military confrontations that lasted into the seventh century.[15] A recurring question throughout this book will be whether and how far these wide-reaching Sasanian goals were strictly limited to the context of the foundation of the empire and attempts to legitimise the rule of their own dynasty, or if Sasanian claims to areas outside Iran were an ideological premise of a programmatic foreign policy that lasted significantly beyond early military conflicts between the two powers.

2: Succession to Achaemenid rule as programmatic foreign policy

The Šāpūr Inscription on the Kaʿba-i Zardušt at Naqš-i Rustam (ŠKZ),
§ 1 The Parthian text

I, the Mazdā-worshipping 'god' Šāpūr, King of Kings of the Aryans and non-Aryans, scion of the gods, son of the Mazdā-worshipping 'god' Ardašīr, King of Kings of the Aryans, scion of the gods, grandson of the 'god' Pābag, the King, am ruler of the Empire of the Aryans.

With regard to our knowledge of Roman–Sasanian relations in the third century we cannot overestimate the significance of an epigraphic testimony that dates to the reign of the second Sasanian ruler, Šāpūr I (240–72), namely Šāpūr's great trilingual inscription on the Kaʿba-i Zardušt ('Cube of Zarathustra') in Naqš-i Rustam, near Persepolis (map 5). The inscription informs us about Šāpūr's conception of himself and his political goals, about the make up of the Sasanian state and about religious matters in the Sasanian kingdom. By analogy with the *Res gestae divi Augusti*, the famous and also epigraphic report of the first Roman emperor, Augustus, the text is called *Res gestae divi Saporis*. Šāpūr I probably composed it himself during the final years of his life, before his son Hormizd had it inscribed after his father's death. Between 1936 and 1939 scholars of the Oriental Institute of

---

[15] Cf. in contrast Strobel 1993: 287–8 and the references in n. 31 below.

Chicago discovered the inscription. In 1940 it was published for the first time. Numerous studies of the text have appeared since then that illustrate the extent to which the inscription complements the Western tradition with its more vague and impressionistic account of the Roman–Persian confrontations. In particular, the inscription draws attention to aspects that authors writing in Greek and Latin neglect altogether. Taken in conjunction with its place of origin and the object inscribed, the content of the text throws significant light on the political goals and rule of the second Sasanian ruler.[16] Šāpūr I uses the title 'King of kings', which had previously been used by the Achaemenid Great Kings.[17] The additional title 'King of Iran and non-Iran'[18] attests to the universal character of Šāpūr's claims, which were among other things also directed against Rome.[19] E. Kettenhofen cautions us that the king does not explicitly claim an old Achaemenid legacy in order to legitimise his political goals vis-à-vis Rome.[20] Šāpūr neither labels his conquests 'former Achaemenid territory' nor does he reclaim the whole area to the Sea of Marmara as Persian legacy.[21] However, the genre of the text may be responsible for the lack of such explicit claims. In his report, the Sasanian ruler displays facts that serve to praise his military and political achievements. M. Rostovtzeff suspected that the inscription followed the official annals of the Sasanian ruling house, which – as was traditional in the ancient Near and Middle East – recorded the king's deeds day by day and year by year. According to this interpretation the inscription is a kind of epitome of an official history.[22] Undoubtedly, the text's main objective is to display Šāpūr as he wanted to be viewed; that is, defeats are omitted, just as they are in the Western tradition of historiography.

Apart from Šāpūr's official title 'King of the kings of Iran and Non-Iran' the inscription contains further Achaemenid reminiscences. We may start with the fact that the text was cut into the Ka'ba-i Zardušt. The building, a kind of tower, was a fire sanctuary built during the reign of Darius I and was located in the valley of Naqš-ī Rustam, an important Achaemenid place of worship (fig. 1). Here the Achaemenids worshipped their former kings in

---

[16] For a bibliography see Kettenhofen 1982: 12–18; 1983: 151–71 and Huyse 1999: 9–11 (vol. 2).

[17] On the significance of this title for the Arsacids see Wiesehöfer 1996: 55–66.

[18] Gignoux 1987: 30–1; Gnoli 1989; Wiesehöfer 2001: 287, 'In *ŠKZ* Shapur uses it to denote all the regions he (temporarily) conquered (Syria, Cappadocia, Cilicia), while he accounts Armenia and the Caucasus region as part of Eran, although they were primarily inhabited by non-Iranian people. Kirdir lists Armenia, Georgia, Albania, Balasagan, as well as Syria and Asia Minor, as regions of Aneran.'

[19] Gnoli 1987: 509–32.   [20] Kettenhofen 1984: 184–5.   [21] Ibid.

[22] Rostovtzeff 1943/4: 20–1; cf. also MacDonald 1979: 77–83.

Fig. 1 The Achaemenid rock tombs at Naqš-ī Rustam and the Kaʿba-i Zardušt
(Gallas, K. (1978) *Iran. Kulturstätten Persiens zwischen Wüsten, Steppen und Bergen*: fig. 34:
drawing in Flandin, E. and Coste, P. (1843–54) *Voyage en Perse pendant les années
1840 et 1842*)

monumental rock tombs.[23] The three languages of the inscription (fig. 2)
also illustrate an attempt to take up Achaemenid traditions. Middle Persian,
Parthian and Greek were the three official scripts in the Sasanian Empire. In
contrast to the Middle Persian text, which was discovered first, the Parthian
and Greek translations of the Middle Persian have been preserved fairly well.
The Middle Persian text was inscribed on the eastern side of the Achaemenid
shrine, the Parthian and Greek texts on the southern and western faces. The
monumental royal inscriptions of the former Achaemenid rulers had also
been trilingual (Babylonian, Elamite, Old Persian).[24] This parallel cannot
be a coincidence.

[23] Cf. Fowden 1993: 29, 'It is unreasonable to maintain that the Sasanians had no knowledge at all of
the Achaemenids. There were, for instance, the visible monuments of the past such as the tombs of
the Achaemenids at Naqsh-ī Rustam, a place that the Sasanian dynasty too regarded as of central
significance and obviously not by coincidence'; cf. also Potter 1990: 372f.
[24] On these Achaemenid trilingual inscriptions see Kent 1953: 116–35; on the origins of the trilingual
documentation see Ghirshman 1965: 248–9; on the Achaemenid royal inscriptions in general see
Koch 1992: 13–28; for a comparison of the three versions and on the 'original' text see Huyse 1999:
182–209 (vol. 2); on the official and spoken languages in the Achaemenid and Sasanian Empires see
Schmitt 2000: 21–42 and 45–7.

Fig. 2 The three languages of the Šāpūr Inscription (*ŠKZ*)
(Schmidt, E.F. (1970) Persepolis III. The Royal Tombs and other Monuments: pl. 9 A–B:
Southeast and Southwest Corner)

In the fourth century the Sasanians still referred to the Achaemenid dynasty in order to legitimise their own territorial claims. The contemporary historian Ammianus Marcellinus, whose knowledge of the situation in the East was extensive, includes a letter of the Sasanian king Šāpūr II (309–79) in his work. In this letter, the king demands that the Roman emperor Constantius II return Armenia and Mesopotamia and in addition to these all territories to the Strymon river and the borders of Macedonia which had belonged to his ancestors.[25] Elsewhere the author reiterates that Šāpūr II claimed territories reaching as far as Bithynia and the coasts of the Sea of Marmara.[26] E. Kettenhofen raises the objection that the Roman historian does not quote Šāpūr literally and that the letter should not be viewed as an authentic testimony. However, there is no reason to believe that the king's letter did not include the phrase _ad usque Strymona flumen et Macedonicos fines_. We would not do the author, who must be accorded high credibility,[27] justice if we see Šāpūr's claims as they are presented in Ammianus as mere 'literary reminiscences'.[28] Most scholars agree that in Roman eyes Šāpūr's references to the borders of the former Achaemenid Empire were a delicate and dangerous political threat.[29]

As Roman–Persian relations progressed in time, there are but few hints that show the East adopting Achaemenid ideology.[30] Be that as it may, in spite of numerous setbacks, the dynamics of the Sasanian Western policies from the third to the seventh century illustrate a desire to restore the Achaemenid borders (**15**).

This interpretation should not lead us to assume that the Sasanians were necessarily the aggressors and responsible for every war they fought with the Romans. In many instances, the activities of the latter were far from 'reactive' or 'defensive'. On the contrary, there is no doubt that Rome repeatedly pursued an offensive policy in the East. However, it seems justified to talk about a programmatic Sasanian foreign policy, which formed the counterpart to the Roman claim to world domination.[31] Scholars correctly point to these rivalling ideological claims to explain how Rome and

---

[25] Amm. XVII.5.3–8.   [26] Ibid. XXV.4.24.

[27] Cf. the important works by Matthews 1989a and Barnes 1998; with regard to the situation in the East see Matthews 1986: 549–64; on the Sasanians as Rome's main opponent in the East see Straub 1986: 218–22.

[28] Kettenhofen 1984: 183–4 and 190; Seager 1997: 253–68; Teitler 1999: 216–23; Trombley 1999: 17–28.

[29] See Rubin 1960: 252 ('ein Politicum von gefährlicher Brisanz'); for a different interpretation see Strobel 1993: 288.

[30] Yarshater 1971: 517–31.

[31] This interpretation is controversial among scholars; see Kettenhofen 1984: 177–90; Wiesehöfer 1986b: 177–85; Winter 1988: 26–44; Panitscheck 1990: 457–72; Potter 1990: 370–80; Gnoli 1991: 57–63; Wolski 1992: 169–87; Lee 1993a: 21–32; Fowden 1993: 24–36; Wiesehöfer 1994: 389–97, esp. 392; Kettenhofen 1994a: 99–108; Roaf 1998: 1–7; Daryaree 2002: 1–14; Shahbazi 2002c: 61–73; Huyse 2002: 298–311.

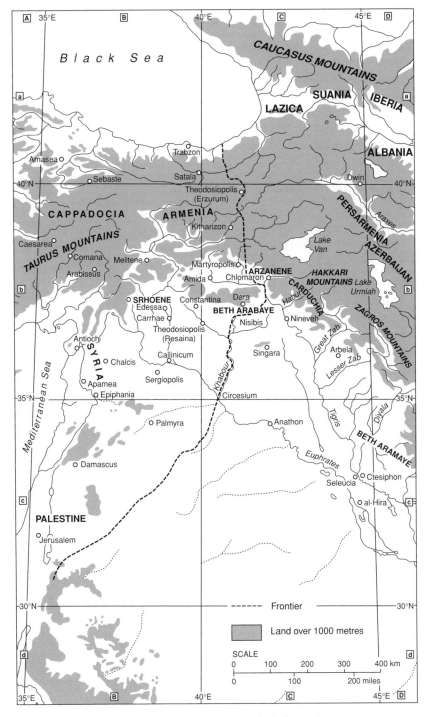

Map 4: The Roman–Sasanian Frontier in late antiquity

Persia consistently failed to become long-term partners on the basis of a mutually accepted international law.[32] In other words, the universal claims on both sides hardly allowed for a peaceful coexistence. They had a tremendous impact on how both sides handled latent conflicts; almost always the enemy's real or apparent weaknesses were met by an aggressive behaviour. Over centuries the borders between Rome and Persia were contested and military confrontations took place almost without interruption.[33]

[32] Grey 1973: 24–40 and Funke 1996: 225–6.
[33] For an overview see Ensslin 1939: 126-37; for the period before AD 337 see Millar 1996: 127–89.

Warfare

3: Sasanian armament and tactics

Heliodorus, Aethiopica IX.15.1–6

(1) The character of their armament is the following. A selected man chosen for his bodily strength wears a helmet[1] that is compact and made of one piece, and it is skillfully crafted to look exactly like a man's face. He is covered by this from the top of his head to the neck except for the eyes in order to see through it; he equips his right hand with a pike longer than a spear, the left is free for the reins. He has a sabre hung by his side under his arm, and he is armed with a corselet not only across his breast but also across the rest of his body. (2) The construction of the corselet is as follows: they forge plates of bronze and iron into a square shape that is a span long on all sides, and they fit one to the other at the edges on each side so that the one above always overlaps with the one below and the one alongside with the one next to run on continuously, and they furnish the conjunction with hooks under the flaps; thereby they create a kind of chiton clad in horny scales, which clings to the body without causing pain and covers it on all sides, tracing each limb and not hindering movement as it contracts and extends. (3) For there are sleeves, and it reaches from the neck to the knee, separated only at the thighs, as much as is necessary to mount a horse's back. Such a corselet it is, a protection against missiles and a defence against all wounds. The greave reaches from the top of the foot to the knee, fastened to the corselet. (4) They fence their horses all around with a similar equipment, tying greaves around the feet, and they bind the whole head tightly with frontlets, and from the back to the belly they suspend on either side a covering plaited in iron, so that it serves as armour but at the same time because of its slackness does not impede the fast pace. (5) Having equipped or rather encased the horse in this way the rider gets on, not leaping up but with others lifting him up because of the weight. When the moment of battle comes, he drives his horse with the rein, applies his spurs and goes with all his force against the enemies, looking like an iron man or like a moving image wrought with the hammer. (6) With its point the pike protrudes a lot, being held up against the horse's neck by a rope. The butt-end is fastened alongside the horse's thighs with a knot, so that it does not

---

[1] Grancsay 1963: 253–62; Overlaet 1982: 189–206.

give way in clashes but supports the hand of the rider, which only gives direction to the blow; the rider, however, exerts himself and presses for the wound to be even harsher; through his force he destroys everyone whom he encounters, and with one blow he may often transfix two.

Maurice, Strategikon XI.1

The Persian nation is wretched, dissembling and servile, but also patriotic and obedient. It obeys its rulers out of fear. Because of this the Persians are capable of enduring their work and engage in wars on behalf of their fatherland. Eager to deal with most serious matters rather by way of counsel and strategy, they pay attention to order and not to courage and rashness. Raised in a hot climate, they easily bear the annoyance of heat, thirst and the lack of food. They are awesome when they lay siege, and even more awesome when they are besieged; they are extremely apt in hiding their pain, in holding out nobly in adverse circumstances and turning these to their advantage. And in negotiations they are irreconcilable so that they do not offer themselves what they want to choose for their own benefit but as recipients are offered this by their enemies. They are armed with cuirass or thorax, bows and swords,[2] and experienced in quick – but not forceful – archery, more than all other warlike nations. Going to war, they encamp within fortified boundaries. When battle arises, they create a ditch and a sharp palisade around themselves; they do not leave the baggage train in this but create the ditch to have a refuge from a critical situation in battle. It is not their practice to let their horses graze but to let them gather their feed from the hand. They are set up for battle in three equal parts, the centre, the right and the left, with the centre having up to 400 or 500 selected men in addition. They do not create an even depth within the formation but try to line up the cavalry in each unit in the first and second line or *phalanx* and to keep the front of the formation even and dense. They place the supernumerary horses and the train a short way behind the main line. When they are in battle against pike men it is their practice to place their main line in the roughest landscape and to use their bows in order that the attacks of the pike men against them are dispersed and easily dissolved by the difficult terrain. Not only before the day of the battle do they like to delay the fighting, in particular when they know that the enemies are well prepared and ready for fighting, encamping on the most inaccessible ground, but also during the battle itself, in particular in the summer, they like to make their attacks around the hottest hour, in order that through the boiling heat of the sun and the delay in time the courage and spirit of those lined up against them slackens, and they make their charges step by step in an even and dense formation, because they walk gently and attentively. They are, however, distressed by the following: the cold and the rain and the south wind, which ruin the force of their bows; a formation of infantry that is carefully composed; a place with an even surface or a bare one because of the charges of pike men; dense fighting because showers of arrows become useless from close by and because they themselves do not use pikes and shields; pressing forward in

---

[2] Rostovtzeff 1943: 174–87; Paterson 1969: 29–32; Overlaet 1989: 741–55 and Masia 2000: 185–9.

battles because they rush to immediate flight and do not know how to suddenly turn against their attackers, as do the Scythian nations; attacks and encirclements as the result of an outflanking on the sides and rear of their formation because they do not place good flank guards in their line to sustain a major attack; often also unexpected nightly attacks against their camp because they place their tents without distinction and at random within the encirclement of the camp. It is thus necessary to line up in battles as the treatise about formations says, namely to choose ground that is even, open and level, so far as possible, which does not have swamps or ditches or shrubs so as not to dissolve the formation. When the army or formation is well prepared do not delay the attack, if it has been firmly decided to fight on that day. In battle, launch the charges and attacks when close to the reach of the bows, even and in dense order, and swiftly, lest through a delay in getting to hand-to-hand combat the enemies, sending a continuous shower of arrows, get to afflict our soldiers and horses with even more missiles.

The two passages are excerpts from two very different sources, each of which provides us with an impressive as well as vivid account of Sasanian armament and tactics.[3] Heliodorus, who tells us that he was a 'Phoenician from the city of Emesa, from the family of the descendants of Helios', is the author of a Greek novel entitled *Aethiopica* ('Aethiopian stories'). The date of this work is uncertain but it was probably composed in the third century, or possibly the second half of the fourth century.[4] As a genre, the Greek novel was extremely popular. The *Aethiopica* tells the love story of a certain Theagenes and an Aethiopian princess Chariclea, whose adventures take them all the way to Delphi.[5] Because of its wide geographical scope this novel is particularly interesting. In our passage the contemporary observer Heliodorus describes the mailed Sasanian cavalry,[6] which underlines the significance of this source with regard to questions of cultural history.

The second source relates to the late phase of Byzantine–Sasanian relations. A work entitled *Strategikon*[7] is attributed to the Byzantine emperor Maurice (582–602), who secured the throne for the Persian king Xusrō II Pārvēz (**34**). This is a manual on military affairs composed in Greek, which contains much information concerning military tactics, the organisation and line-up of the army, military training and the use of armament as well as siege craft and instructions for generals. It is not clear whether the emperor

[3] For a general background see Tafazzoli 2000.
[4] Cf. van der Walk 1941: 97–100 and Szepessy 1975: 279–87; Bowie 1999: 40–1.
[5] See Winkler 1982: 93–158 (also in Swain 1999: 286–350); Szepessy 1984: 432–50; Hunter 1998.
[6] On the Sasanian mailed cavalry see Bivar 1972: 271–91; Michalak 1987: 73–86; Mielczarek 1993: 51–67; Campbell 1999: 339.
[7] For the Greek text see Dennis 1981; for an English translation see Dennis 1985; also Kollautz 1985: 87–136.

Maurice was indeed the author of the work but it is fairly certain that the text originates from some time between the end of the sixth and the beginning of the seventh century. The confrontations with the Islamic Arabs that began in the 630s are not mentioned.[8] Although the so called *Strategikon* of Maurice is one of many comparable military treatises that were composed in the early Byzantine period,[9] it stands out as one of the most important works and adheres to the reality of its time in an exceptional way. Moreover, it is of special value because of its detailed descriptions of foreign peoples and possible opponents, such as the Avars, Slavs and Persians, which provide us with important historical and ethnographical information.

Both texts give insight into the character of Persian armament and battle techniques as well as tactical counter-measures adopted by the Byzantine army.[10] The extremely detailed descriptions of Sasanian armament, techniques and strategies are vivid and accurate, which surprises and impresses the reader. Many of the observations correspond not only with the late antique accounts of particular battles between Byzantium and the Persian Empire[11] but also with the numerous visual testimonies. Many Sasanian silver bowls, finest examples of Persian art and culture, represent the king in full armour and engaged in hunting.[12] The depicted equestrian statue is most likely that of the Sasanian ruler Xusrō II (590–628)[13] because it was found in the grotto of Taq-i Bustan (map 5),[14] immediately below the rock relief representing the investiture of this king. It is not only one of the most important monuments of Sasanian art[15] but also the latest one among the known Sasanian rock reliefs (fig. 3).

The equestrian statue shows the king in full armour.[16] He is armed like a *clibanarius* of the heavy Sasanian cavalry. The equipment of both rider and horse are visible in all details. In 1821 Sir Robert Ker-Porter made a drawing of the relief to illustrate his book *Travels in Georgia, Persia, Armenia and Ancient Babylonia*; in its own way it conveys a good impression of both

---

[8] For a discussion of the date and authorship see Whitby 1988: 242.

[9] Hunger 1978: 329–30.

[10] Cf. e.g. Speidel 1984: 151–6 and Negin 1995: 65–75.

[11] Greatrex and Lieu 2002: 179 and 297 n. 92; Greatrex 1998: 169–85 and 195–207; Wiita 1977: 53–111.

[12] For the most important examples see Ghirshman 1962: figs. 207–11; 247–54; see also Peck 1969: 101–46; Tanabe 1981: 105–18; Wilcox and McBride 1986: 36–48; Harper 1983: 1113–29.

[13] Several scholars have attributed this rock relief to king Pērōz (459–84); cf. Ghirshman 1962: 193; on the interpretation of this relief see also Shepherd 1983: 1086–89.

[14] Ghirshman 1962: fig. 235; on the significance of Taq-i Bustan as a place for royal self-representation see the references pp. 92–3 nn. 87–90.

[15] Fukai and Horiuchi 1962–72; Fukai 1972.   [16] See also Wilcox and McBride 1986: 41.

Fig. 3 Equestrian statue of Xusrō II at Taq-i Bustan
(Ghirshman, R. (1962) *Iran. Parthians and Sassanians*: fig. 235)
(Photo: Ph. Claude Deffarge-Rapho)

the monumentality of the work and the many details eagerly added by the artist (fig. 4).

Testimonies such as the two passages that opened this chapter attest not only to the Western insight into Persian customs and tactics but also to an awareness in the West that the powerful Persian military was well worthy of and in need of investigation.[17] The respect accorded to the Persians

[17] Cf. also Lee 1993a: 103–4.

Map 5: Sasanian Sites

and their army was certainly crucial. Although in general the *Strategikon* displays a hostile attitude towards the Eastern opponent, its author is full of admiration when addressing specific aspects of the Sasanian military. The texts therefore reveal how tough and tenacious the military struggle between the great powers was and how much the relationship centred on strategic advantages and the numerous campaigns fought between the third and the seventh century – campaigns that lasted over decades and moreover demanded long logistic and strategic preparations.[18] On

---

[18] Lee 1989: 257–65 and Whitby 1995: 61–124.

Fig. 4 Sketch of the relief from Taq-i Bustan
(Sir Robert Ker-Porter, *Travels in Georgia, Persia, Armenia, Ancient Babylonia During the Years 1817, 1818, 1819 and 1820*. Vol. II, London 1822, pl. 62)

the Roman[19] as well as the Persian side[20] matters concerning the organisation of the army and its resources were paramount throughout late antiquity.

[19] See Eadie 1967b: 161–73; MacMullen 1980: 451–60; Kaegi 1981a: 209–13; 1982; Turtledove 1983: 216–22; Kennedy 1989: 235–46; Coulston 1990: 139–60; Dixon and Southern 1992; Isaac 1995: 125–55; Kennedy 1996c.

[20] See Inostrancev 1926: 7–52; Frye 1977: 7–15; Coulston 1986: 59–95; Shahbazi 1986: 496–9; Hamblin 1986: 99–106; Nicolle 1996; Tafazzoli 2000.

CHAPTER 3

Military confrontations

Diplomatic contacts and an intensive exchange of information regarding a variety of issues – economy and trade, the security of the borders, religious and cultural matters etc. – formed an important part of Roman–Persian relations. However, it was above all the military confrontations that characterised Rome's relations with her Eastern neighbours. These were as numerous as they were of long duration. Both powers' claim to universal rule pointed out in the previous chapter did not leave any room for a stable coexistence on the basis of international law. Almost inevitably, or rather instinctively, any perceived or real weakness provoked the military initiative of the opponent so that from the third into the seventh century a state of war between the two has to be seen as 'endemic'.[1] The analysis of these military confrontations is therefore predominant in this study, not because of an imbalanced modern view of Roman–Sasanian relations that adopts a 'confrontational perspective' but because of the actual historical events, which were experienced and analysed by the contemporary observers in a similar way. These also emphasise the opposition between West and East and focus on sometimes very elaborate descriptions of a permanent struggle for a powerful position and strategic advantages in the Near and Middle East. This is – and rightly so – reflected in modern scholarship, which has always paid particular attention to questions of peace and war as well as triumph and defeat. Our diachronic survey thus includes a detailed account of the rivalry between the two powers as it is expressed in the numerous military confrontations. The theatres of war included both the Eastern Roman provinces and the Western regions of the Sasanian Empire.

[1] See Hauser's review on Winter and Dignas 2001 (*BMCR* 2002.05.06).

3.1 THE THIRD CENTURY: ORIGINS OF SASANIAN
INTERESTS IN THE WEST[2]

4: Earliest Roman–Sasanian confrontations (230–3)

In the year 230 Ardašīr made his first advance into Roman territory.[3] The Persians besieged Nisibis and undertook raids that led them as far as Syria and Cappadocia.[4] Ardašīr seemed determined to put his political ideas into practice. The Roman emperor reacted with dismay to the Sasanian invasions.[5] On several occasions he sent ambassadors to the king in order to negotiate for a peaceful solution but Ardašīr repeated his aim to re-conquer former Achaemenid territories.[6] A military confrontation was therefore inevitable.

There are but few Western sources that help us with a reconstruction of the events, and the ones that do exist contradict one another. The Eastern tradition does not yield any precise references. Tabarī's remark that Ardašīr was always victorious and that his army had never been defeated is typical.[7] Herodian's elaborate but problematic account[8] is closest to the events in time and allows for a closer analysis.

Herodian VI.6.4–6

(4) When Alexander arrived in Antioch he recovered quickly because after the dry heat in Mesopotamia the much cooler air in the city and its good water supply felt pleasant. He wanted to win back the soldiers' loyalty and tried to appease their anger by promising them a lot of money. He thought that this was the only remedy when it came to regaining the good will of soldiers.[9] He also gathered and prepared a force for a new attack against the Persians, should they cause problems and not give peace. (5) He was informed, however, that the Persian king had demobilised his force and had sent all units back to their homelands. Although the barbarians seemed to have been victorious through the help of some superior force,[10] they were still worn out by the many clashes in Media and the battle in Parthia, where

---

[2] For sourcebooks on Roman–Persian relations in the third century see Felix 1985 and Dodgeon and Lieu 1991.

[3] On the history, origin, course and outcome of this war see Winter 1988: 45–68.

[4] Herodian VI.2.1; Cass. Dio LXXX.3.4; Zon. XII.15.

[5] On the relationship between the two rulers see Potter 1987: 147–57.

[6] Herodian VI.2.4 and VI.4.5 (for an Engl. tr. of these passages see Dodgeon and Lieu 1991: 17 and 19–20).

[7] Tabarī, tr. Nöldeke 21; Bosworth 1999: 17 (820).

[8] Zon. XII.15 is based on Herodian's account. On Herodian see p. 55 n. 10.

[9] These words once more reveal Herodian's critical view of Severus Alexander, whose skills in warfare he tends to judge very negatively.

[10] The expression *ek tou kreittonos* has been interpreted in various ways; cf. Müller 1996: 332; another possible translation would be 'by superiority of military force'.

B l a c k   S e a

40 °E

LAZICA
Petra
GEORGIA

Trapezus

40°N

Theodosiopolis
(Erzurum) ●

Dvin●

Mt Ararat ◦

Caesarea
Mazaca
●

A R M E N I A

C A P P A D O C I A

●Maiferqat

Nımrūd
Dägh

L.Van

●Amıda

Cilician Gates
)(
●Tarsus

Constantına
Edessa ●

Zeugma ●
Carrhae
●

●Dārā
●Nısıbıs

R. Tigris

Greater Zab

Antıoch
●

Resaina
●

A D I A B E N E

Barbalıssus ●
Callınıcum
●

3

Singara
●

Nıneveh ●
Arbela
●

35°N

Hatra ●

Lesser Zab

Cırcesıum ●

Palmyra ●

Dura Europos ●

R. Euphrates

Massıce ●
(Anbār)

Ḥırā ●

Dhū Qār ●

0   300 km

0   200 miles

30°N

40 °E

Map 6: The Roman Near East and the Western Regions of the Sasanian Empire

Map 6: (*cont.*)

many had died and even more had been wounded. For the Romans had not been cowards but had in a way also inflicted great harm on their enemy; moreover, they had been inferior only because they were fewer in number. (6) In fact, almost the same number of soldiers had fallen on both sides and the surviving barbarian soldiers seemed to have won because of their number and not their force. A clear indicator of the barbarian losses is the fact that they remained quiet for three or four years and did not take up arms. When Alexander found out about this, he decided to stay in Antioch; he became more optimistic and lost his fear, and as he was relieved from his concerns about the war he relaxed and enjoyed the pleasures of the city.

Herodian describes the situation after hostilities had ceased in the summer of the year 233. While the Roman emperor Severus Alexander spent his time in Antioch preparing an army for a new attack, he received the news that the Sasanian king had dismissed his soldiers because the Persians had also suffered great losses. Herodian's comments – in particular his remark on the equal numbers of soldiers who had died on both sides – are surprising because this passage is preceded by a detailed account of the hostilities which clearly describes a crushing Roman defeat.[11] The author's psychological characterisation of the Roman emperor tends to be rather schematic. We therefore have to apply caution with regard to Herodian's claim that Severus Alexander's dithering and timid behaviour provoked resentment within the Roman army.[12] However, in spite of inconsistencies in the author's report it looks as if Herodian observed an 'undecided' outcome, which means that matters in the East were not yet settled.[13]

It is difficult to assess the historical accuracy of Herodian's narrative. In particular authors of the fourth and fifth centuries evaluate the outcome of the fighting differently and talk about a great Roman victory.[14] They do not mention Severus Alexander's difficult situation. The biography of the emperor in the *Historia Augusta*, especially, presents him as the triumphant victor. This so-called collection of the *Scriptores Historiae Augustae* includes thirty biographies of Roman emperors and usurpers that cover the time period from Hadrian to Numerianus. The biographies were all composed by the same pagan author towards the end of the fourth century (?) and were not, as they purport to be, a collection of biographies written by six authors during the reigns of Diocletian and Constantine the Great.[15]

---

[11] Herodian VI.5.5–10.
[12] Ibid. VI.5.8 and VI.6.1; on Herodian's tendency to accept stereotypical characterisations and to distort his material along these lines see Zimmermann 1999a: esp. 321–9.
[13] Winter 1988: 63–8.   [14] Fest. 22; Aur. Vict. *Caes.* 24.2.7.; Eutr. VIII.23; Oros. VII.17.7.
[15] On this collection of Latin imperial biographies see especially the commentaries written by an international team of scholars and published as Alföldi, Straub and Rosen 1964–91 and Bonamente, Duval and Paschoud 1991; for further bibliographical references see Johne 1998: 639–40; Birley 1976 with an English translation.

The description of the Persian War of Severus Alexander and the obvious idealisation of the emperor illustrate how problematic these biographies are as a historical source.

Scriptores Historiae Augustae, Severus Alexander 56.2 and 5–8

(2) From the senatorial records of the seventh day before the Calends of October:[16] Senators, we have defeated the Persians. There is no need for long explanations, you should learn only this much, how they were armed and what their contingents were. . .

(5) We scattered 120,000 of their cavalry, we killed 10,000 mailed horsemen,[17] whom they call Clibanarians,[18] in battle and equipped our men with their armour. We captured many Persians and then sold them into slavery. (6) We re-conquered the area between the streams, namely Mesopotamia, which had been given up by that vile beast.[19] (7) We put Ardašīr (I), the most powerful king (not only by name but also in fact) to flight once and for all so that he was seen in flight even on Persian territory, and the king escaped to where our standards had once been taken,[20] leaving his own standards behind. (8) These, Senators, are the facts. There is no need for further explanations. Our soldiers are returning as wealthy men, in light of the victory nobody feels the fatigue.

Scriptores Historiae Augustae, Severus Alexander 57.2–3

(2) This we found in both the annals and many authors. Some, however, claim that he was betrayed by his slave and that he did not defeat the king but fled himself so that he would not be defeated. (3) For those who know the testimonies well there is no doubt that this is against the prevailing view. This minority even claims that he lost his army through hunger, cold and disease, as Herodian states against the prevailing view.

In a fictive speech, the emperor boasts of his military achievements, which present him as the glorious victor over the Persians. The emperor's skills in warfare and his successes are central to the passage. Although the author knows Herodian's account and explicitly names the author, he does not rely on his work and doubts his credibility because Herodian's remarks would spoil the image of the *princeps bonus*.

---

[16] This is a fictive document dating from 25 September 233, which the author of the *vita* claims to cite.

[17] There is no doubt that this number is exaggerated; the origins of these *catafractarii* go back to the sixth century BC. These were heavily armed cavalry from the areas around the Aral Sea who had been integrated into the Seleucid army. Since the time of Hadrian the mailed horsemen also appear in the Roman army; for a description of their elaborate suit of armour see Amm. XVI.10.8 and XXV.1.12; on Persian armour and fighting in general see Wilcox and McBride 1986 and **3** above; on the two powers' military and strategies see Coulston 1986: 77–91; Frye 1977: 7–15.

[18] For equating *catafractarii* and *clibanarii* see Amm. XVI.10.8 and Veg. *Mil.* III.24; whereas the *clibanarii* were soldiers whose horses also wore mailed armour, the horses of the Roman *catafractarii* were not mailed; see **3** above, on Sasanian armament and tactics.

[19] This is a reference to the Roman emperor Elagabalus (218–22).

[20] In 54/53 BC the Roman standards were lost when Crassus was defeated at Carrhae; cf. p. 12 n. 13.

Fig. 5 Coin of Severus Alexander, reverse, 233
(Cohen, H. (1955²) *Description historique des monnaies frapées sous l'empire romain communément appelées médailles impériales IV/2*: Alexandre Sévère nr. 446)
(Cabinet de France. Médaillon de bronze)

The biography follows other much more concise testimonies,[21] which the author of the *Historia Augusta* embellishes rhetorically. Topoi such as the elaborate preparations for the war, the flight of the Persian king, the victory of Severus Alexander and his triumph in Rome appear in the majority of the extant sources; the anonymous author of the biography elaborates on these with much literary freedom and offers the more questionable and remote testimonies in the place of a well-informed and contemporary source. The account is clearly panegyrical.[22] Numismatic evidence attests to a Roman victory and celebrates the emperor's successful return from the East.

The reverse of a coin dated to the year 233 depicts Severus Alexander crowned by the goddess of victory Victoria, at whose feet we see the personified river gods Euphrates and Tigris (fig. 5). The propagandistic character of the image is obvious. Strictly speaking, a representation of the emperor as the master over the two rivers was not correct because this claim did not correspond to the actual frontier between the Roman and the Sasanian Empire. It is noteworthy that the legend (PM TRP XII COS III PP), which shows parts of the typical imperial titulature, does not include the titles *Parthicus maximus* or *Persicus maximus*.[23] No other testimonies confirm Rome's territorial gains as they are suggested by the coin.

---

[21] Cf. n. 14.   [22] Rösger 1978: 167–74.
[23] Kienast 1990: 177–8; on the question whether these titles are attested at all for Severus Alexander see Winter 1988: 60–2; on the liberal use of the terms *Parthi/Persae* see Kettenhofen 1984: 189 and Winter 1988: 227.

In general, the coins of Severus Alexander are based on older types, which the emperor Trajan issued in order to celebrate his successes in the East and which were later also used by Marcus Aurelius as well as Lucius Verus.[24] The choice of these motifs illustrates the aim to depict Severus Alexander as the same triumphant victor over the Persians. After the war in the East further coins were issued whose legends *Victoria Augusti, Iovi Propugnatori, Marti Propugnatori* or *Pax Aeterna Augusti* make it clear that the outcome of the Persian War was to be seen as a victory.[25] This type of propaganda emerged immediately after the events of 233 and was taken up and rhetorically embellished by later authors. An analysis of the source material has thus shown that the outcome of the first Roman–Sasanian confrontation is far from clear.[26] It is neither possible to talk about a splendid Sasanian victory nor to view the Roman emperor as a triumphant victor over the Persians. It rather looks as if each side withdrew their armies and thereby ended the first Roman–Sasanian War because both sides had suffered considerable losses. The Romans retained their positions along the middle Euphrates.

5: Šāpūr I (240–72) at war with Rome

The second Sasanian ruler Šāpūr I (240–72) scored a number of prestigious military as well as diplomatic successes against Rome. In numerous triumphal reliefs he boasts of his victories over his Western opponent. The depicted relief cut into the rock at Bīšāpūr synchronises the successive confrontations with the Roman emperors Gordian III, Philip the Arab and Valerian within one scene (fig. 6).[27] Šāpūr's report of his achievements that was inscribed on the Ka'ba-i Zardušt in Naqš-i Rustam (**2**) also informs us about these wars and describes the events from a Sasanian perspective soon after they took place. First, let us turn to the reign of Gordian III (238–44).

The Šāpūr Inscription on the Ka'ba-i Zardušt at Naqš-i Rustam (ŠKZ),
§§ 6–7 The Parthian text

(§ 6) And as soon as we had become the ruler of the territories, the emperor Gordian conscribed a force taken from the entire Roman Empire, the Gothic and German peoples and marched into Āsūrestān against the Empire of the Aryans and against us; and a great frontal attack took place along the borders of Āsūrestān – in Mišīk.

(§ 7) And the emperor Gordian was killed, and we destroyed the Roman army; and the Romans proclaimed Philip emperor.

---

[24] Gricourt 1965: 319–26.   [25] *RIC* IV² nos. 164; 201; 324; 652.
[26] Wiesehöfer 1982: 445 and 1986a: 373–4.
[27] MacDermot 1954: 76–80; Gajé 1965: 343–88; Mackintosh 1973: 183–203; Göbl 1974; Herrmann 1980; Meyer 1990: 237–302; for an overview over the Sasanian rock reliefs see Vanden Berghe 1984; also Herrmann 2000: 35–45.

Fig. 6 Triumphal relief of Šāpūr I at Bīšāpūr
(Ghirshman, R. (1962) *Iran. Parthians and Sassanians*: fig. 197)
(Photo: John Russel)

According to the *Res gestae divi Saporis* the Roman emperor Gordian III
opened war on the Persians immediately after Šāpūr I succeeded to the
throne.[28] This statement contradicts the Western sources; these mention
several Sasanian invasions into Roman territory, which provoked a Roman
counter-attack.[29] In the spring of 243 the Roman army inflicted a crushing
defeat on the Persians at Rhesaina, between Nisibis and Carrhae, about
which we hear only in Ammianus Marcellinus.[30] In 244 another and this
time decisive battle was fought at Mišīk. According to the Šāpūr Inscription (*ŠKZ*) the Roman army was destroyed in this battle and the Roman
emperor killed. The Persian account clearly links Gordian's death with the
confrontation at Mišīk and thereby differs completely from the Western

[28] On the defensive character of Šāpūr's first campaign against Rome see Sprengling 1940b: 360–71, esp.
     363–4; on the Eastern campaign of this Roman emperor see Kettenhofen 1983: 151–71 and Bleckmann
     1992: 57–76.
[29] SHA *Gord.* 26.6; Synk. 681; Zon. XII.18.
[30] Amm. XXIII.5.17; it is unlikely that Šāpūr I was prepared to hand over Mesopotamia to the Romans
     without fighting.

sources.[31] These talk about Gordian III's victorious activities against the Persians and emphasise that the emperor's successor, the praetorian prefect Philip the Arab, was responsible for Gordian's death.[32] They do not mention the battle of Mišīk. The Šāpūr Inscription alone does not suffice in order to question the entire Western tradition but as the account was composed very soon after the events it cannot be dismissed easily. This is even more so if we consider that the Western authors did not have access to immediate eyewitness accounts but were based on older sources of the third century.[33] There is no doubt that the battle of Mišīk did in fact take place.[34] As it was typical in Eastern historiography to record only victorious events, the battle at Rhesaina does not appear. Western historiography shows the same tendency by on the one hand ignoring the battle of Mišīk, but on the other mentioning the confrontation at Rhesaina and referring to the successful Persian campaign of Gordian III.

The Šāpūr Inscription was composed within thirty years of the events of 244 and we may assume that it would have harmed Šāpūr's credibility to deliberately create a false account; this could not have been in the Sasanian ruler's interest. The rock relief at Bīšāpūr also confirms that Gordian III met his death in the context of the Persian–Roman confrontations (fig. 6).[35] The figure lying under the hoofs of Šāpūr's horse has been identified as Gordian III, and on the Sasanian triumphal reliefs a prostrate figure always symbolises a dead opponent.[36]

Admittedly, neither the *Res gestae divi Saporis* nor the representation on the relief at Bīšāpūr reveal whether the emperor actually died on the battlefield or as the result of a wound he had incurred during the battle. Perhaps the inscription and the visual representation were consciously designed in an ambiguous way in order to insinuate that Šāpūr I was prepared to take responsibility for the emperor's death. Gordian's death was a triumph for the king, which he used in his imperial propaganda. Why would Šāpūr

---

[31] *SHA* Gord. 29–30; Eutr. ix.2–3; Fest. 22; Zos. 1.18–19; Oros. vii.19; on the element of propaganda in the *Res gestae divi Saporis* see Rubin 1998: 177–85.

[32] On the circumstances of Gordian's death see Oost 1958: 106–7; Winter 1988: 83–97; Bleckmann 1992: 66–78; Schottky 1994: 232–5; Körner 2002: 77–92.

[33] York 1972: 320–32 and MacDonald 1981: 502–8.

[34] Maricq and Honigmann 1953: 111–22; at first, it was difficult to locate the place referred to in the Šāpūr Inscription; today it is fairly certain that Mišīk, which was later called Pērōz-Šāpūr (= 'victorious is Šāpūr') is al-Anbār of the Muslim period and situated on the left bank of the Euphrates as far north as Baghdad; for the date and outcome of the battle cf. also Gignoux 1991a: 9–22.

[35] Apart from the bibliographical references in n. 27 see also the monographs (i–vi) on Bīšāpūr that have appeared in the series 'Iranische Denkmäler'.

[36] Cf. Göbl 1974: 12.

claim credit for this death if Gordian III had in fact been assassinated by Philip the Arab far away from Mišīk, as the majority of the Western sources state?

The idea that Philip the Arab was responsible for Gordian III's death thus has to be dismissed. The Western sources share widespread prejudices against Philip the Arab and do not conceal these. It would appear that all versions intend to cover up the military defeat and to blame Philip the Arab for the events of the year 244.[37] Reporting on the fact that the new emperor concluded a humiliating peace treaty with Šāpūr I also served these intentions well (**16**).

In the year 252 a new Roman–Persian War broke out. By 253 the Persians had made a deep advance into Roman territory and inflicted heavy losses on the Romans. Possibly reacting to a Roman counter-attack, they then withdrew without having taken possession of Roman territory. However, in the year 260 the Persians embarked on a new, major campaign about which we learn also from the Šāpūr Inscription.[38]

The Šāpūr Inscription on the Ka'ba-i Zarduš at Naqš-i Rustam (ŠKZ),
§§ 18–22 The Parthian text

(§ 18) During the third campaign, when we advanced against Carrhae and Edessa and besieged Carrhae and Edessa, the emperor Valerian marched against us, (§ 19) and there was with him … (§ 21) a force of 70,000 men. (§ 22) And on the other side of Carrhae and Edessa we fought a great battle with Valerian, and we captured the emperor Valerian with our own hands and the others, the praetorian prefect and senators and officials, all those who were the leaders of that force, and we made all of them prisoners and deported them to Persis.

If we believe Šāpūr's words, the Roman emperor Valerian moved an army of 70,000 men against the king while the Sasanians were laying siege to the Mesopotamian cities of Carrhae and Edessa. In order to commemorate his victory in the most effective way, Šāpūr refers in detail to the make up and size of the Roman army. We learn that during the decisive battle near Edessa not only high Roman officials but also the emperor Valerian himself were captured by Šāpūr 'with his own hands'. We do not know what happened to Valerian afterwards. He must have died in captivity.[39] The Sasanians celebrated this victory, which was one of their greatest successes

---

[37] Cf. York 1972: 320–1 and Pohlsander 1980: 464–5.
[38] On the course of events during this decade see also Tyler 1975.
[39] On the capture of Valerian see Kettenhofen 1982: 97–9; on the inconsistencies in our sources see Alföldi 1937: 62–3 (= 1967: 149–50); Stolte 1971a: 385–6; 1971b: 157–62; Carson 1982: 461–5; Bleckmann 1992: 97–114; Huyse 1999: 10–14 (vol. I) and 82–4 (vol. II).

Fig. 7 Paris Cameo
(Ghirshman, R. (1962) *Iran. Parthians and Sassanians*: fig. 195)
(Photo: Paris, Bibliothèque Nationale, Cabinet des Médailles)

over the Western opponent, as an unparalleled triumph, as they had Šāpūr's preceding victories. On the triumphal relief at Bīšāpūr (fig. 6) Valerian is standing behind Šāpūr's horse. The Sasanian king grasps the emperor's wrist, which nicely illustrates Šāpūr's personal involvement in the capture and also highlights Valerian's submission.

However, in contrast to Philip the Arab, who is represented on his knees before Šāpūr's horse and pleading for peace (16), Valerian appears in a standing position. Considering that Valerian most likely died in Sasanian captivity this contrast is rather surprising. Even at the height of his successes against Rome Šāpūr did not place the emperor Valerian on a level with those on whom he imposed tributary payments, such as Philip the Arab. The fact that Šāpūr refrained from depicting Valerian in a kneeling position suggests that the rulers of both empires could see each other as of equal rank during this early phase of their relations.

The so-called Paris Cameo, on which a duel on horseback between the two rulers symbolises the Sasanian triumph, shows a striking representation of Valerian's capture (fig. 7). Valerian raises his sword against his enemy, whereas his opponent Šāpūr has not drawn his sword. Instead, he seizes the emperor's left hand.[40] Traditionally, 'grasping someone's wrist' symbolises that the person is taken prisoner. The gesture is the same as the one found on the Sasanian triumphal reliefs (fig. 6). It has been argued that the cameo represents the events from a Roman perspective and that the image encourages the viewer to reinterpret the humiliating events by suggesting that Šāpūr achieved his victory not in battle but through a trick.[41] This interpretation is not convincing. In any case, the cameo and all other references to Valerian's capture reveal the deep impression this event left on contemporaries as well as later observers.[42]

The following two examples further illustrate the powerful motif of the victorious Sasanian ruler. Towards the end of the tenth century the Persian poet Firdausi began to collect popular legends and stories of pre-Islamic Iran and to incorporate these in a long epic poem.[43] He dedicated more than thirty years of his life to this work, the so-called Šahnāma ('Book of kings'). As a consequence of his efforts the memory of old traditions and a distinctive pride in the pre-Islamic ancestors and heroes were preserved. No other work of Persian poetry has been illustrated as often as this book, which the German scholar Theodor Nöldeke once appropriately called the 'Iranian national epos'.[44] The miniatures of the Berlin manuscript of 1605, which were commissioned by Shāh 'Abbās I, are particularly impressive.[45] The artistic miniatures and their representations of rulers, royal scenes, duels of Iranian heroes as well as of demons, imaginative creatures or wild beasts express the lifestyle of the Persian nobility of this period. One of the miniatures alludes to the numerous confrontations between Persia and Rome, the great opponent in the West.

In the year 363 the Roman emperor Julian lost his life during his advance against the Sasanian capital Ktēsiphōn (**8**), which forced the Roman army to retreat and to the conclusion of 'an extremely shameful peace'[46] (**18**).

According to the illustration of the Šahnāma the Persian king managed to capture the Roman emperor (fig. 8).[47] Admittedly, there is a confusion of the events that took place during the reign of Šāpūr II (309–79) with those that took place during the reign of Šāpūr I (240–72) because Valerian

---

[40] Gall 1990: 56–9 assumes that Šāpūr II and Jovian are represented.   [41] See Göbl 1974: 15.

[42] Sykes 1921: 401, 'Few if any events in history have produced a greater moral effect than the capture of a Roman Emperor by the monarch of a young dynasty. The impression of the time must have been overwhelming, and the news must have resounded like a thunderclap throughout Europe and Asia.'

[43] For the text see Mohl 1838–55; on the author and his work see also Shahbazi 1991.

[44] Cf. Nöldeke 1892 and 1920.   [45] Enderlein and Sundermann 1988.

[46] Agath. IV.26.7.

[47] Cf. Enderlein and Sundermann 1988: 199 (plate) and 191 (description and commentary); also Wiesehöfer 1996: 226.

Fig. 8 Illustration of the Šahnāma representing the victory of Šāpūr I against Valerian –
Miniatures of the Berlin manuscript, 1605
(Enderlein, V. and Sundermann, W. (eds.) (1988) *Schahname. Das Persische Königsbuch.
Miniaturen und Texte der Berliner Handschrift von 1605*: p. 190)

was the only Roman emperor who ever fell into Sasanian captivity. In the
foreground we see the Roman emperor on horseback, represented as an
elderly bearded man. His hands are tied up and his feet chained together.
Šāpūr, who can be recognised by the honorific parasol, turns his head
towards the Roman emperor as he leads him away in triumph. The Sasanian
ruler is accompanied by his usual train, namely a page holding the parasol,

a standard-bearer, a mounted soldier who leads the emperor's horse and another page walking in front of the king's horse. There is a striking detail at the lower edge of the image where two little trees grow out of the rock. Whereas the left one below Šāpūr grows tall and straight the one next to it on the right below the Roman emperor is bent and wilted. The growth of the two trees corresponds to the different positions of power of the two rulers at the time when the Persians defeated Rome in the year 260. This again corresponds to the victorious Sasanian soldiers depicted at the upper edge of the image; one of these is proclaiming the victory by blowing his trumpet. As a whole it reveals how the Sasanians saw themselves – and claimed to be perceived from the outside – in other words, how the events were interpreted from an 'Eastern perspective'.

In the West the motif of the victorious Sasanian king, who had defeated the Roman emperor, was also transmitted and passed into European cultural memory. Although much later in time, in 1521 the German painter Hans Holbein captured Valerian's humiliation in a pen-and-ink drawing (fig. 9).

Among other scenes from antiquity and representations of the virtues, the drawing complemented the programme of murals for the Great Council Chamber of Basle Town Hall. The setting is contemporary and the names of the main characters are given as inscriptions (Valerianus Imp./Sapor Rex Persarum). Šāpūr uses the emperor as a stool to mount his horse. The scene probably served to remind councillors of the quick reversal of fate and to warn them not to abuse their power.

6: Galerius defeats Narsē in the year 298

Lactantius, De mortibus persecutorum 9.5–8

(5) Spurred on by the example of his grandfather Šāpūr (I), the Persian king Narsē attempted to conquer the East with a great force. (6) At the time, Diocletian, who tended to respond to any unrest with fear and pessimism and who was also afraid that he could share Valerian's fate, did not dare to oppose the king but instead sent him [Galerius] via Armenia while he himself halted in the East and waited to see how matters developed. (7) The former trapped the barbarians, who customarily went to war together with their whole family and were therefore impeded by their numbers and occupied with their luggage,[48] and overcame them without difficulties. After Galerius had put King Narsē to flight he returned with plunder and immense booty and with this brought for himself 'pride', for Diocletian 'fear'. (8) For after this victory he became so arrogant that he even despised the title

---

[48] Several ancient authors agree that the Romans took a large number of members of the royal family as prisoners; cf. e.g. Eutrop. IX.25; Festus 14.5 and 25.2–3; Oros. VII.25.11; only Malal. 12.6–24 (p. 308) mentions that the Persian queen Arsane was taken to Daphne near Antioch on the Orontes.

Fig. 9 The Capture of Valerian. Hans Holbein, Basle, 1521
(Waetzhold, W. (1939) *Hans Holbein der Jüngere, Werk und Welt*: fig. 68)
(Basle, Öffentliche Kunstsammlung; program of murals for the Great Council Chamber
of Basle Town Hall; pen-and-ink drawing, 1521)

'Caesar'. Whenever he read this title in letters addressed to him, a grim expression showed up on his face and he shouted in a terrible voice, 'For how long Caesar?'[49]

Lactantius[50] has no doubts about the political goals of the Sasanian king. Through military successes Narsē (293–302) wanted to acquire new

---

[49] The fourth-century Christian author tries to portray Galerius and Diocletian, who persecuted the Christians, in a negative way. The reproach against Diocletian of being a coward contradicts Diocletian's in fact very assertive course of action at the Eastern frontier. Lactantius also hints at rivalries and tensions between Diocletian and his Caesar, which indeed existed during the later part of Diocletian's reign; cf. Kolb 1987a: 159–76.

[50] Christensen 1980; Creed 1984.

splendour for the Persians, who had been in a defensive position since the death of Šāpūr I. Narsē aspired to take possession of the entire Near and Middle East and threatened many parts of the eastern half of the Roman Empire. Diocletian entrusted the Caesar of the East, Galerius, with the response to the Persian offensive of 296, which presented an immediate threat especially for Syria. There were initial setbacks but in the spring of 298 a Roman offensive opened a new and decisive phase in this Persian War.[51] Near the Armenian city of Satala Galerius forced his way into the Persian camp and inflicted a crushing defeat on Narsē. Lactantius attributes significance to the fact that the kings in the Near East customarily travelled together with their entire household and that this diminished the mobility of the Sasanian army considerably. It was wiped out completely. Galerius captured the royal family including his harem and many treasures. Narsē himself managed to escape with difficulty.

The Roman triumph over the Eastern opponent was celebrated and commemorated on a wide scale. Apart from victory-titles such as *Persicus maximus II, Armeniacus maximus, Medicus maximus* and *Adiabenicus maximus*, which were assumed by all Tetrarchs after 298,[52] coins conveyed the triumphal message.[53] This also applies to a bronze medallion of 298, which was issued for Galerius after his victory against the Sasanians in Siscia (fig. 10).

The legend *Victoria Persica* leaves no doubt that the theme of the medallion is Galerius' triumph over Narsē.[54] On the obverse the bust of Galerius is depicted, on the reverse the mounted Caesar is galloping over two unarmed figures. This detail alludes to the fact that Galerius attacked the Persian camp at Satala by surprise. In the foreground, a woman, a child and a man are visible, who are extending their arms, pleading with Galerius. All figures can be easily identified as Persians by their Phrygian caps. Apparently, Galerius intended to emphasise not only his military victory but also the capture of the king's family and harem. Narsē's extreme humiliation reminds one of Valerian's defeat and capture by Šāpūr I.[55]

In 304 Galerius erected a triumphal arch in Thessaloniki (fig. 11). The dimensions of the monument and its ornamentation make this arch one of

---

[51] On Galerius' campaigns see Enßlin 1936: 102–10; 1942: 40–5; Bleckmann 1992: 135–55; on the chronology of events see also Barnes 1982: 54 and 63.

[52] *CIL* III 824 (= *ILS* 642), III 6979 (= *ILS* 660); on the victory-titles in the imperial titulature of the Tetrarchs see also Barnes 1976: 182–6 and id. 1982: 27.

[53] Cf. e.g. *RIC* VI no. 23 a.b. 26; also Pink 1931: 3, 47, 50. fig. III 59–61.

[54] Garucci 1870: 112–18; Dressel 1973: 306–7.

[55] Schönebeck 1937: 370 places the medallion within the traditional triumphal iconography; in this context see also Pond 1970. Laubscher 1975: 135 observes that the motif follows the typical representation of an emperor's triumph over barbarians; Garucci 1870: 113 suggests that the medallion explains the victory-title *Persicus II* because the military victory and the capture of the royal family can be seen as a 'two-fold' victory over Persia.

Fig. 10 Medallion of Galerius, 298
(Cohen, H. (1955²) *Description historique des monnaies frapées sous l'empire romain
communément appelées médailles impériales VII/2*: Galerius Valerius Maximianus nr. 204)
(Médaillon de bronze)

the greatest Roman triumphal arches.[56] The relief cycles on the monument
depict and glorify the Persian campaign of the year 298. In succession, the
following themes appear: Roman victorious battles, submission and sub-
missiveness, prisoners being brought forward, the end of the war, peace
negotiations, tribute, and again decisive battles and victory. In a large representation of a battle on the north-eastern side of the monument we see
the Romans as victors over the Persians. Foot soldiers frame two mounted
figures, the Roman emperor and the Sasanian 'King of kings'. The representation of the two rulers fighting each other on horseback[57] is part of the
Eastern royal ideology, and as an iconographic motif the royal duel carries
high symbolic meaning. In spite of his defeat, the enemy is not viewed as
submissive but as equal in rank.[58] Although the arch of Galerius attests to
Rome's military superiority over the Eastern opponent,[59] the fact that an
Eastern iconographic motif was chosen and interpreted[60] implies that the
Sasanian king was attributed equal status as a ruler. This is confirmed by
the peace negotiations following the Roman triumph and by the specific

---

[56] Laubscher 1975 and Meyer 1980: 374–444.   [57] Gall 1990.   [58] Chrysos 1976: 16.

[59] The central scene, which depicts the duel between Galerius and Narsē, does not lack details which
express this superiority; Narsē e.g. sits on the skin of a panther, which points to his 'barbarian'
character; the right front hoof of Galerius' horse strides across Narsē's left leg. But this does not
diminish the idea of the equal status of both rulers.

[60] Rodenwaldt 1940: 55–6 points to Galerius' deliberate decision to use the iconographic language of
his enemy. He (56) suggests that the representation on the arch was a monumental response to
Šāpūr's triumphal relief; in contrast see Laubscher 1975: 135.

Fig. 11 The Arch of Galerius in Thessaloniki. Detail from the North-East
(Laubscher, H.P. (1975) *Der Reliefschmuck des Galeriusbogens in Thessaloniki*: pl. 52)
(DAI-Neg.-Nr. 1 D-DAI-ATH-Thessaloniki 257; by Hermann Wagner)

agreements of the *foedus* of 298, which from a Persian perspective can be
seen as acceptable (**17**).

3.2 THE FOURTH CENTURY: THE CONFLICT ESCALATES UNDER ŠĀPŪR II (309–79)[61]

7: Fighting during the reign of Constantius II (337–61)

Sasanian invasions of Roman territory appear to have resumed before the
reign of Constantine the Great ended.[62] The emperor's death on 22 May
337 in the middle of his military preparations delayed the outbreak of the

[61] For a comprehensive survey of the sources related to Rome's relations with Šāpūr II see
Dodgeon and Lieu 1991: 143–274.

[62] Scholars are not unanimous regarding the date of the first siege of Nisibis; see Matthews 1989a: 499
n. 15 and Blockley 1989: 470; on the beginning of the war and its causes see Mosig-Walburg 2002:
329–47.

war[63] but in the following year his son Constantius II, who was entrusted with the rule over the East, led an enormous force against Šāpūr II in order to put a halt to the king's activities in Mesopotamia and Armenia.[64] When in 338 hostilities opened, this was just the beginning of a series of military conflicts that took place during Constantius' reign. Festus, who seems to have been commissioned by the emperor Valens to write a survey of Roman history to the beginning of his reign, summarises the fighting in the East as follows:[65]

Festus 27

(1) Constantius fought against the Persians with varying and indecisive outcome.[66] Apart from the light skirmishes of those positioned along the 'limes' nine pitched battles took place; among these seven were fought by his generals, and he was himself present twice. In the battles at Sisara, at Singara and a second one at Singara, in which Constantius was present, at Sicgara (*sic*), also at Constantia, and when Amida was captured, our state was severely harmed under this emperor. (2) Nisibis was besieged three times but the enemy suffered even greater losses while maintaining the siege. In the battle of Narasara,[67] however, where Narsē was killed,[68] we were victorious. (3) In the night battle at Eleia, near Satara, where Constantius himself was present, the outcome of all activities would have been balanced, if the emperor – although the terrain and night time were adverse – had personally addressed his soldiers, who were in a state of aggressive excitement, and had been able to stop them from opening battle at a most unfavourable moment.[69]

The excerpt is typical for the histories of the fourth century, which, because of the concise character of the narrative, are also labelled 'epitomes'.[70] While numerous other sources describe the course of individual battles in detail,[71] Festus' sparse comments reveal important general characteristics of the fighting between 338 and 361. First, the large number of battles, second, the indecisive outcome of battles and third, the focus on strategically and economically important urban centres in Mesopotamia, such as Nisibis, Singara, Constantia or Amida.

---

[63] On Constantine the Great's plans for a Persian campaign see Fowden 1994: 146–70.
[64] Peeters 1931: 10–47.   [65] On the author and his work see Eadie 1967a.
[66] For a similar assessment see Eutr. x.10.1
[67] Narasara (Hileia) is located at the foot of the Djebel Sindjar, near the modern river Nahr Ghīrān.
[68] Festus is the only author who mentions the death of the Sasanian prince in this battle; according to the Byzantine chronicler Theophanes (*Chron.* A.M. 5815 [p. 20, 21–6 ed. de Boor]) a brother of Šāpūr II named Narsē died in the confrontations with Constantius.
[69] On this night battle at Singara see Mosig-Walburg 1999: 330–84, who dates this confrontation to the year 344; cf. also Portmann 1989: 1–18.
[70] See Den Boer 1972; Schlumberger 1974.
[71] For references with regard to the siege of Nisibis in the year 350, e.g., see Brandt 1998: 161–4.

Although Šāpūr was victorious in the majority of the nine battles mentioned by Festus, he apparently did not gain significant advantages as a result. The oriental limes,[72] which had been fortified during the reign of Diocletian, obviously represented a strong bulwark against the Sasanian attacks. The Persians besieged Nisibis three times in the years 337(8), 346(8) and 350 but were not able to capture the city.[73] Šāpūr's luck in war did not turn until 359, when he took Amida[74] and soon after Singara.[75] According to the contemporary observer Ammianus Marcellinus, who himself barely escaped from Amida, the Chionites fought on the side of the Persians.[76]

At the beginning of the 350s this tribe of the Huns had caused unrest along the northern border of the Sasanian Empire, forcing Šāpūr II to withdraw from Mesopotamia. In fact, the Chionites' activities put the confrontation between Romans and Persians on hold for ten years, during which, however, peace was not officially restored. In 356, while the Sasanians were still engaged in fighting in the East, Constantius II sent ambassadors and a peace offer to Šāpūr II. Ammianus Marcellinus tells us about an exchange of letters in which both parties express their views. Šāpūr II demanded that the Romans return Armenia and Mesopotamia,[77] conditions that were unacceptable for Constantius II. Until the death of this Roman emperor the Sasanians remained a dangerous opponent along the Eastern frontier of the Roman Empire.

8: Julian's Persian War (363)

Julian's Persian War and his death in enemy territory have received much attention among both ancient and modern authors.[78] The excellent accounts by the eyewitness Ammianus Marcellinus[79] and by the fifth-century pagan author Zosimus,[80] who wrote in Greek, give us a detailed knowledge of the events.

---

[72] On the Roman Eastern frontier in late antiquity see Wagner 1985: 67–70.
[73] On the rivalry over this 'strongest fortress of the East' (*orientis firmissimum claustrum*, Amm. xxv.8.14) during the reign of Šāpūr II see Maróth 1979: 239–43; Lightfoot 1988: 105–25; on the date of the first siege see Burgess 1999: 7–17.
[74] Amm. xix.1–9; for a comprehensive treatment see Lightfoot 1989: 285–94.
[75] Amm. xx.6.1–9; see also Lenssen 1999: 40–50.
[76] Amm. xix.1.7 and xix.2.3; on the history of this tribe of the Huns see Schippmann 1990: 38–9.
[77] Amm. xvii.5.3–5 and xxv.4.24; cf. also below pp. 182–4.
[78] On Julian's Persian campaign see Ridley 1973: 317–30; Blockley 1973: 54–5; Arce 1974: 340–3; Wirth 1978: 455–507; Kaegi 1981a: 209–13.
[79] Matthews 1986: 549–64; Fornara 1991: 1–15; Seager 1997: 253–68.
[80] On Zosimus and his work see Veh 1990; Paschoud 1971–1989; Ridley 1984.

Ammianus Marcellinus XXIV.7.1 and 3–6

(1) The emperor therefore discussed a siege of Ktēsiphōn with his chief advisors and then followed the opinion of some well-informed men that this would be bold and inappropriate because not only was the city impregnable by its location but also because the king was expected to arrive any minute together with an enormous force...

(3) But as usual he was greedy for more and did not respect the words of those who warned him; he accused the generals of advising him to let go of the Persian kingdom, which was already almost won, because of laziness and a desire for leisure. With the river on his left and untrustworthy guides leading the way he decided to march quickly into the interior. (4) And as if the fire had been lit with the fatal torch of Bellona[81] herself, he gave the instruction to burn all ships except for twelve smaller ones, which he decided would be useful for building bridges and therefore decided to transport on wagons. He thought that this decision had the advantage of not leaving a fleet behind for the enemy's use and in any case the advantage that (as it had been the case from the beginning of the campaign) almost 20,000 men would no longer be busy transporting and guiding those ships.[82] (5) When then everybody muttered, fearing for his life, and open truth revealed that the army, should it be forced to retreat because the climate was so dry and the mountains so high, would not be able to return to the waters, and when the defectors openly confessed under torture that they had told lies, the order was given to exert all energies to extinguish the flames. As the uncontrollable fire had already spread and had destroyed the majority of the ships, only the twelve ships, which had been set aside to be kept, could be saved unharmed. (6) In this way the fleet had been lost although there had been no need for this, but Julian, who trusted in his 'unified' army, because none of the soldiers were distracted by other duties, advanced with greater numbers into the interior, where the rich countryside furnished supplies in abundance.

Zosimus III.28.3–29.1

(3) They [the Romans] passed a few villages and then arrived at Toummara, where they were all overcome by regret regarding the burnt ships. For the pack-animals, who had suffered hardship on the long journey through enemy territory, did not suffice for the provision of necessary supplies and the Persians had collected as much grain as they could and had hidden this away in the most fortified places so that they could prevent the Roman army from using it. Although they were in this situation, the Romans, when Persian units appeared and they fought a battle, defeated them easily and many Persians died. (4) In the late morning of the following day, however, the Persians unexpectedly attacked the rear guard of

---

[81] Bellona is the wild and cruel goddess of war, who in later times was often identified with the Cappadocian goddess Mâ; cf. Amm. XXXI.13.1 where the goddess intervenes when the Romans are defeated by the Goths at Adrianople (AD 378).

[82] The Byzantine historian Zonaras (XXXI.13) claims that two defectors persuaded Julian to burn the Roman fleet; Lib. *Or.* 18.263 and Zos. III.26.4 also mention the small number of the remaining ships.

the Roman army with their combined forces. Although the soldiers were at first confused and in disorder because the attack had come so suddenly, they took heart and counter-attacked when the emperor, as he used to do, went through their ranks and encouraged them.

(29.1) When it came to a general hand-to-hand combat, he joined the commanders and captains and mixed with the crowd but was then struck by a sword in the decisive moment of the battle and taken to his tent on a shield. He lived until almost midnight and then died, close to having brought on the downfall of Persian rule.

On 5 March 363 Julian left Syrian Antioch with a large force in order to invade Persia. Whereas parts of his army were instructed to attack the Sasanians from the North via Nisibis, Julian crossed the Euphrates at Nikephorion and marched downstream along the left bank of the river. He was headed for the Sasanian capital Ktēsiphōn. Although the Romans made good progress on their march south, which lasted over three months, they obviously were afraid to attack Ktēsiphōn.[83] Against the advice of his generals, Julian decided to cross the river Tigris in order to gain control over important roads in the interior and thereby to improve his strategic position. Ammianus, who in general depicts Julian in a very positive light, criticises the emperor sharply.[84] In particular Julian's decision to destroy his own fleet that was in operation on the Tigris was completely inappropriate from a strategic point of view because, as the author describes, this cut the Romans off from their own fresh supplies. Zosimus also points to the disastrous consequences of Julian's decision and emphasises the problems of provisions, which were exacerbated by the Persian practice of collecting and hiding produce. In this situation the two armies clashed at Samarra;[85] the Romans defeated the Persians but Julian was wounded and died on 26 June 363. With regard to the emperor's death, other sources diverge from these accounts.[86] Whereas the pagan author and admirer of Julian, Zosimus, describes a courageous emperor who was struck down in battle by the enemy, other sources claim that he was the victim of an intrigue.

A Sasanian relief at Taq-i Bustan shows the dead emperor and may indicate that he was killed in battle by his enemy (fig. 12).[87] In contrast to the early Sasanian rulers, who had their rock reliefs carved in the vicinity of Persepolis, from Ardašīr II (379–83) onwards the kings chose the massive rock at Taq-i Bustan (map 5), which rises into a steep summit and is located close to Kermanshah along the road to the Sasanian capital Ktēsiphōn, as the place where they could praise their own deeds.

---

[83] Austin 1972: 301–9.   [84] See Smith 1999: 85–104.   [85] Herzfeld 1948.
[86] On Julian's death see Büttner-Wobst 1978: 24–47; Conduché 1978: 355–80.
[87] See Trümpelmann 1975: 107–11; Sellheim 1994: 354–66.

Fig. 12 Rock relief of Ardašīr II at Taq-i Bustan
(Ghirshman, R. (1962) *Iran. Parthians and Sassanians*: fig. 233)
(Photo: Ph. Claude Deffarge-Rapho)

The relief represents the investiture of Ardašīr II, who is depicted between the highest Zoroastrian deity Ahura Mazda and the god Mithras (characteristically crowned by the rays of the sun).[88] The power of the image is enhanced by the figure lying at the feet of Ahura Mazda and the king, undoubtedly representing a slain enemy. Although the armour is not recognisable, it seems safe to identify the figure as a Roman ruler; as the relief is close in time to the events of the year 363, it is tempting to assume that it is the emperor Julian.[89] This, however, remains speculative.[90]

Soon after the events of June 363 legends formed around the death of the controversial emperor.[91] A plethora of ancient and medieval sources, both pagan and Christian, describe and judge Julian in many different ways.[92]

---

[88] On the Vasanian rock reliefs and the significance of Ahura Mazda within the Zoroastrian religion see the references on pp. 233–36 with fig. 17.

[89] Ghirshman 1962: 190–1 comes to the same conclusion.

[90] Azarpay 1982: 181–7; Nicholson 1983: 177–8.

[91] See Brandt 1998: 180–5 on Libanius' obituary for Julian (*Or.* 17).

[92] For a compilation of these testimonies see Demandt 1989: 106–9.

Julian's death ended the Persian War, which had started in the year 338. The Roman army proclaimed a man from their own ranks the new emperor, Jovian, who quickly agreed to a peace with Šāpūr II (**18**). As Jovian was in a fairly hopeless situation, he had no choice but to accept considerable territorial losses, which turned this peace treaty into a humiliating experience for Rome. In any case, the new emperor was primarily interested in leading his army safely back onto Roman territory.[93] The 'Armenian problem' shattered any hope which the Romans may have entertained of a long peace on the Eastern frontier; however, in the fifth century this conflict was eventually 'resolved' between the two powers.

3.3 THE FIFTH CENTURY: DÉTENTE AT THE ROMAN EASTERN FRONTIER

9: Arcadius (383–408) and Yazdgard I (399–420)

Procopius, De bello Persico 1.2.6–10[94]

(6) When Arcadius, although he was in general not very shrewd, was in this troublesome situation,[95] he devised a plan that guaranteed him both his son and his rule without problems, either after conversations with certain experts (and there tend to be many of such royal advisors) or after having had some divine inspiration. (7) For when he wrote down his will he determined that his son would be the successor to his rule but he designated the Persian king Yazdgard (I) to be his guardian;[96] in this will he urged the king many times to preserve the empire for Theodosius with all his energy and foresight. (8) Having taken care of the succession and also of his domestic affairs in this way Arcadius died. When the Persian king Yazdgard (I) saw this will, which was indeed delivered to him, he (who was already very famous for his extraordinary greatness of mind) displayed a virtue both amazing and praiseworthy. (9) For he did not neglect Arcadius' wishes in any way but established and always kept a profound peace with the Romans and preserved the empire for Theodosius. (10) Immediately, he wrote a letter to the Roman Senate saying that he was not refusing to become the guardian of the

---

[93] Ehling 1996: 186–91.

[94] For an English translation of the preceding paragraphs see Greatrex and Lieu 2002: 32–3.

[95] Arcadius knew that his death was imminent and his only son, Theodosius, was only seven years old. Proc. *BP* 1.2.1–5 describes the emperor's concern regarding both the empire and his son. In this context the author points to the particular threat from Persia and warns that the barbarians could take advantage of the young age of the new Roman emperor and inflict great harm on the Romans.

[96] Scholars have interpreted the term *epitropos* that Procopius uses in this passage in different ways. Blockley 1992: 197 n. 36 sums up, 'While many see Yezdgerd's "guardianship" as no more than a diplomatic nicety...I accept Pieler's view that it was an extension of diplomatic *fraternitas* into executive force via the legacy'; cf. Pieler 1972: 411–33.

emperor Theodosius but that he was threatening war against anyone who would attempt to form a plot against him.

Agathias IV.26.3–7

(3) After that Yazdgard (I), the son of Šāpūr (II) took over rule in Persia, a man who was held in high esteem by the Romans and much talked about. For they say that when the emperor Arcadius was on the point of death and making arrangements regarding his will, as is only human, he made the king guardian and protector of his son Theodosius and of the entire Roman state. (4) For a long time this story has been widely told among us, handed down from generation to generation, and up to the present day it is circulated among both the elite and the common people. However, I have not found this in any document or in any of the historians, and have not even found it in those who give an account of Arcadius' death, with the only exception of the works of the rhetorical writer Procopius. It is not surprising, I think, that he, who was very learned and had read practically every historical work there is, includes a tale that someone else had written up earlier but that I (who knows very little if anything at all) have not come across it anywhere. (5) But I find it very surprising that in his account of this story he does not simply state what was known but that he praises Arcadius and glorifies him as having made such a wonderful decision. For he says that in general Arcadius was not that shrewd but that in this particular situation he proved himself to be sound of mind and to have greatest foresight. (6) It seems to me that whoever admires this does not judge and express praise on the basis of the decision as such but in light of what happened later. For how could it have been right to hand over what is dearest to you to a foreigner, to a barbarian, to the ruler of the most hostile people, to someone whose attitude towards trust and justice was unknown and to someone who on top of everything else erred and held strange opinions in religious matters?[97] (7) If the small child did not take any harm but his rule remained safe and sound because it was protected by his guardian (this was the rule of someone who had not yet been weaned off the breast), one should rather praise the king for his courtesy rather than Arcadius for his plan. However, everybody may form his opinion on this matter depending on his personal views and criteria.

To our surprise, Arcadius' decision to approach the Sasanian king for help in preserving his son's rule is not attested in detail before the sixth century. There are no references in the contemporary authors, although such an intimate cooperation between the Byzantine emperor and his Persian arch-enemy must have raised great attention at the time. It is possible that in retrospect an arrangement of this kind seemed unacceptable when the relations between East and West deteriorated once more during the later part of Yazdgard I's reign (399–421). However, when the two sides grew closer again afterwards, this episode could be revived and found its way into

---

[97] The Sasanian kings were followers of the Zoroastrian religion (**30**).

the literature of a later period.[98] Both Procopius and Agathias tell us that the Roman emperor Arcadius asked Yazdgard I to assume the guardianship for his infant son Theodosius, an episode which certainly underlines the good relations between Byzantium and Persia during this period.[99] In spite of his usual negative attitude towards the Roman emperor, Procopius praises Arcadius for his decision. The historian also expresses his admiration for Yazdgard I, who, from a Roman perspective, had already displayed his greatness of mind when he allowed the Christians in Persia to practise their religion, a gesture which earned him the title 'the infidel' in Arab and Persian historiography.[100] Procopius views Yazdgard I's willingness to grant Arcadius his wish and to maintain peace with the Romans during his reign as the means by which Theodosius acceded to the throne. The chronicle of Theophanes, which was composed between 810/11 and 814, further informs us that Yazdgard sent the Persian eunuch Antiochus to the court at Constantinople to make sure that Theodosius would indeed succeed to the throne.[101]

Agathias comments on the events very differently. It looks as if he questions the authenticity of the arrangements of Arcadius' written testament as Procopius describes them, primarily because, as he points out, they are not confirmed by any other source. In any case, he criticises Procopius for praising Arcadius.[102] Agathias is convinced that the emperor's plan was not wise at all even if Yazdgard in the end did not attempt to attack Theodosius' sovereignty. Regardless of any verdict on Arcadius, in fact no military conflicts between Rome and Persia took place during the entire reign of Yazdgard I.

In the course of relations between the two rival powers, Procopius' episode is not unique (12). Towards the end of the sixth century we observe a father–son relationship between the Roman emperor Maurice and the Sasanian king Xusrō II Parvēz; in this case Byzantium supported the Persian king in his attempts to secure his throne against the rebel Bahrām VI Čōbīn.[103] Here the fictitious family relation between the emperor and

[98] Blockley 1992: 51.
[99] Holum 1982: 83 nn. 18–19; Greatrex 1998: 13; for a detailed analysis of the relationship between the two rulers see Blockley 1992: 46–59.
[100] Cameron 1969–70: 150; cf. also the commentary on 32.
[101] Theoph. *Chron.* A.M. 5900 (p. 79, ed. de Boor); on the important role the Persian Antiochus played in the diplomatic relations between the two powers at the beginning of the fifth century see Greatrex and Bardill 1996: 171–97; for an English translation of the passage see Greatrex and Lieu 2002: 33.
[102] Cf. Cameron 1969–70: 149.   [103] Winter 1989a: 79–88.

the 'King of kings' was no longer a moral category but a forceful political factor.

10: Persian confrontations with the Hephthalites

Procopius, De bello Persico 1.3.1–5

(1) Later the Persian king Pērōz fought a war concerning borderland with the nation of the Hephthalite Huns, who are called 'White Huns'; he gathered a remarkable force and marched against them. (2) The Hephthalites are Huns in fact as much as they are in name but they do not mix in any way with those Huns that we know because they neither occupy land that is adjacent to theirs nor do they even live very close to them; instead they live straight north of Persia where they have a city named Gorgo that is situated on Persian borderland and where the two frequently fight each other over borderland. (3) For they are not nomads like the other Hunnic peoples but have been settling on good land for a long time. (4) For this reason they have never invaded Roman territory, except together with the Median army. They are the only ones among the Huns[104] who have a white skin colour and who are not unpleasant to look at. (5) Neither is their way of life in any way similar to that of the others nor do they lead a savage life like the others do, but they are ruled by one king, have a lawful constitution and deal with one another and their neighbours on the basis of what is right and just, in no way less than the Romans and Persians.[105]

Procopius touches upon the problems faced by the Persians on their North-eastern frontier during the fifth century. The Byzantine historian uses the long peace between Rome and Persia in order to digress; he focuses on the events in the Persian East and gives us an elaborate account of the Sasanian confrontations with their most important enemy during the fifth century, the Hephthalites.[106] Whereas during the third and fourth centuries the Sasanians had been threatened primarily by the Empire of the Kūšān,[107] from the fifth century onwards they had to deal with more and more nomadic tribes, whose individual history and ethnic identity are enigmatic and discussed controversially among scholars.[108] Among these tribes were the Hephthalites, who were called 'White Huns' and who during the fifth

---

[104] The origins of this nomadic people from central Asia are not entirely known; while at some point during the early years of the common era some Hunnic tribes advanced into the Caucasus region, several state formations such as that of the Hephthalites emerged from an Eastern branch of the Huns; Maenchen-Helfen 1973; Harmatta 1997: 159–73; Heather 1998: 487–518.

[105] According to Veh 1970: 459 Procopius' account of the looks, way of life and political order of the Hephthalites is trustworthy and based on good sources.

[106] On the origins of this tribe see Enoki 1955: 231–7; Bivar 1983a: 181–231; Thompson 1996; Frye 1984: 346–51; Lippold 1974: 127–37; Litvinsky 1996: 135–62.

[107] Dani et al. 1996: 163–83.   [108] On the history of Eastern Iran see Alram 1996: 119–40.

century founded a powerful empire in so-called 'Scythian Mesopotamia', between Amu-Darja and Syr-Darja. Procopius points to the non-nomadic lifestyle of the Hephthalites and their political organisation, which distinguished them from the other Hunnic tribes. During the fifth century the Hephthalites were the most dangerous enemy of the Sasanians and forced them to exert all their energies in the East.

Although both Bahrām V Gōr and Yazdgard II had to deal repeatedly with the Hephthalites, they eventually succeeded in fending off their attacks.[109] In the course of these confrontations Yazdgard II suffered numerous defeats between 443 and 450. When after his death in 457 his sons contended for the Persian throne, one of them, Pērōz secured his rule with the help of the Hephthalites. However, this alliance did not last very long. Almost the entire reign of Pērōz was also characterised by fighting with the Hephthalites and by crushing Sasanian defeats.[110] A first phase of confrontations was ended around 469 by a humiliating peace. The Hephthalites held Pērōz' son Kavādh hostage until the Persians offered a high ransom. According to the chronicle of Josua the Stylite the Roman emperor was among those who supported the Persians by contributing money to the war against the Hephthalites.[111]

At the beginning of the 480s Pērōz took up fighting against the Hephthalites in breech of the existing agreements; in 484 the Sasanians suffered yet another crushing defeat and Pērōz met his death in what is now Afghanistan.[112] As a consequence of this military catastrophe the Hephthalites advanced into Eastern Iran, demanded annual tributary payments and intervened repeatedly in the internal affairs of the Persian Empire.

11: The Sasanian monarchy loses and regains power

Procopius, De bello Persico 1.5.1–3

(1) As time went on, Kavādh ruled by force more than before and he introduced innovations into the constitution; among these there was a law which he drafted and according to which the Persians were to have intercourse with their women on a communal basis – a measure that the majority of the population very much disliked. Because of this they revolted against him, removed him from the throne and held him as a chained prisoner. (2) They chose as their king Balāš, the brother of Pērōz, because, as I mentioned, no male offspring of Pērōz was left any more,

---

[109] On these confrontations see Frye 1983a: 143–52 and Luther 1997: 110–24.
[110] Proc. *BP* 1.3.8–1.4.35.
[111] Ios. Styl. 9–10; for English translations of this passage see Watt 2000 and Greatrex and Lieu 2002: 59.
[112] Ios. Styl. 11; on the background and course of events see Luther 1997: 116–24.

and because the Persians are not allowed to appoint a man as king who is by birth a common man, unless it is the case that the royal family is totally extinct. (3) As soon as Balaš had assumed the royal title he gathered the nobility and held council regarding Kavādh (I)'s fate. . . [113]

Political changes and his own socio-political initiatives provoked Kavādh I's downfall. In an attempt to secure his position against the powerful nobility the king grew closer with a man named Mazdak. The so-called 'Mazdakite revolt', which derives its name from this figure, features primarily in the Eastern sources.[114] Many scholars have speculated about and discussed without agreement the possible religious, social and political origins as well as goals of this movement.[115] According to Tabarī's account Kavādh I joined the Mazdakites after ten years of his reign. These, as the author sets out, postulated that all men shared wealth and property equally and that the rich, who possessed too much money, too many women and too much property, should have this surplus taken away from them and instead it should be given to the poor. The king tolerated the severe political unrest and actual raids that took place in consequence of this doctrine. In turn the nobility and clergy decided to depose Kavādh and to imprison him. Procopius confirms Tabarī's words. The nobility replaced Kavādh, who was taken to a 'place of oblivion',[116] with his brother, Ǧāmāsp (497–9), who became the new Sasanian ruler.[117] The sources describe in detail how Kavādh managed to escape from his prison in Hūzistān and found refuge with the Hephthalites. With their help he returned and regained the royal throne.[118] Procopius claims that at this point Kavādh renewed the Sasanian monarchy and henceforth reigned with a firm hand.[119] The political unrest caused by the Mazdakite revolt broke the power of the traditional nobility once and for all.[120] Towards the end of Kavādh's reign his son Xusrō and the Zoroastrian clergy finally persuaded the king to break with Mazdak and to crush the Mazdakite movement. During the reign of Kavādh's successor Xusrō I Anōšārvan (531–79) both the position of the monarch and the Sasanian state as a whole were restored and reached new power.[121]

---

[113] Procopius mistakes Kavādh's paternal uncle Balaš, whose reign (484–8) he dates too late, for Ǧāmāsp (497–9), whom he apparently does not know.

[114] Cf. above all Tabarī's detailed account (tr. Nöldeke 140–7 and 162–3; Bosworth 131–9 [885–888] and 155–6 [897]); see also the references in Wiesehöfer 2001: 208–9 and 294–8.

[115] Klima 1957; Shaki 1978: 289–306; Gaube 1982: 111–22; Yarshater 1983a: 991–1024; Crone 1991: 21–42.

[116] Proc. *BP* 1.5.7.

[117] Tabarī, tr. Nöldeke 140–1 and 143–4; Bosworth 132 (885) and 135 (887).

[118] Ibid. 144–5.   [119] Proc. *BP* 1.6.18.

[120] On the relationship between monarch and nobility during the late Sasanian era see Wiesehöfer 2001: 165–91.

[121] On Xusrō's reforms see the references given above, p. 39 n. 112.

3.4 THE SIXTH CENTURY: THE SASANIANS RENEW THEIR
EXPANSIONIST POLICY IN THE WEST

12: The first Sasanian–Byzantine War (502–32)

The first major Byzantine–Sasanian confrontation of the sixth century began in the late summer of 502 when the Persian king Kavādh I invaded the Roman possessions in Armenia.[122] Although initially the Persians were rather successful and captured the important city of Amida (503),[123] they found themselves more and more in a defensive position.[124]

Kavādh I had no choice but to seek peace negotiations, which in the year 506 led to a first, temporary truce.[125] This, however, did not end the existing tensions, particularly since the Arab allies on both sides continued to raid enemy territory (**25**).[126] It is also remarkable that while the peace negotiations were still going on the Romans introduced measures to improve the protection of their borders, which had to provoke Sasanian suspicion. The following two passages talk about the most significant Roman initiative in this context, namely the fortification of Dārā, which during the course of the sixth century became one of the most important and most contested border cities in Mesopotamia.

Joshua the Stylite 90 (309.12–310.3)

The year 817 (= AD 505/6). The leaders of the Roman army informed the emperor that the troops were being greatly harmed because they did not possess a city located on the frontier. For whenever the Romans made a sortie from Tella or from Amida to make a sweep against raiders in the 'Arab, they were in constant fear wherever they camped of the deceit of enemies. And, again, if they happened to encounter forces which outnumbered them, and they determined to retreat, they had to endure great fatigue since there was no city nearby in which to seek shelter. And because of this the emperor commanded that a wall should be built for the town of Dārā which is situated on the frontier. Stonemasons were selected from all Syria, and they went down there and were building it. The Persians, however, were making sorties from Nisibis and disrupting their work. On account of this

---

[122] For a detailed account of the outbreak of this war and the course of events until 506 see Ios. Styl. 48–101; for a commentary and analysis see Luther 1997: 177–203; Watt 2000: 50–119.

[123] For an account of the siege of Amida see Proc. *BP* 1.7.5–35; cf. also Theoph. *Chron.* 5996–7 (for an English translation see Greatrex and Lieu 2002: 67–8), Ios. Styl. 50–3 and the Syrian chronicle of Zacharias Rhetor (VII.3–5; for an English translation of 4–5 see Greatrex and Lieu 2002: 68).

[124] On the course of events see Greatrex 1998.

[125] Ios. Styl. 71–3; 75–7; 80–2; cf. also Luther 1997: 206–7 and Greatrex 1998: 114–15.

[126] The Romans as well as the Persians punished the Arab tribes for these activities, which amounted to a breach of the recent truce; cf. Ios. Styl. 88.

Pharazman left Edessa and went down and settled in Amida, and he would go out to those who were building and assist them.

Marcellinus Comes a. 518

Dārā, a city of this kind, founded in Mesopotamia.

Dārā, which is a certain estate situated 60 miles south of the city of Amida and 15 miles west of the town of Nisibis paid its proceeds to the church of Amida. The emperor Anastasius thus bought the buildings of this modest village for a fixed sum,[127] with the intention of founding a city there, and he immediately sent first class craftsmen there and gave instructions for it to be built. He then put Calliopius,[128] later patrician of the city of Antioch, in charge of this project. Undoubtedly with admirable perception this man marked out a hill adjacent to a plain by creating a furrow with a light hoe – in order to place the foundations – and on all sides he guarded it with the strongest walls, which were built up to this zone. He also included a river, which is called Cordissus[129] from the estate next to which it originates and winds its way murmuring along; at the fifth milestone it divides the same hill and the new city, gliding forward and forming a mouth on both sides.[130] After it had been decorated with further public buildings, he allowed the city to keep the previous name of the village.[131] The huge watch-tower of this city, which was constructed in an elevated location and was a continuation of the walls, was a tower called the 'Herculean tower' and looked up to Nisibis to the east and back to Amida to the north of it.[132]

The Latin author Marcellinus Comes (Count Marcellinus),[133] who among other works wrote a chronicle covering the years 379 to 518, mentions the proximity of Dārā to the two most important cities Amida and Nisibis and thus points to the special geographical location of the city within the border area between the Byzantine and the Sasanian Empires, which must have been crucial for the emperor's decision to choose Dārā in particular as the location for a powerful fortification. Dārā's city walls and watch towers, which are still visible today (figs. 13–14), attest to the impressive strength of this late antique fortification.[134]

---

[127] As the Church of Amida was the official owner, the emperor had to purchase the village Dārā from her.

[128] On Calliopius see Croke 1984: 86–8.

[129] The easy access to water supply must have been a further reason for choosing this particular place for the fortification.

[130] On the river Cordissus and its position within the city see the detailed account given by Proc. *Aed.* II.2.1–7; *BP* VIII.7.7; see also Whitby 1986a: 739 and Croke 1984: 84.

[131] The city was in fact renamed Anastasiopolis; cf. Croke 1984: 84–5.

[132] On this tower see Croke 1984: 85–6; John of Ephesus mentions it in his account of the siege of Dārā by Xusrō I in the year 573.

[133] On the author and his work see Croke 2001; for an English translation and commentary see Croke 1995.

[134] See in particular Croke and Crow 1983: 143–59; Isaac 1992: 254–5; Gregory 1997: C6.

Figs. 13–14 Dārā: City wall and watch tower
(Photos: M. Stanke)

According to the Syrian author Joshua the Stylite, Anastasius had good reasons for fortifying the border in Northern Mesopotamia at the beginning of the sixth century. Indeed, from a Roman perspective the lack of comparable fortified cities that could provide protection in times of crisis had proven a great disadvantage during the previous military confrontations, in particular as the Persians had such a military base, namely Nisibis.[135] Not only at Dārā, but also at Edessa, Batnai and Amida, Anastasius initiated building activities that served the fortification of these cities. Likewise, he continued to fortify Theodosio(u)polis.[136] In late antiquity, border cities and border fortresses such as Amida, Martyropolis, Bezabde, Singara, Nisibis or Constantina were supposed to carry the main burden of defending the empire in Mesopotamia.[137]

As a whole, the activities of the Romans described above were also responsible for the fact that tensions on both sides continued in spite of serious diplomatic attempts to end the military conflict. Above all, the gigantic fortification of Dārā, which was located in immediate proximity to the border, caused concern among the Persians, who, as Joshua the Stylite suggests, made attempts to stop the project but eventually had to accept it as a *fait accompli*. Numerous sources indicate the haste in which the works were carried out in order to prevent the Sasanians, who at the beginning of the sixth century were still engaged in fending off the Huns and other nomadic tribes, from intervening in the process.[138] From a Roman perspective, building a fortress in the immediate vicinity of the shared border was a strategic necessity. Anastasius must have been aware of the fact that the fortification of Dārā was 'illegal' because according to the treaty of 441 neither side was allowed to build fortresses close to the border.[139] Procopius states that for a while the Persians were placated by promises and monetary gifts.[140]

It is not surprising that from this point onwards Dārā, which was now called Anastasiopolis, became one of the most contested cities in northern Mesopotamia.[141] During the reign of the emperor Justinian the city was further fortified and changed its name once more to become 'Iustiniana Nea'. The great peace treaties of the sixth century (**20**) also feature Dārā as an important point in the negotiations. Although on every occasion the

---

[135] Cf. Luther 1997: 210.   [136] Proc. *BP* 1.10.18–19.   [137] Wagner 1985: 67–70.

[138] Cf. e.g. Proc. *BP* 1.10.15; *Aed.* 11.1.4–5 and see further references in Luther 1997: 201–2.

[139] Proc. *BP* 1.2.15 and 10.16; *Aed.* 11.1.5.   [140] Proc. *BP* 1.10.17.

[141] For a compilation of the sources concerning the important battle of Dārā that took place in June 530 see Greatrex and Lieu 2002: 88–91. After a long siege the city fell to the Persians in the autumn of 573; see ibid.: 147–9 and Turtledove 1977: 205–11.

Romans were able to reject the Persian request to raze Dārā to the ground,[142] they had to concede that a military governor would no longer be based at Dārā.[143] The ruins of Dārā, which serve as wonderful illustrations of the ancient descriptions of the city, in particular those by Procopius, attest to the tremendous – also financial – efforts the Romans made in order to protect the Eastern frontier against their opponent.[144]

In spite of their early successes, the first Sasanian–Byzantine War of the sixth century saw the Persians struggling to defend their empire. In light of the continued attacks of nomadic tribes along the north-eastern frontier Kavādh I, who also faced internal pressures, increasingly feared a continuation of the war with Byzantium. As part of an attempt to secure the succession for his son Xusrō, in 522 the king sought an agreement with the Romans about which we read in Procopius.

Procopius, De Bello Persico 1.11.6–11 and 29–30[145]

(6) It seemed best to him to reconcile with the Romans and to put an end to the war and the reasons for war, on condition that Xusrō became the adopted son of the emperor Justin because this would be the only way to guarantee his rule. He therefore sent envoys and a letter concerning this matter to the emperor Justin in Byzantium. The letter read as follows: (7) 'We have suffered injustice from the Romans, this much you know yourself, but I have decided to abandon all accusations against you altogether because I have come to the conclusion that those men are the greatest victors who although they have justice on their side willingly come off second-best and give in to their friends. (8) However, I am asking you for a favour in return for this, which would establish close kinship and as a natural consequence good-will not only between the two of us but also between all subjects on both sides and which thereby should allow the blessings of peace to flourish. (9) I ask therefore that you make my son Xusrō, who will be the successor to my throne, your adopted son.' (10) When this letter was brought to the emperor Justin he himself was filled with great joy and also Justinian, the emperor's nephew, who was indeed expected to receive the throne from him.[146] (11) And in haste they did everything to create a formal document of adoption, as is the law among the Romans, and they would have done so if Proclus had not stopped them...

---

[142] Proc. *BP* 1.22; Men. Prot. frg. 11.   [143] Proc. *BP* 1.22.16; Men. Prot. frg. 11.
[144] On the ruins of Dārā see Preusser 1911 (1984), figs. 53–61.
[145] For an English translation of 1.11.23–30 see Greatrex and Lieu 2002: 81.
[146] Justin had appointed his nephew Justinian *comes* (519), *magister militum praesentalis* (520) and *consul* (521). When the emperor was terminally ill he had Justinian proclaimed *Augustus* on 1 April 527. After the death of his uncle Justinian's rule was not questioned and he ascended the throne on 1 August 527.

(29) … But when they [the Romans] claimed that Xusrō's adoption had to take place as was proper for a barbarian,[147] the Persians thought that this was not tolerable. (30) Both sides separated and went home, and Xusrō, who had not accomplished anything, went to his father, very bitter about what had happened and vowing that he would punish the Romans for having insulted him.

Procopius bases his account of the diplomatic negotiations at the Sasanian–Byzantine frontier on reliable sources and probably had direct access to the correspondence between the envoys.[148] Just as at the beginning of the fifth century the Roman emperor Arcadius had asked the Sasanian king Yazdgard I to assume guardianship for his son Theodosius (9), in a similar way, Kavādh I now turned to the Byzantine emperor, urging him to adopt his son Xusrō so that his rule would be guaranteed. By his will, Kavādh had designated his favourite son Xusrō to become his successor and thereby had violated the birth-right of his older son Kavus.[149] In order to protect Xusrō against other claimants to the throne Kavādh sought Justin's cooperation.[150]

Kavādh's plans regarding his succession also had an impact on his attitude towards the Mazdakite movement, which he had favoured for a long time and which had become an important element of his social reforms, not least with an eye to strengthening his own position (11). In contrast to Kavus, who was a follower of Mazdak, Xusrō was a declared opponent of Mazdak. It is likely that Xusrō's influence was responsible for the noticeable tensions between the Sasanian ruler and Mazdak from the beginning of the 520s onwards.

Although at first the Roman emperor was very pleased with Kavādh's plan, the negotiations failed in the end.[151] The rejection of the king's proposal by Byzantium did not remain without consequences. Around 528/9, Siyavush, one of the Persian envoys and also one of the most important proponents of Mazdakism in the Sasanian Empire, was executed. Shortly after,

---

[147] Pieler 1972: 399–433 comments on the legal implications that apparently caused Roman doubts with regard to such an adoption. At the time Byzantium moreover envisaged re-conquering the West and propagated Roman world domination, which would have made it impossible to acknowledge the Sasanian king as a ruler of equal rank; cf. Veh 1970: 467.

[148] On Procopius as a significant source for the sixth century see Greatrex 1984; Cameron 1985: 152–70.

[149] Proc. *BP* I.11.1–6.

[150] Luther 1997: 218 points to the difficulties in assessing the authenticity of the failed request for an adoption but argues that the request as such was not implausible, in particular as historical examples (9) existed and the Roman emperor and the king of kings indeed imagined themselves as relatives, an example being Amm. XVII.5.10; on this last aspect see Winter 1989a: 72–92.

[151] Apart from the reasons for this failure given on p. 38 above Veh 1970: 467 points to the fact that the Romans had just started to Christianise the important border area Lazika by the Black Sea and thus to remove it from Persian sovereignty; on this 'Lazic question' see Angeli Bertinelli 1989: 117–46 and Braund 1991: 221–5.

Kavādh did not intervene when Xusrō conspired to have Mazdak removed, too. Earlier, in 526 Sasanian initiatives to establish Zoroastrianism in Ibēria, the majority of whose population was Christian, had triggered new military confrontations.[152]

13: The second Sasanian–Byzantine War (540–62)

Procopius tells us about an embassy that the king of the Goths, Vitiges, sent to Xusrō I before military confrontations began in 540 and whose aim it was to induce the Sasanian ruler to start a war against Justinian. The speech of the Gothic diplomats illustrates both the regional expansion of the conflict between West and East and its world historical dimensions. More and more nations were drawn into the Byzantine–Sasanian confrontations.

Procopius, De Bello Persico II.2.4–11

(4) They [the envoys] appeared before Xusrō and spoke as follows, 'As a rule, it is the case that all other envoys, O king, join an embassy for the sake of their own advantage, but we have been sent by Vitiges, the king of the Goths and of the Italians,[153] so that we speak on behalf of your empire; and now view the following as if he said it to you in person. (5) If someone said, bluntly, that you, O king, had given up your kingdom and all subjects to Justinian, he would rightly say so. (6) For he is a man who by nature strives for change and loves what does not belong to him at all, who is not able to keep things as they are, who has therefore tried to seize the whole earth and has been captured by the desire to take for himself each and every rule. (7) He therefore decided (since he was neither strong enough to go against the Persians on his own nor capable of attacking others while at war with the Persians) to deceive you in the guise of a peace, while he subjugated the remaining powers by force and prepared a huge force against your empire. (8) Already having destroyed the kingdom of the Vandals he subjugated[154] the Maurusians[155] while the Goths stayed out of his way because of a so-called friendship, but now he has come against us with huge sums of money and a lot of men. (9) It is clear that – if he can destroy utterly also the Goths – he will march against the Persians together with us and those whom he has enslaved already, and neither will he respect the name of friendship nor will he be ashamed with regard to the oaths that have been sworn. (10) While you have a chance to save yourself, do not do us any further harm

---

[152] Schippmann 1990: 52 suggests that these initiatives stemmed from Kavādh's desire to show the Zoroastrians in Persia that he was no longer a follower of the Mazdakite movement.

[153] In 537 the king of the Eastern Goths (536–40) had embarked on an offensive in Italy against Justinian's general Belisarius, who had conquered Rome. In March 538 Vittigis had to abandon his siege of Rome and Belisarius advanced to Ravenna. In this situation the king of the Goths campaigned for allies in his fight against Justinian.

[154] In 533/4 Belisarius defeated the Vandals, whose king Gelimer had been supported by the Maureta-nian nobility, and as a result North Africa was again ruled by Byzantium.

[155] This is an older name of the inhabitants of Mauretania in north-west Africa; cf. Polyb. III.33.15.

and do not suffer it yourself but recognise in our misfortunes what will happen to the Persians soon; also understand that the Romans could never be well disposed towards your kingdom but that as soon as they have become stronger they will not hesitate to reveal their hostile attitude towards the Persians. (11) This is the time to use your chance, do not look for it when it has passed. For once a good opportunity has been missed it tends not to present itself again. It is better to take the lead and be secure than to have missed opportunities and to suffer the most shameful fate ever at the hands of the enemy.'

The Gothic envoys, whom Xusrō received at his court in Ktēsiphōn around 538/9,[156] speak of Justinian's aims to unite the whole world under his rule. They warn the Sasanian king that eventually even the Persian Empire will fall prey to Justinian's aggressive attitude if the opportunity to stop him is missed. It is true that the Roman emperor's foreign policy was based on the political idea of a *renovatio imperii*, a restoration of the former Empire. The envoys, however, also had their own interests at heart when they approached Xusrō. In any case, their words fell on fertile ground. Well aware of his own position of power, Xusrō did not hesitate to take action against Byzantium.[157] Disputes between the Ghassanids and Lahmids, Arab tribes supporting the Romans and Sasanians respectively, served as a pretext for war (**25**). Not even a conciliatory letter from Justinian I,[158] who was preoccupied in the West with the Goths and the Huns, could persuade Xusrō to abandon his plans, and in the spring of 540 the Sasanians invaded Roman territory. It is once more Procopius who tells us about this advance.[159]

Procopius, De bello Persico 11.5.1–4

(1) When the winter was already over and for the emperor Justinian the thirteenth year of his reign had come to an end,[160] Xusrō (I), the son of Kavādh invaded Roman territory with a large army at the beginning of spring, and he openly broke the so-called 'eternal peace'.[161] (2) He did not, however, march through the country between the two rivers but left the Euphrates on his right. (3) On the other side of the river there is the last Roman fortress, which is called Kirkesion[162] and which is extremely strong because the Aborrhas,[163] a large river, has its mouth

---

[156] On the dating see Stein 1949: 362–8.
[157] Rubin 1995: 283 argues that even after Xusrō I's reforms the Sasanian army did not quite have the strike force that is commonly believed.
[158] Cf. Proc. *BP* 11.4.14–26.   [159] Downey 1953: 340–8.
[160] The end of the thirteenth year of Justinian's reign corresponds with 1 April 540.
[161] The peace had been concluded in 532; cf. Proc. *BP* 1.22.3.
[162] Kirkesion was the southernmost of the Roman fortresses in Mesopotamia and had been founded as a defensive post by Diocletian and then been fortified with strong walls and towers by Justinian (Proc. *Aed.* 11.6.1–11).
[163] This is the river Chabōras (al-Hābūr).

here and flows into the Euphrates, and this fortress is located right in the corner which the junction of the two rivers forms. And another long wall outside the fortress separates the land between the two rivers there and forms a triangle around Kirkesion. (4) Because of this Xusrō did not want to attack such a strong fortress and was not planning to cross the river Euphrates but rather to march against the Syrians and the Cilicians. . .

Procopius not only comments on Xusrō's determination but also explains the goals of the Persian advance. Apparently, Xusrō was not interested in winning individual positions in Mesopotamia but – as had been the intention of Šāpūr I in the third century (5) – aimed immediately at the heartlands of the Byzantine East. He refrained from an attack on the strong Roman fortress Kirkesion in order to reach Syria and Cilicia as quickly as possible.[164] The element of surprise was not to be spoilt by a long siege, which would have slowed down his advance. Having captured Soura[165] he marched through Sergiopolis and Hierapolis, both of which paid a ransom,[166] and then headed for his actual target: Antioch. The Sasanians took and destroyed the city of Beroia (Aleppo),[167] which was situated between Antioch and Hierapolis, and in June of 540 laid siege to the Syrian metropolis. Procopius describes the siege and capture of the city, which fell into Sasanian hands within days, in detail.[168]

Procopius, De bello Persico 11.10.4–9

(4) But I get dizzy describing such great suffering and committing it to the memory of future times, and I cannot understand how it can be god's will to lift the fortune of a man or a place into the sky but then again to throw it down and to destroy it for no reason, as far as we can tell. (5) For it is not allowed to say that he does not do everything with reason, he who at the time did not mind watching Antioch being razed to the ground at the hands of the most unholy man, Antioch, whose beauty and splendour in every respect may not even now be entirely concealed. (6) The church alone was left after the city had been destroyed, and this through the efforts and foresight of the Persians who were in charge of this task. (7) And there were also many houses left around the so-called cerataeum, not because of the foresight of any human being but because they were situated on the outskirts of the city and not adjacent to any other building so that the fire could not get to them at all. (8) The barbarians also burnt what was outside the wall, except for the sanctuary which is dedicated to St Julianus, and by chance also the buildings

---

[164] Proc. *BP* 11.5.2–4.   [165] Ibid. 11.5.8–26.
[166] Ibid. 11.5.29–33 and 11.6.16–25.   [167] Ibid. 11.7.1–13.
[168] On the Persian conquest of Antioch see Downey 1961: 542–6; Evans 1996: 156–7 and Börm 2006: 301–28.

which had been built around this sanctuary. (9) For the envoys happened to make their stop here.[169]

The fall of Antioch left a deep impression on the Byzantine historian, who was puzzled by the events. It was indeed primarily the conquest of Antioch that made Xusrō famous in the Western world,[170] and the Sasanian ruler added to his reputation by not missing any opportunity to remind the world of his deeds. Not far from the Sasanian capital Ktēsiphōn he built a new city that was modelled upon the conquered city; he named the new foundation Veh-Antiok-Xusrō (= 'Xusrō made this city better than Antioch') and settled Antioch's deported population here (**36**).[171] The capture of Antioch, however, did not bring any resolution but was merely a prelude to further military engagements that lasted for twenty years[172] before in 562 an official peace concluded this second Sasanian–Byzantine War of the sixth century (**20**).

14: The third Sasanian–Byzantine War (572–91) and the Persian expansion into South Arabia

The historian Theophylact Simocatta, who was an imperial prefect and secretary in Constantinople during the reign of the emperor Heraclius,[173] tells us about the outbreak of the third Sasanian–Byzantine War in the sixth century. The author describes how the war spread geographically and points to the many links within the 'international balance of power'.

Theophylact Simocatta III.9.3–11

(3) When the emperor Justinian had passed away to eternity after he had ruled the Romans for thirty-nine years, Justin the Younger became the successor to his rule;[174] he was actually a nephew of the emperor Justinian. (4) In the seventh year of the reign of Justin the Younger[175] the Romans broke the peace treaty[176] because of the king's carelessness, the blessings of peace were disrupted and destroyed, and what came upon the Romans and the Medes was war, which attracts all evils, the harbours, so to say, of all misfortunes, the archetypal destroyer of life, which

---

[169] Elsewhere Procopius describes the restoration of the city, which was called Theoupolis there-after (Proc. *Aed.* II.10.1–25); for Antioch's mixed fortune in late antiquity see Liebeschütz 1972 and Kennedy 1992: 181–98; in general on the history, population and topography of Antioch see Chaumont 1987b: 119–25; Kondoleon 2000 and Huskinson and Sandwell 2004.

[170] Agath. IV.29.5–6.   [171] Ṭabarī, tr. Nöldeke, 265; Proc. *BP* II.14.1–7.

[172] For an outline see Bury 1958: 93–120.

[173] On the author and his work see Schreiner 1985; for an English translation and commentary see Whitby and Whitby 1986.

[174] Justin II reigned from 14 August 565 to 5 October 578.   [175] This is the year 572.

[176] Theophylact Simocatta is referring to the *foedus* of 562 (**20**).

one may appropriately call the rotten part of human affairs. (5) The Romans and Persians had sworn to keep peace for fifty years, but this oath was violated and broken through the great ignorance of the king. And from there the evil course of Roman misfortunes proceeded.[177] (6) The Romans accused the Parthians[178] and announced that they were responsible for the war; they claimed that the Persians had tried to persuade the Homerites (an Indian tribe subject to the Romans)[179] to revolt and that these had suffered terribly under Persian attacks because they had not given in to their offers, once the peace between the Persians and the Roman state had been dissolved. (7) They also complained by saying that the first thing the Persians did when the Turks had sent envoys to the Romans was to corrupt the Alans[180] with bribes in order to do away with the envoys as they were passing through their territory and to prevent their passage; (8) the Romans were looking for a pretext and welcomed a war, and from small and irrelevant beginnings they devised for themselves a long path full of harm.[181] For their love of war did not quite earn them any advantage. (9) The Medes in turn declared that the Romans were the ones who had started the war and they had the following complaints: the Romans had approached the Armenians although these had officially been Persian subjects and had forced them into their own rule,[182] they had also killed Surenes, who had been appointed *climatarchēs*[183] of the Armenian state by the Persian king;[184] (10) moreover, the Romans did not want to pay the customary annual 500 pounds of gold,[185] which the emperor Justinian had agreed to in the peace treaty, because they seemed to think it was unworthy to pay tribute to the Persian king. (11) But this was not the case, rather they had made the payments for the defence of the fortresses, which served everybody's protection, so that the tremendous force of the numerous uncivilised nations would not have the opportunity to attack and destroy both empires.[186]

Surprisingly, Theophylact Simocatta accuses the Roman emperor of having broken the peace that the two powers had concluded for fifty years. He interprets the Roman accusations against the Sasanians, namely that their

[177] For a survey of Roman–Persian relations between 565 and 572 see Turtledove 1977: 120–47.

[178] Cf. above, p. 76 n. 23.

[179] The 'Homerites' were the 'Himyarites' who settled in the Yemen; by mistake the Greek sources label them an 'Indian tribe'; on the history of this Arab tribe see Wissmann 1964: 429–99.

[180] On the Alans, an Iranian people with homes in the northern parts of the Caucasus, see Bachrach 1973; Bosworth 1977: 218–29.

[181] The author, a contemporary observer of Byzantium's desperate situation at the time of Heraclius' confrontations with the Sasanians, blames Justin; cf. also Tinnefeld 1971: 49–50.

[182] In the autumn of 570 Byzantium concluded a treaty with Armenia which was not official until 572 and which was propagated as the *casus belli* by the Sasanians.

[183] 'Ruler over the area'.

[184] This Sasanian official from the family of the Surēn was assassinated on 2 February 572.

[185] It is not clear why Theophylact Simocatta talks about 500 pounds of gold (= 36,000 *solidi*); according to Menander Protector, frg. 11 (*FHG* IV 208) the *foedus* of 562 (**20**) stipulated 30,000 *solidi*; in this context see Güterbock 1906: 63–5.

[186] Schreiner 1985: 279 n. 372 talks about Byzantium and Persia as a world police ('Hüter der Weltordnung').

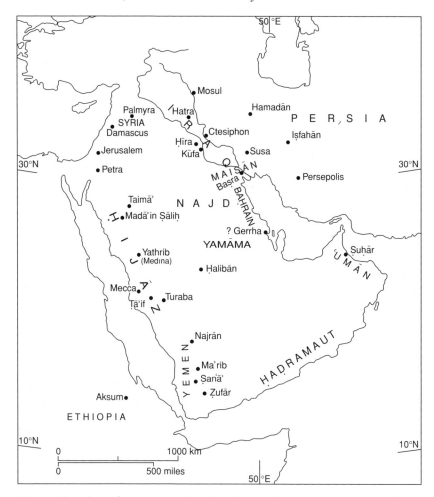

Map 7: The sphere of contact in the Near East between Iran and the Arabs in pre-Islamic and early Islamic times

expansion into south-west Arabia – where the Yemen became a Sasanian vassal state until the rise of Islam[187] – and their intervention in Roman–Turkic diplomatic relations had caused the third great Byzantine–Persian War,[188] as pretexts and he claims that the West was simply eager for war.

Arabia became a theatre of war in the course of the sixth century (map 7). Towards the end of the reign of Xusrō I the Sasanians expanded

[187] Harmatta 1974.   [188] Turtledove 1983: 292–301.

their rule as far as south-west Arabia.[189] This inevitably affected Byzantium's economic interests because the Romans wanted to control the Red Sea and thereby also the lucrative trade with India.[190] The fast spread of Christianity on both sides of the Red Sea, in Ethiopia as well as within the Arabian Peninsula, almost suggested Byzantium as a natural ally of these states.[191] While in Ethiopia the Aksūmites had become Christians and were backing the West, the Himyarites, who at the time were the dominant power in South Arabia, had not yet been swayed by Christianity. In particular the ambitious Jewish Himyarite king Yusuf, who wanted to establish an empire of south-west Arabia, did not refrain from persecuting the Christians.[192] Between 517 and 525 Yusuf's national and religious subversive movement dissolved the previous Aksūmite rule and assumed power. These years were characterised by intensive persecutions of the Christians and by a hostile attitude against Aksūm and Byzantium, which was especially directed against merchants. Yusuf's rule therefore impaired Roman trade considerably.

In 525 a joint force of Romans and Aksūmites struck a decisive blow against the Himyarites. The consequence was a second Ethiopian rule in the Yemen, which lasted into the early 70s.[193] The Aksūmites appointed a new Arab king of the Himyarites, who became a tribute paying dependant of Aksūm. The Romans tried to maintain good relations with both parties, not least because they wanted to win them over to become Roman allies in the continuing war with the Sasanians. Moreover, they wanted to avoid Persian intermediate trade but rather establish a direct route via the Red Sea to India. At the beginning of the 530s the Ethiopian general Abramos achieved Aksūm's independence and founded his own state in South Arabia.[194] Although his enemies approached Xusrō I and urged him to intervene against the new ruler, the political situation in south-west Arabia did not change until Abramos died in the year 570. However, the accelerated spread of the Christian faith during this phase led to a closer

---

[189] Smith 1954: 425–68; Bosworth 1983: 604–12; Müller 1991: 303–31; Shahîd 1995a: *passim*, esp. 723–4 and Morony 2001–2002: 25–37.

[190] It is remarkable that Procopius *BP* 1.19.1 and 1.20.9 tells us about Justinian's efforts to win the friendship of the Aksumites in Ethiopia and of the Himyarites in South Arabia; Wiesehöfer 1998b: 19 sees these contacts with Aksūm and South Arabia, which enabled the Romans to avoid Sasanian territory, closely linked with the Persian offensives in South Arabia.

[191] On early Roman activities in Aksūm see Pigulevskaja 1969: 211–24.

[192] Proc. *BP* 1.20.1.

[193] On the history of Aksūm in late antiquity, especially its attempts to expand into South Arabia, see Munro-Hay 1991; Harmatta 1974: 95–100.

[194] Proc. *BP* 1.20.3–8.

relationship with Byzantium, which was manifested in Abramos' promise to support Justinian I in his battle against the Persians.[195]

When Abramos died affairs in the Yemen became unstable. The Aksūmites were an occupying power in the area. After an unsuccessful attempt to gain support from Byzantium the Himyarites turned to the Lahmid ruler of Hīra, Numān ibn Mundhir. This vassal king acted as a mediator and offered to plead their case before Xusrō I.[196] Allured by the area's wealth and by the prospect of gaining control over south-west Arabia (and thereby inflicting great harm on the Roman trade) the Persian king decided to send an army into the Yemen.[197]

A fragment of a textile worked in the Gobelins technique seems to refer to the successful Persian activities in South Arabia that led to the liberation of the Yemen from Aksūmite domination.[198] On this fragment, which was found at Antinoë in Egypt and is now at Lyons, Egyptian weavers used Iranian motifs (Fig. 15).[199] Among other battle scenes, Persian mounted archers are depicted in combat against a group of black soldiers, who identify an African enemy. In the foreground, a majestic Sasanian king is observing the battle. The textile shows that the celebration of the Sasanian triumph by Persian weavers was copied by Egyptian artists towards the end of the sixth or beginning of the seventh century.

In the Yemen, the Persians appointed a Himyarite as viceroy, who collected taxes and administered the country on behalf of the Sasanian kings.[200] In order to prevent this viceroy from gaining too much power and in order to collect their taxes directly, from the end of the sixth century onwards the Persians appointed a governor, a move which obviously further intensified the Sasanian influence in the region. Only when the Arab conquerors embarked on their advance between 628 and 632 did the Yemen fall into Muslim hands.

The Romans did not immediately respond to the successful Persian attack that ended Aksūmite rule in the Yemen, because their own troops were engaged in several military confrontations along the borders of the Roman Empire. It is difficult to assess to what extent these developments within the Arabian Peninsula were responsible for the outbreak of a new Sasanian–Byzantine War in the year 572. Rather convincingly, Theophylact Simocatta refers to the Persian accusations against Justin, namely that the emperor wanted to free himself from the annual tributary payments

[195] Ibid. 1.20.13.   [196] Tabarī, tr. Nöldeke 220–1; Bosworth 236–7 (946).
[197] Ibid. 221–5 tr. Nöldeke; Bosworth 237–40 (946–9).
[198] Harmatta 1974: 95–106; cf. also Compareti 2002.   [199] Ghirshman 1962: 236.
[200] Tabarī, tr. Nöldeke 236–7; Bosworth 251–2 (957–8).

Fig. 15 Textile fragment from Antinoë in Egypt
(Ghirshman, R. (1962) *Iran. Parthians and Sassanians*: fig. 289)
(Photo: R. Basset)

stipulated in the peace treaty of 562 (**20**).[201] The main reason for the emperor's confidence was the fact that from 568 onwards the Romans entertained diplomatic relations with the Turks. In this year the Persian king turned away Turkish ambassadors who wanted to obtain permission

---

[201] Turtledove 1983: 292–334.

to sell silk in the Persian Empire. In turn, the Turks approached Byzantium and offered the emperor trade relations and safe transport of the precious ware beyond Sasanian territory; they declared that they were willing to fight enemies of Byzantium along all frontiers.[202] Not surprisingly, Theophylact Simocatta mentions Sasanian attempts to undermine these diplomatic contacts. The Persians' fear of an alliance between their two greatest rivals was more than justified.

Although the negotiations with the Turks were delayed until 576 and even then from a Roman perspective did not bring the desired results, in 572 Justin used the first opportunity to start a war against the Sasanians.[203] According to Theophylact Simocatta political unrest in Armenia triggered the war. In the course of a revolt against Persian domination a high Sasanian official, whom Xusrō I had entrusted with the erection of a Zoroastrian fire temple in Dvin, was killed. When the Armenians successfully appealed to Justin II for protection this amounted to a declaration of war.[204]

3.5 THE SEVENTH CENTURY: MIGHT AND DECLINE OF SASANIAN POWER

15: The advance of Xusrō II Parvēz (602–28)

Tabarī, Taʾrīh I 1001–2[205]

When the news that the Romans had broken their allegiance to Maurice and had killed him reached Xusrō, he became furious, and was disgusted by it and was filled with anger. He sheltered the son of Maurice who had come to him as a refugee, crowned him and announced him king over the Romans. He then dispatched him together with strong troops led by three of his commanders. One of them, called Rumiyūzān, was sent to Syria, which he conquered as far as Palestine. . .[206] The other commander, whose name was Šāhin, was the Pādōsbān of the West.[207] He journeyed until he took possession of Egypt, Alexandria and Nubia. He sent Xusrō the keys of the city of Alexandria in the 28th year of his reign. As far as the third commander is concerned, he was called Farūhān and his rank was that of

---

[202] Menander Protector frg. 18.
[203] On the violation of the peace of 562 see Güterbock 1906: 110–16.
[204] Theoph. Simoc. III.9.9; cf. in this context also Schreiner 1985: 278–9 n. 370.
[205] Cf. Bosworth, English translation, notes to the text 317–19.
[206] For the following passage see **33** below.
[207] The title Pādōsbān indicates a high military official; according to Tabarī there were four Pādōsbāns, each of whom was in charge of a fourth part of the empire (corresponding to the four points of the compass); cf. Tabarī, tr. Nöldeke 15 n. 2 and Wiesehöfer 2001: 198; on the Sasanian military in general see Gignoux 1984b: 1–29 and Gnoli 1985: 265–70; for an introduction to the administration of the Sasanian Empire see Demandt 1995: 517–18.

'Šahrbarāz'.[208] Heading for Constantinople he halted at the shore of the Gulf close by, where he set up his camp. At the order of Xusrō he destroyed the land of the Romans out of anger at the insult done to Maurice and to avenge him upon them.

In this brief account the Arab historian summarises the successful Sasanian advances from 603 onwards.[209] During a first phase of the war, which Xusrō II Parvēz declared as an act of revenge for the assassination of his former benefactor Maurice,[210] the Sasanians gained control of Armenia and from there marched on into Cappadocia. Further south their advances were equally successful. Among other conquests were the fortified border cities Amida, Rhesaina, Kallinikos and Kirkesion. All of Mesopotamia fell into Sasanian hands so that the Euphrates became the new border-line between the two empires. Between 608 and 610 Persian troops also pushed their way through Asia Minor and eventually reached Chalcedon. Another contingent marched as far as Caesarea, which remained in Sasanian hands for a year.[211] However, by the beginning of the year 610 the Persians withdrew from Asia Minor.[212]

Political unrest within the Byzantine Empire favoured the Sasanian successes considerably and eventually led to Phocas' downfall. Heraclius, the son of the *exarchos* of Carthage of the same name, became the new ruler of the Byzantine Empire. By now it had also become clear that the Romans were in a weak position in the Eastern provinces because they had exploited these economically and because they were enforcing an orthodox religious policy. The inhabitants of these provinces did not identify with Byzantium any more but accepted the Persians, who adhered to a tolerant religious policy, as their new rulers. In addition, the Roman troops were in a desolate state and no longer in the position to resist any serious attacks. It is thus not surprising that at the beginning of his reign Heraclius sought to come to an agreement with Xusrō II Parvēz (590–628) in order to consolidate his own position as well as that of his empire.

Xusrō II's activities during the following years, however, indicate that the Sasanian ruler was not interested in a settlement. Although his initial aim in the war, namely to avenge his former benefactor Maurice, had been realised when Phocas fell, the weakness of the Byzantine Empire at the time and the successes of his own army raised ambitions way beyond his original goals. He now wanted to beat his great Western opponent into complete submission.[213]

---

[208] Apparently this is a name, not a title; cf. Tabarī, tr. Nöldeke 290 n. 3 and 292 n. 2.
[209] For a chronology of the events to the peace of 628 see Stratos 1968: 103–17 and 135–234.
[210] Cf. pp. 237–41.   [211] Holum 1992: 73–85.   [212] Foss 1975: 721–47 (= 1990: I).
[213] Frendo 1985: 30–6.

Soon after Heraclius succeeded to the throne, he was confronted with serious Persian advances into Byzantine territory. The troops of Xusrō II crossed the Euphrates, once more invaded Syria, raided the countryside and conquered numerous cities, above all Antioch (611).[214] At about the same time Sasanian troops marched via Cilicia into Cappadocia and re-conquered Caesarea, which had been in the meantime liberated by the Romans. Towards the end of the year 612 the situation was more than problematic for the Romans. Apart from the important city of Caesarea, most of Syria was in Sasanian hands, as a consequence of which links and communications with the provinces of Palestine and Egypt were severely impaired. Heraclius therefore had to do everything he could to prevent a split of his empire and the loss of the economically important province of Egypt.

Accordingly, the year 613 was marked by Heraclius' desperate attempts to stop the Persian advance. He sent Philippicus to Armenia in order that he would threaten Sasanian territory from there, while he himself marched south in order to re-conquer Syria. Neither of the two projects was successful and the Roman troops had to withdraw in light of the superiority of the Persian forces. Heraclius returned to Constantinople while the Sasanians continued their expansive policy unchecked. Before the end of 613 they took several Syrian and Palestinian coastal cities, and among these Damascus fell without any opposition. In May of the following year the Persians captured the holy city of Jerusalem after a short siege.[215] The churches were set on fire, murder and plunder swept the city for three days. The Holy Cross was taken to Ktēsiphōn,[216] an act that received much attention by the Arab author Tabarī (**33**) and that caused a spirit of desperation and indignation throughout the Christian world.

During the following period the Persians conquered all of Syria and Palestine, and in 615 Sasanian troops once more reached Chalcedon in Asia Minor and the gates of Constantinople, the capital of the Byzantine Empire.[217] Heraclius' renewed attempts to make peace failed yet again. As the Romans were also attacked from the north, the situation became more and more threatening. The Slavs and Avars were raiding Greece and the Balkan provinces. When in 617 the latter reached Constantinople, the capital was attacked from two sides.[218] The emperor tried to conclude a peace with the Avars but was as unsuccessful as he had been with the Sasanians before. At this point (end of 616) the Persians embarked on an Egyptian

[214] Morony 1987: 87–95 and Russell 2001: 41–71.   [215] Cf. below, pp. 230-1.
[216] Cf. Whitby and Whitby 1989: 156–7 on Chron. Pasch. a. 614 and Mango 1985: 91–117.
[217] On this advance see Foss 1975: 721–47 (= 1990: 1).   [218] Cf. Woods 1996: 259–79.

campaign. They captured Pelousion, Babylon, Memphis and Nikiu without much resistance. After an initial unsuccessful attack, Alexandria was eventually taken by treason. By 619 the Persians had gained control of all of Egypt.[219]

For Byzantium, losing Alexandria was a particularly bitter defeat, since the capital's grain supply was now in jeopardy. For the Sasanians, having conquered Egypt meant control of the entire Near East. Ṭabarī, whose account compresses the sequence of events, conveys the impression that Xusrō II carefully instructed his armies to push in three directions, namely into Syria, Egypt and Asia Minor. The old borders of the Achaemenid Empire seemed restored. It is difficult to assess whether the Sasanians of the early seventh century still knew about the size and dimensions of the empire of their ancestors and if the late Sasanian rulers modelled their foreign policy upon an Achaemenid goal of world domination. However, there is no doubt that in 619 the Sasanian Empire was at the zenith of its powers. Byzantium, in contrast, was threatened from all sides and limited to a defensive policy. Nevertheless, the superiority of the Eastern power did not last for very long. In the year 622 the emperor Heraclius started a counter offensive[220] which formed the beginning of the downfall of the Sasanian Empire.

---

[219] For the exact chronology of the conquest of Egypt see Altheim-Stiehl 1992: 87–96 and 1998: 252–4.
[220] Baynes 1904: 694–702; Oikonomidès 1976: 1–9; Howard-Johnston 1994: 57–87 and 1999: 1–44.

CHAPTER 4

Diplomatic solutions

The persistent military conflicts took their toll of Romans as well as Persians. Already for the third and up to the seventh century our sources attest to attempts to end wars or to even prevent conflicts altogether by way of diplomatic activities. These attempts were serious and showed true interest in a peaceful coexistence beyond the existing rivalries. However, severe defeats in battle, military exhaustion as well as domestic crises were the main reasons why the parties sought a cease-fire and tried to come to agreements.

Numerous peace treaties have survived, and their contents are elaborately described by the ancient authors; moreover, many details regarding embassies during this period convey a vivid impression of the diplomatic relations between the two powers and allow insight into legal practices in the international arena that had developed during the course of late antiquity. An analysis of the diplomatic protocol shows that in spite of any political rivalry both states acknowledged the other's sovereignty and that both rulers were perceived as equals. This chapter in particular points to the efforts towards a reconciliation of differing interests and to conditions under which a peaceful coexistence of neighbours was possible.

16: The peace treaty of 244 between Philip the Arab and Šāpūr I

The Šāpūr Inscription on the Ka'ba-i Zardušt at Naqš-i Rustam (ŠKZ)
§ 8 *The Parthian text*

And the emperor Philip approached us with a petition (regarding the conditions for surrender) and gave us for their souls a ransom of 500,000 *denarii* and became tributary to us; and we therefore renamed Mišīk as Pērōz-Šāpūr ('victorious is Šāpūr').

Apparently Rome's crushing defeat at Mišīk in the year 244 and the death of the Roman emperor Gordian III forced his successor Philip the Arab to seek a peaceful settlement with Šāpūr I. According to the *Res gestae divi*

Saporis the Roman emperor approached the Sasanian king on Persian territory[1] in order to negotiate a peace. Šāpūr tells us that he consented to
the *foedus* under the condition that a high ransom was paid for the release
of the Roman prisoners. The sum of 500,000 *denarii*[2] mentioned in the
inscription suggests a large number and high rank of these prisoners.[3] Not
surprisingly, the Western sources do not include any details regarding the
ransom.[4] They emphasise the territorial agreements,[5] which Šāpūr himself
also alludes to by remarking that the Roman emperor became tributary to
the Sasanian king. His words hint at the political situation in Armenia.[6]
Whereas up to this point Rome had made payments to Armenia for maintaining the fortresses in the Caucasus against nomadic invasions, Šāpūr I
now became the recipient of these payments and thus took over the responsibility for the protection of Armenia against the threat from the north; both
powers were equally interested in this task (**27**). As can be expected from
this propagandistic source, the Šāpūr Inscription emphasises the Roman
emperor's retreat[7] and the new influential position of the Sasanian ruler in
Armenia.[8] What should rather be described as 'Rome's annual subsidiary
payments for the fortresses in the Caucasus' Šāpūr labels as 'tributary payments'. However, there is no doubt that the agreement on the Armenian
question shifted the balance of power in Šāpūr's favour. The majority of
the Western sources judge the *foedus* of 244 as a failure and talk about a
'most dishonourable peace'.[9]

Philip the Arab tried to present the treaty as a success. Coins issued in the
year 244 praise the *pax fundata cum Persis* (fig. 16).[10] Inscriptions dated to the
years 244 and 245 name Philip the Arab as *Persicus maximus* or *Parthicus
maximus* and thus refer to the emperor's triumph over the Sasanians.[11]

---

[1] Winter 1994: 599–602 discusses the venue for the peace negotiations.
[2] These must have been gold *denarii*; cf. Guey 1961: 261–75 and Pekáry 1961: 275–83; regarding the
   character of this payment see Winter 1988: 101–2.
[3] Sprengling 1953: 84.
[4] Zos. III.32.4, who describes the peace as detrimental for Rome, must have been aware of the high
   ransom for Roman prisoners, which may well have had an impact on his evaluation.
[5] Zon. XII.19 talks about the loss of Mesopotamia; Zos. I.19.1 does not mention the loss of any territory.
   The author explicitly states (III.32.4) that the year 244 had not seen any loss of Roman territory;
   according to Euagr. *HE* V.7 Rome had to cede territory in Armenia.
[6] On the cession of territories see Winter 1988: 102–7 and Bleckmann 1992: 76–88.
[7] Kettenhofen 1982: 35 n. 72 raises the possibility that the agreement as far as Armenia was concerned
   featured a kind of 'non-intervention-clause'.
[8] On the Roman–Sasanian battle over Armenia in the third century in general see Chaumont 1969
   and 1976.
[9] Zos. III.32.4.   [10] Cf. Baldus 1971: 31.
[11] *CIL* III 4346; 10619 (= *ILS* 507); 14354/6; VI 1097 (= *ILS* 506).

Fig. 16 Coin of Philip the Arab, 244
(Cohen, H. (1955²) *Description historique des monnaies frapées sous l'empire romain
communément appelées médailles impériales V/2*: Philippe Père nr. 113)
(Cabinet de France. Signifie Argent)

These testimonies obviously form a stark contrast with the military defeat
at Mišīk and the terms of the peace that followed. However, we have to
bear in mind that – given his political and military situation – the Roman
emperor concluded a treaty with the Sasanians that could not have been
any more favourable. Considering the disastrous Roman defeat at Mišīk
Philip the Arab has to be given some credit for having satisfied Šāpūr's
territorial claims by offering to withdraw from Armenia. In light of these
circumstances it would appear justified that the Roman emperor publicly
advertised his *pax fundata cum Persis*.

The events of the year 244 raised the 'national' confidence of the East vis
à vis the world power Rome considerably. The Persians intended to represent their military as well as diplomatic triumph to the world accordingly.
As we learn from the great Šāpūr Inscription, the Persian king changed
the name of Mišīk into the triumphal 'Pērōz-Šāpūr' (= 'victorious is
Šāpūr'), which was certainly an effective starting point for promoting the
victory. In this context the Sasanian rock reliefs may be compared as the
iconographic counterpart to the epigraphic account of the events given
by Šāpūr I. On the majority of the rock reliefs, also on the one at Bīšāpūr,
Philip the Arab is represented in a kneeling position (fig. 6). He is paying

homage to the mounted Sasanian king and offering peace.[12] On another
rock relief at Dārābgerd[13] a shallow rectangular object decorated with a
ribbon is depicted in Šāpūr's right hand, which may be indicating that
the Roman emperor has offered the Persian king an agreement, a draft
of which Šāpūr is holding in his hands.[14] Regardless of any specific interpretation, there is no doubt that Šāpūr concluded a glorious peace with
Rome.

17: The peace treaty of 298[15] between Diocletian and Narsē

Our main source for the peace treaty of 298 is the account of Peter the
Patrician (c. 500–64).[16] In fact, regarding Roman–Sasanian relations in the
third century the narrative of this Byzantine historian is the only testimony
that provides us with details about the provisions of this agreement.[17] Most
likely the author had access to archival material and was thus well informed
of the diplomatic procedures in the year 298. Nevertheless we must bear
in mind that his account is not a copy of the actual agreement but at best
a commentary. The specific terms can only be reconstructed through a
careful comparison with other sources. These, however, are extremely brief
and in contrast to Peter the Patrician yield little information.[18] Moreover,
Peter's elaborate narrative gives fascinating insight into the diplomatic relations between Rome and the Persian Empire towards the end of the third
century.[19]

Peter the Patrician, frg. 13–14

(13) As Apharbān, who was a very close friend of the Persian king Narsē, had been
sent as ambassador, he approached Galerius in supplication. When he had the
opportunity to speak he said, 'It is obvious for all mankind that the Roman and
the Persian Empires are just like two lamps; and it is necessary that, like eyes, the
one is brightened by the light of the other and that they do not angrily strive

---

[12] Göbl 1974: 12.   [13] Hinz 1969: plate 76.
[14] Thus Trümpelmann 1975: 15; in contrast see Göbl 1974: 21, who interprets the *tessera* handed to
Šāpūr by Philip the Arab as a reference to the amount of ransom demanded for the release of the
captured Romans.
[15] For a date of 299 see Barnes 1976: 179–86.
[16] On the author and his work see Blockley 1985b.
[17] The author was interested in this historical event because he was himself a Byzantine ambassador in
the peace negotiations with the Persians during the reign of Xusrō I (531–79).
[18] Cf. especially Fest. 14; for a survey of the sources on the *foedus* of 298 see Winter 1988: 169–71.
[19] Winter 1988: 163–8.

for each other's destruction.[20] For this is not held as a virtue but rather levity or weakness. As they believe that later generations will not be able to help them they make an effort to destroy their opponents.' He continued by saying that it was not necessary to think that Narsē was weaker than the other kings but rather to see Galerius as that much superior to the other kings so that Narsē himself was inferior to him alone, and rightly so, without, however, proving to be lower in dignity than his ancestors. Apharbān added that Narsē had given him instructions to entrust, as they were fair, the right of his empire to the kindness of the Romans; that this was why he was not bringing the oaths by which the peace had to be concluded but was handing everything over to the judgement of the emperor, asking only that his children and wives were returned to him, and he claimed that for their return he would owe the emperor more for his benefactions than if spared by his arms. He was not able to thank him appropriately for the fact that those in captivity had not experienced any cruelty but had been treated as if soon to be returned to their own high status at home. In this context he also reminded the emperor of the changeable character of human affairs. But Galerius seemed to be angry about this remark and, with his body beginning to shake, responded that it was not quite appropriate for the Persians to remind others of the changes in human affairs because they themselves did not cease to use every opportunity to add to human misfortune.[21] 'For you guarded the rule of victory well in Valerian's case, when you deceived him with tricks, took him captive and did not release him until old age and his shameful death, when you, after his death, conserved his skin with some disgusting method and thereby afflicted the mortal body with immortal offence.'[22] The emperor[23] went through all this and added that his mind was not changed by what the Persian embassy tried to convey, namely that he should respect human fate (because one should rather be enraged by this if one considered what the Persians had done), but that he would follow the footsteps of his own ancestors, whose custom it had been to spare their subjects but to fight the ones who opposed them;[24] he told the ambassador to inform his king of the

---

[20] It is striking how much these words resemble those of Xusrō II (590–628) at the end of the sixth century when he approached the Byzantine emperor Maurice in order to win him as an ally against his internal rival Bahrām Čōbīn; Theoph. Simoc. IV.11.1–2 must have based his wording on the chronicle of Peter the Patrician; see also the way Šāpūr II addresses Constantius II in Amm. XVII.5.3 (**34**).

[21] According to Sprengling 1953: 111 Galerius' words are too immediate and lively for an account that was composed 250 years after the events and cannot have been the product of the historian's own imagination.

[22] At this point Galerius recalls the fate of the Roman emperor Valerian, who had been captured by the Persians during the reign of Šāpūr I (240–72) (**5**).

[23] In the Greek text the author uses the title *basileus*, as it was indeed used for a Roman emperor; Galerius, however, had been acclaimed 'Caesar' on 21 May (?) 293; he was acclaimed 'Augustus' in Nicomedia not before 1 May 305; on the title of *basileus* in the early Byzantine period see in general Chrysos 1978: 29–75.

[24] Galerius alludes to Vergil's famous words *parcere subiectis et debellare superbos* (*Aen.* VI.853), which describe a principle of Rome's attitude towards defeated enemies; ironically, the attribute *superbus* describes the Persian ambassador rather well so that Rome's generosity appears even more noteworthy; the reader is also reminded of Festus' statement (25), *Persae non modo armis sed etiam moribus Romanos superiores esse confessi sunt*; see Eadie 1967a: 148.

generosity of the Romans, whose kindness he had challenged, and to hope that soon they [the captives] would return to him by judgement of the emperor.

(14) When Galerius and Diocletian had come together in Nisibis, they took counsel there and agreed to send an ambassador to Persia, Sicorius Probus, an archivist. Narsē received him in a friendly way expecting to hear what had been reported to him. But Narsē also made use of delaying tactics. For as if he wanted the ambassadors who had come with Sicorius to recover (since they were exhausted), he took Sicorius, who knew well what was going on, as far as the Asproudis, a river in Media, until the units who had been scattered here and there because of the war had gathered. And then, in the inner room of the palace, having sent away all others and allowing only the presence of Apharbān and of the *archapetēs* Barsaborsos,[25] the one of whom was the praetorian prefect and the other held the rule over Syme,[26] he asked Probus to deliver his message. The main points of the ambassador's message were the following: that in the eastern region the Romans should receive Ingilēnē together with Sōphēnē, Arzanēnē together with Karduēnē and Zabdikēnē and that the river Tigris should be the boundary line between the two states,[27] that the fortress of Zintha, which was located on the border of Media, should mark the border of Armenia, that the king of Ibēria should owe his royal status to the Romans, and that the city of Nisibis, which lies on the Tigris, should be the place of trade. Narsē listened to these points and – as his present situation did not allow him to refuse any of this – agreed to all of them; with the exception, so that he would not seem to be forced to comply with everything, that he rejected the condition that Nisibis should be the only place for exchange. Sicorius, however, responded, 'This point is a requirement because the embassy does not have full power and no instructions for this have been given by the emperors.' When these matters had thus been settled, Narsē was given back his wives and children, whose pure reputation had been respected thanks to the emperors' love of honour.

Already shortly after the decisive defeat in Armenia, which did not leave the Sasanians any prospects for a military success (**6**), the Persian ruler Narsē sent an ambassador to Galerius. The main objective of this embassy was to achieve the release of the royal family whose captivity would represent an asset for the Romans during the negotiations and at least a significant psychological advantage. The man sent to Galerius by Narsē was Apharbān,

[25] On the title *archapetēs*, which is attested for the Parthian and early Sasanian period, see Chaumont 1986a: 400–1; on Barsaborsos see Chaumont 1969: 120; Felix 1985: 124.

[26] Peeters 1931: 27–8 conjectures *tēn tou Symiou eichen archēn* into *tēn tou sēmeiou archēn*; in this case Barsaborsos, who was able to read, would have acted as secretary to the Great king, which would suggest that there was a written agreement.

[27] Chrysos 1976: 12–14 points to the significance of the term *politeia*, i.e. the 'state' as a construct organised in a specific way in contrast to the royal power (*basileia*). Chrysos argues that the term *politeia* indicates an autonomous state acting in a politically sovereign manner and that in the sixth and seventh centuries Byzantine authors such as Peter the Patrician, Menander Protector and Theophylact Simocatta reserved this term for Rome and the Sasanian Empire whereas other empires and nations were labelled as *ethnē* and *genē*; see also Schreiner 1983: 305–6.

who was the commander of the royal guard and thus a high Persian dignitary and intimate friend of the Sasanian king. On the Roman side the negotiations were led by the *magister memoriae* Sicorius Probus, who was likewise a high official. The Persian ambassador argued that the Roman and Persian Empires were like two lights, two eyes, whose sparkle made each other shine, and they should therefore refrain from destroying each other.[28] Although Apharbān used this metaphor in order to emphasise the equal rank of both empires his words cannot be dismissed as a feeble attempt to show the Sasanian Empire in a better light. The expressive image must reflect his actual view of the relationship between the two states.[29]

Apharbān then went on to appeal to the Romans' sense of humanity and justice. However, when he asked for the Persian captives to be treated well and assured the Roman emperor that this would oblige the great king more than a military victory could, Galerius became very angry and interrupted him. The memory of the death of the Roman emperor Valerian in Persian captivity just a few decades before (5) and the circumstances of his death must have been alive among Romans and Persians alike. Nevertheless, Galerius dismissed the Persian ambassador by promising Narsē that the captives would return soon. The emperor's decision was probably motivated by his respect both for Diocletian's moderate policy and for the Sasanian Empire. The negotiations between Galerius and Apharbān were a prerequisite for the conclusion of a formal peace treaty.

When his negotiations with Apharbān had come to an end, Galerius rushed to Nisibis where he and Diocletian jointly decided on the terms for a formal peace.[30] Afterwards Sicorius Probus went to meet Narsē on Persian territory in order to inform him of these terms. It seems certain that Sicorius Probus and Narsē met in Mēdia but we do not know where exactly on the river Asproudis.[31] The region had been conquered by Galerius after Satala but officially it was still part of the Sasanian Empire. Diocletian's decision to send a middle man to the Persian ruler is surprising; even more surprising, however, is the fact that in spite of the Persian defeat the Roman ambassador crossed the official border and went to meet Narsē in order

---

[28] Cf. also the words placed into the mouth of the Sasanian king Kavādh I by the Byzantine author Ioannes Malalas (18.44 [p. 449]), namely that according to a divine plan Byzantium and the Sasanian Empire were the two centres of civilisation, 'the moon of the West and the sun of the East'; according to Theophylact Simocatta (IV.13.7) Xusrō II wrote to his benefactor Maurice that 'one power alone was not able to shoulder the immense burden of taking care of the organisation of the universe and one man's pulse was not able to steer everything created under the sun'; see also Shahbazi 1990: 591.

[29] For an analysis of this text see Winter 1988: 163–8.

[30] Eutr. IX.25.1; Zon. XII.31.   [31] Enßlin 1942: 42.

to conclude the treaty.[32] In Iranian–Roman relations the venue for peace negotiations was a formal element as important as the accurate diplomatic ceremonial and was also seen to reflect the political balance of power.

Diocletian's policy in the East was shaped by an attempt not to overexert the capacities of the empire, to refrain from expansion and to be content with a restoration of the borders that had been fixed by the Eastern policy of the Severi. In spite of Diocletian's strong position in 298 Rome did not show any aggressive or universal aspirations; instead, Diocletian intended to acknowledge the sovereignty of the defeated Sasanian king. This is illustrated by the place where the *foedus* of 298 was concluded and which was accepted, perhaps even chosen by Rome, together with the moderate terms of the agreement. According to Peter the Patrician Narsē had to give his consent to three important Roman conditions. The first of these concerned territory and a clarification of the situation along the Sasanian–Roman and Sasanian–Armenian borders.[33] Locating the so called 'provinces beyond the Tigris', which had to be ceded to Rome, poses problems (map 8).[34]

Peter the Patrician singles out five regions: Ingilēnē and Sōphēnē geographically comprise the area between the Tigris and the Nymphios. The third province, Arzanēnē, borders these in a south-eastern direction, also situated along the upper Tigris and starting from the eastern banks of the Nymphios.[35] Adjacent to this province are the regions Karduēnē and Zabdikēnē. A comparison with other sources[36] fleshes out our map of the area. The area between the Euphrates and the Nymphios and further east into Karduēnē actually included nine and not five regions.

Moreover, our author's statement that the Tigris was supposed to be the new borderline between the two powers seems to contradict the fact that most areas ceded to Rome were located beyond the Tigris. This is confirmed by the ancient author Festus, who wrote in the fourth century and was thus much closer to the events of 298 than Peter the Patrician. Festus claims that the Romans gained power over five peoples across the Tigris.[37] Ammianus Marcellinus also mentions the *regiones Transtigritanae*.[38] Differentiating between a situation *de-iure* and one *de-facto* may help to explain the diverging accounts of Peter the Patrician and Festus. Whereas the latter describes the official situation which assigns the so called 'provinces beyond the Tigris' to Rome, the Byzantine historian describes the real situation that was created by an administrative practice in these provinces soon after 298.[39]

---

[32] Winter 1994: 603–5.   [33] Winter 1989b: 555–71.   [34] Adontz 1970: 25–37.
[35] On this province see also Whitby 1983: 205–18.
[36] Amm. xxv.7.9.   [37] Fest. 14.25.   [38] Amm. xxv.7.9.
[39] Dillemann 1962: 217–18; see also Felix 1985: 125–6.

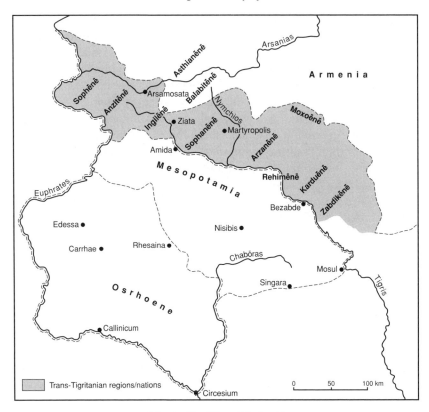

Map 8: The 'Trans-Tigritania'

Ancient authors of the fourth century, who talk about contemporary affairs along the border, refer to the Tigris as the actual borderline.[40] The Romans withdrew to the western banks of the Tigris; in 298 they refrained from constructing a 'proper limes' beyond the Tigris but were content with securing strategically important passes.[41]

Accordingly, the regions beyond the Tigris which were ceded to Rome in 298 did not become new provinces of the Roman Empire but continued to be administered and ruled by Armenian noble families, who, however, were responsible to Rome.[42] Diocletian would not have envisaged a permanent territorial gain for the Roman Empire and left things as they were in

[40] Amm. xvIII.5.3 and 6.9; Iul. *Or.* 1.22 b–c.　　[41] Honigmann 1935: 6–16.

[42] On the administrative structures and the legal status of these Roman–Armenian satrapies and on the special role of the Armenian satraps see Enßlin 1942: 80–3.

Trans-Tigritania. He must have hoped that such a policy of integration would secure the loyalty of the Armenians.[43] In this way, Rome pushed forward the line of defence for the province of Mesopotamia. During the following years, however, we observe new Roman activities with an eye to securing the border region, which illustrate the strategic importance of the area for the West.[44] Another territorial clause poses problems.[45] According to Peter the Patrician the fortress of Zintha, which was supposed to mark the boundary of Armenia, was situated along the border to Mēdia. If we trust the words of the Byzantine historian, the borders of Armenia would have been shifted considerably eastward. In this case, Armenia would have been compensated for the loss of the 'provinces beyond the Tigris' in the area of the Media Atropatēnē (Azerbaijan) at Sasanian expense. It is also possible, however, that the fortress was situated within the border region Ingilēnē, which, as already mentioned, was ceded to Rome and was explicitly named in the treaty because of its strategic importance.

Moreover, any compensation for Armenia by way of a south-eastern extension of its borders is problematic.[46] The overall policy of the Roman emperor speaks against an eastward extension of the borders all the way into the area of the Media Atropatēnē. Diocletian's conservative policy rather aimed at securing the status quo. It is noteworthy that Tiridates III was excluded from the peace negotiations of the year 298 although Galerius owed his military success against Narsē above all to the help of the Armenian king. Diocletian acted in the name of Tiridates III, who apparently did not have any choice but to acknowledge his dependence on Rome. It does not look, therefore, as if Diocletian felt obliged to compensate Tiridates for anything. The latter must have been well aware that his existence depended on the great powers, and this was once more revealed by the treaty of 298.[47]

According to Peter the Patrician the peace treaty also demanded that in the future the king of Ibēria would receive the symbols of his rule from Rome. Narsē thus had to acknowledge a Roman protectorate of Ibēria, which was situated south of the middle Caucasus and north of Armenia.

[43] Barceló 1981: 159 assumes that the long existing *amicitia* between Rome and Armenia was confirmed and that this friendship extended to a wide range of scenarios, such as Rome asking the Arsacid nobility ruling Armenia to protect Roman interests in the East.

[44] Honigmann 1935: 4–5; Enßlin 1942: 54–70 and Lightfoot 1986: 509–29.

[45] Winter 1988: 180–6.   [46] Kettenhofen 1995c: 69–73.

[47] Against this background we have to understand Tiridates III's decision to make Christianity the state religion in Armenia soon after 298. The war against Armenia that began in 312 was the answer to this move, which had such wide-reaching consequences for Armenia's future; on the war against Armenia by Maximinus Daia see Castritius 1968/9: 94–103; on Tiridates and the Christianisation of Armenia see Chaumont 1969: 131–46 and Kettenhofen 1995c: 48–135.

Rome thereby ruled over Kolchis and Ibēria, which together make up the territory of modern Georgia.[48] By placing Ibēria under their supremacy the Romans gained crucial strategic advantages over the Sasanian Empire.

The last paragraph of the treaty of 298 concerned primarily economic questions (see also **28**).[49] The city of Nisibis, which was situated on the Tigris, was named as the only place of trade between the two empires. Peter the Patrician mentions that Narsē complained about this condition whereas he seems not to have shown any reaction against the other terms for peace proclaimed by Sicorius Probus. The king's protest as well as Rome's firm attitude reveal how much importance both sides attributed to this matter. Narsē rejected the clause for good reasons because it entailed that the exchange of goods within Mesopotamia, in particular the local trade along the borders, would be impeded. Correctly, W. Seston interprets this 'economic clause' of the peace treaty as complementing the Roman defence system.[50] The many caravan routes in upper Mesopotamia and in particular the main waterway, the Euphrates, represented natural conditions for intensive trade and also for close contacts between the neighbouring regions of both states. The official frontier between the Roman and the Persian Empires was therefore somewhat artificial. From a Roman point of view, trying to declare Nisibis as the only place for an exchange of goods between the two empires makes sense, also with regard to the safety of the empire (**28**).[51] After Narsē had agreed to Rome's terms his relatives were returned to him.[52] Festus tells us that the king's family had been treated very mercifully and that this impressed the Persians so much that they admitted to being inferior to the Romans not only in arms but also with regard to common decency.[53] It is certainly possible that the return of the captives had been part of the official peace treaty.[54] Apparently the treaty was concluded in the autumn of 298 and was ratified by the signatures of Narsē and Sicorius Probus. It was a *foedus* that fulfilled the technical and legal conditions for an agreement that would bind both parties.

---

[48] Braund 1994: 245–6; on the history of this region in general see Lang 1983: 505–36 and Lordkipanidse and Brakmann 1994: 12–106.

[49] Winter 1987: 47–58 and 1988: 192–9. [50] Seston 1946: 176–7.

[51] According to Andreotti 1969: 217–18 the strict supervision of trade was not crucial for military considerations; cf. ibid. 215–57 for a detailed discussion of the relationship between national safety and the control of trade.

[52] Malal. 12.39 (p. 308); Zon. XII.31.

[53] Fest. 25; Eutr. IX.27.2 and Zon. XII.32 claim that Diocletian paraded Narsē's family in his triumph but these statements must be seen as part of a literary embellishment surrounding the great triumph that Diocletian celebrated in 303.

[54] Cf. Schenk Graf von Stauffenberg 1931: 400.

Most modern scholars interpret the *foedus* of 298 as a great political and diplomatic Roman triumph. In contrast, P. Barceló and R. Klein argue that the final treaty of the year 298 created a situation that was genuinely unacceptable for the Sasanians and hence dangerous. The two scholars talk about a delayed war rather than a real peace, which only lasted as long as it did because for a while the Sasanian king Šāpūr II was preoccupied with domestic and other foreign affairs. They claim that Diocletian's wish to fortify the border revealed how much the emperor was aware of the danger.[55] According to G. Wirth Rome dictated peace conditions that the Sasanian Empire perceived as threatening its very existence.[56] However, such interpretations fail to see the defensive character of Diocletian's policy.

Moreover, we have to look at Sasanian interests from the perspective of the year 298 and not in light of the following events. Considering Narsē's military defeat, what could he have expected from a peace treaty with Rome, in particular given the fact that his family was held captive by the enemy? His goal for the negotiations was the release of the royal prisoners, and in return he seems to have been prepared to accept any reasonable terms. Diocletian's demands must therefore be regarded as moderate and restrained. Only if the emperor had acted differently by claiming more Persian territory or had even refused to release the prisoners – which, considering Valerian's death in Sasanian captivity not long before, might have been considered an option – could one indeed talk of repressions and a treaty that bore the seeds for a new war. As it was, Narsē achieved his main goal in the negotiations, the return of the captives, and from a Sasanian perspective this was a success as much as the fact that Rome waived territorial claims. Narsē certainly accepted terms that entailed significant strategic and economic disadvantages for the Sasanian Empire but in view of the situation in the year 298 this had been inevitable.

An analysis of the peace treaty of 298[57] should also point to the fact that in spite of the military and diplomatic defeat the dignified role of the Persian king and the equality between the 'King of kings' and the emperor were respected. Rome acknowledged the sovereignty of the defeated Sasanian ruler.[58] Likewise, in light of his defeat Narsē gave up Sasanian plans for a world empire. Towards the end of the third century each of the two powers therefore respected the might of the opponent both on a military and a diplomatic level.

[55] Klein 1977: 185 and Barceló 1981: 74.   [56] Wirth 1980/1: 336–7.
[57] Winter 1988: 208–15.   [58] Ziegler 1964: 145 and Chrysos 1976: 1–60.

18: The peace treaty of 363 between Jovian and Šāpūr II

For the most part, Rome's territorial gains and corresponding strategic and economic advantages that resulted from the *foedus* of 298 were lost when Šāpūr II and Jovian concluded a new peace in 363.[59] This time it was the Roman emperor who – in light of his crushing military defeat – had to agree to more or less all conditions for peace named by Šāpūr II. For Rome, losing important strategic positions and cities meant considerable loss of prestige. Many and varied sources ranging from chroniclers and historians to poets, orators and theologians reveal how Rome struggled with this situation, both historically and ideologically.[60] We owe the most elaborate account to the eyewitness Ammianus Marcellinus, who was an officer in the Roman army at the time and participated in a number of wars during his lifetime.

Ammianus Marcellinus xxv.7.9–14

(9) But the king insisted on demanding what, as he called it, was his and what had been taken away a long time ago by Maximianus[61] but really, as the situation required, for our release[62] five regions beyond the Tigris: Arzanēnē, Moxoēnē, Zabdikēnē and also Rehimēnē and Karduēnē together with fifteen fortresses, Nisibis as well as Singara and the Castra Maurorum,[63] a very convenient fortification. (10) And although it would have been ten times better to fight than to hand over any of these, the many flatterers put the timid emperor under pressure by bringing up the dreaded name of Procopius[64] and predicting that if he, after learning of Julian's death, returned with a fresh army, which he commanded, he would easily and without opposition overthrow the government. (11) Without hesitation the emperor, greatly inflamed by these persistent and dangerous remarks, handed over everything they asked for[65] and he barely made sure that Nisibis and Singara came under Persian control without their inhabitants and that the Romans from the fortresses that were to be handed over were allowed to return to our protection.

---

[59] For an analysis of this *foedus* of 363 see ibid.: 25–60; Blockley 1984: 34–7 and Chrysos 1993: 165–202.

[60] See Chrysos 1993: 166–7; Chrysos lists the testimonies related to the peace treaty.

[61] Šāpūr II has Narsē's defeat against Gaius Galerius Valerius Maximianus in 298 in mind (**6**), which resulted in the peace concluded at Nisibis (**17**).

[62] With these words Ammianus Marcellinus refers to the difficult situation of the Roman army, which was still situated in the enemy's territory when Julian died and exposed to the continuing Sasanian attacks.

[63] This important Roman fortification in Mesopotamia, a two days' march away from Dārā, is mentioned by the author elsewhere (xviii.6.9) and also by Procopius (*Aed.* ii.4); see Ball 1989: 7–18 and 2003: 80–1.

[64] This is the usurper Procopius, a relative of the emperor Julian, who had been a general in his Persian campaign and on whom Julian was said to have conferred the imperial title; on 28 September 365 he had himself proclaimed emperor in Constantinople but in May of the following year he was defeated by the emperor Valens.

[65] Eutropius (x.17.3) and Festus (29) also claim that Jovian showed more concern for the preservation of his rule than for the interests of the empire.

(12) In addition there was another dreadful and shameful condition, namely that after the conclusion of these negotiations, our longstanding and faithful friend Arsaces, if he asked for it, should not be given help against the Persians. This was designed with a double purpose, so that a man who with the emperor's instruction had devastated Chiliocomum[66] would be punished and that there would be the opportunity immediately after to invade Armenia without opposition. This is why later the same Arsaces was captured alive and the Parthians under dissensions and turmoils seized the longest stretch of Armenia,[67] which borders Media, as well as Artaxata.[68] (13) After this shameful peace had been sealed distinguished men were given as hostages on both sides so that nothing was done contrary to the agreement during the truce...

(14) Thus a peace of thirty years was concluded and sealed by sacred oaths...

The majority of ancient authors judge the treaty of 363 as one of the most unfortunate treaties that Rome ever concluded with a foreign power.[69] Although Ammianus Marcellinus tends to be critical of the emperor Jovian, his account reveals a balanced view. We learn that the agreement of 363 cancelled important stipulations of the *foedus* of 298, which had been disadvantageous for the Sasanians. From a Roman perspective there was a clear loss of territories that had formed an integral part of the empire. Losing much of north-eastern Mesopotamia, in particular the cities Nisibis and Singara, had an immediate effect on Rome's prestige. Ammianus Marcellinus describes in detail the exodus of the inhabitants of Nisibis and the take-over by the Persians.[70] The urgency of his account reveals how much significance contemporaries attributed to the event and how important the city was for Roman security and trade.[71]

According to the wording of the treaty Nisibis and Singara had to be handed over 'without their inhabitants' (*sine incolis*), which means the cities were taken over 'naked' by their new rulers.[72] Apparently the inhabitants of the two cities were to be spared captivity and deportation.[73] Eutropius and Festus, who composed their *breviaria ab urbe condita* shortly after the events, describe the surrender of Nisibis as a unique event in all of Rome's history.[74]

---

[66] Chiliocomum was a fertile region north of Karduēnē; cf. also Amm. xxiii.3.5 and xxiv.8.4.

[67] On Armenia's and Arsaces' fate during the reign of Šāpūr II see **26**.

[68] This is the capital of Armenia, situated in the left banks of the Araxes river, and the modern Artashat southeast of Yerevan; Diod. xxxi.17a states that Artaxios I built the city in 188 BC; cf. also Plut. *Luc.* 31; Strabo xi.14.6 claims that Hannibal was involved in the foundation of the city.

[69] Fest. 29; Lib. *Or.* 1.134; 18.277–8; Agath. iv.26.6–7; as can be expected, the Christian authors are polemical against the pagan emperor Julian and hold him responsible for the loss of Roman territories.

[70] Amm. xxv.9.1–12; see also Teixidor 1995: 499–510.

[71] Turcan 1966: 875–90.   [72] Malal. 13.27 (p. 336).

[73] On the deportations of Roman prisoners to the Sasanian Empire see **36**.

[74] Eutr. x.17; Fest. 29; in this context see also Bird 1986: 11–22.

On first sight the regulation regarding the so called 'provinces beyond the Tigris' is ambiguous. According to Ammianus Marcellinus Šāpūr II obstinately demanded (*petebat obstinatius*) the return of the territories that had been ceded to the Romans in 298 but was not given all of these: apparently Sophanēnē and Ingilēnē remained under Roman influence.[75] Although the author states that Jovian instantly complied with all demands it would appear that Šāpūr II eventually was prepared for concessions in 363. After Jovian's death the Sasanians pursued an aggressive policy against Armenia, which suggests that Šāpūr II used the first opportunity to achieve with arms what he had not accomplished in 363 (**26**). The two sides failed in their attempt to come to an understanding with regard to the status of the traditional 'bone of contention' Armenia; the stipulation that Armenia henceforth was not to receive Western support did not bring about a long term solution to the problem.[76] Šāpūr II adhered to what was spelled out in the treaty of 363 only as long as Jovian was alive. With the emperor's death Persian attempts to conquer Armenia began and before the end of Šāpūr II's reign an agreement was reached between the two great powers that envisaged the actual partition of Armenia. Shortly after, this was confirmed by a formal agreement.[77]

Our sources do not explicitly mention that the *foedus* of 363 targeted economic considerations or those relating to trade. However, the negotiations regarding the Mesopotamian centres of trade and the influence in Armenia have to be viewed in such a context.[78] The clause that stipulated the surrender of Nisibis 'eliminated the Roman monopoly of the income from the trans-borderia Nisibis'.[79] From the Syriac chronicle of Joshua the Stylite,[80] which was composed in Edessa at the beginning of the sixth century, we learn that the Sasanian king Balāš (484–8) approached the Roman emperor Zeno asking him for financial support for his war against the Hephthalites. Complaining that the taxes of Nisibis granted to Persia many years before were high enough,[81] the emperor refused to pay any money to Balāš although his predecessor Perōz (459–84) had received such payments.[82] According to Joshua the Stylite it was agreed in 363 that the Persians would take possession of Nisibis for 120 years

---

[75] Chrysos 1976: 24; see the commentary by Paschoud 1971–89: 216–20 on Zos. III.31 and Chrysos 1993: 174–7.

[76] On the 'Armenia clause' of the treaty of 363 see Chrysos 1976: 32–6; Blockley 1984: 36; 1987: 223–6 and Seager 1996: 275–874.

[77] Cf. p. 185 n. 56. [78] Winter 1987: 58–62. [79] Blockley 1984: 36.

[80] See **26**, esp. pp. 186–7. [81] Ios. Styl. 18. [82] Ibid. 9.

but that the city would then be returned to its previous masters.[83] This phase ended while Zeno was emperor. When the Sasanians refused to hand over the city new disputes arose. The financial loss incurred by the outstanding taxes remained an issue of contention and were at least in part responsible for the attitude of the Byzantine emperor Zeno (474–75/476–91).

The so called 'Romance of Julian', written by a monk from Edessa and generally dubious as a historical source, contains an interesting remark in this context.[84] The anonymous author states that Jovian agreed to hand over Nisibis for 100 years and that during this period no Christians were persecuted in the Sasanian Empire.[85] The two Syriac sources agree that the clauses of 363 were limited to a fixed period of time. According to Ammianus Marcellinus the peace was concluded for thirty years.[86] It is possible that this was intended to be a time span of 'one generation' and the expected lifetime of the Roman emperor Jovian, who in 363 was thirty years old; he adhered to the terms of the treaty until his death. The discussions regarding the *foedus* of 363 that arose during the fifth century illustrate that the time limit was not simply a diplomatic formula but that it was a real aspect of the treaty which could indeed cause problems later.[87]

In any case, the time limit assigned a somewhat provisional character to the treaty that had been concluded between Jovian and Šāpūr II. Its clauses were not necessarily interpreted as binding and definitive. Given the territorial losses that Rome suffered, this must undoubtedly be regarded as a success for Jovian. It would not appear to be justified, and not even in light of the ceding of Roman territories, to talk about a 'shameful and humiliating peace' for Rome.[88] Although Ammianus Marcellinus tries hard to criticise the Roman emperor for his wrong behaviour in the year 363, he does not fail to notice that during the peace negotiations Jovian was above all interested in securing the release of his troops (*pro redemptione nostra*). After Julian's military catastrophe (**8**) it must indeed have been Jovian's primary goal to see his army withdraw unharmed by Sasanian attacks.[89] He was able to achieve this goal by obligating Rome in the way discussed above.

---

[83] Ibid. 7; on the questionable historical accuracy of this passage see Luther 1997: 99–101.
[84] Luther 1997: 100.
[85] Nöldeke 1874: 285; see also ibid.: 284–92 for a detailed summary of the content and critical commentary (on the basis of Hoffmann 1880 and Wright 1872: no. 918); see also Drijvers 1994: 201–14.
[86] Zos. III.31.1 also mentions a peace of thirty years.
[87] Chrysos 1993: 186.   [88] Agath. IV.26.7.   [89] Cf. Ehling 1996: 186–91.

19: The peace treaty of 422 between Theodosius II and Bahrām V Gōr

The testimonies dealing with the *foedus* of 422[90] pay much more attention to the circumstances of this diplomatic event than the actual content of the treaty. The Greek historian of Syriac descent Malalas, who wrote the oldest surviving Byzantine universal chronicle,[91] tells us about the following remarkable suggestion, which Bahrām V (420–39) made so that a peace could be reached between the great powers.

John Malalas XIV.23 (p. 364)

In this year, the Persian king Bahrām (V) advanced in order to fight a war with the Romans.[92] When the Roman emperor learned about this he appointed the patrician Procopius as *magister militum per Orientem* and sent him out with an army to fight the war. When Procopius was about to open battle the Persian king proposed the following to him. 'If there is one man in your entire army who can fight in single combat one Persian, whom I choose, I shall make peace immediately and in all respect for fifty years and shall give the customary gifts.' When this had been agreed upon, the Persian king chose from the unit of the so-called 'immortal ones'[93] a Persian named Adrazanes and the Romans a certain Goth named Areobindus, a *comes foederatorum*. The two stepped forward, mounted and fully armed. According to Gothic custom, Areobindus also carried a lasso. The Persian attacked first with his lance; Areobindus turned to the right, threw his lasso at him, forced him off his horse and killed him. After this the Persian king concluded a peace. When Areobindus after his victory returned to Constantinople together with his general Procopius, the emperor thanked him and appointed him consul.

It is very unlikely that Malalas' story is authentic and that such events led to the end of the Byzantine–Sasanian War in the year 422.[94] The motif of the duel on horseback, which had a long tradition in Iranian culture, was exceptionally popular in the Sasanian period, when it followed very strict rules and carried moral overtones.[95] Numerous visual representations, for example that of the controversy between Valerian and Šāpūr I (5), confirm

---

[90] Apart from the sources mentioned here see Marc. Com. a. 422; Socr. *HE* VII.20–1.

[91] For an English translation and commentary see Jeffreys et al. 1986; on Malalas and his work see also Jeffreys and Croke and Scott 1990.

[92] Hostilities began in the year 421; from a Roman perspective the battle of 6 September 421 (cf. Marc. Com. a. 421.4) was a success and led to peace in the following year; cf. Luther 1997: 106–7.

[93] In particular the Sasanian cavalry with its heavy armour impressed the West tremendously; cf. Amm. XXIII.6.83; XXIV.6.8; Proc. *BP* I.14.44 also calls these Persian elite units the 'immortal ones'; on the Sasanian army in general see Wiesehöfer 1994: 262–5 and 379.

[94] On these events see Luther's commentary on Ios. Styl. 8 (Luther 1997: 106–7).

[95] Cf. Wiesehöfer 1994: 265.

that the duel symbolised a particular outcome of a historical confrontation. Differing from Malalas, the Byzantine historian Procopius describes the events as follows.

Procopius, De Bello Persico 1.2.11–15

(11) When Theodosius had grown up and reached a certain age and Yazdgard (I) had died because of an illness, the Persian king Bahrām (V) entered Roman territory with a large army; however, he did not inflict any harm but without actually having done anything returned to his own country in the following way. (12) The emperor Theodosius happened to send the *magister militum per Orientem* Anatolius as ambassador to the Persians, all by himself. As soon as he was very close to the army of the Medes, he, on his own, dismounted his horse and on foot went up to Bahrām. (13) When Bahrām saw him he asked those present who this man was who was approaching him. They responded that he was the Roman general. (14) Struck by this extraordinary gesture of honour the king himself turned and drove back his horse, and the entire Persian army followed. (15) Back in his own country he regarded the ambassador with utmost respect and concluded the peace just as Anatolius had asked him to, that is under the condition that neither of the two parties would build any new fortress on their territory in the border area of the other. After they had come to this agreement both sides went about their domestic affairs as they liked.

According to Procopius Bahrām V was impressed when Theodosius II (408–50) sent the high ranking *magister militum per Orientem* as ambassador to him; even more impressed by the ambassador's respectful gestures he decided to withdraw his troops and to conclude a peace. The author seems to get the events of 422 confused with new hostilities during the reign of Yazdgard II (439–57).[96] It was not before this war that the influential Anatolius, who held the supreme command in the East from 433 to around 446, played an important role and was largely responsible for renewing the peace of 422.[97] However, Procopius' account nicely illustrates the crucial impact of diplomatic interaction between the two powers. Codes of honour and gestures of mutual respect were important factors bearing an impact on decisions of war and peace. In this context cross-cultural understanding was necessary and, surprisingly, worked on several levels.

Do either Malalas' or Procopius' episodes reveal the actual outcome of the war? As far as it mattered, one may speculate that the result of the duel in Malalas and Bahrām's compliance with Anatolius' wishes in Procopius

---

[96] Procopius' account is most likely based on the work that Priscus composed during the fifth century. It is possible that Procopius intentionally shortened his source and 'merged' both wars in order to streamline his narrative; cf. Veh 1970: 459.

[97] On the chronology of the peace of 422 and that of 441 see Luther 1997: 101–8.

suggest that the Romans had the upper hand in the fighting.[98] Both sources agree that it was the Sasanian king who sought peace. Bahrām's desire to come to a quick settlement with Byzantium may be linked to the rise of the Hephthalites, who became the greatest danger for the Sasanians during the course of the fifth century (**10**). The sources do not inform us about the content of the peace treaty of 422. As the issue of the Christians had triggered the war in the year 421[99] it is not surprising that Bahrām V had to grant the freedom of their religion to the Christians in the Sasanian Empire. In turn, the Zoroastrians in the Byzantine Empire were allowed to practise their religion – according to K. Schippmann this represents a concession without any practical value.[100] However, Priscus mentions that around 465 a Sasanian embassy to the emperor Leo I (457–74) complained that the fire cult of the Magians who lived on Byzantine territory was impaired, an accusation that was rejected by Leo (**27** Priscus frg. 41.1). It is likely that in 422 both sides agreed to payments for the defence of the Caucasus region. In 441, when these were in arrears, Yazdgard II once more advanced into Byzantine territory.[101] In the same year a new peace was agreed upon, which envisaged mutual support in times of crisis and financial aid for the Sasanians.[102]

In the context of 422 we do not hear about any territorial changes or regulations regarding the borders. This corresponds to the fact that neither side had been able to make major conquests. The mutual obligation not to build new fortifications close to the border was, as indicated above, part of the treaty of 441. However, we can expect that already in 422 there was an interest in reducing the tensions caused by the opponent's armed presence in the border regions that could lead to open conflict. This was also achieved by an agreement not to enter into relations with the opponent's Arabian allies.[103]

The peace was concluded for a remarkably long period, which is symptomatic of the general détente that can be observed between West and East during the fifth century. Whereas Malalas remarks that Bahrām V agreed to

[98] According to Socr. *HE* VII.21.8 the empress Eudoxia composed a poem that was recited during the celebration of the victory.

[99] Marc. Com. a. 420, 3.   [100] Schippmann 1990: 42.

[101] Marc. Com. a. 441, 1; on the possible reasons for this war see Luther 1997: 103 n. 21, who points to a new wave of Christians escaping into Roman territory and an unsuccessful Persian request for their return.

[102] Ios. Styl. 8; on the problems concerning the shared defence of the unsettled Caucasus region see the commentary on **27**.

[103] Malchus, frg. 1; see Luther 1997: 107 n. 34; also Blockley 1992: 57–8; on the role the Arabian allies played within the strategies of the two great powers see in particular **24** and **25**.

conclude a peace for fifty years, another source refers to a 'hundred-years-peace'.[104] Regardless of the exact time limit, the peace that was concluded between Bahrām V and Theodosius II in 422 and renewed in 441[105] introduced a long peaceful period between both empires; this lasted until the beginning of the sixth century, when Kavādh I began to reform the Sasanian monarchy and reopened war against Byzantium.

20: The peace treaty of 562 between Justinian and Xusrō I Anōšarvān

The peace negotiations that led to the conclusion of this *foedus* and the actual treaty mark the highpoint of the diplomatic relations between the two rivalling powers. The narrative of Menander the Guardsman (Menander Protector) is a very comprehensive and reliable source.[106] Unfortunately, the work of this Byzantine historian, who continued the history of Agathias and covered the period between 558 and 582, has survived only in fragments. The author, trained in rhetoric and law, belonged to the entourage of the emperor Maurice (582–602) and thus was well informed of Byzantium's diplomatic relations during this period. He had access to the reports of the Roman ambassadors of the year 562, parts of which he quotes directly.[107] Menander's detailed report reflects the content and language of foreign diplomatic relations in this period. He names all the elements necessary for a successful conclusion of a *foedus*, namely the special status of the envoys, the choice of the venue for the diplomatic negotiations, the ceremonial protocol, the options for communication and the way both rulers addressed each other.[108]

Menander Protector, frg. 6.1 (FHG IV, frg. 11)

In the East and in Armenia a very successful peace seemed to exist, and in Lazika there was an armistice between the Romans and Persians.[109] As the peace had not been fully concluded, but both the Roman emperor and the Persian king had decided to strictly avoid warfare, Justinian sent the *magister militum praesentalis* Peter, so that he could discuss a comprehensive peace treaty with Xusrō (I). After he had arrived in the border region of Dārā and had explained to the king of

---

[104] Soz. IX.4.1.
[105] For the content of the *foedus* of 441 see also Blockley 1992: 61.
[106] For text and translation as well as a detailed commentary see Blockley 1985a.
[107] Men. Prot., frg. 12.
[108] For a detailed analysis of all aspects of this peace treaty see Rubin 1960: 366–73 and Schmidt 2002: 93–136.
[109] Before warfare between the powers had more or less ceased and in 557 the armistice was extended to include Lazika, which was still contested.

the barbaric peoples in the East that he was there in order to act as ambassador regarding a cease-fire on both sides, the Persians also sent an ambassador, who held the title Zich, which is the highest honour among the Persians, and whose name was Yazdgushnasp; he was the chamberlain of the king.[110] The ambassadors thus met in this way and as soon as the leaders of the surrounding areas had also gathered, they called an assembly. And the Roman ambassador Peter, who was an educated man in all respects and also had a good knowledge of the law, declared the following. 'Persians, we are here because the emperor of the Romans has sent us. It should be superfluous to say who our emperor is because his deeds have shown you the man. I am here now in order to transform the already existing peace into a permanent peace. But first I want to point out to you the character and greatness of the state with which you are going to conclude a peace. If, however, I appear to be talking big, looking towards what is advantageous for both states, do not take my long speech badly. For soon it will be clear that my words had to be said and I will be praised after deeds will have shown you the benefit of my words. You are now going to make peace with the Romans. It may suffice to say the word "Romans" because their name should reveal everything else. As you are going to conclude peace with such a powerful state and are not making minor decisions, you now have to make the best and most advantageous choices and in place of the insecure deeds of war welcome as a blessing the most secure thing for all humans, peace. And you should not be deceived by thinking that you were victorious over the Romans, boasting that you captured Antioch[111] and other Roman territories . . .'

At this point the Roman ambassador elaborately points to the advantages of a peace. After Peter's speech the Persian ambassador makes his response in as many words and emphasises above all the greatness of the Persian Empire and the power of the Sasanian ruler Xusrō I.

'If he wants, Xusrō is king over all men, and he does not wear the capture of Antioch like an ornament and as his prime conquest around his neck. Although what we have achieved appears frightful and awesome to you, we nevertheless think that it is not crucial to have been victorious over any of our enemies. For we have been raised to do precisely this, to be victorious, just as the other nations have learnt to be inferior to us. Having destroyed yet another Roman city does not ever tempt us to boast because what can be achieved without any difficulty does not deserve particular praise. And this shall suffice to refute the flood of your keen words. The Romans, however, are doing what they typically do, they ask for peace negotiations before the Persians do. Although you have been inferior to us, you have scored a victory by being fast, having been first in asking for peace. And in this way you conceal your lack of glory in wars, by seeming reasonable although you are really not in the position to sustain battle. If you had hesitated, we would have done this as victors. Nevertheless we start negotiations, as we value peace above everything

---

[110] 'Zich' is a Persian family name; cf. Christensen 1944: 105 n. 3; the Greek sources frequently confuse Persian names and titles in this way.

[111] Cf. **13**.

else. For it is a noble attitude to adjust one's behaviour to what is appropriate.'
After the Zich had spoken these words the interpreters[112] on both sides translated
both speeches and explained their meaning; many words were exchanged between
the two sides, partly in order to gain an advantage, partly in order to boast and
not to appear as the side who was not putting as much effort into the peace.
The Persians demanded that a permanent peace be concluded, and also that they
should be given an annual payment of gold by the Romans for not taking up arms.
Moreover, they would only agree to lay down arms after they had received in one
payment forty times, at least thirty times, the annual sum. The Romans in contrast
wanted to conclude a treaty for a few years only and were not willing to pay for
the peace.[113] This was discussed without agreement for a while and many words
were exchanged, but finally they decided to conclude the peace for fifty years and
that Lazika should be handed over to the Romans. The agreements should be firm
and lasting and valid on both sides, both in the East and in Armenia, and also
in Lazika itself, but under the condition that the Persians should receive for the
peace an annual sum of 30,000 gold coins[114] from the Romans. This was fixed in
a way that the Romans paid in advance the sum for ten years, that is immediately
for seven years and after the period of seven years without delay the sum for the
remaining three years, and subsequently so that the Persians received the required
sum annually...

It was agreed that both rulers should provide the documents which are called
sacrae litterae in Latin and which confirmed everything that had been established by
the ambassadors. And immediately a proclamation of these agreements took place.
In addition it was decided that the Roman emperor should produce a unilateral
document which confirmed that the Romans would give the Persians the additional
sum for three years after the end of the seventh year. The Persian king also had
to give his written consent that, as soon as the Persians had received the required
sum of gold for the three years, the Roman emperor would be given a letter
of confirmation in this regard. The declaration of peace of the Roman emperor
showed the customary prescript and is well known to us. The declaration of the
Persian king, which was written in the Persian language, in Greek translation began
like this: 'The divine, virtuous, peace loving, powerful Xusrō, King of Kings, the
fortunate and pious man, benefactor to whom the gods have given great fortune and
a great kingdom, the giant among the giants, who was designated by the gods, to the
emperor Justinian, our brother.'[115] Thus the prescript but the actual declaration was
the following. I shall give the precise wording because I think that this is necessary
so that nobody can be suspicious claiming that by a change in wording some of the

[112] On the important role of interpreters in the ancient world see Herrmann and von Soden 1959:
24–49.
[113] This passage reveals the fundamentally different interests pursued by the two sides during these and
other peace negotiations. Whereas the Persians are always keen on financial advantages, in particular
regular, long term revenues, in order to protect the borders and to finance their numerous campaigns,
the Romans preferred a short term peace in order to avoid long term financial commitments.
[114] Güterbock 1906: 62–5 discusses the question if the 30,000 gold coins were *solidi*; the *solidus* had
been the most important gold nominal since Constantine the Great; see Brandt 1998: 126–7.
[115] The emperor and the King of kings also address each other as brothers on other occasions; cf. **34**.

truth has been lost.[116] It read: 'We thank the brotherly gesture of the emperor for the peace between the two empires. We have instructed Yazdgushnasp, our divine chamberlain, and have given him full powers. Our brother the emperor has given instruction and power to Peter, the *magister officiorum* of the Romans, together with Eusebius to negotiate and to conclude the treaty. And the Zich and the man whom the Romans call *magister* and Eusebius together negotiated the peace and made agreements; they have concluded the peace for fifty years and all have sealed the statements. According to what the Zich and the *magister* of the Romans and Eusebius have decided, we now confirm the peace and abide by this.' This was the wording. The declaration of the Roman emperor was similar but without the prescript that the Persian royal letter showed. And in this way they ended their conversations...

After this and many other matters had been argued, the terms of the fifty years peace were put down in writing in the Persian and the Greek languages, and the Greek declaration was translated into Persian, the Persian into Greek. On the Roman side the *magister militum praesentalis* Peter, Eusebius and others ratified the treaty, on the Persian side Yazdgushnasp, Surenas and others. After the declarations from both sides had been fixed, they were compared to see whether they corresponded in wording and meaning.[117] Every declaration of the peace treaty was read out. The following points were laid down:

(1) The Persians, Huns, Alans and other barbarians should not have access to the Roman Empire through the pass, which is called Tzon,[118] and the Caspian Gates, nor should the Romans send an army against the Persians in this area or in any other border areas of the Persian Empire.[119]

(2) The Saracens, who were allies of both states, should abide by the agreements and neither should the Saracens allied with the Persians take up arms against the Romans nor those allied with the Romans take up arms against the Persians.

(3) Roman and Persian merchants of all kinds of goods, and suppliers of this type, should conduct their business according to old custom at the determined customs posts.

(4) Ambassadors and public couriers travelling to Roman or Persian territory should be treated according to their rank and in the appropriate way, should receive due attention and not be impeded by any means. They should be allowed to exchange the goods they were carrying without impediment and without any impost.[120]

(5) It was agreed: Saracen and other barbarian merchants should not travel through either of the two empires via unknown routes but travel via Nisibis and

---

[116] With these words Menander Protector tries to underline his own credibility. See Blockley 1985a: 294 n. 39, 'Menander appears to be suggesting that he himself had translated the Pahlavi, but perhaps he merely means that he transcribed the archival translation which he knew would be word-for-word.'

[117] For comments on these rather bureaucratic and cautious proceedings see Miller 1971: 72 n. 69.

[118] Marquart 1901: 106 identified Tzon with the pass of Derbend, which was the route of Hunnic invasions through the Caucasus; see also Gropp 1977; 1619–25; Kettenhofen 1996b: 13–19.

[119] For the crucial importance of the Caucasus region for East–West relations see **27**.

[120] The trading activities of the diplomats may have been a means to cover the costs of the embassies; cf. De Ste. Croix 1991: 129–30.

Dārā, nor should they enter foreign territory without an official permit. If they nevertheless dared to or, rather, engaged in smuggling, and were caught by border officials together with their merchandise, whether Assyrian or Roman, they should be handed over and suffer the prescribed punishment.

(6) Individuals who defected during the war, either from the Romans to the Persians or from the Persians to the Romans, should, if they wanted, be allowed to return to their homes and they should not be impeded in any way. However, those who defected during the peace on both sides, that is those who fled, should not be received by the other side but in any case, even against their will, be handed over to the state from which they fled.[121]

(7) Those who filed a complaint against a citizen of the other state should settle the dispute according to the law either by those who had suffered damage or by representatives in the border areas before officials of both states. This was to make sure that the aggressor made amends for the damage.

(8) It was decided: henceforth the Persians should not complain to the Romans regarding the fortification of Dārā[122] but in the future neither state should erect fortifications, that is fortify any place in the border areas with a wall so that this would not lead to accusations of trouble-making and cause a breach of the treaty.

(9) Neither of the two states should attack or make war on any people or territory subject to the other but without suffering harm or distress they should stay where they were so that these could also enjoy the peace.[123]

(10) They should not occupy Dārā with more units than necessary for the defence of the city. Nor should the *magister militum per Orientem* have his seat here in order that this would not lead to incursions and raids on Persian territory. It was decided that if such harm was done the commander at Dārā should take the responsibility for the offence.

(11) If a city inflicted damage on another city or harmed it in any other way, not according to martial law or with an army but by tricks and secretive theft – for there are shameless people who do such things, which could then create a pretext for war, such cases should be thoroughly investigated and judges[124] from the border regions of both empires should deal with them. It was agreed that if these were not able to put an end to the misfortune that the border cities inflicted on one another the cases should be referred to the commander in the East;[125] if the dispute were not settled within six months and the violated party had not received compensation the offender should be liable to the violated party for a

---

[121] In contrast to Güterbock 1906: 80–3, who assumes that those defectors were members of the upper social milieu, Blockley 1985a: 257 n. 55 refers to the shared interest of both states 'to control the ordinary people in a time of population shortage'.

[122] Justinian's comprehensive building activities both in Dārā and along the Roman Eastern frontier (cf. Proc. *Aed.* 11.3) had frequently led to discrepancies between the great powers.

[123] This clause reveals once more an interest in a comprehensive settlement, which would include territories such as Armenia and Lazika.

[124] Güterbock 1906: 88 assumes that the *dikastai* were local legal magistrates; in contrast see Blockley 1985a: 258 n. 61, 'I prefer either to take δικασταί = *iudices*, the general late-Latin term for provincial governors... or to view them as specially appointed judicial commissioners.'

[125] This is the *magister militum per Orientem*.

double indemnity. If the dispute were still not settled at this point, the violated party should send an embassy to the ruler of the offender. If the violated party had not been compensated by the ruler within a fixed one-year period and had not received the double indemnity, the peace treaty would be broken with regard to this agreement.

(12) This concerned petitions for divine support and prayers: that the god be gracious and an ally forever to the one who loved the peace, opponent and enemy to the insincere and the one intending to violate the oaths.

(13) The agreements should be valid for fifty years and the peace should last for fifty years, the year being reckoned according to old fashion that is ending after 365 days.[126] As mentioned already, it was also determined that declarations were issued by both rulers expressing approval regarding everything the ambassadors had negotiated.

When these terms had been agreed upon, the so-called *sacrae litterae* were exchanged...

After all this had been formally agreed, the two separate declarations were handed to the magistrates in charge, who compared their wording and meaning and immediately made copies of both. The actual treaty was also folded and stamped with a seal and other customary Persian symbols and with the signet-rings of the ambassadors as well as those of the twelve interpreters, six on the Roman side and as many Persian ones. They exchanged the documents. The Zich handed the Persian one to Peter and Peter handed the Greek one to the Zich. In addition the Zich received a Persian copy identical to the Greek one, without any seal, which was supposed to remind him, and Peter respectively. After that they parted, both leaving the border area, and the Zich travelled back to his homeland.

Negotiations

As had been the case when the *foedus* of 298 was concluded, on both sides high ranking officials and experienced diplomats, the *magister militum praesentalis* and the chamberlain of the Sasanian king, were in charge of the negotiations. They were authorised to act with full power. The ambassadors met in a neutral place by the border, close to Dārā, so that neither of the parties was forced into a disadvantageous position even before negotiations began.[127] At the beginning of the talks both sides made an effort to praise the greatness and power of their own empire; then they worked towards an understanding regarding the basic conditions for a peace.

These concerned above all the length[128] and scale of a settlement, and in addition a solution to the Lazic question. After long discussions it was agreed that the peace between the two empires should last for fifty years

---

[126] The Roman and Persian calendars had to be synchronised; see Doblhofer 1955: 215–16.

[127] On the significance of the choice of venue in the context of Sasanian–Roman peace negotiations see Winter 1994: 589–607.

[128] On the payments agreed upon in 562 see Güterbock 1906: 61–5 and Blockley 1985b: 285 n. 61.

and that it should apply to all territories, including Armenia and Lazika. In the past, continuing military confrontations in these regions had prevented a secure peace over and over again. By dropping all claims in this area, the Sasanians did their part to solve the Lazic question; in turn, Byzantium had to agree to substantial monetary payments the amount and conditions of which were a point of contention until, finally, a compromise agreeable to both sides was reached. As soon as these basic conditions for the peace had received mutual consent, the respective documents were produced and sent to both royal courts for ratification. Thereby the foundations for the conclusion of a peace treaty were laid.

After that, further meetings and negotiations between the ambassadors of both empires took place so that all details regarding a permanent settlement could be discussed. The official peace document was composed in Greek and Persian. It is remarkable how much care was used to make this process as accurate as possible. Altogether twelve interpreters were to make sure that each translation had the same meaning and would not allow for different interpretations. The respective documents were compared word for word and sentence for sentence.[129] Menander the Guardsman claims to have quoted *verbatim* the document written by Xusrō I (531–79) in the Persian language and addressed to his 'brother' Justinian (527–65).

Territorial terms

Altogether the Byzantine historian lists fourteen articles of agreement. Several points concern the territorial scope of the peace, which was intended to apply not only to the territories of the Sasanian and Byzantine Empires but in the interest of stability to include further areas. The regulation in article nine according to which the client kingdoms on both sides should not be attacked refers primarily to the Caucasian regions of Ibēria and Albania, which had often been the cause of renewed or continued military confrontations and were the subject of existing agreements (**17**). The Arabian tribes fighting on both sides, namely the Lahmids, who were allies of the Sasanians, and the Ghassanids, who acted on behalf of Byzantium, were addressed in the second article of the treaty.[130] Considering the political as well as military significance of these vassal states for the Sasanian–Byzantine confrontations in particular during the sixth century (**25**), this article makes a lot of sense. The Roman and Persian rulers were to enforce peace among the vassals. This term, however, could have been expected to

[129] On the oral and written components in the formation of a treaty see Täubler 1964: 318–72.
[130] Shahîd 1988: VII.

cause problems because the Arab leaders were not directly involved in the negotiations.

Borders

Further clauses concerned the protection of shared border areas. As conflicts had arisen in particular with regard to this point, the very first article of the *foedus* of 562 addressed the main issue, namely the protection of the Caucasian passes from invasions of the Huns, Alans and other barbarians (**27**). From this point onwards the Sasanians alone were responsible for the defence. In turn, the Romans agreed to refrain from any future troop movements in the Caucasus. Moreover, articles eight and ten addressed the situation of the border city Dārā, a matter that was extremely important from a Roman perspective (**12**).[131] In breach of earlier treaties Justinian had fortified Dārā to the extent that Procopius decribed the city as a bulwark for the entire Byzantine East.[132] The Sasanians now accepted Dārā's paramount status as a fortress, insisting, however, that the number of troops stationed at Dārā would be reduced and that the *magister militum per Orientem* moved his seat from there. In addition, both sides agreed that in the future already existing border cities should not be fortified and offer reasons for wars.

Trade and customs duties

'Economic' clauses can be found also in this treaty.[133] Three articles address economic and trade-related issues but the decisions do not diverge from the principles spelled out earlier (**17** and **28**). According to article three of the treaty, just like before, Sasanian and Byzantine merchants, who had to respect that there was a ban on the import and export of certain goods, were allowed to import goods at a few official customs posts only. As reference was made to previous agreements, Nisibis, Kallinikos and Dvīn (instead of Artaxata)[134] must have kept their preferred status as trade centres. Apparently, the fortress of Dārā, which has already been mentioned,

---

[131] On the negotiations concerning Dārā see Blockley 1985a: 71–2.

[132] In general on the importance of Dārā see Proc. *BP* 1.10.13–16; 1.16.6–8; see Crow 1981: 12–20; also Croke and Crow 1983: 143–59 (= Croke 1992: XI) and Whitby 1986a: 717–35 and 1986b: 737–83; on the fortification of border cities and fortresses see Wagner 1985: 68–9.

[133] Synelli 1986: 96–8 and Winter 1987: 67–72.

[134] During the first half of the fifth century the Armenian metropolis (of trade) Artaxata lost more and more of its significance. Its neighbour Dvīn, which was primarily inhabited by trades- and craftsmen, became the new political and economic centre. According to Proc. *BP* II.25.3 there were numerous merchants who came from India, Ibēria and all of Persia as well as from territories that were under Roman control in order to engage in trade at Dvīn; on the importance of the city as a place of trade see Pigulevskaja 1969: 153 and Manandian 1965: 81–2 and 87–8; with a comprehensive bibliography Kettenhofen 1996a: 616–19.

acquired the same rights. Byzantium gained considerable fiscal advantages from the fact that now a further place within the Roman realm would be dedicated to the exchange of goods. When the Sasanians conquered Dārā in 573, the Roman emperor intended to buy Dārā back or to win the city back in some other way.[135] The Sasanian ruler, however, did not want to return the city under any circumstances and announced that he would never withdraw from Dārā, or from Nisibis.[136] The Persians were not willing to give up the financial advantages that came with controlling the city.

According to article four of the *foedus* ambassadors and those travelling for reasons of state did not have to pay any customs duty for the goods they brought with them and were not subject to any trade restrictions.[137] A similar arrangement had existed in 408/9. However, the diplomats were allowed to stay on foreign territory only as long as necessary.[138] They were thereby prevented from gathering information about the opponent (35). Article five stopped Saracen or other barbarian merchants from entering the Persian or Roman Empire via unknown roads. They were required to go straight to Nisibis or Dārā and to obtain an official permit if they wanted to continue their journey from there. Any violation of these terms or customs fraud entailed legal proceedings. This article concerned merchants from Roman as well as Persian territories and also travellers from nations who were not allies of the great powers, such as tradesmen from South Arabia.[139] This stipulation was designed to stop the smuggling of goods as well as to eliminate any foreign competition for merchants at home and also to prevent Arab tradesmen from engaging in espionage. Above all the geographic conditions to the west and south-west of the Euphrates, where the Syrian Desert represented the actual frontier between the empires, made any strict control of this border area impossible and increased mutual suspicion. Due to these circumstances, foreign trade and national security were politically linked in a way that was characteristic for the economic relations between the Sasanian and the Byzantine Empire, a link that is nicely illustrated by the relevant articles of the *foedus* of 562.

Fugitives of war, reparations, guarantee clauses
Further points dealt with the treatment of the fugitives of war, the payment of reparations as well as the observance of the treaty.[140] Article six permits

---

[135] Menander Protector, frg. 47 (*FHG* IV 250).
[136] Ibid., frg. 55 (*FHG* IV 257).   [137] Antoniadis-Bibicou 1963: 47–8.   [138] Cod. Iust. IV.63.4 (3).
[139] Contacts between the Sasanian Empire and South Arabia, which were primarily initiated by interests in trade, are attested already for the early Sasanian period; cf. Metzler 1982: 190.
[140] Güterbock 1906: 80–3.

defectors to return without punishment. The treaty explicitly mentions, however, that this applied only to persons who had left their country during the war and not to future defectors so that these would not jeopardise home security by passing on information. The long period of war had seen many cases of unrest and raids among the population of the border regions concerned. The controversies between individuals and above all the conflicts between the border cities were to be investigated. According to articles seven and eleven the authorities in charge of the border areas were instructed to mediate in these cases and those responsible forced to pay damages. If an agreement could not be reached the matter was entrusted to higher authorities, which had to come to a decision by a fixed deadline.[141] If the matter had not been settled at the final stage of appeal, which was the appeal to the ruler, this amounted to a breach of the treaty.

Last but not least, the two parties included a 'religious guarantee clause' in order to make sure that the agreed terms would be observed and effective. If Menander the Guardsman uses the authentic words by which the peace was entrusted to divine protection, the treaty displays extremely careful wording also in this respect; the clause compelled both a Christian Byzantium and a Zoroastrian Persia to respect the agreement. The author makes no reference, however, to either hostages of high rank, who would customarily have been part of an official treaty of this type,[142] or to an oath sworn by each ruler.

Conclusion

Who was the 'victor' of the *foedus* of 562 after all? On the one hand, Justinian cannot have been happy with the stipulated large payments, which showed the character of tributary payments and were bound to ruin his prestige. On the other hand, he could claim as a success that the important fortress of Dārā was retained, that the Romans were freed from the financial burdens to do with the protection of the Caucasus passes and that the Sasanians were withdrawing from the territory of Lazika. From a Sasanian perspective it was a considerable loss to give up this strategically and economically important Black Sea region.

Beyond throwing light on the question of how the balance of power was shifted the *foedus* and the actual treaty as transmitted by the Byzantine historian Menander the Guardsman serve as an excellent testimony to the intense diplomatic contacts and the high level of international relations between Byzantium and the Persian Empire in the sixth century.[143] A survey of the individual points addressed in the treaty indicates that all

---

[141] Ziegler 1972: 427–42.   [142] Lee 1991: 366–74.   [143] Verosta 1965: 153–6.

areas of concern that had surfaced at some point since the beginnings of Roman–Sasanian relations in the third century are mentioned. The *foedus* of 562 therefore not only reflects some diplomatic effort to end the military conflict between Byzantium and the Sasanian Empire during the reigns of Xusrō I and Justinian but also gives us detailed insight into the intensity of relations.[144] It was a serious attempt to find a comprehensive solution to all controversial topics in order to stabilise the situation between the two powers. Be that as it may, although the peace was concluded for fifty years it did not last very long. By 572 West and East were at war again.

21: The peace treaty of 628 between Heraclius and Kavādh II Šērōē

Immediately after he had succeeded to the throne, the Persian ruler Kavādh II Šērōē (February – September 628) initiated peace negotiations with Heraclius (610–41). After his victory over Xusrō II Parvēz (590–628) and his advance all the way to Ktēsiphōn at the beginning of the year 628 the Byzantine emperor had decided to withdraw his troops.[145] From 11 March to 8 April 628 he stayed at Gandzak in Azerbaijan.[146] During these weeks he received a letter written by Kavādh II, in which the Persian ruler expressed his desire for peace and which is remarkable in many ways. The text was recorded in the so called Easter Chronicle, the *Chronicon Paschale*, which was composed by an unknown cleric from Constantinople between 631 and 641. It represents one of the most important examples of Graeco-Christian chronography; originally the work covered the time span from Adam to the year 630 but the narrative is preserved only up to the year 628. In particular with regard to the seventh century the *Chronicon Paschale* is a valuable independent source because it includes numerous historical details and draws on many official documents.[147]

Chronicon Paschale a. 628

Copy of the memorandum (written) by Kavādh, the most clement Persian king, who is also called Šērōē, (addressed) to Heraclius, our most pious and god-protected emperor.

From Kavādh Sadasadasach we are sending greatest joy to Heraclius, the most clement emperor of the Romans, our brother.

To the most clement emperor of the Romans, our brother.

[144] Higgins 1941: 279–315; Scott 1992: 159–66.
[145] On the assassination of Xusrō II Parvēz, on the succession of Kavādh II and the events of the year 628, which led to the final Roman victory over the Sasanian Empire, see Stratos 1968: 223–34.
[146] Schippmann 1990: 71.
[147] For a good introduction and English translation of the Greek text see Whitby and Whitby 1989.

'Through fortunate divine providence we have been adorned with the great diadem and have gained possession of the throne of our fathers.[148] As we have therefore been deemed worthy by God of gaining such throne and rule, we have decided, if there is anything that benefits and serves mankind, to accomplish this in so far as possible, and we have, as it was proper, given generous instruction for this to be done. As God has designated us to hold such a great throne and such great rule, we have decided to release every man whom we have imprisoned for whatever reasons. And thereafter we ordered, if there is anything else that benefits and serves mankind and this state and that we were capable of ordering, also this and it has been done. And we made these decisions in order to live in peace and love with you, the emperor of the Romans, our brother, and the Roman state and with the other nations and other princes around us.'

By addressing the Byzantine emperor as his brother the Sasanian king tries to emphasise the equal rank of both rulers.[149] In 590 Xusrō II Parvēz had approached the emperor Maurice (582–602) by using a comparable *captatio benevolentiae* in order to enforce his legitimate claims to the throne against the rebel Bahrām Čōbīn.[150] Kavādh's remark that he owed his throne to God is also very deliberate.[151] The Sasanian king refers to a God in the singular, thereby paying respect to the Christian emperor and creating a favourable atmosphere for the impending peace negotiations. Similarly, in the year 590 Xusrō II had hoped that using a 'Christian vocabulary'[152] would help him with securing Byzantine support in his struggle for the throne.

Considering the weakness of the Sasanian Empire and the military defeat it had just suffered in 628 Kavādh II had good reasons to evoke the familiar themes of the 'family of kings' and the 'legitimacy of rule'.[153] Moreover, he appealed to the Byzantine emperor's clemency and his desire for peace. He emphasises that he himself would do everything to benefit mankind, namely to release all prisoners, and that he wished to live in peace with all other nations.

---

[148] Kavādh had imprisoned his father Xusrō II Parvēz, who in spite of the military defeat had not been willing to conclude a peace with Byzantium; he then had his brothers assassinated and took over the throne in February 628 as Kavādh II Šērōē.

[149] On this address see Oikonomidès 1971: 269–81; the reader is reminded of the exchange of letters between Šāpūr II and Constantius II quoted in Ammianus Marcellinus: *Rex regum Sapor, particeps siderum, frater Solis et Lunae, Constantio Caesari fratri meo salutem plurimam dico.* The corresponding beginning of the response letter reads: *Victor terra marique Constantius semper Augustus fratri meo Sapori regi salutem plurimam dico* (XVII. 5.3). Constantine the Great called Šāpūr II 'my brother' (Eus. *v. Const.* 4.11); it is remarkable that in a letter to the wife of Xusrō I Anōšārvan the Byzantine empress Theodora also addressed her as 'sister' (Malal. 18.61 [p. 467]); for further references see Helm 1932: 385 n. 3; Dölger 1964: 60 points to the general reluctance of the Byzantine monarchy to acknowledge an equal status of any other power and speaks of an enormous concession to the Persian king.

[150] On the relationship between Xusrō II Parvēz and Maurice see Winter 1989a: 79–92.

[151] Whitby and Whitby 1989: 189 n. 491.

[152] Theoph. Simoc. IV.11.   [153] Winter 1989a: 72–92.

Kavādh II entrusted the memorandum to his Persian commander Phaiak and sent him to Heraclius' camp at Gandzak.[154] Unfortunately, Heraclius' response has not survived.[155] We owe a short summary to Nikephoros I, who was patriarch of Constantinople between 806 and 815 and whose earliest work, an account of the period between 602 and 769, incorporates many lost sources of the seventh and eighth centuries. According to Nikephoros Heraclius called Kavādh II his son and assured him that he would never deprive a king of his legitimate throne. The emperor proclaimed that Xusrō II had received divine punishment, which he deserved, and that divine guidance was fostering reconciliation between himself and Kavādh.[156] Heraclius thus also expressed his desire for peace and offered terms that even from a Sasanian perspective were moderate and acceptable.[157]

The emperor entrusted the *tabularius* Eustanthios to work out the details of a peace treaty. After the Sasanian ambassador Phaiak had spent just under a week in the Roman camp Heraclius sent both to the court of Kavādh II.[158] Our sources do not reveal the exact terms of the *foedus* of 628. Only isolated notes and later events allow us to reconstruct the content of the treaty.[159] One important hint comes from Theophanes Confessor, who between 810/11 and 814 continued the incomplete chronicle of his friend Georgios Synkellos and covers the period between 284 and 813.[160] His narrative is generally reliable and was a source for many later chroniclers.

Theophanes, Chronographia 1, p. 327 (ed. C. de Boor)

After peace had been concluded between Persians and Romans in this year, the emperor sent his own brother Theodore together with letters and men dispatched by Šērōē, the Persian king, in order that they send back peacefully to Persia those Persians in Edessa and Palestine, Jerusalem and the remaining Roman cities and that these could pass through Roman territory without harm. The emperor, who had defeated Persia in six years, made peace in the seventh year and returned to Constantinople with great joy.

We learn that Heraclius gave permission for all Persians who were still on Roman territory to make their way into Sasanian territory. He entrusted his brother Theodore with the supervision of this task. Apparently it had been

---

[154] *Chr. pasch.* a. 628.
[155] Cf. the attempts for a restoration of the text in Oikonomidès 1971: 269–81.
[156] Nikephoros 22B–23B (p. 19–20 ed. de Boor); Mango 1990: 15.
[157] Stratos 1968: 237 emphasises the moderate attitude of the Byzantine emperor, 'Heraclios did not make the same mistake as Justinian. He neither wished to humiliate nor to weaken Persia. He was aiming at restoration of the 591 frontiers, as if to show that the Greeks had no thought of conquest. This was why he immediately accepted the peace terms offered by Kavad, the new King of Persia.'
[158] *Chr. pasch.* a. 628.   [159] Rawlinson 1875: 535–6 and 693–4.   [160] Mango and Scott 1997.

agreed that all Persian prisoners would be released and that the emperor would guarantee their safe return.

There is no doubt that the terms of 628 primarily aimed at a restoration of the *status quo ante bellum*. The new borders would be those which had existed between the Byzantine and the Sasanian Empires before the beginning of the war in the year 602. The Persians had to withdraw from all territories they had conquered in Egypt, Palestine, Syria, Asia Minor and in Western Mesopotamia and had to return them to Byzantium.[161] According to Theophanes the Persian troops left these areas during the first year of the reign of Kavādh II.[162] In addition, the Persians had to agree that they would release the captives they had deported to the Sasanian Empire from these areas.[163]

One further aspect must have been particularly important for Heraclius, namely the return of the Holy Cross, which the Sasanians had carried off when they conquered Jerusalem in 614.[164] Its festive restoration in Jerusalem, probably in March 630, earned Heraclius great prestige and made it manifest to the world that a Christian Byzantium had triumphed over a Zoroastrian Sasanian Empire, and this triumph had been sealed by the *foedus* of 628.[165]

---

[161] Rawlinson 1875: 536.
[162] Theoph. *Chron.* AM 6119 (p. 327 ed. de Boor); on the execution of the terms of the treaty see Stratos 1968: 245–56.
[163] Theoph. *Chron.* AM 6118 (p. 327 ed. de Boor).
[164] On the Sasanian conquest of Jerusalem see the references on p. 45 n. 171.
[165] See Stratos 1968: 245–56.

CHAPTER 5

Arabia between the great powers

After the foundation of the Sasanian Empire in the year 224 the two powers had to deal with and administer an Arab world that was divided into three different groups. The first group was the Arab population in the Sasanian Empire, who had already lived in the Parthian kingdom during the Arsacid period and who now inevitably formed part of the Sasanian Empire. They settled in the eastern coastal area of the Persian Gulf, in northern Mesopotamia, where the desert fortress Hatra was the most important centre (map 1) and in southern Mesopotamia, where Hīra, which was located c. 100 miles to the west of the Sasanian capital Ktēsiphōn on the edge of the Arabian desert, had become a new centre (map 2).[1] The second group comprised the Arab population in the Roman Empire, and the third group was formed by the Arabs who lived beyond the Sasanian and Roman territories on the Arabian Peninsula.

The following events and developments illustrate an 'Arabia policy' of the great powers that remained an important component of the foreign relations between Rome and the Sasanian Empire into the seventh century and that both powers designed in a similar way: the inhabitants of Hatra joining the Rome side after 224, the ambitious political activities of the trade metropolis in the Syrian desert, Palmyra, and finally the creation of a system of Arab vassal states.[2]

22: Hatra

During the course of the Roman imperial period one caravan route, which took travellers through the steppes of central Mesopotamia to the north

---

[1] During the Muslim period a distinction was made between al-'Irāq (The South of Mesopotamia) and al-Ǧazīra (The North of Mesopotamia).

[2] Funke 1996: 217–38 (esp. 225–35) discusses the role of individual Arab dynasts and dynasties in the political considerations of the rivalling powers and the systematic creation of vassal states; see also Parker 1986b; Shahîd 1984a, 1984b and 1995a.

and via Singara and Edessa to Zeugma and the river Euphrates, became exceptionally popular. This route was controlled by the desert stronghold of Hatra, which flourished especially during the course of the second century.[3] Although Cassius Dio claims that Hatra was still insignificant during the reign of Trajan, neither large nor prosperous, a city in the middle of the desert and with little and bad water,[4] his statements somewhat disagree with Hatra's impressive temples that were built in the early imperial period.[5] The idea that Hatra did not participate in any significant long-distance trade but owed its wealth to its role as a religious centre within the region is not supported by our evidence.[6] Hatra certainly lay on and profited from the trade route – already described by Strabo – that crossed the Euphrates at Zeugma and went from Mesopotamia to Babylon.[7] Not least the unsuccessful attacks against the city by Trajan and Septimius Severus in the years 117 and 198/9 illustrate the powerful position Hatra had acquired by this time.[8]

The economic and political rise of Hatra[9] is also closely linked to the administrative structures of the Parthian kingdom.[10] As early as in the first century Western observers viewed the Arsacid Empire as joint *regna* rather than a unified state.[11] Especially in the course of the second century Hatra became less dependent from Parthia and instead a loose client relationship with the Arsacid dynasty developed.[12] The increased autonomy is illustrated by the fact that the lords of Hatra, who previously had called themselves 'Sir' (māryā), now adopted the royal title (malkā).[13] Until the beginning of Sasanian rule in the year 224 Hatra was able to preserve this degree of autonomy and also functioned as a buffer state between the Roman and the Arsacid empires. Both in 117 and 198/99 Roman soldiers failed at

[3] In general on Hatra see Drijvers 1977: 803–37; Hauser 1998: 493–528; Sommer 2003a: 44–6 and 2003b: 384–98.

[4] Cass. Dio LXVIII.31.1.   [5] Sommer 2003a: 47–80.

[6] Correctly, Sommer 2003a: 44–6 rejects Young 2001: 192–3.

[7] Strabo XVI.1.27; see also Stein 1941: 299–316.

[8] Cass. Dio LXVIII.31 (Trajan); Herod. III.9 and Cass. Dio LXXVI.12.2 (Septimius Severus); on the two campaigns see Debevoise 1938: 213–39 and 256–62; Birley 1999: 129–45; Rubin 1975: 419–41; Campbell 1986: 51–8; on the fortification of Hatra see al-Salihi 1991: 187–94 and Gawlikowski 1994: 47–56.

[9] For bibliographic references see Hauser 1998: 493–528; Sommer 2003a and b; Kaizer 2000: 229–52; Dijkstra 1990: 81–98.

[10] For an overview see Wiesehöfer 2001: 144–9 and 281–2 with further references.

[11] Wiesehöfer 2001: 144–5 on Plin. *HN* VI.112; Metzler 1991: 22 (now Wagner 2000: 51); on the relationship between local functionaries and the Arsacid lords see also Schuol 2000.

[12] Wiesehöfer 1982: 440; Winter 1988: 34; Hauser 1998: 515–16.

[13] On the controversial chronology and the titles of the rulers of Hatra see Maricq 1955: 273–88; Drijvers 1977: 820–7 and Hauser 1998: 499–503.

conquering the city.[14] Dio's account reveals that Hatra's political situation changed as soon as the first Sasanian king Ardašīr I (224–40) had defeated the last Parthian ruler.

Cassius Dio LXXX.3.1–2

(1) The situation in Mesopotamia was even more alarming and caused deep anxiety among everybody, not only among people in Rome but also everywhere else.[15] (2) For an Artaxerxes (= Ardašīr I), a Persian, defeated the Parthians in three battles, even killed their king Artabanos[16] and then marched against Hatra in order to establish a base from which he could attack the Romans. And indeed, he took the wall but lost many of his soldiers during the siege and therefore turned against Media.

The third-century historian, who was from Nicaea in Bithynia and composed a Roman history from the beginnings of the city to the year 229, informs us about Ardašīr I's attack of Hatra shortly after the change of power in Iran in 224.[17] This campaign against 'pre-Arsacid' Hatra around 226/7, that is, before the beginning of the first Roman–Sasanian confrontations in the years 230–3, was part of the Sasanian conquest of previously Parthian territories after the foundation of the empire in 224[18] and an expression of Ardašīr I's efforts to secure his own power. Cassius Dio also emphasises Hatra's strategic importance in northern Mesopotamia as a base for further military campaigns to the West.

Apparently Hatra was not willing to acknowledge Ardašīr's sovereignty when he tried to integrate the city into the Sasanian Empire. There must have been two reasons for this; first, although Ardašīr had been able to conquer all of Media he had not succeeded in doing the same to Armenia where some Medes had fled.[19] From Hatra's perspective, Parthian rule had not entirely been broken. Secondly, Hatra saw its political and economic autonomy, which the city had gained in the course of the second century, threatened by Ardašīr's desire to consolidate and centralise his rule within the Empire and to remove the power of the vassal kings.

In 226/7 Ardašīr suffered a defeat outside Hatra and had to withdraw. However, his attack had long-lasting consequences because thereafter the

---

[14] Cass. Dio LXVIII.31.1–4 and LXXVI.10.1; Herod. III.9.3–4; on these two campaigns see also Debevoise 1938: 213–39 and 256–62.

[15] Cf. the commentary on 1.

[16] On the decisive battle between Ardašīr and the last Arsacid ruler Artabanos IV, which took place on 28 April 224 in the plain of Hormizdagān, see Schippmann 1990: 15.

[17] We also read about Ardašīr's activities against the caravan city in Tabarī, tr. Nöldeke 18–19; Bosworth 15–16 (820).

[18] Wiesehöfer 1982: 445–6.   [19] Cass. Dio LXXX.3.3.

Hatraensians, who had been Rome's enemies during the Arsacid period, now sought cooperation with Rome against the common opponent, the Sasanians. Rome and Hatra allied themselves in the following years[20] and the city became part of the Roman defence strategy along the Eastern frontier, developments which enhanced Rome's strategic position in northern Mesopotamia considerably. Latin inscriptions that have been found in Hatra attest the presence of Roman soldiers in the city during the reigns of Severus Alexander (222–35) and Gordian III (238–44).[21] Roman activities after 230 such as the building and repair of streets and fortresses in the vicinity of Hatra further reveal Roman interest in using the city as an outpost against the Persian enemy and as part of its defence system.

The military alliance between Rome and Hatra weakened the Sasanian position in a region that was strategically important as well as from the point of view of trade. This situation inevitably provoked a reaction from the rising Eastern power and eventually Hatra was not able to withstand the Sasanian expansion of power. When the Persians conquered Hatra in the year 240[22] the political balance of power in this region was affected significantly and this entailed new military confrontations. In the Roman–Sasanian peace treaty of 244 (**16**) the Roman emperor Philip the Arab (244–9) presumably gave up the Roman protectorate of the territory of Hatra and, urged to do so by Šāpūr I, recalled his troops from there.[23] Ammianus Marcellinus describes the Hatra of the year 363 as an old city in the middle of the desert, which had been deserted a long time ago.[24] The example of Hatra was not unique. J. Wiesehöfer explains that Hatra's fate was typical for that of buffer states between the great powers. They often rose as a result of the strategic and political interests of their patrons but as often were crushed between them.[25] Not quite identical but comparable was the situation of Palmyra, which played an important role in the Iranian–Roman confrontations.

23: Palmyra

Pliny, Naturalis Historia v.88[26]

Palmyra, a city that is privileged by its location, the high quality of its soil and its pleasant waters, is encircled on all sides by wide sandy deserts and lies – as if separated from other countries in a natural way – on its own between the two

---

[20] On this alliance see Hauser 1998: 516–19.   [21] Oates 1955: 39–43 (nos. 79–81).
[22] Cf. the references on pp. 19–22, nn. 9-12.   [23] Winter 1988: 103–4.   [24] Amm. xxv.8.5.
[25] Wiesehöfer 1982: 447.   [26] On this passage see Kaizer 2002: 36.

greatest empires of the Romans and the Parthians, thus in a conflict always the first point of interest on both sides. The distance between Palmyra and Parthian Seleucia, which is called '(Seleucia) on the Tigris',[27] is 337 miles, between Palmyra and the nearest Syrian coast 203 miles and between Palmyra and Damascus 27 miles less than that.[28]

Pliny the Elder wrote a comprehensive natural history, which was an encyclopaedic work comprising several hundred Roman and Greek technical authors and composed according to subject groups. We learn from his passage on Palmyra that the city, just like Hatra, owed its wealth and significance to its geographical situation. Its prominent location between Rome and Iran (map 9) attracted the attention of both powers, in particular during military confrontations.[29]

As contacts between Rome and the Parthian kingdom developed, Palmyra, which had always played a key role with regard to the trade in the Near and Middle East, gained more and more importance. Especially during periods of peace Palmyra thrived and developed into a flourishing trading metropolis in the East of the ancient world. Modern travellers are still impressed by its numerous magnificent monuments, among these the famous temple of Bel, the main Palmyran deity,[30] which reveal not only a rich religious life but also the prosperity of the city.[31] Undoubtedly, the city was a crucial mediator for the trade between the great powers Rome and Iran[32] because the Roman East was the main recipient of the goods traded in Palmyra, above all the luxury goods that came from China and Arabia and travelled along the Silk Road, but also goods from India (**28**).[33]

From a Roman perspective Palmyra was also attractive because of the strategic role it could play. The city was supposed to represent an outpost

[27] Around 300 BC Seleucus I founded the city to become the capital of the Seleucid Empire. Although the city, which is located 40 miles north-east of Babylon on the right bank of the Tigris, had to cede this privileged status to Antioch on the Orontes in 293 BC, it developed and flourished as an Asian trade centre. In 165 Seleucia was burnt down during the Parthian War of Lucius Verus. Ktēsiphōn, which was situated across the river and is mentioned by Polybius (v.45.4) for 221 BC for the first time, was heavily fortified after the Parthian War of Septimius Severus and became the new capital of the Sasanians.

[28] These distances are somewhat exaggerated; the units are *stadia* that have been converted into miles.

[29] On the significance and history of Palmyra see Février 1931; Michalowski and Gawlikowski 1966–85; Frézouls 1976; Drijvers 1977: 837–63; Browning 1979; Teixidor 1984; Bounni and Al-As'ad 1988; Laurenti 1995; for further references see Kaizer 2002.

[30] On the religious life of Palmyra see Drijvers 1976; Teixidor 1979; Gawlikowski 1990: 2605–58 and Kaizer 2002.

[31] On the topography and architecture of Palmyra see Schlumberger 1935; Gawlikowski 1973; Will 1983: 69–81.

[32] On Palmyra's role as a trading centre in general see Drijvers 1977: 837–63; Drexhage 1982: 17–34; Teixidor 1984; Gawlikowski 1994: 27–33 and 1996: 139–45; Young 2001: 136–86; Luther 2004: 327–51.

[33] Cf. App. *Civ.* v.9.

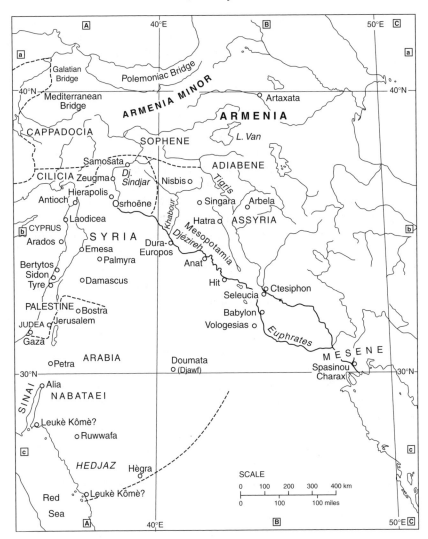

Map 9: Palmyra and the Roman East in the second century

against both the Parthian kingdom and the many Arab tribes in Syria.[34]
Because of its mediating role in the world of trade Palmyra was interested
in maintaining good relations with Parthia but the city preferred to attach
itself to Rome, the most powerful military power in the area. Palmyra's

[34] Shahîd 1984a: 22–4.

special status is expressed in the city's title *Hadriana*, which it received after Hadrian's visit in 129.[35] Citizens of Palmyra could be granted Roman citizenship.[36] In 212 the Roman emperor Caracalla raised Palmyra's status to that of a colony and granted the city the *ius Italicum*. Further privileges linked to this new status included the right to raise and dispose of taxes.[37]

The defeat of the Parthian kingdom at the hands of the rising Sasanian dynasty represented a threat not only for Rome. Similar to Hatra, Palmyra feared that its position could be jeopardised by the new power in the East. Above all, the fact that the founder of the new empire, Ardašīr I (224–40) was expanding into the north-eastern areas of the Arabian Peninsula affected Palmyran interests. When the king occupied Spasinu Charax on the Šatt al-'Arab the city lost immediate access to the Persian Gulf and thus its lucrative trade with India, one of its most important sources of income.[38] In general, Palmyra therefore developed a hostile attitude to Persia and simultaneously formed a bond with Rome. Because of its crucial role in the military confrontations between the two great powers from the middle of the third century onwards the city gained tremendous power and eventually became an empire in its own right.

During this period the history of the city was directly linked to the ruling family in Palmyra, the Iulii Aurelii Septimii. It was mainly Septimius Odaenathus who laid the foundations for Palmyra's expansion of power in the 260s and 270s. In an inscription dated to April 252 he is described as *vir clarissimus*, which was the title typically used during the imperial period for members of the senatorial order. Moreover, he was called the 'Lord of Palmyra' (*exarchos*).[39] Considering Palmyra's municipal order that assigned supreme administrative power to the *strategoi*, this title reflects a remarkable concentration of power in the hands of one individual. In several inscriptions from 257/8 Odaenathus was addressed not only as *vir clarissimus* but also as *vir consularis*.[40]

Odaenathus' rise is closely linked to Palmyra's intervention in the Roman–Sasanian confrontations during the reign of Šāpūr I (240–72).[41] In 253 Odaenathus inflicted a first defeat on a Sasanian unit. It looks, however, as if Šāpūr had dismissed Odaenathus' attempts to form an alliance

---

[35] Schlumberger 1939: 63–4 (no. 3).   [36] Strobel 1989: 74.

[37] In general on the economic and political structures of Palmyra see Zahrnt 1986: 279–93; Brodersen 1987: 153–61 and Matthews 1984: 157–80.

[38] Cf. the references on p. 19, with n. 8.   [39] Gawlikowski 1985: 257, no. 13.

[40] Ibid. 254–5, nos. 5–8; on these ranks and Odaenathus' membership in the Roman Senate see Strobel 1989: 74–5.

[41] On Odaenathus' activities, which are difficult to trace, see Kettenhofen 1982: 122–6.

with Persia before the Palmyrene lord was granted the position of *vir consularis*.[42] In light of the 'crisis' of the Roman Empire, which reached its peak around the middle of the third century, this development turned out to be extremely advantageous for Rome. Concerted actions of Palmyra and Persia would have entailed severe consequences for Rome.[43] Because of the growing tensions between the great powers it was impossible for Palmyra to adopt a neutral position. This is why Odaenathus once more tried to get closer to Rome. The anonymous author of the *Historia Augusta* (c. 400) reveals how significant the military activities of Odaenathus were for Rome's policy in the East.

Scriptores Historiae Augustae, Tyranni triginta 15. 1–4

(1) If Odaenathus, the Palmyrene prince, had not seized power after the capture of Valerian when the resources of the Roman state were exhausted, the East would have been lost. (2) As it was, after having assumed for the first time the title 'King' he gathered an army and then set out against the Persians together with his wife Zenobia, with his oldest son, whose name was Herodes, and with the younger sons Herennianos and Timolaos.[44] (3) First, he brought under his power Nisibis and most of the East together with all of Mesopotamia, after that he forced the defeated king himself to flee. (4) Finally, he pursued Šāpūr (I) and his children all the way to Ktēsiphōn, captured his concubines and also made a great amount of booty.

Although this *chronique scandaleuse* of Roman emperors is a problematic historical source (4), we cannot but agree with the ancient author that Rome was only able to retain its Eastern provinces because of the help of the Palmyrene lord Odaenathus. We learn that after Valerian (253–60) had been captured by Šāpūr in the year 260 (5) Odaenathus gathered an army and advanced against the Persians. In the second half of the year 260 he started a first counter-attack.[45] The military successes in Mesopotamia mentioned in the *Historia Augusta* were part of another Persian campaign (262–4), upon which Odaenathus embarked at the instigation of the emperor Gallienus (260–8), using Palmyrene as well as Roman troops. In particular Odaenathus' previous involvement in suppressing the attacks (260–1) against Gallienus' reign[46] persuaded the emperor to give him full powers with regard to the war in the East.

---

[42] Petr. Patr., frg. 10; cf. on this source Kettenhofen 1982: 72–3 and 124.
[43] Thus Alföldi 1939: 178.
[44] On the question whether these names are fictive see Hohl 1976–1985: 365 n. 1 on SHA *Tyr. Trig.* 27.1.
[45] On Odaenathus' Persian campaigns see De Blois 1975: 7–23; Kettenhofen 1982: 122–6 and Bleckmann 1992: 122–9.
[46] On these events see Strobel 1993: 246–56.

In the year 262 Odaenathus succeeded in reclaiming the territories in Mesopotamia previously gained by the Sasanians. In particular the loss of Nisibis and Carrhae amounted to a serious defeat. Moreover, twice Odaenathus' troops advanced all the way to Ktēsiphon (262; 264?) and devastated large parts of Mesopotamia.[47] However, they did not manage to capture the Sasanian capital, contrary to what the *Historia Augusta* might indicate. Apparently only the area surrounding the capital, which was successfully defended by the Persians, was raided. Nor is the capture of the royal harem confirmed by other sources. Be this as it may, there is no doubt that Odaenathus' advance enabled Rome to restore the *status quo ante bellum*. Gallienus granted Odaenathus the title of *imperator* for his successes. The emperor also appointed him commander over the entire East and he became *corrector totius Orientis*.[48]

In Gallienus' name Odaenathus now governed the territories that he had reconquered from Šāpūr. He probably held his *imperium maius* over the Eastern Roman provinces from the Pontic coast all the way to Palestine.[49] He became indispensable to the Roman emperor and to the defence of the Roman Eastern frontier.[50] With regard to Palmyrene trade interests it was above all important to restore direct access to the Persian Gulf.

Odaenathus' death in the spring of 267 not only freed Šāpūr I from a powerful opponent but was also a benchmark in the history of Palmyra. Up to this point the city had sided with and been loyal to Rome, and its power had increased steadily. Odaenathus' official successor was his ten year-old son Vahballāthus on whose behalf his mother Zenobia (267–72) ruled the city. Within a short period of time she became the actual ruler of Palmyra and 'governed almost the entire East like a man'.[51] Gallienus must have taken advantage of Palmyra's unstable situation entailed in the change of rule but the threat from the Goths in the West prevented the emperor from pursuing an active policy in the East.[52] Apparently Rome and Palmyra found some sort of *modus vivendi* also during the reign of Claudius II (268–70). Coins issued by both the Roman emperor and the Palmyrene ruler indicate a policy of *rapprochement*.[53] Palmyra retained its significance for the protection of the Roman Eastern frontier against the Sasanian Empire.

---

[47] Cf. Strobel 1993: 249–50.
[48] SHA *Gall.* 10.1–2; on Odaenathus' titles see Chrysos 1978: 51–2; Swain 1993: 157–64; Potter 1996a: 271–85.
[49] Strobel 1993: 249.
[50] On Palmyra's role as the most important Roman outpost against the Sasanians see Funke 1996: 226–7.
[51] SHA *Gall.* 13.5.   [52] Alföldi 1939: 177–8.
[53] Mattingly 1936: 95, 102 and 109.

However, when in 270 Palmyra sent troops to Egypt, embarked on a campaign into Asia Minor advancing to Ankyra and Chalcedon and conquered the Roman province of Arabia the break with Rome was final.[54] When the emperor Aurelian (270–5) began his reign Palmyra's sphere of influence was at its peak, reaching from Alexandria in Egypt to the Hellespont.[55]

Officially, Zenobia also broke with Rome; in 271/2 the joint mints with Aurelian ceased.[56] By issuing coins with the title 'Augusta' or 'Augustus' for herself and her son, without including Aurelian, Zenobia postulated her own imperial rule and proclaimed Palmyra's independence from the Roman Empire.[57] Her aggressive policy did not remain without a response. In the year 271 Aurelian, whose hands had been tied by revolts in the empire and barbarian invasions, turned against Palmyra. At Antioch and at Emesa he scored a decisive victory against the Palmyrene army and in 272 he forced Palmyra to surrender.[58] Whereas Zenobia herself was captured the city was spared by Aurelian. However, shortly after he had left the area the emperor was informed of an uprising in Palmyra, which made him return and besiege the city once more.[59] The title *Palmyrenicus maximus*, which is exclusively attested for Aurelian, celebrated the victory.[60] The emperor had managed to restore his rule in this region.

With regard to Zenobia's fate the sources are not unanimous. Whereas the Greek historian of the fifth century, Zosimus, claims that Zenobia died on the journey to Rome,[61] the majority of our sources tell us that she was paraded through Rome during Aurelian's triumph and that she lived in the vicinity of Rome for some time after.[62] Once more the *Historia Augusta* deserves special attention in this context. The *Lives of the Thirty Tyrants* include a letter attributed to Aurelian and addressed to the Roman Senate in which the emperor defends himself against accusations that he had celebrated his victory over a woman like a victory over a military leader.

Scriptores Historiae Augustae, Tyranni triginta 30.4–11; 24–6

(4) A letter by Aurelian survives which bears testimony regarding the captured woman. For when he was criticised by certain people because he, the strongest

---

[54] Zos. 1.50; for the difficult chronology of the events see Strobel 1993: 256–60.

[55] Millar 1971: 1–17; Equini Schneider 1993 and Stoneman 1992.

[56] On these mints see the references in Strobel 1993: 265.

[57] On the legends S ZENOBIA AUG and IMP C VAHBALLATHUS AUG see *RIC* v 2: 584, nos. 1–2 and 585, nos. 1–8; see also Drijvers 1977: 851–2 and Strobel 1993: 265–6.

[58] Downey 1950: 57–68.

[59] Zos. 1.61; see Bowersock 1983: 130–7 and Shahîd 1984a: 22–5, 151–2.

[60] *CIL* v 4319 (= *ILS* 579); cf. also Kettenhofen 1986: 143–4.

[61] Zos. 1.59.4.   [62] SHA *Tyr. Trig.* 24.4; *Aur.* 33.1–2; Eutr. IX.13; Fest. 24.

man, had paraded a woman in his triumph like some general,[63] he defended himself in letters to the Senate and the Roman people by giving the following explanation, (5) 'I hear, Senators, that I am being accused of having performed an unmanly act by parading Zenobia in triumph. Those who are criticising me would praise me to the sky if they knew what kind of woman she is, how prudent in her way of thinking, how consistent in her actions, how firm with the soldiers, how generous when the situation requires it, how harsh when discipline is called for. (6) I may well say that she was even responsible for Odaenathus' victory over the Persians and for the fact that he advanced all the way to Ktēsiphōn after he had put Šāpūr (I) to flight. (7) I may add that the woman spread such fear among the peoples of the East and of Egypt that neither the Arabs nor the Saracens or Armenians dared to move against her. (8) And I would not have spared her life, had I not known that she did the Roman Empire a great service by preserving her rule in the East for herself or for her children.[64] (9) May those who are not pleased by anything, therefore, hold their nasty tongues. (10) For if it is not appropriate to defeat a woman and to lead her in triumph what do they say about Gallienus, on whom she placed shame by ruling her empire as well as she did? (11) What about the deified Claudius, this revered and honoured leader, who, as they say, allowed her to enjoy her rule while he himself was busy with his campaigns against the Goths? And he was well advised and clever to do so in order that he could achieve more securely what he had set out to do while she guarded the borders of the empire in the East.'[65] (24) And so she was led in triumph displaying a splendour that the Roman people had never seen before. She was adorned with gems so huge that she suffered from the weight of her jewelry. (25) For it is said that the woman, although she was very strong, stopped very often, saying that she was not able to bear the weight of her gems. (26) Moreover, her feet were bound with gold and also her hands bound by golden chains, even around her neck she wore a golden chain, by which a Persian buffoon[66] led her.

Although the author credits Zenobia with Odaenathus' military successes against the Persians, he is justified in pointing to her advances into Asia Minor, Arabia and Egypt. There is no doubt that the passage reflects Zenobia's actual position of power as it was widely acknowledged in antiquity.

The description of the triumph is certainly exaggerated and embellished with novelistic elements. E. Merten points out that the motif of the oriental queen who can barely carry the weight of her gemstones was a familiar topos in contemporary novels and rhetoric.[67] However, there is no reason to reject the idea that Zenobia was indeed paraded in Aurelian's triumph. Although

---

[63] SHA *Aur.* 26.3 and 5; Zos. 1.55.3.　　[64] Gaudemet 1970: 94 and n. 47.

[65] The author of the *Historia Augusta* clearly tries to ignore Zenobia's ambitious claims for power; she appears only twice in the *Life of Claudius* (4.4 and 7.5).

[66] On this *scurra Persicus*, who was Zenobia's own servant, see Straub 1980: 243–4.

[67] Merten 1968: 134; cf. ibid. 132–40 for detailed comments on this passage.

we cannot make firm statements about Zenobia's fate it becomes clear that she inspired people's imagination. Ancient observers compared her to Cleopatra. These comparisons corresponded to Zenobia's own claim for Palmyrene rule and laid the ground for further stories about the queen.[68]

Aurelian reveals that he spared Zenobia's life because of her deeds for Rome and thus recalls the special role Palmyra played in the history of Roman–Sasanian relations. As long as Palmyra sided with Rome the city contributed significantly to the protection of the Roman East and thus helped to maintain the political *status quo*.[69] When Palmyra was destroyed an important buffer state between the great powers disappeared.[70] In the following period the Romans were forced to protect their borders themselves, both against the Sasanians and against the Arabs in this region. Although the fall of Palmyra left a vacuum barely filled by Rome, the great powers continued with their Arabia policy. Rome as well as the Sasanian Empire sought to win allies among the Arab rulers of the border territories by the Syrian and Arabian deserts. These were supposed to fend off nomadic tribes and could also be directly included in the military confrontations between Rome and Persia. Although this proxy policy did not reach its peak before the sixth century, the foundations for such a development were already built during the third century.

24: The Arab prince Imru'ulqais between Romans and Sasanians

Hatra and Palmyra controlled the numerous nomadic Arab tribes of the steppes around them in a way that the great powers were not or hardly able to.[71] They protected the traffic of goods, and they achieved economic prosperity and along with it political power.[72] The fall of the Parthian Empire changed this situation fundamentally. The destruction of Hatra by the first Sasanian ruler Ardašīr I in the year 240[73] led to a vacuum of political power in the central Mesopotamian steppe, which significantly jeopardised the transport of goods in this area. The destruction of Dura-Europos by Ardašīr's successor Šāpūr I[74] amounted to the loss of a further

---

[68] See Kornemann 1947: 288–313.   [69] Nakamura 1993: 133–50.

[70] On the consequences of this see Funke 1996: 228–35.

[71] Isaac 1993: 114–15 (= Isaac 1998: 422–3) assumes that the Roman Eastern limes was above all designed to control the nomads in the Roman Empire; see also Sommer 2003a: 83 and n. 48; in general on the function of 'frontier lines' in the East see Isaac 1992: 408–16; on the general discussion regarding the strategic aims of the Roman policy in the East see ibid.: 372–426 and Sommer 2004: 96–8.

[72] On the crucial role of the caravan cities for long-distance trade see Millar 1998a: 119–37; on caravan cities in general see Rostovtzeff 1932.

[73] Chaumont 1979: 217–37; Wiesehöfer 1982: 437–47.

[74] Rostovtzeff 1943: 17–60; James 1985: 111–24; Mac Donald 1986: 45–68; Gilliam 1941: 157–75; Millar 1996: 445–71; 1998b: 473–92; Pollard 2000 s.v. and 2004: 119–44.

important centre of trading and trans-shipment.[75] Neither in Hatra nor in Dura-Europos did new settlements emerge afterwards.

More than anything else, however, the conquest of Palmyra by Aurelian in the year 273 and the end of Palmyrene rule were decisive.[76] Within a few decades the established local powers in Syria and Mesopotamia had disappeared, and the vacuum they had left was not filled by either of the two great powers.[77] As a consequence, the infrastructure and protection that the autonomous centres Hatra and Palmyra had provided for the entire Eastern trade collapsed. The geographer Strabo refers to the possible problems this caused for the individual merchant who had to cover long distances safely. As part of his description of the trading routes in Mesopotamia he mentions that the nomadic or semi-nomadic Arabs along the Euphrates demanded such high tolls that several routes had become entirely unprofitable.[78]

In the fourth century the risks for travellers in the region were still enormous. According to Hieronymus, nomadic Saracens were notorious in the barren country along the public road between Beroia and Edessa. Travellers formed larger groups in order to resist the threat but this did not always help. In much detail the church historian describes how the nomads, riding horses or camels, attacked a group of about seventy travellers, robbed them and then disappeared.[79] From the end of the second century onwards Rome reacted to these dangers with a stronger military presence in the Eastern provinces.[80] However, in particular the introduction of a new saddle for camel riders during the fourth century increased the threat posed by the now extraordinarily mobile and united Saracens. Interestingly, in the first century Palmyra made use of a militia made up of camel-riders, cavalry, mounted archers and light infantry, which was in charge of protecting not only the territory of Palmyra but also its trading routes against raids.[81]

In many ways the history of Hatra and Palmyra thus illustrates the crucial role Arabia played in Roman–Persian relations as early as in the third

---

[75] It is unclear, however, if the decline of Dura-Europos as a trans-shipment centre for the Palmyrene long-distance trade began earlier, possibly linked to the presence of Roman garrisons in the city. The ports of both Anath, where soldiers from Palmyra were based (see Driven 1999: 35 n. 137) and Kirkēsion (Will 1992: 89) would have been other options.

[76] On the end of Palmyrene rule, the conquest of Palmyra and the fall of the city see Downey 1950: 57–68; Bowersock 1983: 130–7; Shahîd 1984a: 151–2; Stoneman 1992 and Hartmann 2001: 375–87.

[77] On the consequences of the fall of Palmyra for the policy of the great powers see Funke 1996: 228–30.

[78] Strabo XVI.1.27.

[79] Hier. *Vit. Malchi* 4; on this text see Fuhrmann 1977: 41–89.

[80] Kuhnen 1999: 220; Mayerson 1989: 71–9.   [81] Hartmann 2001: 54 and n. 40.

century. Odaenathus' activities on behalf of Rome (260–6/7) reveal the impact of individual Arab leaders and how much these could further their own position. The early Persian attempt to include Arab tribes outside their territory in their political strategies accelerated this development.[82]

During the reign of the first Sasanian king Ardašīr I, Hīra was the other important centre apart from Hatra (map 10).[83] For the numerous Arabs in this region the fall of Arsacid rule entailed a period of change. According to the author Tabarī many Arab tribes did not want to remain on Sasanian territory because they feared that they would lose their autonomy under Sasanian rule.[84] When towards the end of Parthian rule the people of Hatra concluded an alliance with the Romans (**22**) Ardašīr I turned his attention to Hīra. Here the family of the Lahmids, who had been of importance already during the Arsacid period, were the focus of attention. During Ardašīr's reign the leading man was 'Amr ibn 'Adī.[85] Ardašīr I wanted to cooperate with him in order to weaken Rome and to control new Arab Bedouin tribes. Tabarī informs us about the position of the son and successor of 'Amr ibn 'Adī, Imru'ulqais as follows.[86]

Tabarī, Ta'rīh 1 833–4

After the death of 'Amr b. 'Adī b. Nasr b. Rabī'a, one of his sons called Imru'ulqais al Bad was at that time a governor of Šāpūr I,[87] then of Hormizd I and (finally) of Bahrām I, ruling over the frontier territory of the Arabs of Rabī'a, Mudar and the other tribes who lived in the deserts of Iraq, the Hiǧāz and of Mesopotamia. He was the first of the kings of the clan of Nasr b. Rabī'a and the governors of the Persian kings to convert to Christianity. According to Hišām b. Muhammad, he lived as a vassal king in his district for 114 years,[88] of which 23 years and one month were under Šāpūr I, one year and ten days under Hormizd I, three years, three months and three days under Bahrām I, and eighteen years under Bahrām II.

If Tabarī is right, Imru'ulqais was appointed Sasanian governor over the Arabs in the vast deserts of 'Irāq, Hiǧāz and Mesopotamia during the

---

[82] For a survey of this development see Bosworth 1983: 593–612 and 1985–7: 201–3.

[83] On Hīra's role in particular with regard to the protection of the Sasanian Western frontier see Bosworth 1983: 597–604 and Shahîd 1971a: 462–3.

[84] Tabarī, tr. Nöldeke, 23–4; Bosworth 20–2 (822).

[85] On 'Amr ibn 'Adī, whose historical biography escapes us for most parts (in contrast to that of his successor Imru'ulqais), see Rothstein 1968: 39–40; Pellat 1971: 450 with further references.

[86] On Imru'ulqais see Bowersock 1983: 138–47.

[87] In the Arabic text 'of Šāpūr son of Ardašīr'; for ease of understanding here and below the conventional names and numbers of the Sasanian kings are used.

[88] This must be one of the frequently attested 'oriental exaggerations'; Arabic sources often show legendary years of age with regard to the birth and death of individual rulers. It could also be the case, however, that mistakes were made when the manuscripts were copied.

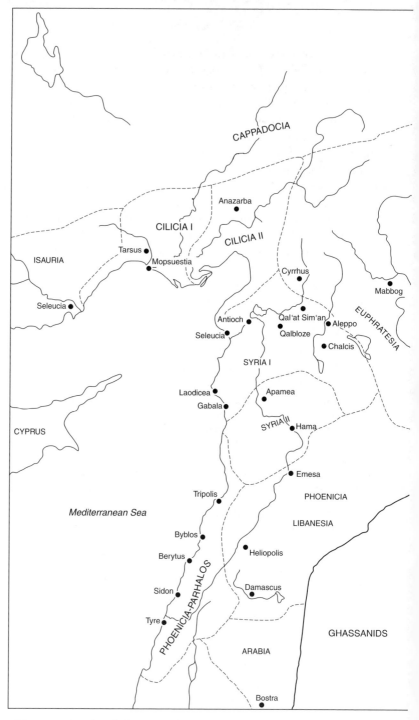

Map 10: Lahmids and Ghassanids along the Roman–Sasanian frontier

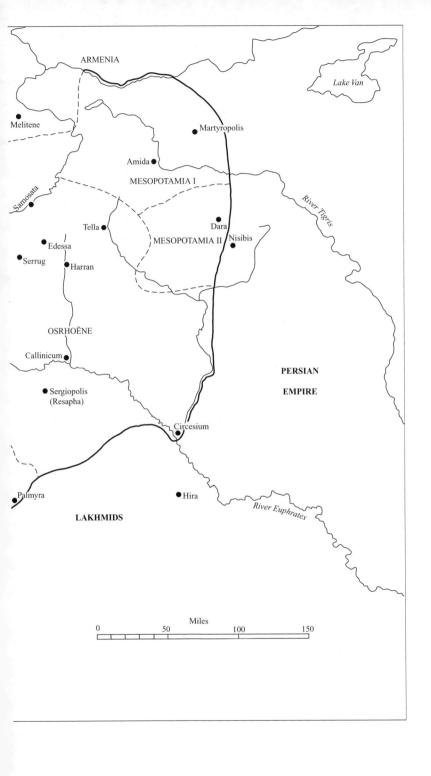

ARMENIA

Lake Van

Melitene

Martyropolis

Amida

MESOPOTAMIA I

Samosata

Tella

Dara

Edessa

MESOPOTAMIA II

Nisibis

Serrug

Harran

River Tigris

OSRHOËNE

Callinicum

PERSIAN

Sergiopolis
(Resapha)

EMPIRE

Circesium

Palmyra

Hira

River Euphrates

LAKHMIDS

Miles

0   50   100   150

reign of Šāpūr I (240–72). This meant that he controlled the Arabs living within the Sasanian Empire. Imru'ulqais' political activities, however, are discussed without agreement among scholars. In particular the statements made in the grave inscription of this Arab ruler do not correspond with Ṭabarī's account. The former was discovered by the French scholars R. Dussaud and F. Macler in 1901 when they found an inscription in the rubble of a completely destroyed mausoleum southeast of an-Namarā (modern Jordan), carved into a large basalt block. Originally the block had served as a door-lintel of the entrance to the grave. It is the oldest Arabic inscription that has been found so far and also the only one that was incised in the Nabataean alphabet. Since its first publication in 1902 it has received much attention from both epigraphists and historians.[89]

According to the inscription the Arab ruler Imru'ulqais died on the seventh day of the month Keslül in the year 223 (= 328). The dating formula uses the era of Bostra, an Arabic centre in the north-western part of the Arabian Peninsula.[90] Imru'ulqais' name, descent and title are given. The Arab ruler had the right to call himself 'king of all Arabs'.[91] With regard to the Roman–Sasanian relations it is noteworthy that Imru'ulqais appears as a Roman client king and that he took measures to make this relationship with Rome last beyond his death.[92] On first sight the alliance between Rome and Imru'ulqais seems to contradict the role accredited to him by Ṭabarī, namely that of Sasanian governor. It would appear, however, that he changed sides at some point, probably during the reign of the Sasanian king Bahrām III (293), so that his sphere of influence shifted to the West. Henceforth he was a Roman client king and in this role allowed to call himself 'king of all Arabs', as we learn from his grave inscription. We can only speculate about his motives for the 'change of front'. According to Ṭabarī Imru'ulqais was a declared Christian but this can hardly have been the main reason. It is more likely that his decision was motivated by the unstable situation that arose after the death of Bahrām III. Given that he had been the king's supporter and could expect the new Persian ruler Narsē to be hostile he must have decided to escape.[93]

---

[89] For the text and a German translation see Altheim and Stiehl 1965: 312–32; for a more recent – but problematic – English translation and interpretation see Bellamy 1985: 31–51.

[90] After the Nabataean empire had been integrated into the Roman Empire in 105/6 Bostra became the capital of the newly created Roman province of Arabia; at this point the era of Bostra was established.

[91] Funke 1996: 231 has pointed out that this is the first instance where the legitimacy of rule stems from a pan-Arabian ideology.

[92] Altheim and Stiehl 1965: 316–17; according to Bellamy 1985: 34–5 and 46 Rome assigned special titles to the Arab vice kings appointed by Imru'ulqais and thereby turned them into rulers by Roman authority. As *phylarchs* they were supposed to protect Roman interests in this region.

[93] Thus Altheim and Stiehl 1965: 320.

His example did not alter the general Persian policy and the Sasanians continued to entrust individual Arab rulers with the control of the restless Arab tribes along their borders.[94] In the so called Inscription of Paikuli, an inscription of Narsē (293–302), we read that once more a 'king of the Lahmids' paid his respect to the Sasanian king on the occasion of his accession to the throne.[95] Apparently the Persians had put him in charge as an allied vassal along their Western frontier so that he would continue the tasks carried out by Imru'ulqais before.

It thus looks as if – corresponding to the Persian policy – the Romans also tried to protect their own border by using local Arabs as commanders in these areas. Inevitably this 'Arabia policy' extended the geographical scope of the conflict between the great powers and introduced a new element to the Roman–Iranian relations. Whereas henceforth the Sasanians always entrusted one powerful family, namely the Lahmids, with the protection of their interests in the Arab territories, the Romans always used several *phylarchs* who, in return for pay, performed services that helped with the protection of the border and controlling the restless Arab tribes. This rather loose state of dependence, which is alluded to in the grave inscription of Imru'ulqais, did not change before the beginning of the sixth century when the Ghassanid dynasty became to Byzantium what the Lahmids had been to the Sasanians for a long time.[96] In the sixth century the 'proxy policy' of the great powers, that is the policy of including Arab rulers in their own political considerations, reached its peak.

25: 'Proxy policy': Lahmids[97] and Ghassanids[98]

Procopius, De Bello Persico 1.17.40–41 and 45–48

(40) . . . For Alamoundaros was a very smart man and very experienced in war, extremely dedicated to the Persians and exceptionally daring to the effect that he thwarted Roman interests for almost fifty years. (41) From the borders of Egypt to Mesopotamia he raided every territory where and from where he captured all things, one after the other. . .

(45) To sum up: this man was the worst and most dangerous enemy for the Romans. The reason for this was that Alamoundaros was the only one holding the

---

[94] See Mayerson 1989: 71–9.
[95] Humbach and Skjaervo 1983: § 92 (p. 71 ed. Skjaervo); Skjaervo 1983: 126; on this second great epigraphic statement by a third-century Sasanian ruler see Kettenhofen 1995c: 1–47.
[96] On the importance of the Lahmids for the protection of the Sasanian Western frontier against the Bedouins of the Arabian–Syrian desert see Nyberg 1959: 316–26.
[97] Rothstein 1968 and Shahîd 1986: 632–4.
[98] Nöldeke 1887b; Kawar 1957–8: 232–55 and Shahîd 1965: 1020–1.

royal title and thus ruling over all Saracens in Persia, which meant that he was able to use the entire army at any time in order to attack whichever parts of the Roman Empire he desired. (46) However, neither one of the Roman generals, who are called *duces*, nor one of the commanders of the Saracens allied with the Romans, who bear the title *phylarchs*, possessed enough power to oppose Alamoundaros with his men. For none of the units present in these territories was strong enough to be the enemies' equal. (47) This is why the emperor Justinian made Arethas, the son of Ğabala, who ruled the Saracens in Arabia, the leader of as many tribes as possible and thereby honoured him as never before among the Romans. (48) However, in the following period Alamoundaros did not thwart Roman interests any less than before, that is rather more, because whenever he attacked or when they competed with each other Arethas was either markedly unsuccessful or deserted his men very quickly. For we know very little about him. And thus Alamoundaros had the opportunity to loot the entire East without any resistance and for a long time, in particular as in addition he simply reached a very old age.

During the reigns of Kavādh I (488–97/499–531) and Xusrō I Anōšarvān (531–79) al-Mundir III, whom the Greek sources call Alamoundaros, was the leader of the Lahmids. Procopius' account emphasises how much this Arab ruler posed a threat for Byzantium. Only when the Byzantine emperor Justinian (527–65) established a client relationship with the Ghassanid dynasty similar to the one that existed between the Lahmids and the Sasanians, did the situation change.[99] In 529 Justinian placed the famous ruler al-Hārit V ibn Ğabala, whom Procopius calls Arethas, at the head of as many tribes as possible.[100] The centre of his rule was in Gabīyā, close to Damascus, and his sphere of influence reached as far as the Red Sea (map 10). He was also given the title of king and must have ruled over all Arabs in Syria. Justinian's intentions are obvious. He wanted to set up a counterpart to the Lahmids, who were pursuing Persian interests most successfully.[101] During the sixth century the relations between the two dynasties, siding with the Byzantine and Sasanian side respectively, were characterised by permanent military confrontations.[102]

Procopius gives a comprehensive account of the continuing quarrels and fighting and also comments on their military consequences for the confrontations between West and East. Alamoundaros acted as the leader of a Persian army[103] and Arethas' soldiers reinforced Justinian's troops.[104] We are also told that Arethas gathered a large army which he used to support

---

[99] On the Byzantine–Arabian relations during the sixth century see Vasiliev 1935–50 and Shahîd 1995a; on the violent proxy war fought between the kingdoms of the Lahmids and Gassānids during the following period see Funke 1996: 232–5; Whittow 1999: 207–24.

[100] Kawar 1959: 321–43.   [101] Casey 1996: 214–22.   [102] Devreesse 1943: 263–307.

[103] Proc. *BP* 1.18.1 and 9.   [104] Ibid. 1.18.7 and 35.

the activities of the Roman troops and to raid Sasanian territory.[105] As he was much feared by the Romans, these planned their activities carefully around possible attacks by Alamoundaros.[106] Moreover the Ghassanids and Lahmids fought each other directly without any Roman or Persian involvement.[107]

Procopius indicates that the great powers used the Arabian allies merely as a means to an end in order to pursue their own military interests.

Procopius, De bello Persico II.I.I–5

(1) Shortly after Xusrō (I) learnt that Belisarius had also started to win over Italy for the emperor Justinian,[108] and – although he was no longer able to conceal his plans – wanted to find a way how to break the peace treaty by way of a clever excuse. (2) He took counsel with Alamoundaros in the matter and instructed him to come up with reasons for a war. (3) The latter then accused Arethas of having violated borderland, started hostilities in spite of the peace and in this way attempted to attack Roman territory. (4) He claimed that he himself was not violating the peace treaty between the Persians and Romans because neither of the two parties had included him in the peace. (5) And this was true because not in a single instance were the Saracens, as they were subsumed under the name 'Persians' or 'Romans', named in the declarations.

Apparently Xusrō I wanted an excuse for a new war with Byzantium. In 540 – when Justinian seemed occupied with activities in the West – he thus provoked confrontations between the Lahmids and Ghassanids. The Persian ruler did not perceive this as a violation of the so-called 'eternal peace' (*eirēnē peras ouk echousa*),[109] which had been concluded shortly before between Byzantium and the Sasanian Empire, because the treaty of 532 did not explicitly mention the Arabian allies.[110] In this way the two powers, who were each striving for strategic advantages, had retained their liberty to move. In practice, however, the attacks of Alamoundaros, who accused his opponent Arethas of violations of the border, became the *casus belli* and in 540 this led to the outbreak of the second Byzantine–Sasanian War in the sixth century.[111] In light of these events it is even more remarkable that the

---

[105] Ibid. II.19.11–18.   [106] Ibid. II.16.17.

[107] Ibid. II.28.12–14; on these activities, of which the great powers in general approved, see Vasiliev 1950: 274–83; Rubin 1960: 272–3 and 310–11 and Shahîd 1971b: 240–2.

[108] In 535, after the victory over the empire of the Vandals in North Africa (533/4), the most powerful of Justinian's generals, Belisarius, was put in charge of the war against the Eastern Goths in Italy. After several victories in southern Italy he entered Rome on 10 December 536.

[109] Proc. *BP* 1.22.3; cf. also the references in Luther 1997: 219 n. 425.

[110] On the *foedus* of 532 see Güterbock 1906: 37–56 and Greatrex 1998: 213–21.

[111] On the events of the year 540 see Greatrex 1998: 218–21.

Arabian allies were explicitly included in the peace when in 562 the great powers tried to end the war and to establish an overall peace (**20**).

This may suffice to illustrate the important role the Arab Saracens played in the confrontation of the great powers. The end of the Lahmid dynasty once more reveals the significance of the client relationship for the Sasanians and the consequences for the course of Sasanian history. Whereas the Lahmid subjects had converted to Christianity for a long time, their rulers had remained pagans. Only the last Lahmid king Numān III (580–602)[112] professed himself a Christian.[113] This may have contributed to the break with the Persian king Xusrō II Parvēz (590–628) as much as the fact that Xusrō accused the Lahmid king of lacking support against Bahrām Čōbīn. By treason Numān III was lured to the court of Xusrō II and assassinated.[114] The Lahmid monarchy ended with the death of Numān III. Xusrō II entrusted an Arab of non-Lahmid descent with the tasks previously carried out by the Lahmid dynasty. Alongside this new ruler a Sasanian governor was appointed.[115] In the eyes of the Sasanian ruler the Lahmids had obviously gained too much power. Although Xusrō II had liberated himself from an inconvenient vassal, he had destroyed the balance of power in the region. In the following period, the protection of the South-western borders of the Sasanian Empire against the attacks of nomadic Arab tribes, which had been one of the most important tasks of the Lahmids, was lacking. As a result, several Arab Bedouin tribes formed an alliance and probably in 604 destroyed a Sasanian army at Dū Kār. From a Sasanian perspective this defeat was rather insignificant but the battle had important psychological effects on the Arabs. The victory showed them how powerful they could be when they cooperated. A few years later the Arabs united under the banner of Islam, put an end to the Sasanian Empire and rose to become the new power in the Near and Middle East.[116]

---

[112] Shahîd 1995a: 486–7 (vol. 1).   [113] Rothstein 1968: 139–43 and Preißler 1975: 47–8.
[114] Shahîd 1995b: 119–20.   [115] Rothstein 1968: 119–20.
[116] Preißler 1975: 54 and Funke 1996: 234.

CHAPTER 6

Shared interests: Continuing conflicts

Although Roman–Persian relations were dominated by military conflicts or diplomatic activities concerning these conflicts, there were a number of issues that showed points of contact between the two powers, which, however, could themselves become the starting point for further tensions. These are above all economic and trade related issues, the protection of the frontier and the integration of territories that had been contested for centuries. It is noteworthy that the contemporary authors always give their accounts on the basis of an 'imaginary opposition' between Occident and Orient, which creates a typical 'perspective of confrontation'. One cannot fail to notice the prejudices the Roman historians held against the 'oriental barbarians'. Such commonplaces, which found their way into Western literature many centuries ago, and which were embellished in numerous subsequent accounts given by those travelling between the cultures – soldiers or diplomats, scholars or philosophers, artists or missionaries – have had a tremendous impact on modern views until the present day. The second part of this book thus emphasises the contrary, namely the efforts to reconcile differences, the openness for cooperation between the powers and the solutions that were found in the process and thereby to gain a deeper understanding of Roman–Sasanian relations.[1] Given how the rivalries between Rome and Persia persisted and how difficult in particular the geographical conditions in the border regions were, these solutions can indeed be called innovative and forward-looking. At times, they certainly helped to stabilise the difficult political situation in the contested border territories along the Euphrates and Tigris.

26 Armenia

It is not easy to say what exactly 'Armenia' was in (late) antiquity, let alone to pinpoint the origins of those settling in the territorial entity between

---

[1] In this context see also chapter 9 'Exchange of information', below.

the Black and the Caspian Seas that may be referred to as 'Armenia' by contemporary or modern authors.[2] The meaning of 'Armenia' varies, and this not only according to date and context but also according to perspective, which means that at any given point the Armenians themselves would have had a very different view from those adopted by the Romans and Persians.[3] From the beginning of Roman–Iranian relations, however, Armenia was an object of rivalry between both powers, and for good reasons (map 11).

Because of its geographical location, the highland of Armenia to the south and south-west of the Caucasus was a focal point throughout antiquity: it was the area through which the majority of traffic from the Near East to Asia Minor passed and it was close to the strategically important Caucasus passes (**27**). Apart from being a transit area, Armenia had remarkable economic resources.[4] Among others, there were the gold mines of Pharangion,[5] mentioned by both Procopius and Malalas and famous already during Strabo's lifetime.[6] Accordingly, during the peace negotiations for the so-called 'eternal peace' in 530/31 Kavādh I insisted on these mines being returned by the Romans.[7]

Armenia benefited not only from its 'natural' resources but also from its important role in trade. Among those who travelled to Greater Armenia – the larger part of the country, which, as we shall see, came to be controlled by the Sasanians – in order to engage in trade were merchants from Persia as well as from Syria and Palestine.[8] Procopius provides us with a description of the most important Armenian city in the sixth century, Dvīn.[9] The Byzantine historian mentions a densely populated landscape surrounding the new capital, which was also the economic centre of Armenia. He also refers to fertile plains used for breeding horses. According to the author, merchants came from neighbouring Ibēria, from almost anywhere in Persia and even from faraway India.[10]

Armenia's human resources were equally significant and resulted from the idiosyncratic structure of Armenian society. Considering the sporadic

---

[2] For an excellent summary of early Armenian history see Garsoïan 1997a: 63–94 and 1997b: 95–116; for a sequence of maps see Hewsen 2001.

[3] For a cautious assessment with an emphasis on the 'diversity and incongruity' of anything 'Armenian' see the forthcoming article by Greenwood.

[4] On the economic resources of Armenia see Redgate 1998 (repr. 1999): 83–7.

[5] Proc. *BP* 1.15.26–9; Malal. 18.50–1 (pp. 455-6).   [6] Strabo XI.14.9.

[7] Chaumont 1987a: 433 correctly interprets this as an indication 'that their exploitation yielded large profits for the Sasanian government'.

[8] Malal. 18.63 (p. 469). Armenia's intensive trade with the neighbouring regions during late antiquity may be confirmed by the large variety of coins found in the area; for references see Chaumont 1987a: 433.

[9] Manandian 1965: 81–2.   [10] Proc. *BP* 11.25.1–3.

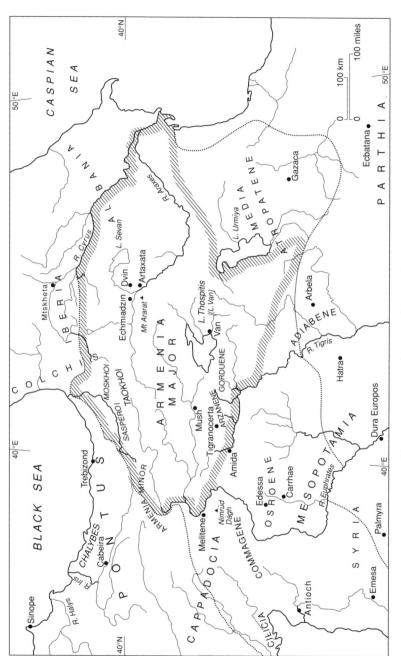

Map II: Armenia at the time of the Parthian Empire

character of our evidence, it is problematic to use the term 'feudal system'.[11] However, the relationship between the king, who had his own resources, and the hereditary Armenian nobility, the *naxarars*, was characterised by obligation as well as independence. There was also intense competition between and within the princely families, whose prestige and landed property varied but was often immense.[12] Below the nobility, the rest of the population was primarily made up of peasants who owed military and labour service to the respective families and ultimately to the crown. The contingents at the king's disposal were impressive and enhanced by monetary contributions owed by the princes.[13]

To the west of the river Euphrates, Lesser Armenia (Armenia Minor), belonged to the Roman Empire from early on. Since Diocletian and Constantine this part of Armenia formed the provinces Armenia I and II. In contrast, Greater Armenia (Armenia Maior), was often the reason for military conflicts between Rome and Iran. Although both sides showed the desire to resolve tensions peacefully, both also wanted to gain power in this strategically important region. The following account by Suetonius goes back to an earlier period of Roman–Parthian relations,[14] but it illustrates Armenia's delicate situation between East and West – a situation that remained difficult throughout late antiquity.

Suetonius, Nero 13

(1) Among the spectacles that he staged I may well also report on the entrance of Tiridates into the city. As foggy weather had prevented him from showing the man to the people on the day determined by the edict, he produced this man, the king of Armenia, who had been persuaded to come by great promises, when the next possible opportunity arose; cohorts in full armour were displayed around the temples in the Forum, he sat in a curule chair by the rostra in the attire of a triumphant general and surrounded by military symbols and standards. (2) And at first he let the king, who was approaching via a sloping platform, go down on his knees, then he kissed him after he had raised him with his right hand, and finally he took his *tiara* away, as the king had asked him to, and replaced it with the diadem,[15] while a man of praetorian rank translated the words of the suppliant and announced them to the crowd. Then he led him to the theatre and placed

---

[11] Redgate 1998: 97–8 on Toumanoff 1963: 34–144 and Adontz 1970: 343–61.
[12] See Thomson 1999: xiii–xiv; Garsoïan 1997a: 76–9; somewhat speculative Chaumont 1987a: 433.
[13] Cf. Redgate 1998: 99 with further references.
[14] On the history of Armenia during the Parthian period see Bedoukian 1980; Chaumont 1987a: 420–6; 1990: 19–31; Kettenhofen 1998: 325–52; see also Schottky 1989.
[15] The *tiara* is a Persian headgear. Among the Parthians, it was the prerogative of the kings, who alone were allowed to wear the battlemented *tiara*, often decorated with stars; the diadem was the royal symbol granted and acknowledged by the Romans.

him, who once more adopted the demeanor of a suppliant, on his right. Because of this he was hailed as imperator, and after laying a laurel wreath in the Capitol he closed the double doors of the temple of Janus, indicating that no war was left anywhere.[16]

In the year 54 the Parthian king Vologaeses I (51–76/80) had appointed his brother Tiridates (52/54–60 and 61/66–72) as king of Armenia. This move had threatened Roman interests and triggered war with Rome. Although the Romans mobilised a large army in order to deal with the 'Armenian conflict', a solution was reached only through a mutual agreement that led to the events described by Suetonius. Right after the last battle in Armenia, which had taken place at Rhandeia, Tiridates had paid tribute to Nero before the emperor's image and taken off his diadem, which Nero himself returned to him three years later as part of a solemn ceremony. Suetonius depicts the events as a spectacle that illustrated Rome's greatness and superiority, a representation that matches his efforts to praise Nero as a triumphant victor. What we do not immediately see, however, is that after a series of unsuccessful military activities the Romans had to waive their claims for direct rule in Armenia; this was compensated for by the willingness of the king to acknowledge that henceforth any Armenian king would be an official dependant of Rome. At least in the year 66 the solution proved to be a successful reconciliation of interests, which had a stabilising effect. By agreeing on such a partition of sovereignty over Armenia both sides came to terms with the fact that neither could rule in Armenia without respecting the interests of the other. Ultimately, however, Armenia remained a Parthian vassal state because the Parthian kings did not allow the Romans to prescribe who would be the Arsacid on the Armenian throne. While the investiture of the Armenian king was reserved to the Roman emperors, the actual choice lay with the Parthian king.[17]

Armenian history after Tiridates I is not well documented. We can say, however, that for the next 150 years the situation was more or less peaceful and closely linked to the state of Roman–Parthian relations.[18] When tensions between the great powers increased, this entailed turbulence for Armenia. The following passage reveals how much the foundation of the Sasanian Empire in the year 224 affected affairs within Armenia itself as well as its role as a cause for conflict between West and East.

---

[16] This was the customary symbolic act that indicated the end of war.

[17] Chaumont 1987a: 424.

[18] On the episodic character of Armenian history and the difficulties of 'reconstructions' see Garsoïan 1997a and 2004; see also Redgate 1998: 88–94.

Agathangelos, History (ed. Thomson) §§ 18–20[19]

(§ 18) At the eclipse of the era of the Parthian kingdom, when sovereign rule was taken from Artabanos son of Vałarš at his murder by Ardašīr son of Sasan – who was a noble from the province of Stahr, who had come and united the Persian forces,[20] who then scorned and rejected the sovereign rule of the Parthians and were pleased to choose the lordship of Ardašīr son of Sasan – when the sad news of his death had reached Xusrō, the king of Armenia – who was second in the sovereign rule of the Persians, because whoever was the king of Armenia was second in the sovereignty of the Persians[21] – although he soon heard the sorrowful news, he had no time at all to complete preparations for warfare. After this, he returned in great sadness at the course of events, because he had not been able to accomplish anything; in great distress and at the completion of these matters, he turned and went to his own country.

(§ 19) Now at the start of the next year, Xusrō, the king of Armenia, began to organise his army and to collect a force,[22] gathering the forces of the Albanians and the Georgians, opening the gate of the Alans[23] and the pass of Čor,[24] bringing the forces of the Honkʻ,[25] in order to campaign in Persian regions and attack the regions of Asorestan,[26] as far as the gates of Ktēsiphōn. Having ravaged the whole land, he brought populous cities and prosperous towns to ruin and left all the inhabited land empty and devastated. He was attempting to eradicate and destroy utterly, to overthrow the foundation; he was aiming to expunge the traditional institutions of Persian sovereignty. He made an oath at the same time to seek revenge with great resentment for their [i.e. the Parthian] loss of sovereignty...

(§ 20) For because of his close kinship to that house, he himself was also greatly dejected, that they had submitted and entered into service, acknowledging the kingdom of the Stahracʻi,[27] and had joined with him. And although Xusrō arranged

[19] On this passage see also the references in Thomson 1976: 454–6; for a brief survey of Armenian historiography see Thomson 2001: 106.

[20] On Ardašīr and his career see Wiesehöfer 1986a: 371–6.

[21] On the close relations between the Armenian Arsacids and the Parthians see Chaumont 1969: 25–47; on the representation of the Arsacids in the Armenian sources see Kettenhofen 1998: 325–53.

[22] Cf. the account of Moses of Chorene II.71–9, who describes Xusrō's support for the last Parthian king Artabanos against Ardašīr; for discussion of this extremely problematic source see Chaumont 1969: ch. 2 and Toumanoff 1969: 251.

[23] This refers to the Dariel pass, the main route through the Caucasus; cf. the commentary on **27**, esp. p. 188 n. 70.

[24] This is the Derbend pass by the Caspian Sea (= Caspian Gates).

[25] The Honkʻ are the Huns, which is an anachronistic term at this point and reflects the fifth-century perspective of the author; he has the Kūšān in mind, who at the beginning of the third century were active along the North-eastern frontier of the Parthian Empire.

[26] This is a frequently used geographical name for Sasanian Mesopotamia.

[27] Istakhr is the main religious centre of the Sasanians in the Persis, a region in south-eastern Iran; although there are no archaeological remains, the sources agree that from the late Parthian period onwards it was home to a fire sanctuary of the goddess Anahita. According to tradition, the ancestral founder of the Sasanian dynasty, Sasan, presided over this sanctuary, which therefore was directly linked to the rise of the Sasanians; see Wiesehöfer 2001: index s.v. (Istakhr) and the glossary in this volume.

an embassy, [urging] that his relatives should come in support and should stand against them with his kingdom, and that help would be given to him from the regions of the Kūšān and from that border and from their own country, by brave peoples and military forces, that they would come in support, the houses, the chiefs and nobles and family-heads of the Parthians, did not pay heed because they had accepted and submitted to the sovereign rule of Ardašīr rather than the sovereignty of their own relative and brother.

During the Parthian and Sasanian eras the history of Armenia was closely linked to that of Iran.[28] Accordingly, the testimonies of Armenian historiography are very valuable for us, not least because they yield numerous details regarding the history and culture of the Sasanian Empire. However, frequently these sources show a pro-Armenian or rather anti-Iranian bias and – as they were composed during a later period – also confront us with problems of chronology.[29] This applies above all to the early phases of Sasanian history. The passage above is an excerpt from an Armenian history, several revised editions of which have survived under the author's name 'Agathangelos'. Although the author claims to have been an eyewitness during the reign of Tiridates the Great (who ruled until c. 330), his work is most likely a compilation of the fifth century. Agathangelos describes the reaction in Armenia immediately after the Arsacids had been overthrown by the Sasanians.[30] Xusrō, the king of Armenia and brother of the last Parthian king, feared that the events would jeopardise his own position. Being of Arsacid offspring himself, he did not want to acknowledge the Sasanian dynasty and sought allies in order to continue the fight against the Sasanians.[31] Agathangelos' list of Xusrō's various initiatives in the Caucasian region once more points to Armenia's geo-strategic significance, which steered the activities of the great powers in the region. However, Xusrō's efforts were unsuccessful. In the face of the resolute actions of the first Sasanian king the initial resistance against Ardašīr within the Sasanian Empire broke down quickly.

---

[28] For a historical survey see Chaumont 1987a: 423–38.

[29] As the Armenian script was invented between 410 and 420 and did initially not have any biblical focus the work cannot predate c. 450; see also Wiesehöfer 2001: 156.

[30] On the conflicting accounts of Western and Armenian historiography and the resulting difficulties in establishing a chronology of the events in Armenia see especially Schottky 1994: 226–31; cf. also Toumanoff 1969: 233–81.

[31] Cf. Chaumont 1987a: 426, 'The dynastic upheaval in Iran transformed the political scene in Armenia. The Armenian sources state that the country's king at the time was Khosrov "the Great". He was probably a close relative of the last Parthian monarchs, and he evidently wanted to make his realm an Arsacid bastion against the Sasanians. Since his own forces were too weak, he needed Roman support and remained resolutely pro-Roman.'

Ultimately, Armenia could not escape the ambitions of the early Sasanian rulers. Xusrō's successor on the Armenian throne, his son Tiridates, had to flee and seek refuge in the Roman Empire. After Ardašīr had tried already in 227 to take possession of Greater Armenia,[32] from 252/53 onwards the country became part of the sphere of influence of the Sasanians, who followed the Parthian tradition of appointing a member of their own dynasty as king of Armenia. Hormizd-Ardašīr, the oldest son of the second Sasanian king Šāpūr I became the 'Great king of Armenia'.[33] He was the only member of Šāpūr's family who was allowed to use the title of 'Great king', a circumstance which reveals the important role Armenia played for the Sasanian dynasty. During the reign of Šāpūr I's successor, Hormizd I, Armenia continued to be ruled by a Sasanian satellite king, probably the youngest son of Šāpūr I, Narsē.[34] It looks as if this phase of Sasanian rule introduced some internal stability in Armenia, which among other aspects involved an assimilation of local religion and orthodox Mazdaism.[35]

However, in the face of the changing balance of power towards the end of the third century we observe renewed Roman attempts to increase their influence in Armenia. Bahrām II (276–93) had to accept that Diocletian invested Tiridates III and thereby once more a descendant of the Arsacid dynasty as Armenian king, whose rule, however, was at first limited to Lesser Armenia.[36] As a consequence of Narsē's catastrophic defeat by Galerius in the year 298 (**6**) and the resulting peace treaty of Nisibis strategically important regions in southern Armenia became part of the Roman sphere of influence (**17**); moreover, with Roman support Tiridates extended his rule to all of Armenia. As Tiridates 'the Great', he captured a very special place in Armenian history because during his reign the country turned to Christianity.[37] Although the historical circumstances are complex and the reconstruction of the 'story' subject to speculation,[38] one may say that 'Armenia' became the first ever Christian state, not long before a similar change took place in the West. Against the opposition of the Armenian nobility, who largely followed Iranian traditions, the country increasingly opened up to Western influence. The Armenian churches and monasteries

---

[32] Widengren 1971: 758.   [33] Cf. *ŠKZ*, Greek text, ll. 40–1.

[34] Cf. Humbach and Skjaervo 1983: III 1, 28, 32 and 45; III 2, 10–11, 36 and 72.

[35] Chaumont 1987a: 426, with reference to Moses of Chorene II.77.

[36] For details cf. Winter 1988: 145–51.

[37] Soz. II.8.1; on the controversial dating of this crucial event within Armenian history – often the years 313 or 314 are given as the date but many Armenians prefer the year 301 – see Ananian 1961: 43–73 and 317–60.

[38] There was already a Syrian current of Christianity that had percolated into southern districts; see Garsoïan 1997: 81–3.

built during late antiquity and in particular the early Middle Ages can still be admired today, which has led to the assumption that Armenia contributed to the development of Christian religious architecture in general.[39] The following passage attests to the consequences of Tiridates' decision for Armenia's position between Rome and the Sasanian Empire.

Moses of Chorene (ed. Thomson) III.5[40]

Copy of the letter of the Armenians
'Head-bishop Vrt'anēs and those bishops under him and all the nobles of Greater Armenia, to our lord Constantius, emperor, autocrator, Greeting.

Remember the sworn agreement[41] of your father Constantine, which was [made] to our king Tiridates; and do not give this country of yours to the godless Persians, but assist us with forces, in order to create as king the son of Tiridates, Xusrō. For God has made you lord not only of Europe but also all the Middle-lands, and respect for your power has reached the ends of the earth. And we ask that your rule may expand more and more. Be well.'

On hearing this, Constantius sent Antiochus, the overseer of his palace,[42] with a substantial force and purple robes with a crown and a letter which had this original:

Letter of Constantius
'Augustus, autocrator, emperor Constantius, to you the great Vrt'anēs and all your countrymen, greetings.

I have sent to you a force in assistance and the order to make as king for you Xusrō, son of your king Tiridates, so that, having been established in good order, you may serve us faithfully. Be well.'

As is the case with the history of Agathangelos, the work of Moses of Chorene confronts us with serious chronological difficulties, and this with regard to its date of composition as well as the sequence of the narrative. Moses himself claims to have composed his work in the fifth century and to have been a contemporary of St Maštoc'. The debate over the date is ongoing but recent scholarship has forcefully argued in favour of a date of composition in the eighth or ninth century.[43] As far as the narrative itself is concerned, in many places the work contradicts the information given by other authors. Nevertheless, the text throws much light on the situation of Armenia during the first half of the fourth century. After the victory of

---

[39] See Redgate 1998: 113–39.
[40] On this passage see also Thomson 1980: 257–8.
[41] Such an 'agreement' is also referred to by Agathangelos 877, 'Similarly with great happiness he showed love for king Tiridates as a dear brother especially because of his knowledge of God; furthermore he made a treaty with him, holding the faith which was in Christ the lord as the common denominator, so that they might preserve assuredly and for ever a steadfast friendship between the kingdoms' (tr. T. Greenwood); see also *Epic Histories* III.21.
[42] Cf. Thomson 1980: 258 with n. 3.   [43] See Thomson 1980: 1–61; Mahé and Mahé 1993.

Galerius over the Sasanians in the year 298 Tiridates had been placed on the Armenian throne as a Roman client king. Presumably he had supported Rome's anti-Christian policy during the reign of Diocletian, and when he decided to convert to Christianity and the Christian religion became the official, publicly promoted religion also in the Roman Empire, this brought the two states even closer.[44] In contrast, the relationship with the Zoroastrian Sasanian Empire was bound to deteriorate dramatically.[45] The persecutions of the Christians in the Sasanian Empire that began during the reign of Šāpūr II clearly reveal that the relationship between West and East was changing for the worse after the Constantinian revolution. Accordingly, Moses of Chorene's letter of the Armenians to the Roman emperor Constantius stems from the fear that the Sasanians would renew their attempts to take possession of the country. The petition for military support against the claims of the 'godless Persians' is now accompanied by a reference to the emperor's duty to act as the patron of Christianity as a whole.

Elsewhere we also hear about the emperor's all-embracing care for the Christians, which applied also to the Christians in the Sasanian Empire and inevitably irritated the Persian king (**31**). Numerous sources attest to the continuing confrontations between the followers of the Christian faith and those of the Zoroastrian fire cult, which provoked intervention by the great powers in Armenia. The changes with regard to the religious affairs in Armenia meant that the already explosive situation in this region was aggravated. It is thus not surprising that Šāpūr II's far reaching political ambitions also took aim at Armenia.

Ammianus Marcellinus XXVII.*12.1–4*[46]

(1) The Persian king, the now aged Šāpūr (II),[47] who from the very beginning of his reign had always been tempted by raids, seemed well disposed to us with his people for a short while after the death of the emperor Julian and after the shameful peace[48] was struck; but then he spurned the promise of the agreements made under Jovian and laid his hand on Armenia in order to bring it under his rule as if the validity of the agreements had been erased. (2) At first he used various tricks and inflicted fairly light harm on this densely populated country by soliciting some of

---

[44] Again, scholars do not accept this reconstruction of events unanimously; see above, p. 128 with n. 47.

[45] According to Chaumont 1987a: 427, 'Christianization tended to strengthen Armenia's link with the Roman Empire and to set back the Iranian cultural influence.'

[46] For another English translation that includes the following paragraphs see Greatrex and Lieu 2002: 21–2.

[47] The author describes events of the last years of Šāpūr II's long reign, the years after 367.

[48] This is the peace treaty of 363 which was concluded between Jovian and Šāpūr II (**18**).

the influential men and satraps or by surprising others with unexpected raids. (3) Then he used a carefully calculated mix of flattery and perjury in order to get at King Arsaces himself. He gave instructions to take the king, who had been invited to a banquet, to a secret door, to tear his eyes out and to bind him in silver chains, which among this people is held as a consolation in the punishment of men of rank, if only a small one;[49] then he had him banished to a fortress called Agabana,[50] where he was tortured and then punished with death by the sword. (4) After that, so that his perjury would not leave anything undefiled, he expelled Sauromaces, who ruled over Ibēria by Roman authority, and handed over the rule over the same people to a certain Aspacures; he even crowned the man in order to show how much he disrespected our authority.[51]

In February of 364 Jovian died unexpectedly and Šāpūr II embarked on an offensive against Armenia.[52] In the above passage, Ammianus Marcellinus criticises the Persian advance sharply. The author emphasises Šāpūr II's aggressive policy and his intention to conquer the areas that his ancestors had controlled. It is noteworthy that Ammianus' words contradict his own account of the peace of 363 (xxv.7.12; **18**) according to which the Romans broke the treaty when they refused to support Armenia in the event of a Persian invasion. Be that as it may, the Persian king met with strong opposition in Armenia. Whereas the Armenian Christians tended to support the West and the still numerous Zoroastrians sided with the Persians, the interests of the almost independent 'feudal' nobles were not as clear cut because the latter above all wanted to retain their autonomy. Ammianus mentions that it took Šāpūr II until 367 to capture and execute the Armenian king Arsaces, and this only by resorting to a ruse. Arsaces' son and successor to the throne, Papās, fled and sought protection from the Roman emperor Valens. Šāpūr II mustered a large force and took possession of large parts of Armenia. He also tried to expand Sasanian influence to the north, into Ibēria, by deposing Sauromaces, whom Rome had invested with power in Ibēria, and to install a man of his own choice, a certain Aspacures, as the new ruler.

Rome reacted to this development without delay. Shortly after the peace agreement of 363 both powers were at war again. In 371 the armies of Šāpūr II and of the Roman emperor Valens confronted each other in open

---

[49] Cf. Hdt. iii.130 and Curt. v.12.20.
[50] Proc. *BP* 1.3.7 mentions this fortress and calls it the 'place of oblivion'.
[51] When Ibēria was to be divided between Sauromaces and Aspacures in 370 (Amm. xxvii.12.16–17) Šāpūr II objected vehemently (Amm. xxx.2.2). The Sasanian king used the war against the Goths fought by the emperor Valens in order to expel Sauromaces once more from Ibēria in 378 (Amm. xxx.2.4 and 7).
[52] Gutmann 1991: 162–91.

battle. The outcome was not decisive but the armies withdrew to Ktēsiphōn and Antioch respectively. When Šāpūr II was informed that the claimant to the Armenian throne Papās, on whom he had hoped to exercise great influence, had been assassinated (374),[53] he tried to approach Valens in order to find a common solution to the Armenia problem. The following passage tells us about the agreement that was reached by the great powers. Its anonymous author wrote his work, which has mistakenly been attributed to P'awstos Buzand/Faustus of Byzantium, in the 470s in the Armenian language. Going back to local oral traditions, in an epic style, the source describes the history of the late Arsacid dynasty in Armenia.

Epic Histories VI.I

After the death of the commander of Armenia Manuēl, no one could confirm the reign of Aršak (Arsaces) over the country; instead many of the Armenian nobles left the court and went to the king of Persia and surrendered to him the country of Armenia. And they requested from him a king [who was] an Arsacid. And he consented with great joy on his part to give by his word (a king) from the same line, from the Armenian Arsacid royal house, and through him to seize for himself the country of Armenia. Therefore he found a youth from that house named Xusrō and he placed a crown on his head and gave him as his wife his sister Zruanduxt and placed at his disposal all the forces of his authority. And he gave his deputy Zich as a tutor for king Xusrō. And they went and reached the country of Armenia. When king Arsaces saw them, he left the place and travelled and went to the borders of the Greeks. And the king of the Greeks was assisting Arsaces and the king of the Persians was assisting Xusrō.

Then the forces of the king of the Greeks came in support. And king Arsaces was around the district of Ekeleac and the Persian forces and king Xusrō were in the district of Ayrayrat. Then envoys and messengers of the two kings, of the Greeks and of the Persians, shuttled back and forth between them. And as a result the king of the Greeks and the king of the Persians decided to make a joint agreement with one another, and they resolved that it would be better to divide the country of Armenia between themselves; for they said, 'Since this powerful and wealthy country is situated between us, it would be better if we were able to disorder and ruin this kingdom. First let us divide it into two through these two Arsacid kings, whom we have installed; then let us try to nibble away at them, to impoverish them, to intervene and reduce to submission so that they shall not be able to raise their heads between us.'

And they approved this plan and they divided the country into two. The portion on the Persian side belonged to king Xusrō and the portion on the Greek side belonged to king Arsaces. But many districts, being eaten away from these, were

---

[53] Amm. XXX.1.1–23.

cut off on this side and that side and only a small part from both countries was left to the two kings.[54]

However the two kings of Armenia, Arsaces and Xusrō, who was Suren, the districts of the kingdom of Armenia remained on both sides between them. And the two Arsacid kings, having introduced boundaries between the two parts, were established in peace, and the land of Armenia was in two parts, with two kings; they submitted in each portion to their respective king. But the portion of Xusrō was larger than that of Arsaces. And many districts were separated from both of them. And the kingdom of Armenia was diminished, divided and scattered. And from that time on, it declined in importance.

As we do not have any contemporary sources on the so called partition of Armenia, this late source is our most important testimony. The text confirms on the one hand the already existing division of Armenia into two parts, one within the Roman, the other within the Persian sphere of influence, on the other hand the desire of the great powers to dissolve the Armenian monarchy and to divide up the country between the Roman and the Sasanian Empires. Both sides had learnt that tensions repeatedly flared up because Armenian issues had not been resolved and wanted to find a mutually acceptable and permanent solution. The contemporary historian Ammianus Marcellinus confirms this assessment of the situation by describing how the Sasanian king urged the emperor Valens to get rid of the notorious trouble spot, Armenia.[55] Initially Valens refused but eventually gave in to Šāpūr's urging. The fact that the Goths were about to invade Roman territory along the Danube forced the emperor to retreat from the Eastern theatre of war. In 363 Armenia, which had been the reason for numerous conflicts between West and East since the beginning of Roman–Iranian relations, was factually divided into two spheres of influence: the Sasanians took possession of Greater Armenia, and Rome was assigned Lesser Armenia, which comprised only a fifth of the size of Greater Armenia. Soon after, this partition of Armenia was officially confirmed during the reign of Šāpūr III (383–8).[56] During the following years the situation stabilised. Whereas in c. 390 the Romans replaced Arsaces with a *comes* in charge of the administration of the areas under Roman rule while preserving a considerable degree of autonomy for this part of Armenia, the Sasanians left the monarchy intact and as a subject of the Sasanian king

[54] This alludes to the Armenian territorial losses in the South and East, where land was ceded to the Albanians and Sasanians; cf. Toumanoff 1963: 132.

[55] Amm. III.2.2.

[56] About this treaty on the partition of Armenia see Doise 1945: 274–7; Stock 1978a: 165–82; Blockley 1987: 222–34; Gutmann 1991: 230–2 and 260 with further references; Greatrex 2000: 35–48.

a descendant of the Arsacid dynasty continued to rule the Persian sector of the country. In 428, however, the situation changed when Bahrām V. Gōr (420–39) decided to depose king Artashes (Ardašīr) as well as the head of the Armenian Church, the *catholicos* Sahak, and to appoint a Persian governor who would henceforth administer Armenian affairs.[57] Sahak was replaced initially by an Armenian Surmak, and then by two Syrians. This final loss of independence and an anti-Christian policy pursued by the Sasanian rulers in the following period led to a split within the ranks of the Armenian nobility into pro- and anti-Sasanian factions; moreover, during the course of the fifth century numerous military conflicts arose between the Armenians and the Sasanians.[58] Two Armenian authors, Lazarus of Pharp, whose history was composed around 500, taking up where the *Epic Histories* end and continuing to 485, and Elišē, who wrote his *History of Vardan and the Armenian War* around 570, describe the last unsuccessful revolt of the Armenians against the Sasanian overlordship in 450/51 and the ensuing fate of the Armenian captives in the Sasanian Empire.[59] The following passage by the Syrian chronicler Joshua the Stylite shows that the tense situation in Armenia continued to bear an impact on the relations between Byzantium and Persia.

Joshua Stylites 21 (249.15–23)

Now, when the Armenians who were under the rule of Kavādh heard that the Romans had not replied to him with a truce, they took heart and were encouraged, and they uprooted the fire shrines that had been built in their country by the Persians, and they killed the Magians in their midst. And Kavādh sent against them a certain *marzban*,[60] with an army, that he might punish them and again force them to worship fire; but they fought with him and destroyed both him and his army. They sent envoys to the emperor in order to submit to him, but he was not willing to receive them, so that it might not be supposed that he was provoking the war with the Persians.

The author of these lines wrote a very detailed and informative description of Roman–Sasanian conflicts, and in particular those of the fifth century. His work is one of the oldest examples of Syriac historiography and also yields much information regarding the social and economic climate in

---

[57] Cf. Chaumont 1987a: 429, 'Thereafter the government of Armenia was conducted by marzbans, who were sometimes picked from the Armenian nobility. The first marzban appointed by Vahram was Veh-Mihr-Sapur.'

[58] On a detailed analysis of the military as well as diplomatic activities see Yuzbashyan 1986: 51–5 (in Russian with an English summary) and Luther 1997: 141–4.

[59] Cf. Thomson 1982 and 1991.

[60] Title of the governor of a border province and military commander of the Sasanian border troops.

Edessa and the surrounding area at the beginning of the sixth century as well as the history of the Sasanian Empire during the reigns of Pērōz, Balāš, Kavādh I and Ğāmāsp.[61] The passage throws light on the inner affairs of Greater Armenia,[62] which were closely linked to the increasingly complex and difficult foreign policy of the Sasanian Empire. Here, the growing threat in the East by the Hephthalites affected internal affairs. The 'crisis' reached a first peak when in the summer of 484 the Hephthalites defeated the Persians and killed King Pērōz (459–84). The situation was exacerbated by severe financial problems. According to Joshua the Stylite the two successors of Pērōz, Balāš (484–8) and Kavādh I (488–97/499–531) were forced to approach the Western opponent and ask for gold from the imperial treasury. Kavādh's aggressive tone was unmistakable – the king threatened Byzantium with war should his request be turned down.[63] Nevertheless, both Zeno and his successor Anastasius refused the desired financial support.

Unrest in Armenia was thus also an expression of the internal problems of the Sasanian Empire at the beginning of the rule of Kavādh I, which led to confrontations with various peoples along the borders of the empire.[64] Joshua the Stylite specifically points to the Armenian unwillingness to accept Persian attempts to convert them to the Zoroastrian faith.[65] The destructions of the fire temples – symbols of Persian rule – and the assassination of numerous Magians by Armenians triggered war. Initial Sasanian attempts to consolidate their rule by military action were unsuccessful. It is not a coincidence that the upheavals in Armenia were accompanied by the Armenians' desire to establish diplomatic contacts with Byzantium and to procure Roman protection, a scenario that once more illustrates Armenia's delicate role between the two great powers. Ultimately, if there was such 'conscious' reasoning, Armenia could only 'survive' through an alliance with either of the two opponents. Anastasius, however, refused any help for Armenia because from a Persian perspective this could have been viewed as an intervention in Sasanian affairs and thus a valid reason for war. The emperor's decision reflects an attitude that applies to the fifth century as a whole, namely for Byzantium to hold back along the Eastern frontier of the empire rather than to risk any aggressive behaviour towards the Eastern opponent. Armenia was thus left to its own devices. The Armenians' attempt to ally themselves with Rome had also been motivated by religion

---

[61] Cf. Luther 1997: 1–4. [62] For the general background see Thomson 2000: 662–77.
[63] Ios. Styl. 18 and 19. [64] Luther 1997: 145.
[65] On the rigorous Sasanian religious policy in Armenia under Yazdgard II and Pērōz see Chaumont 1987a: 429–30.

as well as a desire for more autonomy. The plan failed but the unrest in Armenia further weakened the monarchy of Kavādh I. Conflicts broke out within the Sasanian Empire, and eventually Kavādh I was deposed.[66] Only with the help of the Hephthalites did he manage to return to the throne in 498/99. Shortly after, Anastasius once more refused to grant financial support to the king, which triggered the outbreak of the first Byzantine–Sasanian War in the sixth century (**12**). Apparently Kavādh remembered well that the Armenians had revolted against Sasanian rule a decade earlier – the first Persian attack in August 502 targeted the capital of Lesser Armenia, Theodosio(u)polis.[67] Once more Armenia was the setting for a war between Byzantium and the Sasanian Empire.[68]

27: Protection of the frontier

The following comments focus on an area that was of exceptional strategic importance in antiquity and played a crucial role in relations between Rome and its Eastern neighbours: the Caucasus (map 12).[69] Only very few routes existed by which this region between the Black and the Caspian Seas, characterised by its huge mountain ranges, could be crossed. Apart from the coastal routes along the Black Sea and along the Caspian Sea the most important pass was the so-called Caucasian Gates.[70] These *portae Caucasiae* are different from the *portae Caspiae*, which are situated south of the Caspian Sea and often confused with the former in the ancient sources. The *portae Caucasiae*, however, a narrow passage through the Caucasus, are the only route to Ibēria and this is why they are sometimes also called *portae Hiberiae*. Procopius describes how the Huns settling in the Transcaucasus and as far as the Maeotic Lake (Sea of Asov) invaded Persian as well as Roman territories through this pass, which was set there by nature just as if made by the hand of man. The author explains that their horses did not come to any harm nor did they have to take detours or overcome

---

[66] On the so-called Mazdakite revolt and its consequences for inner affairs in Persia see **11**.

[67] Ios. Styl. 48; Malal. 16.9 (p. 398); Zach. *HE* VII.3 (22.15–22); cf. also Luther 1997: 178–9 and Greatrex 1998: 79–80.

[68] On the political and religious situation in Armenia during the reign of Kavādh I see Chaumont 1987a: 430–2; on the general history and culture of Armenia in late antiquity see Redgate 1998 (repr. 1999): esp. 140–64 and Thomson 1999: XI–XXX.

[69] Toumanoff 1954: 109–90; Lang 1962: 25–8; Braund 1986: 31–49 and 1989: 31–43; Dabrowa 1989: 77–111; Dreher 1996: 188–207.

[70] Luther 1997: 105 n. 29 locates two strategically important passes through the Caucasus, namely the so-called Alans' Gate or Dariel pass, situated to the north of Tiflis (= *portae Caucasiae*), and the Derbend pass, the Caspian Gates, to the Persian Atropatēnē.

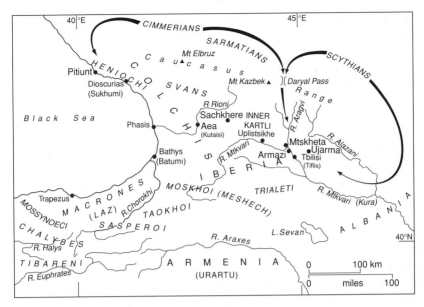

Map 12: The Caucasus

precipitations; that when they went through other passes they did so with great difficulty, had to change their horses and were forced to make great detours through steep territory.[71]

The great powers showed great interest in the Caucasian countries because they were hoping to engage in trade in the area[72] while staying off the enemy's territory and also because of the necessity to protect the frontier against attacks from the north. Already during the Arsacid period the Transcaucasian peoples had represented a lingering force that was easily mobilised and intervened in the rivalries of the areas in the Caucasus and along the Caspian Sea and seriously affected the balance of power.[73]

Ibēria was a small but because of its location an important country, which represented a bulwark against the peoples attacking from the north (map 12).[74] The fact that they controlled the *portae Caucasiae* enabled

---

[71] Proc. *BP* 1.10.3–8; in this passage Procopius also confuses the Caspian with the Iberian Gates; Veh 1970: 465–6 and Standish 1970: 17–24.

[72] Cf. the references on p. 202 with n. 147.   [73] Halfmann 1986: 43; Toumanoff 1971: 111–58.

[74] On the trade related aspects of controlling Ibēria see Magie 1919: 302–3 and Charlesworth 1970: 106; on the geographical situation of Ibēria see Hewsen 1992: 128–41; Kettenhofen 1995c: 22–3.

the Romans to intervene before the Persians could form political alliances with northern nomadic peoples. During the first and second centuries cooperation between Rome and Ibēria proved advantageous for both states, and this at a time when the Romans were confronted by the Parthian expansion westwards and their political interests in Armenia were at stake. The peoples in the mountainous regions south of the Caucasus also feared the Parthians, who were thus the common enemies of Rome and Ibēria. While the Ibērians hoped that close contacts between the two would secure their own freedom, the Romans saw these contacts as a means to stop the Eastern power from invading this strategically important region.

The end of Parthian rule did not change the situation. Common interests in the Caucasus intensified the relations between Rome and the Sasanian Empire.[75] As part of the *foedus* of 244 between Philip the Arab and Šāpūr I the Roman emperor was obliged to make annual subsidiary payments to the Sasanian king (**16**), money which had previously been used for the protection of the fortresses in the Caucasus. This meant that Šāpūr I was henceforth responsible for maintaining the Caucasian passes. The regulations of 244 also entailed that the Roman emperor had to withdraw from this strategically important region where the Sasanians now gained much influence. In the military confrontations of the following period the Ibērian king may have fought on the Persian side; in the great Šāpūr Inscription the Ibērian king is listed among the subjects of the Persian king[76] and in the Inscription of Paikuli he is still among those who show reverence to Narsē at the beginning of his reign.[77]

Only when Narsē was defeated and the two powers concluded the treaty of 298 (**6** and **17**) did Rome regain hegemony over the important countries Kolchis and Ibēria, which form modern Georgia. The sixth-century Byzantine historian Peter the Patrician states that the rulers of Ibēria had to receive the symbols of their power from Rome.[78] The territories which Šāpūr I had conquered in this part of the Caucasus had therefore been lost by the end of the third century. In 298 Diocletian achieved obvious strategic advantages and thereby continued the existing policy of protecting Roman interests around the Black Sea and of securing the Caucasian passes. It is doubtful whether the Caucasus region was also an issue in the agreements of the year 363 (**18**). However, John the Lydian, who wrote his

---

[75] On the Sasanian interests see Yuzbashian 1996: 143–64.
[76] *ŠKZ* § 44 (p. 355 ed. Back); on the successes of Šāpūr I in the Caucasus see Kettenhofen 1982c: 42–3.
[77] *Inscription of Paikuli* § 92 (p. 71, ed. Skjaervo).
[78] Petr. Patr. frg. 14 (*FHG* IV 189).

work *De magistratibus* during the first half of the sixth century, conveys this impression.[79]

John Lydus, De magistratibus III.52

As the ankles of the Caucasus are split by nature – towards the sun when it rises under the constellation of the Lion at the narrow beginning of the Caucasus, towards the north wind by the Caspian Sea, an entrance was created for a barbarian people settling around Hyrkania but unknown both to us and the Persians.[80] Through this entrance they attack Persian territory in the East, Roman territory in the North. And as long as the Romans were in control of Artaxata and also of further territories they were present there and thus used to go against them. But when during the reign of Jovian they had given up this and many other territories[81] the Persians were not strong enough to protect their own and the previously Roman territory and therefore on both sides Armenia was constantly afflicted by unbearable unrest.[82] In consequence then after the luckless reign of Jovian talks took place between our *hyparch* Salutius[83] and the most eminent Persians, and later with Yazdgard,[84] to the effect that both states would share the costs and establish a fortress at the described entrance and set up a garrison in these places in order to stop the barbarians from pouring through. However, as the Romans were occupied by their wars in the West and North the Persians – being closer to the attacks of the barbarians – were forced to erect a fortress there, which they call Biraparach in their language,[85] and stationed troops there. And no enemy managed to come in.

John the Lydian, who was born in Philadelphia (Lydia) and became a teacher of rhetoric in Constantinople, is the author of several works; to some extent his accounts are confused and often superficial but they nevertheless provide important information on cultural and administrative aspects of the Roman Empire. In particular the author's knowledge of the situation in the eastern Roman Empire seems excellent. The above passage comes from a work that not only informs us about Roman officials during the republic and the imperial period into late antiquity but also frequently refers to geography and natural history. In spite of evident chronological inconsistencies[86] Lydus' narrative throws light on the special geographical

---

[79] On the author and his work see Carney 1971; for text and English translation see Bandy 1983a and b.

[80] John Lydus must be referring to the *portae Caucasiae*.

[81] On the *foedus* concluded between Jovian and Šāpūr in the year 363 see **18**.

[82] On the 'partition' of Armenia between the great powers see above, pp. 184–6 with n. 56.

[83] As *praefectus praetorio Orientis* Salutius played a major role in the successful conclusion of the peace treaty of 363.

[84] Luther 1997: 105 n. 28 suggests that this man is neither Yazdgard I (399–421) nor Yazdgard II (439–57) but an otherwise unknown Persian diplomat who led the negotiations with Salutius; such negotiations would then have taken place before Salutius left office, that is before 366–8.

[85] This fortress must be identical with the Iuroeipaach mentioned by Priscus, frg. 41.1 (= *FHG* IV 105).

[86] For a detailed analysis see Blockley 1985a: 63–74 and Luther 1997: 104–8.

and political role the Caucasus region played between the two great powers. Three aspects are crucial: first the dangers posed by invasions of the 'barbarians', secondly the fact that by themselves neither Rome nor the Persian Empire were able to guard the Caucasus region and thus to protect their own territory and, thirdly, the necessity to make arrangements for the protection of the frontier together, to guarantee this by official agreements and in particular to assign and agree on the financial contributions of each side.

In this context the ancient author also refers to the peace treaty of the year 363 (**18**). He confirms once more the loss of important strategic positions that Jovian had to accept after Julian's catastrophic defeat in his Persian War (**8**). As after 363[87] the Romans withdrew from the Caucasus extremely slowly, the Persians thought that they had to increase their efforts to protect the region. John the Lydian seems to indicate that the Romans henceforth no longer met their financial obligations with regard to the Caucasus.[88] In the end the Persians could not accept the fact that the Roman payments had ceased and they decided to invade Syria and Cappadocia.[89] It is also significant that the author refers to negotiations regarding the costs for building a fortress in order to protect the *portae Caucasiae* and for setting up a garrison. However, it would appear that it did not come to an official agreement.

In spite of the hostile atmosphere between Rome and Persia, both shared an interest in fending off bellicose nomadic tribes. However, an agreement to that effect would have had to be based on an alliance that most probably did not form until the beginning of the fifth century, and not, as John the Lydian claims, as early as 363.[90] Certainly from the end of the fourth century and with the increasing frequency of the attacks by the Huns, which posed a serious threat to the West and the East, the protection of the Caucasian passes became a crucial issue for both great powers.[91] This was still the case when in the following period Rome had to turn to the more and more pressing problems along the frontiers along the Rhine and the Danube and the Sasanians alone often had to bear the financial burden of protecting the Caucasus region. As a consequence the relations tended to deteriorate and the outbreak of the wars of 421–2 and 441 (**19**) was directly linked to

---

[87] The confrontations between Valens and Šāpūr II in Ibēria between 362 and 378 (Amm. XXVII.12.1–2 and XXVII.30.2–3) reveal that the great powers continued to fight over the country; cf. also Chrysos 1993: 183.

[88] Luther 1997: 105–6.   [89] Lyd. *Mag.* III.53.

[90] Synelli 1986: 106–20.   [91] Chrysos 1993: 183.

the fact that the Romans had failed to comply with the Persian request to contribute to the protection of the Caucasus.[92]

An account given by Priscus from Thracian Panion (c. 420 to after 474) regarding a Persian embassy to the Byzantine emperor Leo I (457–74) nicely illustrates the concerns. Priscus is the author of a lost Byzantine history, which covered the events between 434 and 474; the work primarily yields information on the confrontations between Byzantium and the Huns but also gives us insight into the balance of power between Romans, Persians, Huns, Hephthalites and the Lazes. The surviving fragments are assembled in the *Excerpta de legationibus* by Constantinus Porphyrogenitus (905–59).[93] Priscus himself participated in two embassies sent to Attila, the king of the Huns, in 449 and to Rome in 450 by Theodosius II (408–50) and therefore must have known the contemporary diplomatic events quite well.

Priscus frg. 41.1 (= FHG IV, frg. 31)

There was also an embassy from the Persian king complaining that some of their people were seeking refuge with the Romans . . . They also requested that the Romans contributed money for maintaining the fortress Iuroeipaach, which is situated by the Caspian Gates,[94] or at least commanded soldiers to its protection because they would no longer bear the costs and protection of the place by themselves. For if they withdrew the attacks of the tribes in the area would bear an impact not only on the Persians but also on the Romans. They added that it was also necessary that these supported them with money for the war against the so called Kidarite Huns; for it would be to their own advantage if they defeated this people and did not let them enter the Roman Empire. The Romans responded that they would send someone[95] who would discuss all these matters with the Parthian king.[96] For neither were they receiving refugees nor did they keep the Magians from practising their religion. With regard to the protection of the fortress Iuroeipaach and the war against the Huns, they claimed that the Persians had taken these on in their own accord and did not have a right to request money from the Romans.

The ambassadors referred to the Kidarite Huns, who during the reign of King Pērōz (459–84) represented a serious threat primarily to the Sasanians.[97] Leo therefore tried to delay the negotiations. According to another passage in Priscus, in 467 the emperor rejected a new Persian request to

---

[92] Luther 1997: 106.

[93] Doblhofer 1955: 11–82 and Blockley 1983: 222–377.

[94] Priscus confuses the Caspian Gates at Derbend with the *portae Caucasiae*.

[95] The Romans sent the *patricius* Constantius to enter negotiations with Pērōz (459–84), which ended without any actual results; cf. Priscus frg. 41.3 (= *FHG* IV 106).

[96] Priscus refers to the Sasanian ruler Pērōz.

[97] Blockley 1985a: 66 and Luther 1997: 112–16; see also Blockley 1981: 121.

support the fortress Iuroeipaach by sending either money or troops, saying that each side should defend their own country and maintain their own fortresses.[98] In contrast, during the first half of his reign the Byzantine emperor Zeno (474–5/476–91) did make subsidiary payments to Pērōz, although these should probably not be labelled 'tribute', as the Syrian chronicler Joshua the Stylite clarifies in his detailed account.[99]

Immediately after the death of the Sasanian king (484) the payments for the fortification of the Caucasian passes ceased.[100] This led to new tensions. When in the year 502 Kavādh I (488–97/499–531) asked the emperor Anastasius (491–518) to send him money for his battle against the Hephthalites,[101] the emperor's rejection led to the outbreak of the first Byzantine–Sasanian War in the sixth century.[102] Apparently, the Persian ruler had offered Anastasius one of the Caucasian fortresses in turn; during the peace negotiations in the spring of 531 Kavādh I accused Anastasius of having been the aggressor by saying, among other things, that the emperor had not been willing to 'acquire' the Caspian Gates. If he had done so, he would have had to maintain an army there for all times and bear a great financial burden in order to fend off the barbarians.[103]

Both the question of how the costs for maintaining the Caucasian fortresses would be met and the cessation of the annual payments triggered many new conflicts way into the sixth century.[104] It is thus not surprising that when Justinian I (527–79) and Xusrō I (531–79) tried to put an end to the second Roman–Persian War in the sixth century in 562 (**20**) the diplomatic efforts towards a comprehensive agreement also focused on the protection of the shared border and its defence against the bellicose nomadic peoples attacking from the north. According to Menander the Guardsman the Persians agreed to march against invasions of the Huns, the Alans and other barbarians in the Caucasus region whereas the Romans promised not to send troops into the area and thus to give up any influence in the region.[105] This means that the Persians, who had firmly established their military presence in the Caucasus by the sixth century,[106] were now willing to defend this insecure border by themselves without insisting on

---

[98] Priscus frg. 47 (= *FHG* IV 107).

[99] Ios. Styl. 8; see the detailed commentary in Luther 1997: 101–8; also Blockley 1985a: 66–7, 'The insistence of Joshua that the payments made by Zeno were no tribute suggests that some thought they were, perhaps because the Persians had attempted to convert an occasional payment into a regular.'

[100] Ios. Styl. 18.

[101] Proc. *BP* 1.7.1–4 and Ios. Styl. 20 and 23; on Kavādh's requests see Blockley 1985a: 68.

[102] Greatrex 1998: 73–119.   [103] Proc. *BP* 1.16.4.   [104] Blockley 1985a: 68–74.

[105] Menander Protector, frg. 11.   [106] Kramers 1935–7: 613–18.

compensation from Byzantium. This agreement stayed in place until the end of the relations.[107]

28: Economy and trade

Although the numerous military conflicts between Rome and the Sasanian Empire impeded uninterrupted trade, both sides showed a strong interest in close economic relations. Primarily in order to secure the revenues from customs duties they designed a diplomatic framework which established the conditions for a regulated exchange of goods. Numerous treaties that were concluded between the empires and their details on economic and trade related issues attest to this.

When relations between Rome and the Parthian kingdom intensified it was above all luxury goods from the Far East, in particular silk and silk products, which were traded at great profit and therefore important goods of trade in East and West.[108] The ancient sources reveal the wide range of goods that were imported from the East and had to be declared, for example spices, incense, gems or even wild beasts and enslaved Indian eunuchs.[109] They also attest to the wider circulation of these goods.[110]

The fourth-century Latin work of an anonymous author, the so called *Expositio totius mundi et gentium*, gives a description of all territories of the ancient world and their populations, including trade and its products.[111]

Expositio totius mundi et gentium 19 (pp. 153–4, ed. Rougé)

After these there are the Persians, who are the neighbours of the Romans. The history books say that they are particularly bad and brave in war... in all other respects, however, they are said to have everything in abundance; for the nations neighbouring their territory are given the opportunity to engage in trade and therefore they themselves also seem to have plenty of everything.

In this passage the anonymous author, who draws on an unknown Greek source,[112] emphasises the Sasanian trade policy. For rather selfish reasons they permitted the neighbouring peoples to engage in trade as they pleased. The Sasanians made good profit from the exchange of luxury goods, not only silk but also precious stones, spices, incense and ivory. The traditional trade route was the famous Silk Road (map 13),[113] which went from China

---

[107] Blockley 1985a: 72.   [108] Cf. Young 2001.
[109] *Dig.* xxxix.4.16 (7); cf. also Pigulevskaja 1969: 78–9.
[110] On the wide range of goods that entered the Roman Empire see Miller 1969: 34–109; in general on the Roman eastern trade see Raschke 1978: 604–1378; Loewe 1971: 166–79.
[111] Rougé 1966 and Drexhage 1983.   [112] On the author see Pigulevskaja 1969: 46–50.
[113] Haussig 1983 and Klimkeit 1990.

via Central Asia, Horāsān and Northern Persia to Mesopotamia from where the goods could then be shipped to the Black Sea and the Mediterranean.[114] Trade relations between the Graeco-Roman world and the Far East and India existed already during the early Principate. In late antiquity these contacts intensified.

Until late in the third century the most important trade route from the Persian Gulf to the centres of the Roman province of Syria and the Mediterranean ports followed the river Euphrates.[115] There are early attestations to the transport of goods to Nikēphorion-Kallinikos via the Euphrates, and from there to the markets in Edessa, Batnai or Harran, from where the merchants transported their merchandise to the Mediterranean centres.[116] Isidorus of Charax, who was a geographer of the Augustan period, gives us a detailed description of the major trade routes and bases for supplies. According to the author the traffic of goods went from the Parthian capital Seleucia on the Tigris/Ktēsiphōn to the Roman Empire via the trading centres along the Euphrates, namely Neapolis, Anath,[117] Bēlesi Biblada,[118] Phaliga, Nikēphorion, to Zeugma.[119]

The intense trade between the Far East, India and the Persian Gulf did not cease after the fall of Hatra (**22**) and Palmyra (**23**); Persian traders themselves participated in the lucrative trade with India.[120] After 273 at the latest, possibly already after the fall of Hatra, the traffic of goods may have shifted towards the Tigris river, and as a result this waterway, which so far had been rather insignificant for trade purposes, became much more attractive.[121] This view is supported by the decision of 298 to make Nisibis the only centre for an exchange of goods.[122] Because of a lack of archaeological investigation along the Tigris we do not have any immediate testimonies for such a 'shift' of trade but new studies show that there were significant demographic movements from the Hatrene towards the Tigris.[123] Intensified settlement patterns throughout late antiquity can be observed also

---

[114] Bivar 1970: 1–11.
[115] See Young 2001: 188–90.   [116] Chaumont 1984: 63–107.
[117] Kennedy 1986: 103–4 and Kennedy and Northedge 1988: 6–8.
[118] Kennedy and Riley 1990: 224–5.
[119] Isid. of Charax *Mansiones Parthicae* 1; on this source see Chaumont 1984: 63–107 and Luther 1997: 237–42.
[120] Williams 1972: 97–109; Whitehouse and Williamson 1973: 29–49; Whitehouse 1996: 339–49 and Morony 2004: 184–8.
[121] This development also affected strategic considerations; according to Amm. XXIII.3.1 before embarking on his Persian campaign Julian had to decide at Carrhae whether to take the route along the Tigris or along the Euphrates.
[122] See Millar 1996: 483–4, who argues that the peace of 298 indicates a possible shift of trade from the Euphrates to the Tigris.
[123] Hauser 2000: 187–201.

for the parts of the Tigris that were under Roman control,[124] and these must have been a consequence of the increased significance of the Tigris for trade. However, as the ravines created by the course of the river become very narrow, hardly any transport of goods would have been possible above the Roman camps Castra Maurorum[125] and Bezabde.[126] Moreover, along this part of the Tigris the extremely barren mountain ridge of the Tūr ʿAbdīn (Mons Masius) to the West must have impeded regular trade so that goods going upstream must have been taken no further than Bezabde, most likely only to Castra Maurorum, from where they would have been transported along the southern edges of the Tūr ʿAbdīn to Nisibis.

In light of these topographical premises Nisibis, which was located in the northern Mesopotamian plain on the upper reaches of the Chabōras/Chabūr,[127] almost inevitably became the new centre for long distance trade.[128] There were then several routes on which goods could be transported from Nisibis to Syria, via Edessa and Zeugma for example. In contrast to the ʿcaravan citiesʾ Hatra and Palmyra the Roman *colonia* Nisibis, which was also the seat of the Roman governor of the province of Mesopotamia, was no longer the guarantor for an extended network of traffic but a huge trans-shipment centre. The *Expositio totius mundi et gentium* confirms the city's exceptional role.

Expositio totius mundi et gentium 22 (p. 156, ed. Rougé)

Mesopotamia, however, has many different cities of which I shall name but the most exceptional ones. There are, then, Nisibis and Edessa, which possess the best men in every respect, both clever merchants and good hunters. Above all they are wealthy as well as equipped with all sorts of goods. For they acquire their goods directly from the Persians, sell them throughout the entire Roman Empire and then engage in trade with the goods they purchase there, except for bronze and iron because it is not permitted to sell bronze and iron to enemies.[129] These cities, which will always remain standing through the wisdom of the gods and the emperor and

---

[124] On the location of Castra Maurorum see Ball 1989: 7–18 and 2003: 18–19.

[125] Ball 2003: 80–1.

[126] For a long time it has been suggested that Bezabde was located in the Turkish–Syrian border area close to Cizre; see Lightfoot 1983: 189–204; for new surveys locating Bezabde 13km further north see Algaze 1989: 248–52 and 1991: 191–2.

[127] On the course and navigability of the Chabōras/Chabūr see Tardieu 1990: 103–35.

[128] Also important because of its geographic location was Singara, a point of intersection between the course of the upper Chabōras/Chabūr towards the Tigris and along the route from Hatra to Nisibis; on Singara see Oates 1968: 97–106 and Kessler 1980.

[129] For the export embargo on *aeramentum et ferrum* see also Herodian IV.18; *Dig.* XXXIX.4.11; *Cod. Iust.* IV.53.1 (4); on further export embargos ibid. IV.41.1–2 and IV.63.2.

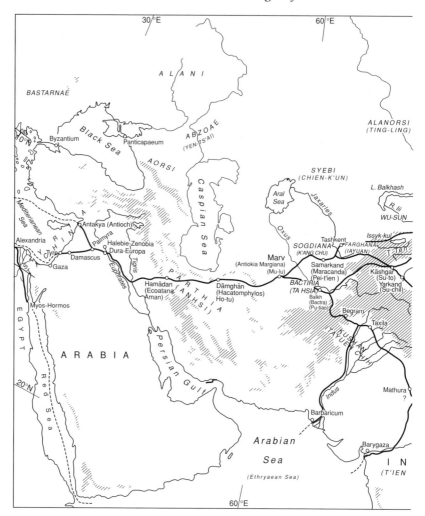

Map 13: The Silk Road from China to the Roman Orient

which have famous walls,[130] in war always thwart the bravery of the Persians;[131] they are enthusiastic about their business and well engaged in trade with the entire province.

[130] In late antiquity city walls were considered as *sanctum* and could not be mended or changed without explicit permission by the emperor; cf. *Dig.* 1.8.9.4, 1.8.8.2 and 1.8.11; on this issue see Winter 1996: 205–6.
[131] The Sasanians had attacked Nisibis repeatedly during the reign of Constantius II (7).

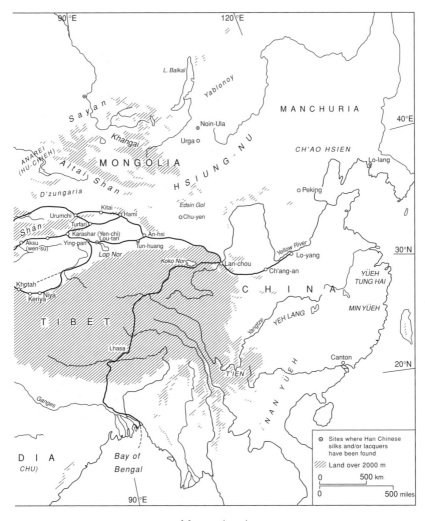

Map 13: (*cont.*)

By the fourth century Nisibis was thus a crucial centre of trade and also
played a great strategic role. As the passage suggests, for the purpose of
defending the Roman Eastern frontier the city served as an essential fortress.
Ammianus Marcellinus speculates that had it not been for Nisibis – *orientis
firmissimum claustrum* – at this point the Roman East would have been
under Sasanian rule for some time.[132] Quite consistently, the same author

[132] Amm. xxv.8.14.

labels the *foedus* of 363 (**18**) and the cessation of Nisibis to the Persians as 'humiliating agreements' accepted by Jovian.[133]

But why did Rome insist in 298 (**17**) to make it the *only* place for the exchange of goods between West and East? There may have been several reasons. The fact that the treaty of 298 made Nisibis the only place of trade – in an area where numerous caravan routes and traffic routes existed – inevitably channelled the Sasanian trade. However, the changes initiated by Rome with an eye to centralisation did not bear that much impact on the trade of the sought after luxury goods from the Far East because these had always been exchanged in the great centres of trade such as Nisibis. The changes affected above all the local trade in the border areas and the exchange of goods within Mesopotamia. The individual tradesman, merchant or peasant who had offered his ware at the nearest market now had to decide whether to expose himself to the risks of the long and exhausting journey or not. According to the treaty of 298 merchants had to take their goods, sometimes covering long distances, all the way to Nisibis where Roman merchants received them.

When Roman merchants received goods from the Far East and from India that had travelled through Persian territories into the border regions along the Euphrates and Tigris,[134] they had to pay customs duties fixed by the Eastern power. Some scholars believe that the revenues accumulated in this way allowed the Sasanians to build up their army, to conscribe Arab mercenaries and finally to expand westwards.[135] For the Romans the fact that their only overland trade with China and India was via the Sasanians entailed high costs in peace time and a cessation of the eastern trade in times of war.[136] In order to secure its eastern trade the Romans therefore were primarily interested in breaking the Sasanian monopoly as mediators for the exchange of goods along the Roman Eastern frontier and in acquiring trade centres outside the Persian Empire.

Accordingly, the Romans intended to limit the activities of Persian merchants and to control these. Moreover, they were interested in fixed prices as well as their own revenues from customs duties, which were normally

---

[133] Ibid. xxv.7.13.

[134] For some time Sasanian merchants monopolised the trade in the Persian Gulf and the Indian Ocean so that the Sasanians were able to control the trade with India; cf. Williams 1972: 97–109; Whitehouse and Williamson 1973: 29–49; Whitehouse 1996: 339–49.

[135] Haussig 1959: 138.

[136] In late antiquity Roman maritime trade between the Red Sea and India therefore became more and more important; cf. Sidebotham 1986a: 16–36.

raised by cities that had customs offices.[137] It is thus not surprising that in 298 the Roman ambassador Sicorius Probus insisted on Nisibis as the only place of trade in Mesopotamia. Fiscal considerations must have been responsible for including this clause in the treaty because in consequence every Sasanian merchant had to pay customs duties if he wanted to sell his goods in Nisibis, which at the end of the third century was part of the Roman sphere of influence.[138] We cannot say with certainty how high these customs duties were. It is possible that the Sasanians now had to submit 25 per cent instead of the customary 12.5 per cent of the selling price.[139] By imposing high customs duties Diocletian intended to break the Persian monopoly on the silk trade and to add a counter weight to the prices dictated by the Persians.

While the Roman line of reasoning seems clear and financial advantages on the Roman side possible, it is difficult to estimate how far the decision of 298 had an overall effect on the Sasanian state budget.[140] It looks as if the clause did not diminish the revenues of the Sasanian state because it did not lose its freedom to impose customs duties from traders either when they entered the Sasanian Empire or when they sold their goods within Persian territory.[141]

Nisibis was vehemently contested during the fourth century[142] but still retained its role as a trans-shipment centre after 363 when the city fell into Sasanian hands.[143] Ammianus Marcellinus' elaborate description of the exodus of its inhabitants and the take over by the Persians illustrates how much the loss of this city shocked contemporaries.[144] Not surprisingly, when relations once more deteriorated during the sixth century, the Romans built the city of Dārā-Anastasiopolis facing Nisibis and transformed it into a massive bulwark during the reign of Justinian. This was meant to be the Western counterpart to Nisibis.[145]

---

[137] Manandian 1965: 77; in general on trade related aspects in the diplomatic relations between West and East see Winter 1987: 46–74.

[138] Andreotti 1969: 215–57.

[139] Cf. *DNP* s.v. Zoll: 830 for further references; on late antique taxation in Syria and Mesopotamia see Pollard 2000: 213–18 and Jones 1964: 824–7.

[140] Blockley 1984: 33 emphasises the financial advantages for Rome, 'The result of this was that the Romans would garner all the income from taxes of the lucrative eastern trade.'

[141] In Winter and Dignas 2001: 210 the authors emphasised the financial losses for the Sasanians but have changed their view since; on the Sasanian economy in general see Morony 2004: 166–94.

[142] Festus 27.2; on the confrontations during the reign of Šāpūr II see Maróth 1979: 239–43 and Lightfoot 1988: 105–25.

[143] Amm. xxv.7.19–14 (**18**); see also Chrysos 1993: 165–202.

[144] Amm. xxv.9.1–12; for context and interpretation see **18**.

[145] For details, references and a photograph of the modern – still impressive – ruins of Dārā see figs. 13–14.

The *foedus* of 298 also forced Narsē to acknowledge the Roman protectorate of Ibēria (**17**), an area south of the central Caucasus and north of Armenia through which the upper and middle Kyros was flowing. Diocletian intended to expand the Roman sphere of influence to the north-east in order to create new routes for the Eastern trade which would circumvent Sasanian territory in the north. The emperor's ambition to regain power over Ibēria was closely linked to the role of this area as a transit area. Repeatedly the Romans had become painfully aware that the most important overland trade routes in the East of the ancient world, by which the sought after luxury goods from the Far East reached the large Roman centres along the eastern coast of the Mediterranean, went through Sasanian territory. The Persian supremacy by sea, in particular in the Persian Gulf, which was the starting point for the lucrative trade with India,[146] must have further strengthened the key role the Sasanians played with regard to the Roman eastern trade. The Romans therefore tried to establish firm bases along the Black Sea and in the Caucasus in order to create new land routes for an extended eastern trade, primarily with China.[147] To some extent their attempts to maintain diplomatic relations with Armenia and the Caucasus had to do with the hope that the peoples in this region would help them to obtain important luxury goods, above all silk and silk products. The significance of the areas in the Caucasus and around the Caspian Sea with regard to trade has been suggested as a motive for the expansion of a Roman Eastern policy during the Parthian period[148] and has been acknowledged for some time as a cause for confrontations between Byzantium and the Sasanian Empire during the fifth and sixth centuries.[149] This significance very much also applies to the situation at the end of the third century.

Until the treaty of 363 (**18**) when Šāpūr II (309–79) made the emperor Jovian (363–4) revise the central aspects of the *foedus* of 298 (**17**) the agreements of this treaty continued to be legally valid. Ammianus Marcellinus states, however, that during the reign of Constantius II an annual market existed in Batnai where Indian and goods from Seran were offered and the author also praises the magnificent goods of the city of Kallinikos.[150]

---

[146] On the Sasanian contacts with India, specifically by sea via the Persian Gulf see also Wiesehöfer 1998a: 19–20 and Daryaee 2003: 1–6.

[147] On possible trade routes to China which went through the Caucasus and bypassed Sasanian territory in the north see Herrmann 1966: 18–19 and 26–7; cf. also Thorley 1969: 215 and Wissemann 1984: 166–73; on the Sasanian attempts to stop trade along the northern route of the Silk Road see Haussig 1983: 161–82.

[148] Wissemann 1984: 166–73.

[149] Pigulevskaja 1969: 155–8; Harmatta 2000: 249–52.

[150] Amm. xiv.3.3 and xxiii.3.7; cf. also Kirsten 1959: 558 and Synelli 1986: 89; on Batnai as a centre of trade see Kissel 1998: 171–2 and De Ligt 1993: 74.

The consequences of making Nisibis the only place in the border area for the exchange of goods were thus less dramatic for Roman merchants than they were for their Sasanian counterparts. The same impression is given by the anonymous author of the *Expositio totius mundi et gentium* when he names not only Nisibis but also Batnai and Kallinikos (far west of Nisibis) as important centres of trade.[151]

It would be helpful to know to what extent the political climate throughout the centuries altered the trade relations between Rome and the East. Until the end of the Parthian kingdom the 'international' trade along the Eastern frontier of the Roman Empire had flourished without any restrictions. Economy and trade had never been an issue in Parthian–Roman peace treaties.[152] For the period of Roman–Parthian relations we observe active trade between the two powers and Roman contacts with the ports of India from where Chinese silk was imported into the Roman Empire.[153] When the Sasanian Empire was founded in the year 224 a new development began, which presented entirely different premises for the relations between East and West. Immediately after the fall of the Arsacids Ardašīr I (224–40)[154] occupied Spasinu Charax on the Šatt al-'Arab and thereby restricted Palmyrene activities in a provocative way, which in turn had a negative effect on Roman trade interests.[155]

During the following centuries the rivalry between both states did not allow for a free development of trade between Rome and the Sasanian Empire. An increasingly suspicious attitude towards the neighbouring state led to closed borders where a type of frontier police were to guarantee that trade regulations were adhered to.[156]

According to instructions from the reign of Theodosius I the *comes commerciorum* was the only person permitted to acquire and sell (raw) silk from the barbarians.[157] This official, who was also largely in charge of assessing import and export duties,[158] was responsible for ensuring that

---

[151] On the history and significance of Edessa in late antiquity see Kirsten 1963: 144–72; Segal 1970; Ross 2001.

[152] Ziegler 1964: 87–8.

[153] Raschke 1978: 641–3 and 815–47; Wissemann 1984: 166, however, points to possible difficulties for Rome resulting from the mediating role played by the Parthians.

[154] Cf. above, p. 19 with n. 8 and Drexhage 1988: 70–6 and 139–40.

[155] Wagner 1985: 12.

[156] *Cod. Theod.* VII.16.2 (410); cf. also Güterbock 1906: 71–2 and Segal 1955: 127.

[157] *Cod. Iust.* IV.40.2; see Stock 1978b: 602 n. 10.

[158] *Cod. Theod.* IV.13.8–9 (381); all duties (import, export and transit) went to the *comes sacrarum largitionum*, who supervised the trade within the empire and in particular border traffic; cf. *Cod. Iust.* IV.63.2 (374) and 6.

official bans on the export of certain goods were respected, above all the export of arms, iron, gold, wine and oil.[159] He thus supervised the Roman foreign trade and acted according to Diocletian's goal of linking national security with a regulated trade.[160]

The *Codex Iustinianus* tells us about a constitution *de commerciis et mercatoribus* by the emperors Honorius and Theodosius II (408/9), which was addressed to the *praefectus praetorio Orientis* Anthemius[161] and which sums up official guidelines for the trade between Byzantium and the Persian Empire – guidelines that remained valid until their relations ended altogether.[162]

Codex Iustinianus IV.63.4

It is by no means permitted that merchants, neither subjects of our empire nor of the Persian king, hold markets[163] outside the places that were agreed on together with the mentioned nation at the time when the peace was concluded in order that they do not find out about the secrets of the foreign kingdom in an inappropriate way.[164] (1) Henceforth no subject of our empire shall dare travelling further than Nisibis, Kallinikos and Artaxata in order to acquire or sell goods, nor shall anybody expect to exchange goods with a Persian but in the named cities. Both sides who contract with each other shall know that goods sold or acquired outside these places will be confiscated by our most sacred government, that these goods and the price that was paid or exchanged shall be lost and that they themselves shall be exiled for life. (2) Regarding their appearance at transactions that took place outside the mentioned places judges are also punished with a payment of thirty pounds of gold, [and also those] via whose territory a Roman or Persian travelled to the forbidden places for the purpose of trade. (3) However, this does not apply to those who accompanied Persian ambassadors sent to us at any time and carried goods for the purpose of trade; out of humanity and respect for an embassy we do not deny these the right to engage in trade also outside the fixed places, unless they use the embassy as a pretext in order to spend more time in any province and

---

[159] Ibid. IV.41.1 (370–5); IV.41.2 (455–7); IV.63.2 (374); cf. also *Dig.* XXXIX.4.11; *Cod. Theod.* VII.16.3 (420); *Expositio totius mundi et gentium* 22 (p. 156 ed. Rougé); also Karayannopoulos 1958: 168 and De Laet 1949: 477–8.

[160] On the *comites commerciorum*, who existed only in the provinces that bordered foreign territory (cf. for the Eastern Roman Empire *Not. Dign. Or.* XIII.6–9), and their responsibilities; De Laet 1949: 457–9; Pigulevskaja 1969: 83–4; on their changing responsibilities from the end of the fifth century onwards see Karayannopoulos 1958: 159–68, esp. 164–5.

[161] On the life and activities of Anthemius, who around the turn of the century, prior to his appointment as *praefectus praetorio* (404), was ambassador at the court of the Sasanian king and contributed significantly to the good relations between East and West during this period, see Clauss 1981: 147; *PLRE* 2: 93–5; Synelli 1986: 93–4 and 172.

[162] On this source see Antoniadis-Bibicou 1963: 115 and 194.

[163] The wording '*nundinas exercere*' is discussed in De Ligt 1993: 53–4.

[164] On the issue of espionage by merchants and diplomats see also **35**.

do not accompany the ambassador on his return to his own country. When these engage in trade they shall be rightly afflicted with the punishment resulting from this sanction, and also those who do business with them and those with whom they stayed.

The constitution refers to a *foedus* concluded with the Sasanians in the past. This must be the treaty of 298 between Diocletian and Narsē (**17**), and it looks as if the stipulations regarding trade were still valid in 408/9.[165] According to the constitution of 408/9 the exchange of goods was limited to the cities of Nisibis, Kallinikos and the Armenian metropolis Artaxata (map 3).[166] Espionage by foreign merchants was much feared and punished harshly, with exile, the confiscation of the merchant's goods or his personal property. Already Ammianus Marcellinus states that Roman border traffic was strictly controlled in order to prevent Romans from escaping to the enemy's territory and thereby from passing on important information to the opponent.[167] On the basis of the geographical location of the three cities we can infer how the flow of goods was channelled. The trade beyond the Tigris was supposed to flow via Nisibis, the trade with and through Armenia[168] via Artaxata and the trade with the more southern regions along the Gulf, especially with the numerous Arab tribes in Syria, via Kallinikos.[169]

The fact that the constitution and its sanctions address both Roman and Sasanian merchants is significant because it shows that Sasanian interests are also represented. In 408–9 two of the three places designated for the exchange of goods, namely Nisibis and Artaxata, were situated within the Sasanian realm of power. We are thus dealing with an international settlement or rather its points of execution that needed the consent of the Sasanian ruler Yazdgard I (399–420). This explains why this imperial constitution was not included in the *Codex Theodosianus* of 438.[170]

From the perspective of the great powers, restricting trade to a few centres was an important step towards securing the shared border.[171] In the

---

[165] Winter 1987: 64–5.
[166] On the significance of Artaxata as an international trading centre see Manandian 1965: 80–1.
[167] Amm. XVIII.5.3.
[168] In general on Armenia's role for the trade in the eastern parts of the ancient world see Manandian 1965.
[169] Cf. on Kallinikos as a flourishing trading centre p. 202 with n. 150.
[170] Güterbock 1906: 75; Bury 1958: 212 even talks about a treaty with the Sasanian Empire 'which secured peace on the Persian frontier'.
[171] Thus also Pollard 2000: 216 who points to the 'preference of centralization' as a typical phenomenon in late antiquity.

year 422, very close in time to the *foedus* between Bahrām V Gōr and
Theodosius II (**19**), an edict was issued according to which trade between
the two empires was permitted only in places that had been designated
in earlier constitutions.[172] Attempts to circumvent the official regulations
of 408/9 may have triggered new legislation and a confirmation of their
content.[173] This corresponds with the warning not to host foreign merchants without the knowledge and consent of the *comes commerciorum*,
which was issued at the same time.[174] Finally, three articles of the elaborate
treaty concluded between Xusrō I Anōšarvān and Justinian I in 562 (**20**)
addressed decisions regarding economy and trade. These adhered to the
general guidelines that had already been fixed in 298 and 408/9 and that
remained valid until the end of the Byzantine–Sasanian relations in the
early seventh century. The economic rivalry between Byzantium and Persia
continued in spite of the peace. However, the increasing hostilities, in particular the Sasanian offensives at the beginning of the seventh century (**15**), no
longer allowed for a regulated and uninterrupted flow of trade between both
states.

The following conclusions may be drawn: from the end of the third
century onwards economic aspects also guided the diplomatic interaction
between the two empires. Attempts to deal with economic questions led
to political contacts.[175] Trade related interests, above all the assessment of
customs duties, gained more and more significance as they both intensified contacts and increased rivalries. Given the increasing ideological and
military tensions between the empires a free exchange of goods without
state intervention and control ceased to exist. In contrast to their predecessors, the Sasanian kings did not accept any Roman superiority but
pursued an active expansionist foreign policy; with the treaty of 298 (**17**)
Diocletian reacted to this by introducing a policy that linked foreign trade
with Rome's security. This policy became characteristic for the economic
relations between (East-) Rome and Persia.

Numerous constitutions and treaties confirm a consistent policy on
both sides, always accompanied by Roman attempts to establish multiple alliances with the prospect of creating new trade routes by land and
by sea that would avoid Sasanian territory.[176] According to the Byzantine
historian Menander Protector the start of diplomatic relations between

---

[172] *Cod. Iust.* IV.63.6. praef.; cf. also De Laet 1949: 458–9 and Karayannopoulos 1958: 167.
[173] Karayannopoulos 1958: 160–1.   [174] *Cod. Iust.* IV.63,6, praef.
[175] On the shared economic interests of the great powers see also Frye 1972: 265–9.
[176] In this context cf. esp. Pigulevskaja 1969; also Eadie 1989: 113–20; Sidebotham 1989: 485–509 and
     1986a: 16–36 and 1986b.

Byzantium and the Turks in the year 568 (**14**) was mainly motivated by the Roman interest in importing the precious silk from the Far East without any Sasanian involvement.[177] In this context, Procopius describes an attempt made by Justinian (527–65) in the year 552 to introduce the breeding of silkworms into the Byzantine Empire.

Procopius, De Bello Gothico IV.17.1–8

(1) Some monks, who were visiting from India around this time[178] and who saw that the emperor Justinian was keen for the Romans not to have to buy silk from the Persians anymore, approached the emperor and promised that they would take care of the silk issue in a way that the Romans would no longer have to purchase it from their own enemies or any other people. (2) They claimed that they had spent some time in a country that was situated beyond most of the Indian settlements and that was called Serinda[179] and that they had found out exactly how it would be possible to produce silk in the Roman Empire. (3) When the emperor enquired persistently and tried to find out whether their story was true, the monks told him that a type of worm produced the silk and that nature was their teacher forcing them to work continuously. (4) That it was, however, impossible to bring the worms here alive but that their offspring were easily transported. They explained that the offspring of these worms were an innumerable number of eggs from each one; (5) that men buried these eggs long after they were produced in dung and by warming them for sufficient time they made the living animals. (6) After their speech the emperor promised to reward the men with large gifts and he persuaded them to put their words into practice. (7) Then they travelled once more to Serinda and brought the eggs to Byzantium, they managed to transform them into worms in the prescribed way and fed them on mulberry leaves; and it was to their credit that from then on silk was produced in the Roman Empire. (8) This is, then, how matters stood between the Romans and the Persians concerning the war and with regard to the silk.

It is revealing that the monks from India promised Justinian they would solve the 'silk problem' in a way that Byzantium would never again have to purchase silk from the hostile Sasanians. Their own manufacture of silk would have entailed many advantages for the Romans because this would have lowered the drain of gold from the empire. Moreover, the state's purple dye-works would profit tremendously from this development because an even and reliable provision of the raw material would henceforth be

---

[177] Menander frg. 18; cf. also the Byzantine contacts with Aksūm and South Arabia (Proc. 1.19.1–2 and 1.20.9–13); esp. **14**.

[178] This is the year 551.

[179] Serinda is the land of the 'silk people' who are called *Serae* or *Sêres* and who are the same as the Chinese; the Chinese had known silk since the third millennium BC but had kept its production a secret into the first millennium BC; it reached the West above all via the 'Silk Road'.

guaranteed.[180] Accordingly, Justinian gave full support to the monks' plan to import the eggs of the silk worms. Although in the following period Byzantium gained some independence from the Persian intermediate trade[181] this development was certainly not the end of the silk trade with the Far East.

Although official regulations aimed at controlling the trade, there was – far away from interstate politics – room for free economic and personal exchange. This becomes clear from the writings of Procopius. In his description of the Armenian border region Chorzanē the Byzantine historian points out that the population of neither Sasanian nor Byzantine territory feared each other but rather intermarried, held markets together and shared agricultural products.

Procopius, De aedificiis III.3.9–12

(9) On the way from Kitharizon[182] to Theodosio(u)polis and the other Armenia[183] lies a region called Chorzanē; it extends over a march of three days and it is not separated from Persia by a lake, a river or mountains, which would impede the crossing of a pass but the borders of the two merge. (10) Because of this the inhabitants, whether subjects of the Romans or of the Persians, do not fear one another or suspect mutual attacks but even engage in intermarriage, hold common markets for their daily needs and run their farms together. (11) Whenever the military commanders on each side lead an army against the other because their rulers instructed them to do so they find their neighbours unguarded. (12) The densely populated settlements are very close to each other and from old times there were no mounds anywhere.

It becomes clear that the 'border' between Romans and Sasanians was not a heavily fortified 'limes', which prohibited any contacts. The Tigris and the Euphrates or the wide areas of the Syrian Desert formed natural borders that in the course of the centuries often marked the political borders between East and West but nevertheless allowed contacts between the people who lived in the border regions. A common language, customs and way of life furthered close relations among the population. In this context once more a link between trade and religion can be observed. In particular in times of peace the personal contacts between the numerous Christians and Jews who lived beyond the Euphrates and their fellow-believers in the West

---

[180] Veh 1978: 1091–2.　　　[181] Lopez 1945: 1–42 and Wada 1970.

[182] Kitharizon was situated in the region of Asthianēnē, which was adjacent to the Sophanēnē (map 8) and here was the seat of the second *dux Armeniae*; its precise location is uncertain; cf. Howard-Johnston 1989: 203–28.

[183] For the distinction between *Armenia Minor* and *Armenia Maior* see above, p. 176.

stimulated the trade between East and West.[184] N. G. Garsoïan summarises the situation well, 'For all the antagonism and suspicion present, channels of transmission were available most of the time, the frontier was in no sense hermetic and an official *modus vivendi* had been elaborated between the two rivals.'[185]

[184] On the significance of the individual religious communities with regard to trade see Ziegler 1964: 89 and Lieu 1992: 97–106; on the Jews in particular see Neusner 1965–70.
[185] Garsoïan 1983: 575.

CHAPTER 7

Religion: Christianity and Zoroastrianism

From the third century onwards the religious policy of the great powers formed an important part of Roman–Persian relations. Evidently, there was an interaction between religion and foreign relations, and developments in West and East not only were of the same character but also took place simultaneously. This means that Rome and the Persian Empire dealt with religious matters in a comparable way and that the state of religious affairs in the East and in the West affected the neighbour's course of action. In particular after the dramatic religious changes during the reign of Constantine the Great the conflict between the now Christian Rome and the Zoroastrian Sasanian Empire escalated, also ideologically.[1]

29: Religion and kingship in the Sasanian Empire

First, let us examine the situation in the Sasanian Empire.[2] Here, the doctrine of Zarathustra[3] became the privileged religion and developed into a supporting pillar of Sasanian kingship. Zoroastrianism was therefore the religion of the Sasanian rulers and furthered by them in an exceptional way. The religious development aimed at and entailed a concentration of royal power and a centralisation of rule.[4] This formed a stark contrast to the situation during the Parthian rule. During the Parthian period religious matters in Iran were characterised by an extremely tolerant attitude of the state towards other religious movements to the effect that Eastern

---

[1] Modern scholarship distinguishes between Zarathustrianism and Zoroastrianism. The latter term designates the religion as it had developed in the later, especially the Sasanian, period, in contrast to the original religion established by Zarathustra.
[2] Cf. the relevant chapters in Duchesne-Guillemin 1964; also 1983: 874–97 and Schippmann 1990: 92–102 and Wiesehöfer 2001: 199–221.
[3] On Zarathustra and his doctrine see Boyce 1984a and 1982; de Jong 1997; Stausberg 2002 (on the Sasanian period 205–62); on the controversial dating of Zarathustra's life see Shahbazi 2002b: 7–45 (between the end of the 2nd millennium BC and the 7th/6th century BC).
[4] On Zoroastrianism under the Sasanians see Duchesne-Guillemin 1983; further references in Wiesehöfer 2001: 288–9.

and Hellenistic cults mixed profoundly.[5] Just as in other regards, after the change of rule in 224 we observe a politically motivated return to old Persian traditions. The beginning of Sasanian rule therefore was an important benchmark in the religious history of Iran. All Sasanian kings explicitly declared their faith in Ahura Mazda.[6] There is no doubt that the 'Iranisation' observed with regard to politics and society also applied to religious affairs. The following two passages give insight into the relation between the Sasanian state and the Zoroastrian 'state cult'.[7]

Masʿūdī, Murūǧ 1 § 586

My son, religion and kingship are brothers who cannot do without each other, for religion is the foundation of kingship and kingship is religion's protector. And that which does not have a foundation collapses and that which does not have a protector perishes.

So called 'Will of Ardašīr I', ed. Grignaschi 49[8]

Know that kingship and religion are twin brothers each one of which cannot do without its partner. For religion is the foundation of kingship, and kingship is the protector of religion. Kingship cannot do without its foundation, and religion cannot do without its protector, for that which has no protector perishes and that which has no foundation collapses.

The author of the first Arabic text, Masʿūdī, lived in the tenth century. He tells us about Ardašīr I (224–70) advising his son and successor Šāpūr I (240–72) to make religion the foundation of his monarchical rule. Accordingly, he should show himself as the protector of religion.[9] Around the same time the author Ibn Miskawayh transmits the so-called 'will' of the founder of the Sasanian Empire, Ardašīr I, which is a late Sasanian fabrication.[10] In this passage, too, the close link between kingship and religion is expressed, if not without alluding to the fact that the 'twins' are actually rivals.[11] In the eyes of both authors religion as the foundation of the empire has priority over kingship, which merely functions as the 'guardian' of religion.

---

[5] Boyce 1987: 540–1 and Wiesehöfer 2001: 149.
[6] On this supreme deity, the 'wise, omniscient lord', who represented the light and the truth, see Boyce 1985: 684–7.
[7] Gignoux 1984a: 72–80.
[8] The same text with only minor deviations can be found in Caetani 1909: 102.
[9] This is also expressed in the so called 'letter of Tansar', 'Church and state stem from the same body and are inseparably linked' (tr. Boyce 33–4); see also Wiesehöfer 2001: 170. 211; the 'letter of Tansar' – we have a neo-Persian translation of an Arabic translation going back to a source from the late Sasanian period – claims to be a letter written by Ardašīr's 'religious advisor' Tansar (Tōser), who is known through the Zoroastrian tradition.
[10] Grignaschi 1966: 70.   [11] On the metaphor see Shaked 1990: 262–74.

Testimonies such as these convey the impression that already during the third century a form of 'state religion' existed in the Sasanian Empire, based on the excellent relations between the Zoroastrian priesthood and the Sasanian rulers.[12] Apparently king and state owed their power and legitimacy to the religion, just as vice versa, religion and 'church' needed the king as their protector and guarantor. The idea, however, that from the third century onwards a Zoroastrian 'state church' was firmly established in the Sasanian Empire raises doubts; although they go back to Sasanian traditions, the relevant surviving passages within the Arabic–Persian historiography were obviously composed not before the late or post-Sasanian period.[13] Ph. Gignoux summarises correctly: '(I)t appears then that the sacred alliance between kingship and religion is but a literary theme which developed mainly after the Sāsānian period and ... under Islamic influence which attempted, sometimes successfully, the symbiosis of these two powers.'[14]

With regard to the third century the idea of a Zoroastrian 'state religion' is thus as problematic as the label 'church' (in the sense of an organised and hierarchically structured institution), in particular as the term originally designated a specific historical phenomenon solely referring to Christianity.[15] Nevertheless, the hierarchical structures within the Zoroastrian community of the Magians and within the Christian Church are comparable. In both, tiered religious honours and titles with fixed responsibilities had emerged.[16] This 'system' was characterised by a strict separation of clerics and lay people, by a strictly regulated promotion to certain offices and a decreasing level of democratic elements, which had been unknown to early Christianity. The responsibilities and power of the Zoroastrian priest Kartēr are similar to those of a bishop in the Christian Church. In the West as well as the East there was a trend towards a concentration of power and towards monarchical power. While handing all spiritual and administrative responsibilities to the bishops, this development consistently and increasingly excluded the people and the aristocratic powers of the clergy.[17]

Whereas during the third century the strong link between kingship and religion in the East represented a model to the West, during the fourth and fifth centuries the emergence of an ecclesiastical hierarchy in the West affected the development of a 'religious administration' in the East. Christianity and Zoroastrianism therefore differed fundamentally from all other religions, cults and philosophical schools, which lacked a corresponding organisation. Moreover, they alone consistently rejected all other religious

---

[12] See also Bier 1993: 172–94, esp. 181–4.   [13] Wiesehöfer 1993: 362–82, esp. 367–8.
[14] Gignoux 1984a: 80.   [15] Wiesehöfer 1993: 362–82.
[16] See Paul 1983: 107.   [17] Cf. ibid. 109.

movements, which paved the way to the enormous success of these two world religions in the Roman and Sasanian Empire respectively.

30: The Sasanian kings as patrons of Zoroastrianism

Numerous testimonies of the third century already depict the early Sasanian kings as 'patrons' of Zoroastrianism.[18] During the reign of Bahrām II (276–93) the most powerful priest within this religion was Kartēr. In several inscriptions (at Sar Mašhad, Naqš-i Rustam and Naqš-i Rajab), which were composed in the Middle Persian script and show an almost identical wording, Kartēr describes his career under the early Sasanian rulers, namely under Šāpūr I (240–72) and his successors.[19] Apart from the great Šāpūr Inscription (*ŠKZ*), these inscriptions are our most important sources for the study of Zoroastrianism in the Sasanian Empire of the third century.[20]

Kartēr's inscriptions at Sar-Mašhad, at Naqš-i Rustam, on the Kaʿba-i Zardušt and at Naqš-i Rajab, pp. 405–10 (ed. Back)

And from the beginning, I, Kartēr, saw great pains and labour for gods and rulers and for the sake of my own soul, and I set up many fire (sanctuaries) and Magians in Ērānšahr . . . flourishing; and also in ʿAnērānšahr fire (sanctuaries) and Magians, present in the territory of the non-Aryans where the horses and people of the King of Kings went – the city of Antioch and the territory of Syria and the provincial territory above Syria . . . [a list of the territories conquered by Šāpūr follows] – also there, commanded by the King of Kings, I established the Magians and fire (sanctuaries) that existed in those provinces.

According to Kartēr, during his campaigns against Rome he established fire sanctuaries in order to introduce the Zoroastrian fire cult in areas outside Iran (= ʿAnērān). The priest had accompanied the Sasanian king on his campaigns in the West. If we can trust his words, the king instructed him to reorganise the Zoroastrian cult in the conquered western territories. Hereby Šāpūr I probably intended to tie these areas closer to the Sasanian Empire and to include them in his sphere of interest. However, there is no proof that the king aimed at an 'Iranisation' of the provinces in Asia Minor that had formerly been part of the Achaemenid Empire.[21]

The fire motif possessed great significance in the Zoroastrian religion. It symbolised purity and virtue and for the Zoroastrians was the 'reflection of truth'. The rituals employed in the worship of the fire were mainly carried out in fire sanctuaries.[22] Numerous testimonies confirm the close relation

---

[18] Mosig-Walburg 1982.   [19] For further references cf. Huyse 1998: 109–20.
[20] Back 1978: 384–489; MacKenzie 1989: 35–72 and Gignoux 1991b.
[21] Thus Widengren 1961: 11.
[22] Erdmann 1941 and Schippmann 1971; Kaim 2004: 323–37.

between the Sasanian king and the 'fire'. In the Šāpūr inscription at Naqš-i Rustam the king thanks the gods for supporting his campaigns by referring to the dedication of fires marking his victories.

The Šāpūr Inscription on the Kaʿba-i Zarduŝt at Naqš-i Rustam (ŠKZ) § 51
The Parthian text

Just as we take great care now for the affairs and worship of the gods and are the '*dastgerd*'[23] of the gods and with the help of the gods sought and took possession of all these countries, and in addition became famous and brave, (in this way) the one, who will come after us and will be successful, shall take great care for the affairs and worship of the gods, so that the gods will help him and make him their own 'dastgerd'.

Šāpūr I points to his numerous fire dedications, to his support of the fire cult and the priesthood, and he thereby emphasises his close relationship with the gods. Just like the Zoroastrian priest Kartēr, the Sasanian king also explicitly states that he owed his military success in the West to the goodwill of the gods. Both texts illustrate a close link between politics and religion at this point. By furthering Zoroastrianism the Persian ruler attempts to unite his 'nation' – possibly with an eye to the battle against the opponent in the West.[24] In the end, strengthening and spreading the Zoroastrian religion also served to legitimate and enhance royal power. These and further activities of Šāpūr I were therefore part of a 'religious policy'. At the end of the inscription the king encourages his successor to follow his zeal with regard to religion. All rulers should appease the gods, become the protégés of the gods, look after religious matters and, just like Šāpūr I himself, endorse the Zoroastrian religion. In accord with the support received by Zoroastrianism in general, over the course of time Zoroastrian priests gained considerable power. The fact that Zoroastrianism became the official religion of the empire facilitated the emergence of a fixed hierarchy and differentiation within the priestly cast. The religious titles attested by Kartēr's inscriptions reveal an increasing significance of their holders during the third century.[25] Comparable to the realm of politics, where a few noble families occupied the high civil and military ranks, the Zoroastrian religious community was based on a hereditary priesthood that was kept within one family. However, a Zoroastrian 'state church' and a corresponding 'religious administration' did not exist before the fourth or – more developed – fifth century.[26] This development was facilitated by

---

[23] The term '*dastgerd*' refers to the close relationship between the ruler and the gods; cf. Huyse 1999: 180–1 (vol. II); Henning 1958: 96 translates the term as 'Schützling' (= protégé); cf. also Back 1978: 504 n. 199.

[24] Decret 1979: 130–1.   [25] Grenet 1990: 87–94.   [26] Gignoux 1983: 253–66.

the fact that Sasanian kingship was particularly weak in this period; from the fifth century at the latest, Zoroastrianism was firmly established also on an institutional level.

As the example of Kartēr has shown, already during the third century a Zoroastrian priest could achieve great power and influence.[27] During the reigns of Bahrām I (273–6) and Bahrām II (276–93) he seems to have been at the peak of his power. His epigraphical 'biography' at Naqš-i Rustam, which has a strong propagandistic character comparable to the Šāpūr Inscription (*ŠKZ*), impressively illustrates his rise in power.[28]

Kartēr's inscriptions at Sar-Mašhad, at Naqš-i Rustam, on the Ka'ba-i Zardušt and at Naqš-i Rajab, pp. 414–16 (ed. Back)

And after . . . Bahrām (II) . . . had become ruler, instigated by his love for Ohrmezd and the gods and for the sake of my own soul, he elevated my rank and honour in the empire, and he gave me the rank and honour of the magnates, and at his court and in every province, in every place, in the entire empire, in the worship of the gods he made me even more powerful and independent[29] than I had been before.

Already while serving Šāpūr I Kartēr proudly claimed to have established many fire sanctuaries in 'Ērān' and 'Anērān'. However, during the reign of the second Sasanian king religious minorities were not yet persecuted. Whereas the reign of Šāpūr I was characterised by caution – religious minorities were tolerated, the rivalling Manichaeism was attractive for many[30] – the situation of the non-Zoroastrian religions deteriorated under the successors of Šāpūr I. Kartēr describes the attempt to destroy all other religions and to spread Zoroastrianism as the only legal religion.

Kartēr's inscriptions at Sar-Mašhad, at Naqš-i Rustam, on the Ka'ba-i Zardušt and at Naqš-i Rajab, pp. 419–28 (ed. Back)

And the false doctrines[31] of the Ahreman (Angra Mainyu) and of the dēws (= demons)[32] disappeared from the empire and were expelled.[33] And the Jews, Buddhists, Brahmans (= Hindi), Nazarenes, Christians, Baptists and Manichaeans were broken up, and their idols were destroyed and the dwellings of the dēws were annihilated and turned into places and seats of the gods.

---

[27] Cf. the references above, p. 27 n. 48; also Sprengling 1953.   [28] See Gignoux 1991b.

[29] In KSM the order of the two comparatives is exchanged.

[30] Brown 1969: 92–103; Sundermann 1986: 40–92 and 239–317; Hutter 1988; Lieu 1992; id. 1994; on the special relations between Mani and the Sasanian ruler Šāpūr and the rivalry with Kartēr's Zoroastrian priesthood see Hinz 1971: 485–99; Russel 1990: 180–93; also Hutter 1992: 152–69.

[31] This means 'dogma', in particular of the non-Mazdā-followers, thus 'false doctrine'.

[32] Back 1978: 508 n. 256 talks about 'demons, false gods'.

[33] Differently Back 1978: 414; cf. also MacKenzie 1982: 285.

Apart from Zoroastrianism there were many groups of different faiths in the Sasanian Empire, namely Jews, Buddhists, Hindi, Mandaeans, Christians and Manichaeans. To some extent these were severely persecuted by the Magians. Kartēr intended to restore the 'right order', which translated into sanctions against those who did not follow 'orthodox Zoroastrianism'. In particular the Christians, Jews and Manichaeans, who adhered to the so-called 'supranational' religions, faced coercive measures by the Zoroastrian priesthood.[34] From Kartēr's perspective and that of the Magians it was above all Manichaeism which represented a serious rival to their own religion because during the third century it enjoyed great success also outside Iran. In 277 the founder of this religion, Mani, was captured. R. Ghirshman refers to reasons for the persecution of the followers of non-Zoroastrian religions that we have touched on already, 'The problem of an imperial religion must have arisen ... at a time when the young Empire was winning success in foreign policy and needed to mobilize all its national forces for the struggle with Rome.'[35]

But already Narsē (293–302) turned his back on the religious policy of his predecessors. The fact that the persecution of religious minorities ceased can be attributed partly to an attempt to limit the increasing power of the Zoroastrian priestly caste but must primarily be seen in the context of the renewed conflict with Rome (**6**). In the West, we observe a simultaneous persecution of Manichaeans, followers of a faith that was certainly associated with the Persian opponent (**31**).

31: From Diocletian to Constantine – Religious change in the West and the consequences for Roman–Sasanian relations

Diocletian's Edict against the Manichaeans, 297 (or 302[36]): Collatio legum Mosaicarum et Romanarum xv.3.1–8

The emperors Diocletian and Maximianus, *Augusti*, and Constantius and Maximianus,[37] the finest *Caesars*, send greetings to the proconsul of Africa, Julianus. A very leisurely life tends to encourage people in a community to transgress the limits of human nature and incites them to introduce some kind of empty and despicable superstitious doctrine, so that by making their own erroneous judgement they seem to sway also many others, my dearest Julianus. (2) But the immortal gods in their providence intended to stipulate that what is good and right should

---

[34] Wiesehöfer 1993: 362–82; on the persecutions under Bahrām II see Schwaigert 1989: 42–4.
[35] Ghirshman 1954: 315.   [36] For a date 302 see Barnes 1982: 169.
[37] This is Galerius (**6**), whose full name was Gaius Galerius Valerius Maximianus; Diocletian made him 'Caesar' on 21 May (?) 293.

be acknowledged and applied by the counsel and decisions of many virtuous, eminent and very wise men[38] (it is against the right order to step against and oppose this), and that the ancient religion may not be questioned by a new one. For it is the greatest crime to open to debate what was once decided on and defined by the forefathers and what develops steadily and has its fixed place.[39] (3) We are therefore intent on punishing the stubborn and deprived minds of the most useless people: for these are people who try to replace the old religions with new and unheard-of sects in order to – through their own false judgement – cast out what we were once given by divine providence.[40] (4) The Manichaeans, about whom you reported to Our Serenity with much insight, as we have heard, have come into existence and entered our realm only recently from our enemy, the Persian people, just like new and unexpected portents, and they commit many crimes here because they disturb quiet peoples and certainly also inflict harm on civilised states; and we have to be afraid that, as tends to happen, by scandalous customs and the bad laws of the Persians over the course of time they will try to infect people of a more innocent nature, modest and quiet Romans and our whole empire with their malign poison. (5) And as everything you set out so well in your report about their religion by our statutes is obviously a crime and crazy lies, we have decided to punish these with deserved and appropriate punishments. (6) For we give order to punish the authors and leaders severely and to burn them in the flames together with their abominable writings; we give instruction that the followers who remain stubborn receive capital punishment and we decide that their property will be confiscated by the imperial treasury. (7) If officials or people of considerable rank or influence have joined this unheard-of, despicable and utterly infamous sect or the doctrine of the Persians you will take care that their property will be taken over by our imperial treasury and that they themselves will be handed over to the mines at Phaeno or Proconnesus.[41] (8) In order, therefore, that this superfluous pestilence can be removed from our most blessed times, may Your Devotion hurry in carrying out our orders and decisions. Given in Alexandria on the day before the calends of April.[42]

The so-called 'Edict against the Manichaeans' was issued by the emperor Diocletian either in the year 297, during the Persian War and before the peace of 298 (**17**) was concluded, or after this event in 302.[43] It has been transmitted in the *Collatio legum Mosaicarum et Romanarum*, a compilation

---

[38] As part of their invectives against Christianity, Celsus (e.g. Orig. Centr. Cels. praef. 5) and Porphyry (e.g. frg. 1) also referred to famous and learned men who had postulated the worship of the traditional gods.

[39] This reminds one of the famous speech of Maecenas by Cassius Dio (LXX.36.1–2), in which the ancient author postulates not to tolerate those who failed to worship the proper gods.

[40] These words reflect an attitude and religious policy among Diocletian and his colleagues that formed the background for the renewed persecutions of the Christians under the tetrarchs.

[41] The island of Proconnesus, situated in the western part of the Sea of Marmara, was famous for its marble quarries; in late antiquity the island's city of the same name was a bishop's see and a place of exile.

[42] This is 31 March.   [43] Seston 1940: 345–54 (= Widengren 1977: 374–84).

of selected Roman legal norms and those of the Old Testament, which was composed towards the end of the fourth century probably by a Christian loyal to Rome.[44] The edict turns against a religion originating from an empire that had been utterly hostile to Rome for a long time. The connection is evident – the laws and customs of the Persians are condemned and criticised en bloc.

Although the outbreak of a new Roman–Sasanian war under Narsē (**6**) may have triggered the activities agains the Manichaeans,[45] one cannot fail to notice that the edict against the Manichaeans was part of a comprehensive attempt for religious restoration, which on the one hand aimed at a restoration of the traditional cults, on the other hand postulated an immediate link between the welfare of the state and the benevolence of the gods.[46] The claim that the old religious order was inviolable served to legitimise the official persecutions of the Manichaeans as well as to justify the return to the religion of the ancestors.

The revival of the Roman 'national' cults formed an important part of Diocletian's reforms, which sought to overcome the 'crisis' of the Roman Empire. In order to stabilise the basis of Roman monarchical power these reforms included not only a decentralisation of rule – the tetrarchy was established[47] – but also the construction of a firm bond between the ruler and the Roman gods, above all the supreme god Jupiter. This bond was taken as serious enough to fight religions not willing to serve and sacrifice to the emperor, who was the first representative of Jupiter on earth. Diocletian's goals were similar to those of Constantine later: linking emperor and supreme god, legitimising his rule as an expression of god's will and establishing a state religion as the basis of and unifying factor within the state.[48]

After Constantine,[49] the fact that religious questions affected foreign relations put the conflicts between the now Christian Rome and Zoroastrian Persia on a new level.[50] Constantine's promotion of Christianity to the extent that it became the official religion in the Roman Empire affected the Persian attitude towards both the Christians and Rome.[51] The consequences

---

[44] For a partial German translation see Guyot and Klein 1994: 186–9 and 348–9; cf. Schwarte 1994: 203–40 and Kolb 1995: 27–31.

[45] Wiesehöfer 1993: 372–3.

[46] On the goals of Diocletian's religious policy see Kolb 1988: 17–44; 1995: 27–31 and Brandt 1998: 25–6 and 92–101 with further references.

[47] Kolb 1987a and Brandt 1998: 20–1 and 57–101.   [48] Paul 1983: 198.

[49] Girardet 1998: 9–122.   [50] Wiesehöfer 1993: 376–9.

[51] On the history of Christianity in the Sasanian Empire see Asmussen 1983: 924–48; Atiya 1991: 252–6; Schwaigert 1989: 1–11.

for the Christians in the Sasanian Empire were severe as they were declared enemies of the state, Roman auxiliary troops, and soon after were officially persecuted – for political rather than religious reasons.[52]

In turn, the attitude of the Roman emperors towards the Persian Christians was also influenced by the religious policy of Constantine the Great (306–37). In his *Life of Constantine,* the Greek Church father Eusebius of Caesarea (Palestine), who was very close to the emperor,[53] quotes a letter which Constantine wrote to the Sasanian king Šāpūr II (309–79) on behalf of the Christians in the Persian Empire.[54]

Eusebius, Vita Constantini iv.8 and iv.13

(8) When the Persian king also deemed it worthy to win Constantine's friendship through an embassy and sent gifts indicating his desire for friendship and peace, the emperor, too, wanted to form an alliance with him; he surpassed the king, who had obliged him with his honours first, in an exceptional way with his counter gifts.[55] When he found out that the churches of God were numerous among the Persians and that very many communities had joined the herds of Christ, he rejoiced and displayed – as if the common protector of everything – also there his solicitude for all. He will now express this in his own words which he used in a letter to the Persian king, recommending them with utmost diligence and zeal to his care. This letter, which was written by the emperor himself,[56] is circulated among us in Latin but translated into Greek it should be more accessible to the readers.[57] It reads as follows . . .

(13) 'You can imagine with what joy I heard that also many fine areas of Persia are adorned with this group of people, I mean the Christians (for it is on their behalf that I am speaking), just as I desire. May many blessings be granted to you, and in equal amounts blessings to them, as they also belong to you; in this way the almighty Lord will be a father to you, merciful and benevolent. I now commend these to you, because you are so powerful, I place them in your care, because your piety is as eminent. Love them according to your customary humanity; for by this expression of your faith you will procure an immeasurable gratification for yourself and for us.'

[52] Brentjes 1978: 245; on the ambivalent situation of the Christians see Blum 1980: 11–32 and Brock 1982: 1–9 (= 1984: 1–19).

[53] See Barnes 1981 and Winkelmann 1991.

[54] On this letter see Dörries 1954: 125–7; Vivian 1987 and Girardet 1998: 75–6.

[55] The embassy referred to by Eusebius dates to the year 324, that is after Constantine had defeated Licinius and become the sole ruler of the empire; it would appear that soon after (around 325) Constantine approached Šāpūr II; on the dating of the letter (324, 325 or 327) see DeDecker 1979: 100; Barnes 1985: 131; Vivian 1987: 87–129.

[56] For Warmington 1986: 94 this letter is the only 'surviving verbatim example of an imperial diplomatic document from a Roman emperor'; in contrast Vivian 1987: 70–7, who questions the authenticity of the letter as being a document composed by Constantine himself.

[57] Greek was the preferred language in the Eastern Roman Empire, also with regard to foreign relations; cf. Balsdon 1979: 135.

Constantine urges Šāpūr to look after the Christians and to become their protector. It is not certain whether the letter – as transmitted by Eusebius – is historical or not. The content, however, is characteristic for Constantine's view of history and of himself as a Christian emperor. Clearly, Eusebius wants to depict Constantine's concern for Christianity as a whole. Such ambitions, however, which included also the Christians in the Sasanian Empire, were to find Šāpūr's disapproval and to evoke opposition.

The Persian War (7) that broke out during the reign of Constantius II (337–61) was accompanied by continuing systematic persecutions of the Christians in Persia. When in 338 after a long unsuccessful siege of Nisibis Šāpūr II had to retreat, persecutions of the Christians began soon after and lasted for forty years.[58] Numerous acts of martyrs from the period after the thirty-first year of the reign of Šāpūr II (= 340/41) have been preserved.[59] The Bishop Mārūtā of Maiperkat was probably the editor of a collection of Syrian martyr texts.[60] At the beginning of the fifth century he was a Byzantine ambassador at the Persian court. In the year 410 he presided over the Synod of Seleucia, which reorganised the Christians in Persia; in the aftermath many relics from the persecutions of Šāpūr II's reign were taken to Seleucia.[61] The acts of the martyrs confirm that after the death of Constantine the Great (337), Šāpūr II began to put pressure on the Christians and to destroy the churches within his realm of power.[62] The following martyrology of Simon, the *metropolitēs* of Seleucia-Ktēsiphōn, deserves special attention.

Martyrologium of Mar Simon, Acta martyrum et sanctorum,
ed. P. Bedjan II 135–6

Let us begin, then, with the history of the persecution and killing of those holy martyrs whose names we have recorded above. In the year 655 of the reign of Alexander, which is the year 296 after the crucifixion of our Lord, that is the year 117 of the reign of the Persians, which is the year 31 of Šāpūr the king, son of Hormizd (= AD 340/41), Šāpūr found an opportunity, after the blessed Constantine emperor of the Romans died, to pick a quarrel with his sons, because they were young, and [so] he was continually going up to raid the land of the Romans.[63] And for this reason he was especially stirring up hatred against the servants of God who were in the territory under his dominion, and he was longing and scheming to find a pretext for the persecution of the faithful. And he contrived a stratagem to crush

---

[58] On Šāpūr's persecutions of the Christians see Schwaigert 1989: 103–75; also Rist 1996: 17–42.
[59] Devos 1966: 213–42; Wiessner 1967 and Vivian 1987: 93–103.
[60] Braun 1915: XII–XIII.   [61] On the synod of 410 see Müller 1969: 227–45.
[62] See Braun 1915: 6.
[63] On the Roman–Sasanian confrontations during the reign of Constantius II see 7.

with a double levy all the Christians who were in the dominion of the Persians. And he wrote an edict from Bēth Hūzāyē to the governors of Bēth Arāmāyē,[64] as follows: 'Immediately you see this our, the gods', commandment in this text of the prescript which we have issued, arrest Simon the chief of the Nazarenes, and do not release him until he has put his seal to a document and agreed upon his life that he will collect and hand over a double poll-tax and a two-fold levy from the whole people of the Nazraye which is in our, the gods', land and lives under our rule. Because we, the gods, have the hardships of war, but they have delights and luxuries, and although they live in our land, they share the doctrine of Caesar our enemy. These things have been written by Šāpūr the king from Bēth Hūzāyē to the governors of Bēth Arāmāyē.' And when the king's edict reached them they arrested the blessed Simon Bar Sabbā'ē, and these words that had been written by the king they read out before him, and they demanded that he carry out these things that had been written.

The passage illustrates that from Šāpūr II's perspective the Christians were a 'Roman advance guard'.[65] Apparently after he had suffered setbacks in the fight against Rome the king had intended to impose higher taxes on the Christians in order to finance the continuing war with the Romans. Here as elsewhere the source emphasises the close bond between the Christians in the Sasanian Empire and their 'fellow believer', the Roman emperor and enemy of the Persian king. From an Eastern perspective this situation entailed the risk of espionage and of transmission of secret information.[66] When Simon refused to comply with the exertion of higher taxes and when the Sasanian king feared a Christian revolt against his rule he initiated systematic persecutions of the Christians in the entire Sasanian Empire.[67]

32: The situation of the Persian Christians during the reign of Yazdgard I (399–420)

Socrates VII.8.1–20

(1) Around this time Christianity also spread in Persia for the following reasons. (2) Between the Romans and Persians frequent embassies constantly take place; varied, however, are the reasons why they constantly send embassies back and forth (3) This necessity then also at the time entailed that Mārūtā, the bishop of Mesopotamia, whom I mentioned briefly earlier, was sent to the Persian king by

[64] Bēt Hūzāyē and Bēt Arāmāyē are geographical names referring to the areas Hūzistān and Assyria.
[65] Wiesehöfer 2001: 202; cf. also 1993: 378.
[66] See Shahbazi 1990: 589 who states, 'In Iran devotion to the Christian faith thus appeared as allegiance to a hostile political power and Šāpūr II regarded such developments as threats to the security of his empire.'
[67] Asmussen 1983: 940.

the Roman emperor. (4) The Persian king found the man very pious and treated him with honour, just as it befitted a man loved by god. (5) This irritated the Magians who had much power over the Persian king; for they feared that he might persuade the king to become a Christian.[68] (6) For with his prayers Mārūtā cured his chronic headache, which the Magians had not been able to treat successfully. (7) The Magians therefore devised a trick; as the Persians worship the fire but the king was used to worshipping the eternal fire in a particular house,[69] they hid a man under the floor at the time when the king used to pray and instructed him to utter that the king had to be expelled because he had committed an impious deed because he thought a Christian priest could be 'god beloved'. (8) When Yazdgard (I) (this was the name of the Persian king) heard this, he wanted to send him away although he much respected him, (9) Mārūtā however, who was indeed a god-beloved man, focused on his prayers, through which he found out about the deceit devised by the Magians. (10) He said to the king, 'Don't be deceived, king. But when you go in and hear the voice you will dig up and find the deceit; for it is not the fire that is speaking but a human device causes this.' (11) The Persian king followed Mārūtā's instructions and went back into the house where the eternal fire was. (12) When he heard the same voice again he gave the order to dig up the ground; and the one who had produced the supposedly divine voice was caught. (13) The king was extremely angry and made the Magians pay for their deed; then he promised Mārūtā that he could build churches where he wanted; this is why Christianity spread among the Persians. (14) At that time Mārūtā left Persia and returned to Constantinople; but soon after he was sent back again in the context of an embassy. (15) Again the Magians thought of tricks in order that the king would not receive the man; they produced some bad odour wherever the king tended to appear. They slandered the followers of Christianity by saying that they caused this. (16) As already before the king had been suspicious of the Magians, he was very keen to find the culprits and again the ones who had caused the bad odour were found among them. (17) This is why again many of them were punished; the king, however, held Mārūtā in even higher esteem. (18) And he loved the Romans and welcomed their friendship; and he nearly converted to Christianity after Mārūtā had passed a further test, together with Ablaas, the bishop of Persia. (19) For by spending their time with fasting and praying, these two drove out a demon that was torturing the king's son. (20) But Yazdgard died before he fully converted to the Christian faith; the throne fell to his son Bahrām (V), during whose reign the peace between Romans and Persians was broken, as I shall report a little later.

The account of the ecclesiastical historian Socrates (c. 380–440) reveals how important the reign of Yazdgard I (399–420) was for the evolution of

[68] At this point and later on in the text (cf. esp. 18–20) Socrates tries to point out the superiority of the Christian faith; it would have been impossible for a Sasanian king to convert to Christianity as the Sasanian ruler was a 'Zoroastrian ruler' *qua* office.

[69] In the Sasanian period there were various types of fires, also one that symbolised the royal rule; on the terms used for individual fires and a possible hierarchy among them see the references in Schippmann 1990: 102; on the 'fire of the king' see Wiesehöfer 2001: 166–7.

Christianity beyond the borders of the Byzantine Empire. Socrates Scholasticus continued the Church History of Eusebius to the year 439; his work includes numerous documents, resolutions of Councils, imperial letters as well as those of bishops and is therefore a reliable source full of important information.[70] In particular, the author emphasises the crucial role of the bishop Mārūtā, who in his role as Roman ambassador contributed much to the good relations between Arcadius and Yazdgard I (**9**).[71]

According to Socrates Yazdgard I gave him permission to build churches wherever he wanted. Mārūtā managed to restore an organised Christian community which had been destroyed by the persecutions of Šāpūr II.[72] His influence was crucial when as a result of the Synod of Seleucia-Ktēsiphōn in the year 410, at which Church officials from the Byzantine Empire also participated, the Persian Church received a new hierarchical organisation and its own ecclesiastical law.[73] This laid the foundations for a separation of the Persian Church from the Christian Church elsewhere. After another Council on Sasanian territory took place in 424, the Persian Church gained permanent independence from the patriarch in Antioch.[74] The successful activities of bishop Mārūtā increased the number of Christians in the Persian Empire considerably. Even members of the Sasanian nobility turned to Christianity.

However, the growing influence of the Christians in the Sasanian Empire provoked opposition, above all by the Zoroastrian Magians. Socrates alludes to religious tensions which eventually led to new persecutions of Christians towards the end of the reign of Yazdgard I (399–420).[75] The Greek ecclesiastical historian and bishop of Cyrrhus, Theodoret, provides us with more detailed information regarding the beginning and the reasons for these persecutions. His *Church History*, which covers the period from 325 to 428 and was completed in 450, is also full of documents and an extremely important source for the religious history in the East during the fourth and fifth centuries.

Theodoret, Historia ecclesiastica v.39.1–6

(1) Around this time the Persian king Yazdgard (I) fought his war against the churches, using the following pretext: there was a certain bishop Abdas, who was virtuous in many respects. With unnecessary zeal this man destroyed a *pyreion*.

---

[70] See Leppin 1996. [71] Frye 1983a: 144; Asmussen 1983: 940 and Sako 1986: 59–61.
[72] On the fate of the Christians in the Sasanian Empire during the fourth and fifth centuries see Hage 1973: 174–87 and Gero 1981.
[73] Sachau 1907: 72–3. [74] On the Council of 424 see Müller 1969: 233 and 1981: 298.
[75] van Rompay 1995: 363–75.

The Persians, however, call their fire sanctuaries '*pyreia*' because they believe that the fire is divine. When the king was informed about the deed by the Magians he sent for Abdas. (2) He scolded him and ordered him to restore the pyreion. Abdas rejected this and said he would do this under no circumstances. The king threatened that he would destroy all churches and eventually actually carried out his threat. For first he had this man of god executed and then he gave instructions to destroy the churches.

(3) I, however, claim that the destruction of the *pyreion* was inappropriate. (4) For when he came to Athens and saw the city adorned with idols the holy apostle did not destroy any altars revered by them but with words he revealed their ignorance and showed them the truth.[76] Nevertheless I quite admire the fact that he did not restore the temple he had destroyed but chose death over doing this and I deem it worthy of the martyr's crown. For worshipping the fire or erecting a sanctuary for it seem to me the same.

(5) From here the storm took its beginning and created the cruellest and wildest waves against those set in their faith. And although it has been thirty years since,[77] the waves are still there because it is rekindled over and over again by the Magians as if rekindled by strong winds. (The Persians call those Magians who worship the elements as divine. I have described their doctrine in another work[78] in which I also responded to their questions.) (6) After the death of his father, Bahrām (V), the son of Yazdgard (I), inherited together with his rule his father's war against the right faith; and when he died he also handed over both of these closely linked to his own son.[79]

According to Theodoret the destruction of a Zoroastrian fire sanctuary by the bishop Abdas triggered the destruction of all churches in the Persian Empire as well as the capture and execution of Christians. It is noteworthy that the author tries to explain the significance of the fire and thus to make the Persian religion more accessible to his Greek audience. He judges the violation of a fire temple as an inappropriate and anachronistic deed. The author's words have to be seen in the context of the pro-Christian attitude displayed by the Persian ruler Yazdgard I over a long period of time. However, Theodoret claims that the bishop's behaviour was used as a pretext by the king in order to take action against the Persian Christians. Moreover, he states that in the end it was the Zoroastrian Magians who were continuously striving for the destruction of the non-Zoroastrian religions.

The latter remark refers to the ambitions of the Zoroastrian clergy and its problematic relationship with the Sasanian kingship, which during the

---

[76] On St Paul's stay in Athens see Acts 17.16.

[77] The persecutions of Christians, which had started around 420 during the reign of Yazdgard I (399–421), thus continued into the last years of the reign of Yazdgard II (439–57).

[78] This work (*ad quaesita Magorum*), which Theodoret mentions repeatedly (*ep.* 82 and 113), has not survived.

[79] This is Yazdgard II.

course of the fifth century became more and more dependent on the wielders of power. It would appear that also in the year 420 Yazdgard I, who because of his long standing tolerance with regard to Christians and Jews received the title 'the Infidel' in the Eastern literature,[80] gave in to the Magians. The persecutions, which began during the reign of Yazdgard continued under the rule of his successor Bahrām V Gōr (420–39). In his ecclesiastical history Theodoret talks about how the Christians were tortured to death.[81] Although in 422 Romans and Persians concluded a peace (19) which guaranteed the freedom to practise one's religion in both empires, the following period saw new persecutions in the Sasanian Empire.[82]

33: Religion and politics during the sixth and seventh centuries

In the sixth and seventh centuries, no less than before, dealing with religious matters formed an important part of Byzantine–Sasanian relations; religion could bear an impact on armed conflicts (15) and was the subject of agreements and treaties between the powers. Menander Protector, who wrote a detailed account of the specific terms of the peace treaty concluded in 562 between the Sasanian king Xusrō I Anōšārvān (531–79) and Justinian (20), finishes his report with agreements that relate to the situation of the Christians in the Persian Empire.

Menander Protector, frg. 6.1 (= FHG IV, frg. 11)

When these issues had been agreed upon and ratified, further agreements were made,[83] namely regarding the Christians in the Persian Empire. They should be allowed to build churches as well as engage in worship without fear, and to sing their hymns of praise without impediment, as it is customary also among us. For they should neither be forced to convert to the religion of the Magians nor to praise the traditional Persian gods against their will. The Christians in turn should not attempt in any way to convert the followers of the Magian religion to our faith. The Christians should be allowed to bury their dead in graves, as it is customary among us.

Apparently this was a separate agreement, which was concluded after all other issues had been agreed upon. The wording at the beginning of the passage suggests that there may have been an independent treaty guaranteeing the Christians the full freedom to practise their religion and to build

---

[80] Nöldeke 1887a: 103.   [81] Thdrt. *HE* v.39.7–24.   [82] Asmussen 1983: 942.

[83] The Greek verb used here is *nomizein*, which in a legal context refers to a usage prescribed by the force of law.

churches.[84] However, any attempts to convert Zoroastrians to the Christian faith were strictly prohibited. Political considerations must have led Xusrō I to consent to these 'Christian rights', which must have been proposed by Justinian.[85] Demographical reasons had been largely responsible already for the early deportations of Christian prisoners to the Sasanian Empire (36).[86] The fact that Xusrō granted these substantial privileges to a religious minority also reflects a tolerant attitude that can be seen elsewhere (37).

As the agreement applied to the situation within the Persian Empire only, it was dealt with separately. However, the number of Christians affected by it must have been considerable. K. Schmidt claims that the passage represents the first ever international regulation concerning the protection of religious minorities.[87] This is impressive but may be due to transmission. In the peace treaty of 422 the Christians in the Persian Empire had been granted the freedom to practise their religion, and the Zoroastrians in turn were guaranteed the same privileges in the Byzantine Empire (19).

As a consequence of the Christological controversies within the Church in the West, the Councils of Ephesus (431) and Chalcedon (451) prompted many Nestorian Christians to take refuge in Persia. These were certainly no longer seen as 'enemies of the state' and not persecuted in the way other Christians had been in the fourth century during the reign of Šāpūr II (309–79) (31). On the contrary, they were perceived as opponents of the Byzantine emperor, who in spite of several attempts had failed to restore the unity of the Church in the Eastern provinces. In the year 428 the new patriarch of Constantinople, Nestorius, supposedly pleaded with the emperor Theodosius, 'Help me destroy the heretics, and I will help you destroy the Persians.'[88]

The tensions between the Nestorians and the monophysites, who were seen as non-loyal subjects of the Sasanian king, could be felt also in Persia. The Syrian author and anti-Chalcedonian bishop of Constantinople, John of Ephesus (c. 507–86), to whom among other works we owe a collection of 58 biographies of contemporary 'holy men and women', records the words of a Nestorian bishop held before the Sasanian king Kavādh I

[84] Güterbock 1906: 93–105.   [85] Guillaumont 1969–70: 41–66.
[86] See also Wiesehöfer 2001: 200–1, who argues that the deportations of numerous Christians by Šāpūr I did not take place for religious but rather for economic and demographical reasons and that the king – although unintentionally – thereby contributed to the spread of Christian ideas and Christian communities in the Persian Empire.
[87] Cf. Schmidt 2002: 131.
[88] Socr. *HE* VII.29.5; see also Greatrex and Lieu 2002: 259 n. 61, 'How much significance should be attached to the patriarch's words is uncertain, however: Socrates at least was critical of his pronouncement . . . and his tenure of office was short.'

(488–97/499–531). In his speech the bishop accused the monophysites in the Sasanian Empire of being traitors because, as he argued, their faith and rites resembled those of their fellow-believers in the Roman Empire. Kavādh I reacted by giving instructions to persecute all orthodox monophysites in his empire.[89] Similarly revealing are the words with which Barsauma,[90] one of the most influential Christians in Persia during the fifth century, addressed king Pērōz (459–84), 'Only if the faith of the Christians in the lands of the Greeks is different will their heart and mind focus on you.'[91] Moreover, the Nestorian Arabic *Chronicle of Se'ert* in its own characteristic way reflects the close relationship between the Persian Christians and the Sasanian monarchy.[92] Not least the fact that the Sasanian rulers made use of Christian bishops as advisors and ambassadors (**35**) illustrates their privileged role at the Persian court.[93]

Xusrō II (590–628), who owed his throne to the Christian emperor Maurice (582–602), once more issued a statement to the Christians in which he allowed them to build churches and permitted anybody with the exception of the Magians to adopt the Christian faith. According to Tabarī he did so by referring to the agreement of the *foedus* of 562. In this context the author also points out that in 562 the Byzantine emperor had promised to treat the Sasanians in the Roman Empire well and to allow them to establish fire sanctuaries.[94] The pro-Christian attitude of Xusrō II[95] is also nicely illustrated through a remarkable episode recorded by the Byzantine historian Theophylact Simocatta:

Theophylact Simocatta v.14.1–10

(1) In the third year,[96] however, he even approached Sergius, a man who had been most active in Persia, that a child by Seirem be given to him. When not much later this had indeed happened for him, he once more fairly rewarded his benefactor with gifts. He dispatched a letter, written in Greek. Word for word, the letter read as follows:

(2) 'To the great martyr Sergius, Xusrō, King of kings. I, Xusrō, King of kings, son of Xusrō, have sent the gifts together with the patten not for men to see, and not in order that from my words the greatness of your most sacred name shall be

---

[89] Joh. Eph. *Lives, PO* 17.142; see also the references in Greatrex and Lieu 2002: 52.
[90] See also above, p. 36 with n. 95.
[91] According to Barhebraeus *Chron. eccl.* III.65.16–7; cf. Wiesehöfer 2001: 296.
[92] See e.g. *PO* VII.2.147.5 (Scher).   [93] See in general Sako 1986 and below, pp. 250–1 (**35**).
[94] Tabarī, tr. Nöldeke, p. 287; Bosworth 314 (1000).
[95] On Xusrō's attitude towards Christianity see McCullough 1982: 157–62; on the situation of the Persian Christians in the sixth and seventh centuries see also Brock 1982: 18–19.
[96] This is the third year after Xusrō II took over the throne, i.e. 27 June 592 to 27 June 593; for a discussion of this dating see Schreiner 1985: 318 nn. 766–7.

known, but because the truth about what has happened has been acknowledged and the many favours and benefactions that I have received from you. For I am lucky that my name may be displayed on your sacred vessels. (3) During my stay at Berthemaïs,[97] I asked from you, holy man, to come to my help and that Seirem conceive a child in her womb. And as Seirem is a Christian and I am pagan, our law does not allow us the freedom to have a Christian wife. (4) I wanted to be considerate to you and because of this I disregarded that law: I held and hold her among my wives every day in legitimacy, and therefore I resolved now to ask your goodness that she conceive a child in her womb. (5) And I asked you and at the same time gave instruction in order that, if Seirem conceived a child in her womb, I would send the cross that she wears to your most holy house. And in order that I and Seirem have this mark for the remembrance of your name, holy man, we hold on to this cross. (6) We have resolved to send instead of the cross its value, which does not extend 4300 *milaresia* staters,[98] 5000 staters. (7) And from when I held this wish within me and was considering this until we got to Rhesonchosron[99] not more than ten days passed, and you, holy man, not because I was worthy but because of your goodness, appeared to me in a vision during the night, and three times you said to me that Seirem had conceived in her womb. (8) And in the same vision I answered you three times, saying, "Good, good." And because of your sanctity and mercy, because of your most holy name, and because you grant what you have been asked for, from that day on Seirem did not experience what is customary for women. (9) I, however, was not in doubt with regard to this but trusted your words because you are holy and truly grant what you have been asked for. When she did not have to bear womanly matters anymore, I learned from this the power of the vision and the truth of what you had said. (10) Immediately I dispatched the same cross and its value to your most holy house, giving order that from its value one patten and one drinking vessel be made for the praise of the divine mysteries, but of course also that a cross, which is owed, be fixed to the revered table, and an incense burner, solid gold, and a Hunnic curtain decorated with gold.'

The fact that Xusrō II married a Christian woman is certainly remarkable. In the later Persian literature this wedding received much attention and became the subject of many later Persian romances.[100] Many sources call Seirem (or Shirin) Greek but she was actually from Khuzistan.[101] Syrian sources even give a detailed description of the wedding ceremony and reveal,

---

[97] Euagrius and the vulgate MSS falsely give the reading Beramaïs; it must be the area of Bēt Arāmāyē in lower Mesopotamia; see Whitby and Whitby 1986: 151 n. 73 and Schreiner 1985: 318–9 n. 770.

[98] 'Stater' is used in the sense of 'coin', whereas 'milaresion' refers to the type of metal, in this case silver coins.

[99] This place has not been identified; Peeters 1947: 31–2 suggests upper Mesopotamia, a town close to Dārā.

[100] Bosworth 1999: 312 n. 729.

[101] Christensen 1944: 475–6; Bosworth 1999: 312 n. 729 refers to the authority of the *Anonymus Guidi*, who claims that she was of Aramaean origin, from the district around what was later al-Basrah; on the author see below.

for example, that bishops and clergy formed part of her train; moreover, Xusrō built for her places of worship dedicated to St Sergius and Mary, the mother of Jesus.[102] We find the most elaborate account regarding Seirem in the so called *Chronicle of Guidi*, which was composed in Syriac in the 660s. This is the anonymous work of a Nestorian author, who probably wrote in Khuzistan (hence it is also called *Khuzistan Chronicle*). After the historiography of Theophylact Simocatta there are few reliable sources that describe the events along the Eastern frontier of the Byzantine Empire. A source such as the *Chronicle of Guidi*, which dates from a period very close to the end of the Sasanian Empire, is therefore extremely valuable.[103] The text shows that Seirem was also a political factor and personally exerted influence on the appointment of the catholicos Gregorius (605–9).[104] Most likely, the marriage between Xusrō and Seirem did not meet with approval by the Zoroastrian nobility. Theophylact Simocatta seems to allude to this when, in an earlier passage, he mentions that the king debased the customs of the Babylonians when he slept with the Christian Seirem.[105] In our passage, the author explicitly states that such a marriage was against the Sasanian laws. Nevertheless Xusrō II chose St Sergius to sanction his plans and rewarded him generously. Just as Theophylact Simocatta does, many other sources attest to the king's benefactions to the shrine of Saint Sergius.[106]

Aside from the Seirem episode, the Persian king's affinity to Christianity surfaces in further Western as well as Eastern sources. According to these the patriarch of Antioch, Anastasius, consecrated three churches that had been built upon the Sasanian ruler's initiative.[107] Xusrō is said even to have worshipped Christian relics. According to Theophylact Simocatta when the Roman ambassador Probus, bishop of Chalcedon, was dispatched to Ktēsiphōn the king summoned him to the palace and asked to see the image of the Mother of God.[108] As the bishop carried a representation with him, he allowed the king to take a look at it. Xusrō knelt in front of the panel and claimed that the figure represented on it had appeared to him and told him that she was granting him the victories of Alexander of Macedon.[109]

---

[102] Cf. ibid.
[103] Guidi 1903; for an English translation of the first part, which covers the period between the death of Hormizd IV in the year 590 and the end of the Sasanian Empire, see Greatrex and Lieu 2002: 229–37; on the dating of this text see Hoyland 1997: 182–5.
[104] See the references in Greatrex and Lieu 2002: 317 n. 55.
[105] Theoph. Simoc. v.13.7.   [106] See the references in Greatrex and Lieu 2002: 176–8.
[107] Flusin 1992: 101–2.
[108] The incident once more attests to the important function of bishops as diplomats in late antiquity (see **35** below).
[109] Cf. Theoph. Simoc. v.15.9–10.

However, the claim that Xusrō II himself converted to Christianity[110] is not supported by any evidence.[111] The remarkable privileges enjoyed by the Christians in this later phase confirm the earlier and consistently favourable situation of the Persian Christians during the first phase of Xusrō's reign. They are, of course, also a consequence of his good relationship with the Byzantine emperor Maurice, who according to Tabarī even gave his consent to a marriage between the Persian king and his daughter Mary.[112] It is highly doubtful that such a wedding ever took place, and for good reasons most scholars question Tabarī's account on this point.[113] It rather looks as if the many references to a union between Mary and Xusrō are an expression of literary fiction based on the marriage between Xusrō and the Christian Shirin.[114]

Ultimately, the rift between the Persian Christians and the Byzantine Church had paved the way for the advantageous situation of the former in the Persian Empire. Difficulties arose only when from the end of the sixth century onwards conflicts with other theological movements, above all with the Monophysites,[115] arose for the Nestorians and threatened their position in the Sasanian Empire. This was aggravated by the last and long lasting military confrontation between West and East during the reigns of Heraclius (610–42) and Xusrō II Parvēz (15). At this point the religious antithesis between a Christian Byzantium and a Zoroastrian Persia surfaced again and bore an impact on the military conflict. When in the year 614 the Sasanian commander Romiuzan besieged Jerusalem, one of his main goals was – according to Tabarī – to capture the Holy Cross and to transport it to Ktēsiphōn:

Tabarī, Ta'rīh 1 1002

He reached the city of Jerusalem and captured its bishop, and whatever priests and other Christians were there because of the wooden cross, which had been placed in a golden chest and buried in a garden with a vegetable plot sown on top of it. He harangued them until they brought him to its location. He dug it up with his (own) hand, took it out and sent it to Xusrō in the 24th year of his reign.

---

[110] Tabarī, tr. Nöldeke, 287 n. 2; Bosworth 314 (1000); also Shahbazi 1990: 592.
[111] Shahbazi 1990: 591 states, 'It is certain, however, that any attempt to convert Persia to Christianity would have run counter to deeply rooted popular sentiment.'
[112] Tabarī, *Ta'rīh* 1 994; tr. Nöldeke 283; Bosworth 305; cf. also Tabarī, *Ta'rīh* 1 999; Bosworth 311–12.
[113] See e.g. Garsoïan 1983: 579.
[114] Goubert 1951: 179–82; *PLRE* III s.v. Maria (6) and Bosworth 312 n. 729; Greatrex and Lieu 2002: 315 n. 21 claim that 'the later oriental tradition transformed Mary into a daughter of Maurice'.
[115] See Frend 1979: on Xusrō II's attitude towards monophysitism see Spuler 1961: 192 and Asmussen 1983: 946–7.

Tabarī's dramatic account makes it easy to imagine how the return and resurrection of the cross in the spring of 630 was celebrated as a great triumph.[116] During the advance of the Islamic Arabs, which led to the fall of the Sasanian Empire, the Persian Christians fought alongside the conquerors. It is possible that they felt their religion had greater affinity to that of the Arab tribes than to the religion of the Zoroastrian Sasanian kings,[117] from whose tolerant attitude they had benefited for centuries.

[116] See the references on p. 49.   [117] See Wiesehöfer 2001: 204–5.

CHAPTER 8

Emperor and 'King of kings'

34: Concepts of 'legitimate rule' and the 'family of kings'[1]

Although the military confrontations between Rome and Persia continued over centuries and their ideological differences were irreconcilable, it is evident that both 'world powers' from early on acknowledged the other's claims to being of equal rank. In particular the relationship between the individual rulers and the way they treated each other are good indications for this. Examining this relationship allows us to gain insight not only into the state of diplomatic relations and the political balance of power but also into the degree of mutual respect that existed between the two rulers at a given point.[2] In this context one should pay special attention to two fundamental ideas, namely the legitimacy of the ruler's status and the notion of a 'family of kings'. Ammianus Marcellinus records an exchange of letters between Constantius II (337–61) and Šāpūr II (309–79), which clearly reveals that the two perceived each other's rank as equal to their own. The Sasanian king addresses the emperor with the following words:

Ammianus Marcellinus XVII.5.3 and 10

(3) 'I, King of kings, Šāpūr, comrade of the stars, brother of the Sun and the Moon,[3] am sending many greetings to my brother, the Caesar Constantius.'[4]

The emperor's response begins as follows:

(10) 'I, Constantius, victor by land and by sea, always *Augustus*, am sending many greetings to my brother, King Šāpūr.'

By the middle of the fourth century war between Rome and Persia had been going on for quite some time without substantial gains on either

---

[1] For a detailed discussion of this theme see Winter 1989a: 72–92.
[2] On the representation in the Byzantine authors see Diebler 1995: 187–217.
[3] On the Persian king as ruler of the stars see Widengren 1976: 231.
[4] Cf. Syme 1968: 41.

side (7).[5] In the year 356 peace negotiations had begun. In their written exchange, both Constantius II and Šāpūr II tried to set out their conditions for peace. Given how tense relations between Rome and Persia were during this period, the way the two rulers address each other is remarkable.

Both kings explicitly place the other on an equal level and clearly show mutual respect. The idea of a 'brotherhood of kings' was far more than a stereotypical formula used to comply with the diplomatic protocol. The two rulers shared the idea that as rulers of their empires – brother of the sun and the moon[6] – they partook in cosmic occurrences and therefore possessed an aura that removed them from life on earth.[7] As a concept, the notion of a 'family of kings' existed throughout the history of Roman–Sasanian relations (9). West and East agreed on this notion, which contributed to a mutual acknowledgement of the other's sovereignty and compliance with an emerging international law. However, this did not reduce concrete political conflicts between the two; in the same letter Šāpūr demanded that the Romans return Armenia and Mesopotamia, conditions that were unacceptable for Constantius II.[8]

The modern observer may not be surprised to see Rome on an equal footing with the Sasanian Empire and the emperor equal to the 'King of kings' but was this true from both perspectives; that is, did the West acknowledge the Eastern Empire and its ruler accordingly? In this context it is crucial to examine whether the legitimacy of the emperor's rule and the corresponding legitimacy of the Persian king's rule – postulated and acknowledged in West and East – could be used to establish something like a 'brotherhood' between the two. The notion of a 'legitimacy of rule' was paramount for the Sasanian monarchy.[9] Already in the context of the foundation of the Sasanian Empire the theme has a special place. The legend, as it was told in the so called *Book of Deeds of Ardašīr*, a sixth-century work that was composed in the Middle Persian language, reflects a late attempt to legitimise the rule of the Sasanians in Iran.[10] The following summary may suffice.[11]

The last Parthian king, Artabanos IV (213–24) invited Ardašīr to his court to be educated there. One day a young girl, who was favoured by

---

[5] On the military conflicts during this period see above, pp. 88–90.
[6] Cf. Malal. 18. 19–20 (p. 449) for a letter by Kavādh I in which he addresses the Byzantine emperor Justinian with similar words.
[7] On Sasanian kingship in general see Wiesehöfer 2001: 176.
[8] See 7 above.   [9] Sundermann 1963.
[10] On the *Kārnāmak i Artaxēr i Papakan* (Book of Deeds of Ardašīr, son of Papak) see Nöldeke 1878: 22–69; DeMenasce 1983: 1187–8 and Yarszhater 1983b: 379–8.
[11] For the following cf. the German translation of the text in Nöldeke 1878: 35–47.

Artabanos, revealed a secret to Ardašīr. According to her words, the wise men and astrologers had warned Artabanos that a new king would rule and that someone who would take flight within the next three days would acquire greatness, power and victory over Artabanos. Upon hearing this Ardašīr took flight together with the girl. Immediately Artabanos and his men pursued them. Travellers told Artabanos on his way that a ram would follow Ardašīr. When he asked his chief Magian how to interpret this, the latter responded, 'This is the majesty of rule; it has not reached him yet but we have to rush. It is possible that we will be able to get hold of him before it will have reached him.' On the following day Artabanos and his horsemen were informed by a caravan that they had seen someone on horseback together with a ram. Now the chief Magian told Artabanos, 'May you be immortal. The majesty . . . has reached Ardašīr; there is no way to get hold of him now.' After that Artabanos turned back and sent out a large army to march against Ardašīr. After extensive fighting Ardašīr, who possessed 'the radiance of the royal majesty', was victorious and killed Artabanos.

The 'radiance of the royal majesty', the *xvarna*,[12] which in this case was symbolised by the ram, is thus closely linked with the royal family. Apparently, only the one who was able to get hold of the *xvarna*, who literally possessed this 'royal radiance', was called to be king. It becomes clear that the question of legitimacy was central to the confrontations with the last Arsacid ruler, Artabanos IV. Possession of the 'unreal' *xvarna* gave entitlement to kingship and also provided the factual power to aquire the throne. Moreover, there were certain prerequisites for a legitimate rule, namely to be a descendant of the Sasanian dynasty and to enjoy a special relationship with the supreme god. Several rock-cut reliefs depict Ardašīr's investiture as 'King of kings' by Ahura Mazda, the supreme Zoroastrian god.[13]

On the rock-cut relief at Firuzabad Ardašīr I is reaching for a diadem, which Ahura Mazda is handing to him as a symbol of his power (fig. 17). The gesture indicates that rule is transferred from the god to the king. Ardašīr's inscriptions also reveal a desire to legitimise his rule by divine approval. In a trilingual inscription from Naqš-i Rustam we read, 'This is the image of his Zoroastrian majesty, Ardašīr, the King of kings of Eran, whose descent is from the gods, the son of his majesty, the king Papak.'[14] 'Ardašīr's efforts to present himself as a god-related and devout Mazda-worshipper, and as the possessor of the divinely given *xvarrah*, his claim to legitimacy as a worthy scion of the Iranian (mythical) kings, his successful propaganda against the rightfulness of the Parthians and their proper place in the sequence of

[12] On the motif of the *xvarna* (*xvarrah*) and its importance for the Sasanian monarchy see Wiesehöfer 2001: 176.
[13] On the rock-reliefs of Ardašīr see Girshman 1962: 122–34.   [14] Translation Huyse.

Fig. 17 Rock relief at Naqš-i Rustam representing the investiture of Ardašīr I
(Ghirshman, R. (1962) *Iran. Parthians and Sassanians*: fig. 168)
(Photo: Roman Ghirshman)

Iranian history, prove the importance of the Achaemenid legacy to the mind of the early Sasanians.[15] Examining the late phase of Roman–Sasanian relations reveals how much the notion of the legitimacy of royal rule influenced the relationship between the states in general and patterns of behaviour between the emperor and the 'King of kings' in particular.

Towards the end of the reign of Hormizd IV (579–90) the Sasanian Empire was in a difficult position, with regard to both internal and foreign affairs.[16] Above all, the Turkish Hephthalites posed a serious threat along the Eastern frontier of the empire.[17] The Sasanians owed it to the support of the powerful general Bahrām Čōbīn that in the spring of 589 the Western Turks suffered a decisive defeat and became tributary allies.[18] When shortly afterwards, Persia faced a period of political unrest, Bahrām Čōbīn decided to revolt. Hormizd IV was imprisoned and his son Xusrō II Pārvēz was enthroned in February of 590.[19] The deposed king Hormizd was given a last opportunity to speak before the highest officials of the empire. According to the Byzantine historian Theophylact Simocatta he addressed them with the following words:

Theophylact Simocatta IV.4.7–13

(7) But I see also that the glory of my ancestors is bespattered today by the unholy acts that you have committed against me, ancestors who should have been honoured like immortals because of the godlike guard that is kept over their descendants every day. (8) Although among you the law of nature has been overthrown and laws of the state have been erased, the order of the monarchy has been trampled down, the presidency of justice has disappeared and vengeance for suffered violence is gone, I shall not forget good royal behaviour but shall tell you out of benevolence towards the existence of the dynasty what will be beneficial for the Persian state. (9) Satraps and all of you gathered around this royal place, develop a common strategy against the rebellion, and do not tolerate that a monarchy that is proud and extremely powerful, old and very awesome to those inhabiting the world, continues to be insulted. (10) Otherwise, you will destroy a great empire and will turn over the starting point of many victories, cast down the peak of highest glory and tear up a monarchy that is most resilient, and as a consequence you Persians will be deprived of your fortune, once power has been taken away from you and the laws of the monarchy have been made invalid because of the rebellion. (11) For revolt is the precursor of disorder, and disorder equals anarchy, and anarchy, which takes its

---

[15] Wiesehöfer 1986a: 376; on the royal image in the Sasanian period see Abka'i-Khavari 2000.
[16] See Frye 1983a: 162–4.   [17] See Bivar 1983a: 215.
[18] On Bahrām Čōbīn see Shahbazi 1989: 519–22.
[19] For the relevant testimonies see Greatrex and Lieu 2002: 172–4; see also Whitby 1988: 292–6; Frendo 1989: 77–88; on the controversial chronology regarding the beginning of Xusrō II's reign see Higgins 1939: 51–2; 1955: 97, who dates Xusrō II's crowning to 15 February 590.

origin from rebellion, is the start of dissolution[20] ... (13) If, therefore, you do not scatter the rebels you will lead the monarchy into servitude, and you will be a plaything for the nations ...

Above all, Hormizd criticises the fact that the Sasanian monarchy has not been treated with the deserved respect. The aspects emphasised in the speech, namely 'the order of the monarchy', 'the royal laws' and especially the concern 'for the existence of the dynasty', illustrate how crucial the legitimacy of the future king and the continuity of monarchical rule were in the eyes of contemporary historians. However, his words did not save Hormizd – he was assassinated.[21]

Attempts by the legitimate successor of Hormizd IV, Xusrō II Pārvēz, to come to an agreement with Bahrām Čōbīn failed, and on 9 March 590 the latter became the new Sasanian king Bahrām VI Čōbīn. Never before in the history of the Sasanian Empire had anyone but members of the Sasanian dynasty held the throne. Given his lack of power at the time, Xusrō II had to take flight and to seek help from the Byzantine emperor Maurice. Both Xusrō and Bahrām Čōbīn were willing to cede large territories to Byzantium in turn for support. The Byzantine reaction to these offers and the emperor's final response illuminate the relations between the empires, in particular between the two rulers. The decision was by no means unanimous but rather accompanied by vivid confrontations.[22] In the eyes of the Senate it was Maurice's duty to prioritise the interests of his own empire. Accordingly, it would have been best to leave the Sasanian Empire to its own devices rather than to restore ordered rule. This seemed to be the long awaited opportunity to defeat the main enemy along the Eastern frontier of the empire. Although the public shared this view, Maurice decided to support Xusrō II in his attempts to regain the Sasanian throne. His decision is even more remarkable if we consider that it entailed new military confrontations rather than peace along the eastern frontier of the empire and that Roman soldiers fought alongside the Sasanian 'arch enemy'. Once more a letter recorded by Theophylact Simocatta helps us to better understand the situation. In a rather humble fashion, Xusrō II turns to the Byzantine emperor:

---

[20] On this 'dissolution of the state' see the remarkable parallel in Plato *Leg.* 945c; for a detailed interpretation of this passage see Kaegi 1981b: 132–3.

[21] Cf. Whitby 1988: 294–5.

[22] This conflict within Byzantine leadership is not mentioned in the Greek sources but – along with the typical poetic elaboration – it is indeed reflected in the Eastern sources; cf. Firdausi tr. Mohl, vol. 7, 109–39; according to Theoph. Simoc. IV.14.1 Xusrō II immediately received military support from Byzantium; in fact, however, the king had to wait for the requested aid for several months; cf. Higgins 1941: 310 n. 88.

Theophylact Simocatta IV.II.2–II

(2) God saw to it that the whole world would be lit up from above and from the beginning by two eyes, namely by the most powerful Roman Empire and by the wisest rulers of the Persian state. (3) For by these greatest powers the disobedient and bellicose nations are winnowed, and man's way of life is well ordered and always guided.[23] . . . (5) And just in these days the most destructive demons have come upon the Persian state and have effected awful things: they have led slaves into war against their masters, subjects against their kings, disorder against order, what is not appropriate against what is decent, and they have abundantly furnished all enemies of goodness with weapons . . . (6) For Bahrām, the most disgusting slave, who was hailed by our ancestors and was conspicuous, and who has not lived up to the greatness of his fame, has skipped away towards destruction; having wooed kingship for himself, he has disturbed the whole Persian state, and he does and endeavours everything in order that he may extinguish the great eye of power, (7) and that then the uncivilised and evil-doing nations may acquire licence and power against the most peaceful Persian kingdom, then finally in the course of time also irrepressible force over your tributary nations – and this a force that does not come without a lot of brutal outrage.[24] (8) It is thus appropriate for your peaceful providence to extend a saving hand to a kingdom infested by robbers and tortured by tyrants, to support a power that is in the process of being destroyed, and to construct in the Roman state the motives for salvation, as if universal trophies, and to announce yourselves the founders, saviours and physicians of the Persian state. (9) For the most powerful kings always have to put into practice all that pertains to justice . . . and be an example that it is not allowed to arm slaves against their masters . . . (11) May the angels of God, who grant the good things, preserve your kingdom irreproachable and free from tyrants.

Once more Xusrō's words are based on the idea that both states were equals,[25] and that this equality also applied to the Persian king[26] – his own legitimate rule – and the Roman emperor. Only if the 'most powerful kings' showed joint responsibility for their rule, the 'good order' would be

---

[23] For comparison see Petr. Patric. frg. 13, who records the words of the Persian ambassador Apharbān before the Roman Caesar Galerius, 'It is obvious for all mankind that the Roman and the Persian Empires are just like two lamps; and it is necessary that, like eyes, the one is brightened by the light of the other and that they do not angrily strive for each other's destruction. For this is not held as a virtue but rather levity or weakness. As they believe that later generations will not be able to help them they make an effort to destroy their opponents'; see above **17**.

[24] At this point the king includes a clear reminder that the Sasanians contributed significantly to the protection of the borders against the tribes attacking from the north and via the Caucasus; the stability of the region was as crucial for Byzantium; cf. **27**.

[25] Contemporary authors always acknowledged the Sasanian Empire as a '*politeia*'; relations were based on the experience of a 'Realpolitik', which meant that (East) Rome regarded the Eastern power as its equal; cf. Schreiner 1983: 301–6.

[26] In contrast, contemporary literature displays a strong suspicion against the Persians as a people and against the Sasanian king; cf. e.g. Theoph. Simoc. IV.13.1; from Theophylact Simocatta's perspective, which was influenced by the long confrontation between Heraclius and Xusrō II, a relationship of mutual trust seems to have been impossible; see also Whitby 1988: 294–5.

preserved. 'Chosroes believes that both Empires are of divine right, designed by eternal providence for protection of civilization and foreseen in its plan as the lights in the firmament.'[27] At the end of his letter, Xusrō calls himself the son of the emperor[28] and thereby tries to evoke the concept of the 'family of kings' as well as to take advantage of the good personal relationship between the rulers of both empires. Although a 'fictive' father-son relationship may suggest a difference in status, the possibility of this diplomatic gesture implies an equal rank between the two rulers. It is remarkable that Maurice does not fail to pick up on Xusrō's preferred 'scenario' and in a subsequent letter also addresses the king as his son.[29]

After he had sent the letter to Maurice, Xusrō also dispatched ambassadors with specific proposals for the negotiations. Again the ambassadors appealed to the emperor's disposition towards solidarity with the king as the legitimate Persian ruler. They acknowledged that through the design of the rebel Bahrām Čōbīn the great Persian Empire was close to its downfall but argued that the Romans would display a lack of sense if they wished this to happen.[30] They continued their speech with the following explanation:

Theophylact Simocatta IV.13.7–21

(7) For one power alone is not able to shoulder the immense burden of taking care of the organisation of the universe and one man's pulse is not able to steer everything created under the sun. (8) For unlike the oneness of the divine and first rule it is not ever within us to take the earth, which is in a state opposed to that of the order above, steered here and there towards the unstable by human beings who by nature are in a state of flux, and whose views are most useless because of their convergence towards the worse . . . (13) What luck would it then bring to the Romans, if the Persians are deprived of their power and hand over their rule to another tribe? What mark of honour would the Romans acquire for themselves, if they reject as suppliant a king who is the most illustrious and bravest of all kings on earth? . . . (15) How will you accomplish anything more worthy of a king than this during your entire time of your rule? . . . (20) We have learnt that the usurper has also sent ambassadors to you, asking to have as a partner the one who has not committed any fault and cleverly devising all but that a ruler together with a fugitive slave carry out a revolution. What could be more inglorious and more abominable than this for the Romans? (21) What kind of foundation of your trust will he sustain for his promises, a man who has principles of greatest unfairness and who has mobilised a force against his benefactors, who endorses every kind of evil-doing in order that he may deprive of his monarchy a ruler who has not committed any injustice?

---

[27] Higgins 1941: 309.
[28] Theoph. Simoc. IV.11.11; according to Theoph. *Chron.* A.M. 6081 (p. 266, 13, ed. De Boor) Xusrō II had been adopted by Maurice.
[29] Theoph. Simoc. V.3.11; see also Theoph. 266.13.   [30] Theoph. Simoc. IV.13.5–6.

M. Whitby summarises the ambassadors' appeal as 'a rhetorical expansion of the themes of Chosroe's letter (IV II)'.[31] Apparently the rhetoric worked: the emperor granted Xusrō II the requested support and declared war on Bahrām. The reasoning behind the decision is revealing:

Theophylact Simocatta IV.14.2

... because the emperor thought it unworthy of Latin rule to provide arms for criminals and to brave danger for what was not good just because of the number of promises, and that the Romans would follow the most shameful principle and be branded with immortal blame for ever.

It was thus the idea of legitimate rule that led Maurice to support whom he saw as the lawful leader against a rebel who had claimed the throne on false grounds. The emperor must have been confident that his principles would have applied also to his own rule as the legitimate heir of the Justinian dynasty. In the spring of 591 Xusrō II mustered Byzantine troops and embarked on a campaign against Bahrām Čōbīn.[32] The subsequent military confrontations in the Sasanian Empire led to the fall of Bahrām Čōbīn, who fled to the court of the Turkish Khagan where he was assassinated shortly after.[33] The legitimate Sasanian ruler was restored to the throne and a formal peace was finally concluded between Rome and Persia, who had been at war since 572.[34]

During the following years Maurice and Xusrō II appear much more committed to each other than they would have been through the peace agreements alone. The close personal relations between the two rulers outlived the short phase of the united campaign against the rebel on the Persian throne, and the ideological consequences are striking. 'Previous to 590, Rome claimed exclusive dominance of the earth; thenceforth she agreed to divide the world into two equal shares. She reserved the West for herself, the East she assigned to Persia. Her eternal enemy was to become her eternal friend, each with a distinctive outlook on life, each with a peculiar culture and civilization.'[35] This situation, however, was as fragile as the life of each of the two rulers.

When in the year 602 Maurice was assassinated by Phocas, Xusrō II went to war against Byzantium. His decision corresponds with his close bond to his former benefactor Maurice and shows remarkable parallels with the

---

[31] Whitby 1988: 121 n. 50.
[32] On the joining of Roman and Persian troops and the decisive battle at Ganzaka see Theoph. Sim. V.11–12; on the date of the battle see Higgins 1939: 53–4.
[33] On the events in the Sasanian Empire, the flight and end of Bahrām Čōbīn see Christensen 1944: 445.
[34] On the peace of 591 see Greatrex and Lieu 2002: 174–5.   [35] Higgins 1941: 314–15.

events of the years 590/91. According to Tabarī Xusrō II became extremely angry when it was reported to him how the Romans had betrayed Maurice and killed him. He received Maurice's son, who had fled to him, crowned him and declared him the new monarch of the Romans.[36] Theophylact Simocatta explicitly states that for Xusrō Phocas' usurpation dissolved the good relationship between Romans and Persians and triggered war.[37] From a king's perspective, just as the monarchy in the Sasanian Empire had been threatened in 590/91 by a usurper, Phocas' activities and reign of terror in 602 questioned the imperial rule and asked for solidarity between legitimate rulers. Xusrō's decision to go to war against Phocas triggered the last great confrontation between Romans and Persians (**15**).

There is no doubt that until its downfall the Sasanian Empire remained the *natio molestissima* for Rome – which ultimately had to be destroyed.[38] One of the main reasons for this was the fact that the Sasanians rejected Rome's claim for universal rule.[39] However, a Sasanian 'King of kings' could be acknowledged and respected by a Roman emperor as a much honoured equal, and this status was not threatened by the universal claims of the world power Rome. The West and the East shared a basic consensus regarding a legitimacy of rule, and this not only manifested itself as a strong ideology of rule but could turn into 'Realpolitik' – certainly carrying force as a political argument. Ultimately this consensus therefore facilitated the emergence of an international law binding sovereign states on the basis of principles that are still applied today.

---

[36] Tabarī, tr. Nöldeke 290; Bosworth 317 (1002).

[37] However, at the very end of his work Theoph. Simoc. (VIII.15.7) states as explicitly that the events in Byzantium were merely a pretext for Xusrō II in order to open war against the West; cf. Garsoïan 1983: 578 and Blockley 1985a: 74.

[38] Amm. XXIII.5.19.   [39] See the commentary on **1** and **2**.

CHAPTER 9

Exchange of information between West and East

Between neighbours and rivals there were plenty of opportunities to learn about the political strategies and customs of the other.[1] In this context, it must be emphasised that a transfer of technology and a curiosity with regard to the foreign culture can be observed in both directions. Scholarly literature often refers to a 'difference in the degree of civilisation' between West and East – this is not justified. The title of this chapter has therefore been chosen deliberately in order to stress an 'exchange' rather than a one-sided process. To give but one example: on many occasions the Sasanian Empire functioned as a mediator of cultural possessions from the Far East and India, which were eagerly received by the West.

The opportunity for exchange was not limited to the official political and administrative realms. It can be observed in particular with regard to the border regions (map 14), namely Mesopotamia and Armenia or border cities such as Dārā, Amida and Nisibis, where a frequent change of rule took place. 'Enmity did not isolate the two empires from each other ... A common language ... and identical customs prevailed on either side of the frontier, linking together related populations split asunder by political accidents.'[2] In particular the geographic conditions in Armenia and Mesopotamia as well as to the west and south-west of the Euphrates, where the Syrian Desert formed the actual border between the great powers, prevented any strict control of this part of the frontier. Vast mountain ranges or wide plains, which were rather an impediment for close communication, and also the rivers Tigris and Euphrates formed natural borders, which during the course of the centuries also marked the political borders between West and East. However, in spite of many attempts to regulate these, there were numerous contacts between the populations of the border areas. Moreover,

---

[1] For a general survey of Byzantine–Iranian relations providing the background for this chapter see Shahbazi 1990: 588–99; on the 'diffusion of ideas' through various channels see Matthews 1989b: 29–49.
[2] Garsoïan 1983: 569–70.

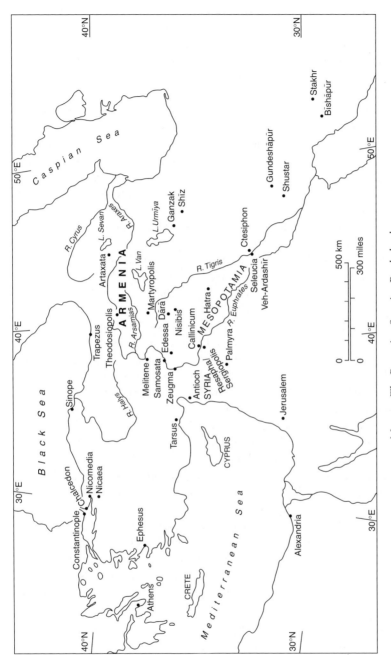

Map 14: The Byzantine-Sasanian Borderlands

the course of the two major rivers and their many branches provided good opportunities for tradesmen and travellers to cover even long distances.[3]

Because of the character of the landscape, also marked by the ethnic and linguistic diversity of its inhabitants, the outer frontier of the Eastern part of the Roman Empire cannot be compared to the strong and continuous fortification of the 'limes' to the north and west of the Roman Empire. Recent scholarship has correctly pointed to the special character and permeability of this part of the Roman frontier, which is rather a supervised military zone with a mixed population on both sides and a Romanised upper class contrasted by nomadic as well as settled inhabitants. It is argued that this peculiar make up of the border region always showed an 'open' character and that no ruler would have been in the position to disrupt or interdict underlying continuities.[4]

With regard to trade relations between the two powers, it has become clear that there was a close link between aspects of trade and security, which can be observed already for the year 298.[5] Both states made efforts to control the flow of goods but rather than being guided by financial reasoning – such as aiming at higher customs duties – they sought to protect an often 'invisible' border along the Mesopotamian–Syrian limes. Unfortunately, the unsatisfactory archaeological exploration of important fortifications as well as the ancient infrastructure in this region does not allow us to further strengthen this argument. In spite of several recent and excellent surveys of the history and culture of the Roman Near East it remains true that among the provinces of the Roman Empire Mesopotamia and Osrhoene are the least explored and documented provinces. No excavations with the specific aim of illuminating the Hellenistic and Roman periods have taken place in the most important cities such as Edessa, Amida, Carrhae or Nisibis. Nor do we know nearly enough about the Roman border fortresses or the road system. The barren landscape, the climatic conditions and the political situation of the past decades have prevented any closer examination of this area, and this represents a major desideratum. Recent surveys and archaeological studies in northern Syria and Mesopotamia as well as along the Roman Tigris, often initiated in response to threats posed by the construction of dams, have revealed the wide insight gained by a continuation of the work. A better knowledge of the genesis and structure of settlements, of road systems and their use in late antiquity would also throw light on many

[3] Cf. Millar 1998a: 119–37; for the importance of this aspect with regard to trade see also **28**.
[4] Whittaker 1994: 99–101 and von Wickevoort Crommelin 1998: 272–3.
[5] See above, **28**.

questions regarding Roman and Sasanian policies along the Euphrates and Tigris.

However, there is no doubt that it was precisely these areas where exchange took place or was initiated, be it through official channels and diplomatic activities or through other modes of interaction between the two cultures. In what follows we want to examine how and via which channels the observed exchange of information took place. Which groups were able to gain from such communication, which ideas and attitudes were transmitted, and, not least, who were the carriers of information relating to the opponent? Undoubtedly, diplomatic exchange, to which we have already repeatedly referred, features prominently when it comes to the transmission of detailed knowledge about the neighbour.[6]

35: Diplomacy and espionage

Constantinus Porphyrogenitus, De ceremoniis aulae byzantinae 89–90
(Reiske pp. 398–410)

(89) What needs to be observed when a great ambassador of the Persians arrives.

It is necessary that when a great ambassador is announced, the *magister* sends to the border area an illustrious magistrate or *silentarius* or tribune or also one of the notables or *magistriani*, or he may send whomever he resolves worthy of the arriving person, in order that he receives him and guides him safely through Roman territory. The one who is sent gets [p. 399] to Nisibis, and he greets him, and if he has a letter of the emperor, he hands it over to him, (if not, one by the *magister*), and he urges him to come in. Possibly the *magister* does not write either, but the invitation arises solely through the *mandata*, to the effect that he come with good spirit and in good health. And he goes out with him. It is necessary that the magistrates of Dārā meet him together with their soldiers in the border area and that they receive the ambassador and his men. And if there is something that needs to be talked about at the border, it is talked about, because the magistrate from Nisibis is accompanying him together with a Persian force as far as the border. If there are no talks, it is still by all means necessary that he accompanies him together with a force and that whereas the Romans receive him and those with him, the other Persians remain on Persian territory, and that he alone with his retinue gets to Dārā and be attended to. It is the duty of the magistrates of Dārā to show much alertness and foresight so that the Persian force does not come along by some pretext of the ambassador, and in turn follows him and captures the city by ruse. But the magistrates must give much thought to this force [p. 400] and must be secretly watchful and prevent such scheme. As is customary, the *ducici*[7]

---

[6] See Blockley 1980: 89–100; Sako 1986; Lee 1986: 455–61 and 1993a: 166–84; Scott 1992: 159–66.

[7] Reiske's Latin translation explains this term as '*homines ad officium ducum illorum thematum, per quae traiectus fit, pertinentes*' (p. 400).

cover the expense of the journey here for up to 103 days. For this many days have always been determined as sufficient for an ambassador making his way up [to Constantinople], and as many for his return. It happens that he is slow on his way, and the emperor gives instructions to the effect that he is given a supplement. The record of what has been given to him is kept in the *scrinium* of the barbarians.[8] And according to the agreements that were concluded when Constantine became praetorian prefect five horses were assigned to him, and 30 pack animals. If the emperor wants to give him special attention, he gives order that he be assigned much more. If he wants to honour him as well, he must send for him and receive him through one of the highly ranked men in Galatia and Cappadocia, and to provide food for him. Likewise, he must send to Nicaea to host and look after him there. It is necessary that when he gets close to Antioch,[9] the *magister* also sends a *magistrianus*, who has to meet and greet him, and to find out how he is being guided through Roman territory. If the emperor wishes, he does this once and then a second time, that is he both writes to him and greets him, and asks him how he is being guided. It is necessary that pack animals are ready for him at Helenopolis and also light vessels, in order that, if he wishes, [p. 401] he may go to Nicomedia on foot, or if he wishes, may get across in the light vessels, and there it is absolutely necessary that horses and pack animals are ready for him, in order that they receive him and take him to Chalcedon. In Chalcedon the magister has to provide lodgings both for him and his men, and to send the *optio*[10] of the barbarians and to set aside for him sufficient expenses for the day, or even days that he spends in Chalcedon. And as his host he sends gifts to him. It is the *magister*'s duty to immediately send someone to greet him, and to ask how his journey was, and that he was not recovering from anything, and simply to entertain him as much as possible. It is necessary that his lodgings in the city are prepared in advance as is appropriate for the rank of the man and for the group that he brings along, and that in there are for him beds, linen, ovens, fireplaces, tables and buckets to carry water and to be of service with regard to the other dirty tasks. But the *comes privatorum* bears the expense of the bed linen according to a billet of the *magister*, or rather the *sacellarius* of the emperor (for now this duty has been transferred to him). The *praefectus urbis* [p. 402] bears the expense for the beds, drinking vessels, tables, ovens and pots, again according to a billet of the *magister*. The men of the arsenals provide the fireplaces. The men from the workshops are also assigned to him by the supervisor. And the bath of the house, in which he is to live, has to be made ready, or close to this, in order that, whenever he wants, he himself and those with him can take a bath, and the bath is at their disposal alone . . .

(90) What should be observed during the other days with regard to the ambassador.

The emperor, once he has read the letter, when he wants to, allows the *magister* to inform the ambassador that he may come to the palace on the following day. He

---

[8] On the *scrinium barbarorum* see Clauss 1981: 137.

[9] On the question whether this is Antioch in Pisidia or the capital of Syria on the river Orontes see the references in Greatrex and Lieu 2002: 275–6 n. 8.

[10] The *optio* could be either a military official or an ambassador.

himself may inform him, if he wishes, through a *silentiarius*, that he may come, and a silence takes place, and the arms are held up and the *labaresioi* stand by, and when he comes forward the *magister* receives him into his *schola*, and he leaves him seated and gets up, and he indicates (his arrival) to the emperor; he receives him inside, either in the portico or in the Augusteum itself.[11] If the ambassador has gifts of his own, he announces this a day before through the *magister*, in order that they may be received, and if the emperor allows this, he shows them to the *magister* in the *schola*, and they are recorded for him. And it is necessary [p. 409] that the *magister* goes to the emperor in advance to show him the record of the gifts. And the ambassador, if he wants them to be received, goes in and asks the emperor, in order that he may receive his gifts. And if the emperor allows this, his men come in, bearing his gifts, and a similar procedure takes place with regard to the royal gifts, and a conversation takes place. It is essential that the emperor again remembers the king of the Persians and his disposition continuously and in a positive way, and if there is peace, they also talk about that kind of thing, and the emperor dismisses him, and he awaits the *magister* outside, and the *magister* comes out, bids him farewell and dismisses him himself. On the other days he sends for him, and they discuss matters. And if he decides to do so, he allows the *magister* or other magistrates together with him to talk with the ambassador outside. If there is complete friendship between the states, the king has to send someone to visit him continuously and to find out how he is, and also to send him food, and gifts of friendship during our holidays and during his special days, and to entertain him in all sorts of ways.

Numerous and wide-ranging works of literature are accredited to the Byzantine emperor Constantine VII Porphyrogenitus (905–59), who from 949 to 959 ruled as monarch.[12] The author's aim was to acquire knowledge on a number of different topics, to put it to paper and make it accessible for practical purposes. His work *De ceremoniis aulae byzantinae* is an encyclopaedia compiled on the basis of the records in the imperial archives; it is tremendously important with regard to the protocol at the Byzantine court and the administrative hierarchy of the Byzantine Empire. It is an example of a genre that was popular during the ninth and tenth centuries, namely the *Taktika*, handbooks made up of lists of Byzantine offices and titles that were instructive if one wanted to learn about and follow royal protocol. Obviously, these texts are also a valuable source for the modern historian as they provide much information about the administration and bureaucratic hierarchies of this period. The passage gives detailed instructions concerning the arrival of a high ranking Persian diplomat and most likely has to do with the journey of the Persian ambassador Yazdgushnasp

---

[11] For the archaeological remains of these buildings see Bardill 1999: 216–30, esp. 227, with further references on the role of the Augusteum in entertaining officials.

[12] On the author and his work see Toynbee 1973; Sevcenko 1992: 167–95.

to the imperial court at Constantinople.[13] Around the middle of the sixth century this man played a crucial role for the diplomatic relations of the two great powers.[14] His input was also essential for the conclusion of the peace treaty of 562 (**20**). On the Roman side, the most significant diplomat of this period was Peter the Patrician,[15] who wrote a detailed account of Yazdgushnasp's mission, which must be based on an official protocol and was clearly used by Constantine Porphyrogenitus in his work.

The protective measures taken immediately after the crossing of the border are remarkable. In particular the instructions concerning Dārā must result from actual Sasanian attempts to get hold of this strategically important fortification by way of some ruse. In spite of an armistice agreed upon in 545 Xusrō I was determined to control Dārā.[16] In 547 the Persian ambassador Yazdgushnasp was travelling to Constantinople together with a large entourage; on his way he was supposed to capture Dārā with the help of the Persian troops stationed at Nisibis. The plan failed because the Romans made sure that Yazdgushnasp did not enter the city with more than twenty of his men; without causing any offence he continued his journey to Constantinople where he was received by Justinian and honoured with numerous gifts.[17] It looks as if the protective measures mentioned by Constantine Porphyrogenitus with regard to the arrival of Sasanian diplomats also applied to the following period. A set of Roman officials had to make sure that Persian ambassadors entered Roman cities as individuals accompanied by only a few men and that the Persian soldiers remained on the other side of the border.

Apart from aspects of security, the passage reflects the great amenities and the privileged role enjoyed by the ambassadors both during their journey across foreign territory and during their stay in the cities they were travelling to, in general the capitals of the respective states. It is not surprising that such 'special treatment' brought along many opportunities to acquire information about the 'opponent'.[18] The following two episodes related by Procopius illustrate this process exceptionally well:

Procopius, De bello Gothico II.2.1–3

(1) At this point Vitiges, the leader of the Goths, who had suffered severely from the war, sent two envoys to him [Xusrō I], in order that they persuade him to

---

[13] With regard to the controversial date of Yazdgushnasp's embassies see the references in Greatrex and Lieu 2002: 275 nn. 5–6.

[14] See above, pp. 139–41.   [15] On Peter the Patrician see above, p. 122 on **17**.

[16] On the fortification of Dārā see pp. 100–4 with figs. 13–14.

[17] This episode is recorded by Procopius (II.31–44).   [18] See Tinnefeld 1993: 193–213.

lead an army against the Romans;[19] he did not send Goths, however, in order that they would not immediately be recognisable and spoil the plans, but two Ligurian priests, who had been bribed to get involved in this deed. (2) The one, who seemed to be of higher integrity, went on this embassy giving himself the appearance and name of a bishop (although entitled to neither), the other followed him as his servant. (3) On their journey they moved through Thracian territory where they recruited an interpreter of the Syriac and Greek language and then entered Persian territory without having been noticed by the Romans. For as this happened during a time of peace[20] these were not guarding the area meticulously.

Procopius, De Bello Gothico IV.15.1–2 and 19–20[21]

(1) In Byzantium Xusrō (I)'s envoy Isdigusnas[22] met with the emperor Justinian in order to talk about the peace and spent a considerable period of time there. (2) After much dispute they finally agreed that there should be a five-year-truce within the hegemony of each ruler but that there should be frequent embassies between both sides, with the envoys going back and forth safely during this period in order to settle the disagreements regarding Lazika[23] and the Saracens[24]...

(19) Isdigusnas, however, appropriated more revenues than any envoy before him and returned, as I believe, as the wealthiest Persian to his home country. For the emperor Justinian had placed the highest honours upon him and gave him large monetary gifts before he dismissed him. (20) He was the only envoy who was never supervised; he and the barbarians with him (and there were a large number of them) rather enjoyed great freedom. During the entire period they were allowed to meet and converse with whom they liked, to move around anywhere in the city, acquire and sell whatever they wanted, conduct all business and do so with utmost freedom, just like they would in their own city; no Roman followed or accompanied them or dared to observe them, as was normally the case.

Procopius confirms that when Yazdgushnasp stayed in Byzantium he enjoyed much freedom and his movements in the capital were not monitored at all. However, the passage also suggests that contemporary observers were aware of the dangers that such privileges for foreign diplomats could

---

[19] On the political background to this embassy see **13**.

[20] The first Sasanian–Byzantine war of the sixth century (**12**) had been ended in 532 by the so-called 'eternal peace' (Proc. *BP* 1.22.3).

[21] On IV.15.19–20 see Tinnefeld 1993: 207–8.

[22] Elsewhere (Menander Protector, frg. 11 [see **20**]) this man is called Yazdgushnasp; see above.

[23] Proc. *BP* 11.28.6–11 states that in the year 545 Xusrō I did not want a peace but merely a truce and that he, moreover, explicitly refused to return Lazika; the hostilities that arose before the end of the agreed truce actually focused on this Black Sea region.

[24] As a rule, the Lahmids and Ghassanids (**25**) were excluded from the peace negotiations of this period so that the vassal states were able to continue their military confrontations, which also happened after the truce of 545; cf. Proc. *BP* 11.28.12–14; the *foedus* of 562 (**20**) was the first one to address also the situation of the Arabs.

entail.[25] According to a military treatise called *Peri Strategias*, which was most likely composed in the sixth century,[26] foreign ambassadors who had travelled to Constantinople were supposed to be treated well but also to be closely observed, in particular if they were representatives of powerful states.[27]

In 538/9 the Gothic envoys, who were accompanied by an interpreter, travelled unimpeded through Byzantine territory on their way to Persia. Interestingly, Procopius refers to the fact that one of the two Ligurian priests pretended to be a bishop. Precisely because of their high status, bishops played a significant role for diplomatic relations throughout late antiquity. The example of the Mesopotamian bishop Mārūtā has already shown how much responsibility a bishop functioning as Byzantine ambassador could have and how Church officials could influence foreign policy (**32**).[28] Moreover, in particular the bishops in charge of the border regions often acted on behalf of the cities and population directly affected by the military confrontations. The Greek ecclesiastical historian Socrates records the deeds of the bishop of Amida Acacius, who became quite famous in this role in the early fifth century. When the Romans refused to allow 5,000 starving Sasanian prisoners to return to their homes, he made an attempt to use funds of the Church in order to pay the determined ransom. Socrates summarises, 'This deed of the exceptional Acacius impressed the Persian king even more because the Romans showed themselves as being victorious in both warfare and good works. The Persian king is said to have wanted Acacius to come before him in order that he may have the pleasure of seeing the man; Theodosius gave instructions for this and the meeting actually took place.'[29] The bishop's activities are yet another testimony for the good cross-border relations at the beginning of the fifth century,[30] and they also reflect a remarkably active role of bishops, who repeatedly intervened in the political events of their times. This is confirmed by a passage in Ammianus Marcellinus according to whom the bishop of Bezabde (in the vicinity of Amida) tried to act as mediator when the city was besieged by Šāpūr

---

[25] On military and political intelligence in the Roman world see Austin and Rankow 1995; see also Ezov 2000: 299–317.

[26] On the discussion regarding the date of this work see Greatrex and Lieu 2002: 128; the authors themselves, however, argue in favour of the tenth century.

[27] *Peri Strategias* 43.1–13 (= *Peri Presbeias*); for text and translation see Dennis 1985.

[28] See also Sako 1986.

[29] Socr. *HE* VII.21.1–6. On Acacius' visit to the Sasanian court in 422 see Sako 1986: 78–80 and Blockley 1992: 58.

[30] Cf. Greatrex and Lieu 2002: 43, who also point out, 'The actions of Acacius described by Socrates were in effect a reciprocal gesture for the return of Roman prisoners captured from the Huns by Yazdgerd I.'

II. However, not even his perseverance and private conversation with the Persian king motivated the latter to abandon the siege, and the city was ultimately captured by the Sasanians.[31] The author indicates that at times such diplomatic initiatives of bishops were criticised and viewed with suspicion. He states that the bishop was suspected of having given advice to the Persian king as to which parts of the city wall should be attacked. The suspicions seemed justified when the enemy's siege engines targeted weak and dilapidating walls and it looked as if they had been guided by people with inside knowledge of the city.[32]

The episode reminds the reader that in a different context the privileged status of envoys and the knowledge gained in this way could also be used in the preparation for military conflicts.[33] Whereas to some extent this was inevitable and had to be accepted as within the limits of diplomatic activities, the great powers sought to keep a check on acts of espionage[34] and defectors. Given the lively trade between the great powers the fear of espionage often concerned foreign merchants. High fines were stipulated in order to deter them from engaging in such activities (**28**). In particular Ammianus Marcellinus, a man who knew the situation in the East exceptionally well, provides us with much insight into the strict control of the border traffic in order to stop Romans who sought refuge on the enemy's territory because they might transmit crucial information to the opponent. The following passage sketches the activities of a Roman who decided to flee the empire for private motives.

Ammianus Marcellinus XVIII.5.1–4

(1) A certain Antoninus, formerly a wealthy merchant, then an accountant of the *dux* of Mesopotamia and finally *protector*, an experienced and intelligent man who was well known throughout those territories, had got into serious debt through the greed of certain people; he realised that he would suffer more and more injustice by standing up against the powerful people because his opponents had more money and were inclined to bribe those who were investigating the case. In order not to play right into their hands, he therefore turned to more cunning ways and admitted to the debt, which by way of a shady deal was passed on to the imperial treasury.[35] And already at this point he had unbelievable plans; secretly he searched

---

[31] Amm. XX.7.7–9.   [32] Amm. XX.7.9.

[33] Proc. *BP* II.31–44; see Lee 1993a: 109–28.

[34] Lee 1993a: 170–82; on potential espionage by Christians in the Sasanian Empire see the reference in the *Chronicle of Arbela II* p. 77, ll. 7–9 (tr. Kawerau); on this see Lieu 1986: 491–5 and Wiesehöfer 2001: 202 and 295–6.

[35] It looks as if Ammianus is trying to excuse Antoninus' activities; he portrays him as the victim of fiscal exploitation; this corresponds to the author's general critical attitude with regard to the fiscal policy of the Roman authorities.

through the organs of the state and, as he knew the script of both languages,[36] turned to accounting: he took down which and how many troops were positioned in which places and where and when they would march, ready to fight battle, and he also made eager inquiries whether the supplies of arms and provisions and other supplies for the war were abundant. (2) While he was thus gathering information about the inner affairs of the entire East, namely about the distribution of troops and their pay in Illyria, where the emperor was held up by the difficult situation, the deadline arrived by which he had to pay the money that he had under threat of violence acknowledged in writing as debt. As he anticipated that he would be exposed to all sorts of dangers and as the *comes largitionum* put more and more pressure on him to comply with the demands of the other one, he made incredible efforts to escape to the Persians together with his wife, his children and everything that was dear to him. (3) In order not to raise the attention of the soldiers guarding the border, for a small sum he bought an estate in Hiaspis, a place right on the river Tigris. Because of this trick, nobody dared to ask him, the owner of a large estate, what he was doing in the most remote part of the Roman border territory; and with the help of servants who were both loyal and knew how to swim he conducted secret talks with Tamsapor,[37] who at the time was a *dux* and in charge of all the areas on the opposite bank; as he had been known before, he and all his possessions were ferried over on barges in the middle of the night with the help of agile men from the Persian camp, and although so much unlike a Zopyrus still similar to a Babylonian traitor.[38]

Apparently Antoninus had used his social and political rank, his education and language skills in order to acquire comprehensive insight into Roman internal affairs in the East. It is thus not surprising that the Sasanians showed an interest in the man and that the Persian satrap Tamsapor, whom Antoninus had known already before,[39] helped him in every possible way to escape to Persian territory. After his successful flight in the year 359, Antoninus became one of the most important advisors of the Sasanian ruler Šāpūr II during his campaigns of 359 and 360 against Rome. Throughout the books 18–20 of Ammianus Marcellinus' work he plays an important role.

   The historian Agathias, who was from Myrina in Asia Minor, tells us about very different ways of acquiring knowledge about the other culture.

---

[36] These are Greek and Latin.

[37] This name, which consists of the royal name and the adjective 'tam' (= strong, powerful), is a name of honour and indicates the high rank of the official; our sources mention Tamsapor also as a persecutor of Christians during the reign of Šāpūr II; cf. Peeters 1925: 276–7.

[38] During the reign of the Achaemenid king Darius I (522–485 BC) a Persian Zopyrus had gone to Babylon in order to worm himself into the confidence of the people there and afterwards play the city into Darius' hands (Hdt. III.153–8); Lib. *Or.* 12.74 compares Antoninus with the Spartan king Demaratos who in the early fifth century had fled to the court of Darius I (Hdt. VI.70).

[39] Amm. XVIII.8.5–6.

Agathias II.27.8 and IV.30.2–4

[II.27.8] Also in this respect I have recorded precisely what they themselves wrote down, and, I believe, it is particularly appropriate to mention all this in the present work. In what follows I shall therefore – when necessary – give a detailed account, even though this means that I shall include long lists of names, and those of barbarians, some of whom have not even achieved anything noteworthy.

[IV.30.2] As I promised, I have given a comprehensive chronology of the Persian kings and a list of the years of their reigns. I think that this list is very accurate and exact because it is based on Persian books.[40] (3) For the translator Sergius[41] went there and persuaded the guards and administrators of the royal records[42] to make the relevant documents available to him (for I frequently asked him to do so); he claimed that he wanted to see them for no purpose other than that what they knew and appreciated would also be recorded among us, and they therefore were happy to comply, thinking that they were doing a good deed, which would bring fame to their kings, if it were known also among the Romans which and how many kings there had been and how they had taken care of their succession. (4) Sergius, however, recorded their names and dates, and the more important events[43] that took place during their reigns and then carefully translated them into Greek (for he was the best translator around, admired even by Xusrō (I) himself and acknowledged as a specialist in his field in both states). After he had made an accurate translation he handed everything over to me, in a conscientious and friendly way, and he encouraged me to use the material for the purpose it had been given to him. And this has now happened.

Agathias' work on the reign of Justinian continued Procopius' *Histories* but was never finished. In five books he covers the years between 552 and 558.[44] Apart from comprehensive ethnographical and chronological digressions

---

[40] On the question of sources used by Agathias for his digression on Persia see Cameron 1969–70: esp. 109–10 and 161–2. 'Evidently Agathias did not suspect that Sergius' information was not quite what it purported to be, nor did he realize that it was in some places contaminated with a Syrian bias' (161).

[41] Sergius was probably Syrian; as Syriac was a kind of 'mediating' language between the Greek and the Persian world (cf. e.g. Proc. *BP* II.2.3) Syrians were often used as interpreters. However, when referring to his sources Sergius explicitly talks about *Persikai bibloi*, which were certainly composed in the official language of the Sasanian Empire, namely Middle Persian.

[42] From the Achaemenid period onwards the Persians had kept such annals; cf. Hdt. VII.100.1 and VIII.90.4; Thuc. I.129.3; Diod. II.32.4. The Sasanian annals, whose middle-Persian title (xvatāi-nāmag) means 'book of rulers' or 'book of lords', were the official chronicle of the Sasanian Empire. They began with the reign of Xusrō I (531–79), who drew on earlier records and added new information. After his death these annals were continued to the reign of Yazdgard III (632–51). None of the original Middle Persian text has survived. We get an idea of this 'book of rulers' only through later Arabic and neo-Persian books, especially through the revised translations made by authors of the ninth and later centuries.

[43] It looks as if Sergius did not produce a full translation of the material but made excerpts or summarised the records as he saw appropriate.

[44] For an English translation see Frendo 1975; on Agathias and his work see also Cameron 1970.

the main theme of his narrative are the Roman wars against the Francs, Goths and Sasanians.[45] Agathias points to his efforts in gathering precise information from official Persian sources.[46] Access to these he owed to the activities of the translator Sergius, who was held in high esteem by Xusrō I (531–79) and whom the author asked to translate the Persian documents into Greek. Agathias may have claimed to have had access to the archives of the Sasanian kings in order to make his account more trustworthy; however, even if this is a false claim, it is remarkable that the scenario could have been possible.

As the above examination has shown, contacts took place via diplomats, spies, refugees, exiles and historians who were interested in foreign cultures and whose names we often know. The mediators were also 'unemployed philosophers' as well as Christians and Jews in the Sasanian Empire because of their close contacts with their fellow-believers in the Roman Empire. They all found their way into the neighbouring empire and furthered the exchange of ideas and knowledge between the two cultures, above all within the border areas and in Mesopotamia.[47]

36: Deportations: Enforced resettlement of prisoners

Moreover, in the context of the Persian conquests numerous people were deported into the Sasanian Empire.[48] Together with these, Western ideas and culture reached Iran. Already Šāpūr I (240–72) boasted in the epigraphic record of his deeds that as a consequence of his victorious campaigns in the Roman Eastern provinces he had deported innumerable people from the Roman Empire and resettled them in the Persis, in Parthia, in the Susiane, in Mesopotamia[49] and all other provinces.[50] The deportations of a large number of Romans to the Sasanian ancestral homelands after the victory over the emperor Valerian in 260 and the assignment of Roman prisoners to several cities in Iran are confirmed by a Nestorian chronicle, the so-called Chronicle of Se'ert, which was composed in Arabic. This text stems from a period soon after 1036 and is not only significant for our knowledge about the religious situation in Iran but also an important source with regard to the Sasanian–Roman relations.[51]

---

[45] On the Persia-excursus see Cameron 1969–70: 69–183.   [46] See Suolathi 1947.
[47] Matthews 1989b: 29–49.   [48] Lieu 1986: 475–505 and Kettenhofen 1994b: 297–308.
[49] See Simpson 2000: 37–66.   [50] ŠKZ, § 30 (pp. 324–6 ed. Back).
[51] Decret 1979: 93–152.

Chronicle of Se'ert, PO IV 220–1

In the eleventh year of his reign Šāpūr son of Ardašīr entered the land of the Byzantines, where he remained for some time laying waste to many towns. He defeated the emperor Valerian and took him prisoner, taking him to the land of the Nabataeans, where he fell ill from grief and died. Then (and) the bishops whom the wicked Valerian had exiled returned to their sees. When Šāpūr left the Byzantine lands he brought with him captives whom he settled in Iraq, Ahwaz, Persia and in the cities founded by his father. He himself founded three cities, giving them names derived from his own. The first of them lies in the land of Maišan, he named it Sod Sapor, and is now called (this is) Deir Mahraq. The second one is in Persia and is still (up to our time) called Šāpūr. He also rebuilt Gundēšāpūr, which had been demolished and called it Antišāpūr. This name is a mixture of Greek and Persian and it means: 'you are the opposite of Šāpūr'. He founded a third city on the Tigris river and he gave it the name Marw Habur and currently this is Ukbura and its surroundings. In these cities he settled a number of captives, distributing among them lands to cultivate and houses to live in, and because of this the number of Christians in Persia increased. Monasteries and churches were built. Among the settlers were priests taken captive in Antioch who settled in Gundēšāpūr. They elected Azdaq from Antioch as their bishop because Demetrius, patriarch of Antioch, had fallen ill and died of grief.

The author gives a detailed list of the Persian territories and cities where the Roman prisoners were settled. According to the chronicler the resettlements led to an increase of the Christian population in the Sasanian Empire.[52] Tabarī also talks about the deportations under Šāpūr I.

Tabarī, Ta'rīh I 827–8

Then he passed from there (Nisibis) to Syria and Roman Anatolia and conquered a great number of cities. It is said that Cilicia and Cappadocia were among the territories that he took, and that he besieged a king who happened to be in Anatolia called Valerianus in the city of Antioch, captured him, and took him together with a large group that was with him and settled them in Gundēšāpūr. It is mentioned that he forced Valerianus to build the dam at Sostar at a width of one thousand cubits. The Roman had it constructed by a group sent to him by the Romans. He made Šāpūr promise to release him after he had finished building the dam. It is said that he took from him great wealth and that he set him free after he cut his nose off. It is also said that he killed him.

Tabarī's words suggest that there were many skilled workers among the Roman prisoners. In fact, among the Roman prisoners who were settled

---

[52] On the Christianisation of Sasanian Iran after the deportations and on the consequences of this development for the Roman–Sasanian relations see Decret 1979: 91–152 and Wiesehöfer 1993: 369.

in Iran, primarily in the modern provinces Fārs and Hūzistān, there were numerous architects, technicians and craftsmen,[53] who during the following period participated in the building projects of Šāpūr I. Their skills were important for the construction of bridges, dams, roads and palaces. One of the most famous building projects was most certainly the dam of Sostar (Shushtar), which Tabarī mentions and which was located on the river Karun in the province of Hūzistān. Its ruins can still be seen today and attest not only to the grandeur of the monument but also of Šāpūr I's efforts to make use of Roman experts on irrigation systems in order to exploit the fertile soil of this region for everybody's benefit.[54]

Both Tabarī and the Chronicle of Se'ert also mention the foundations of cities by the Sasanian king. Analogously to other Sasanian foundations of cities the king often chose names that testified to his victories.[55] In most cases the name of the king was part of the name of the city. Many of the Roman captives came from the Syrian metropolis Antioch. The majority of these were deported to the city Veh-Antiok-Šāpūr (= 'Šāpūr made [this city] better than Antioch'). The city later developed into the intellectual centre GundēŠāpūr (= 'the weapons of Šāpūr'). In this case Šāpūr restored and extended an existing settlement, which was renamed to become GundēŠāpūr soon after 260.[56]

Yet another remarkable example is Bīšāpūr (= 'the beautiful [city of] Šāpūr'), which the king founded in the Persis after his victory over Valerian.[57] The city was modelled on the plan of a Roman military camp. Its first inhabitants were mostly Roman soldiers who had been taken captive in the year 260. It looks as if the foundation was an attempt to integrate the captives and to facilitate their life far away from their home country. In fact, we do not hear of confrontations between the Iranian population and the new settlers.[58]

In Bīšāpūr, the 'Sasanian Versailles',[59] one notices a remarkable influence of Western craftsmen on Iranian art. Many of these were among the Roman prisoners but there were also volunteers, who had been attracted by the good pay and the exceptional prestige of the royal project – the royal buildings made up a quarter of the whole city.[60] Above all the Western influence

[53] Schwaigert 1989: 19–20 and 23–33.
[54] Ghirshman 1962: 137 with fig. 174 and O'Connor 1993: 130 with fig. 106; in general cf. Rahimi-Laridjani 1988.
[55] On the Sasanian foundations see Metzler 1982: 183–212.
[56] Potts 1989: 323–35 and Sayı lı 1991: 1119–20; on the history of the city cf. Abbott 1968: 71–3; Schöffler 1979: 28–9; Shahbazi 2002a: 131–3; Richter-Bernburg 2002: 131–3.
[57] Ghirshman 1962: 138–9.   [58] Metzler 1982: 226.   [59] See Ghirshman 1956–71.
[60] Porada 1980: 197 and Lieu 1986: 479.

Fig. 18 The great hall of the palace in Bīšāpūr
(Ghirshman, R. (1962) *Iran. Parthians and Sassanians*: fig. 177.179)
(Photos: Paris, Museum Louvre, model by A. P. Hardy)

can be seen with regard to the throne room in the royal palace of Bīšāpūr
(fig. 18).

The altogether sixty-four recesses were decorated with Greek key-
patterns, leaf-scrolls and dentils, which give a Western ambience to the
room. The themes of the floor mosaics reveal that the Roman artists modelled the room on the famous repertory of the mosaics of Antioch and
North Africa.[61] However, the models imported from the West were never
reproduced stereotypically but rather 'adapted by local artists to Iranian
tastes and traditions'.[62]

It is impossible to estimate how many Romans were resettled by Šāpūr
I but given that he conquered thirty-six cities in the year 260 the number
must have been large. Deportations were not uncommon in antiquity.[63]

---

[61] Ghirshman 1962: 140–1.
[62] Ibid. 141; see also Shahbazi 1990: 594–5, who lists numerous examples illustrating the reciprocal
influence of Western and Eastern art; on Roman models for the design of the Sasanian rock reliefs
see Azarpay 1981–2; on the reception of Western motifs in Persian art see also Goldman 1989: 831–46.
[63] Oded 1979; on a list of deportations in Iran ranging from Cyrus I (550–529 BC) to Xusrō II (AD
590–628) see Peeters 1924: 305–9; on mothodological considerations see Olshausen 1997: 101–7; see
also Kulesza 1994: 221–50.

Fig. 18 (*cont.*)

To give but a few, one is reminded of the Babylonian captivity of the Jews or the 10,000 Roman prisoners who according to Plutarch were deported to Iran by the Parthians after the battle of Carrhae.[64] The Romans also deported Persian prisoners of war. Cassius Dio, for example, tells us that after the capture of the Parthian capital Seleucia-Ktēsiphōn the emperor Septimius Severus (193–211) moved 100,000 Parthian captives to the West.[65] During the third century the Romans had hardly any opportunity to deport Persian prisoners of war into the empire because in most instances they found themselves exposed to Sasanian attacks and in a defensive position. In the context of their famous defeat of Narsē (293–302), however, we hear about Diocletian (284–305) deporting colonies of prisoners from Asia to Thrace.[66] Galerius (305–11) must have taken these captive after his victory over Narsē in Armenia, when the entire Sasanian camp including the royal family fell into his hands (**6**). In an encomium for the Roman emperor Constantius II (337–61) the orator Libanius mentions Roman attacks on Sasanian territory during which important cities were captured and the entire population deported to Thrace.[67] The author also states that the deportations served to commemorate Rome's victory and gave the emperor an opportunity to display his generosity and compassion.[68] These words suggest a difference between Roman and Persian deportations. S. Lieu argues that 'unlike the Sassanians, the Romans had no coherent plan of settlement for these prisoners and did not seem to have any economic aim in their deportation beyond using them as cheap farm-labourers. The main objective of the deportation was clearly propagandistic.'[69] While this may be true, the deportation of Persians certainly continued into the late phases of Roman–Sasanian relations. Several sources attest to the deportation of the Persian population of Arzanene to Cyprus in the year 578.[70]

With regard to the East, the weak phase after the death of Šāpūr I meant that the flow of Roman prisoners to the Persian Empire ceased. Not before the reign of the powerful Persian king Šāpūr II (309–79) and his many successes against Rome did deportations become more frequent again.[71] The economic motives of the Sasanian kings that could be seen already with regard to the deportations of Šāpūr I are confirmed by the so called *Martyrology of Pusai*, the Syriac testimony of a Christian martyr

---

[64] Plut. *Crass.* 31.8. [65] Cass. Dio LXXV.9.4. [66] *Pan. Lat.* VIII. (V).21.1.
[67] Lib. *Or.* 59.83–4. [68] Ibid. 59.85. [69] Lieu 1986: 487.
[70] Ioh. Eph. *HE* VI.15 provides us with the most detailed account; but cf. also Theoph. Simoc. III.15.13–15, who mentions 100,000 prisoners of war.
[71] Amm. XX.6.7; on the deportation of Roman prisoners by Šāpūr II see Lieu 1986: 495–9.

who lived during the reign of Šāpūr II, when comprehensive persecutions of Christians took place in the Sasanian Empire (**31**).

Martyrology of Pusai under Šāpūr II, Acta martyrum et sanctorum,
ed. P. Bedjan, II 208–10

This illustrious Pusai was one of the descendants of the captives whom Šāpūr the son of Hormizd[72] had brought from the territory of the Romans and had settled in the city of Vēh Šāpūr which is in the province of Fārs, for the father of this Pusai had arrived in that captivity.[73] He was a person at ease with his way of life in this world, and was a believer in Christ before he was taken captive. He lived, then, by order of the king, in the city of Vēh Šāpūr, and he made himself a native in it, and married a Persian woman from the city, and converted her, and baptised his children, and raised and instructed them in Christianity. Now when this king Šāpūr the son of Hormizd, he who stirred up the persecution against the churches of the east,[74] built Karhā d-Lādān and brought captives from various regions and settled them in it, it was also pleasing to him that from all the peoples of the cities which were in the territories of his dominion he should bring thirty families, more or less, and settle them among them, so that through the mingling of their people the captives should be bound by their families and by their love, so that it should not be easy for them to return by flight, a few at a time, to the territories from which they had been taken captive.[75] Now Šāpūr planned this by his cunning, but God in his compassion made use of it to bring about good, for through the mingling of the captives with the peoples he captured the peoples for the knowledge of truth, and made them disciples on the way of verity. Like the other families whom they brought from various regions and settled in Karh, by the command of Šāpūr son of Hormizd, so also they brought [families] from the city of Vēh Šāpūr which is in Fars. Among these whom they brought from Vēh Šāpūr they also brought the blessed Pusai, and his wife and children, and brothers and sisters, and the people of his household, and they settled them in Karhā d-Lādān. Pusai was a skilled craftsman, and was especially expert in the making of woven cloth and in the embroidery of gold filigree. And he was one of those craftsmen whom king Šāpūr gathered together from all the peoples, the captives and his own subjects, and made into a single, multi-tiered, guild, and he established a workshop for them beside his palace in Karhā d-Lādān. Now the blessed Pusai, because he was excellent at his craft, was praised before the king, and he was continually giving him honours and great gifts. Indeed, after a short time he made him chief craftsman, as day by day the man grew in honour and praise.

---

[72] According to Braun 1915: 58 n. 2 this must be a confusion and refer to Šāpūr I, son of Ardašīr, during whose reign many Roman prisoners of war were deported to the Sasanian homelands.

[73] On Pusai see Schwaigert 1989: 155–9.

[74] On the persecution of Christians during the reign of Šāpūr II (309–79) cf. pp. 220–1 (**31**).

[75] This refers to the desire of the deported population to return to their home countries.

The text once more illustrates a Persian interest in resettling prisoners of war, whose knowledge and skills could be an asset.[76] It was thus a matter of acquiring not only a work force as such but also the knowledge of specialists, and the main beneficiary of this process was the king, who continued to make use of those he had captured 'with his own hands'.[77] There is no doubt that the use of Roman prisoners contributed considerably to improving the infrastructure of the Sasanian Empire.[78] One of the consequences of the resettlements of large numbers of Roman prisoners was – to say it in modern terms – a 'transfer of technology', which guaranteed an economic upturn for Sasanian Iran.[79]

Deportations of Romans continued into the sixth century. The following two passages refer to activities of Xusrō I (531–79). After his conquest of Syrian Antioch in the year 540 the king resettled the inhabitants of this metropolis to the city Vēh-Antiok-Xusrō, which he founded in the vicinity of the Sasanian capital Ktēsiphōn.[80]

Procopius, De bello Persico II.14.1–4

(1) Xusrō (I) founded a city in Assyria,[81] in a place that was a day's march away from the city of Ktēsiphōn; he named it 'Xusrō's Antioch' and settled all captives from Antioch there, for whom he even had a bath and a hippodrome built and whom he provided also with other comforts. (2) For he brought along the charioteers and musicians from Antioch and other Romans. (3) Moreover, at public expense he took more care in catering for these people from Antioch than was customary for captives, and (he did so) for their entire life, and gave orders to call them 'the royal ones' so that they would not be responsible to any magistrate but the king alone.[82] (4) When one of the other Romans had escaped and managed to seek refuge in Xusrō's Antioch and when one of the inhabitants claimed that he was a relative, the owner was no longer allowed to remove this captive, not even if one of the highest ranking Persians happened to have enslaved the man.

---

[76] On this passage and specifically on the consequences of the deportations for the spread of Christianity see Brock 1982: 4 and 14–15.

[77] Cf. Metzler 1982: 214 and 219–20. [78] Wiesehöfer 1993: 369.

[79] For this link between a 'transfer of technology' and captivity, also with regard to the Roman–Sasanian relations, see Stoll 1998: 254–70.

[80] Theoph. Simoc. v.6.10; cf. also Güterbock 1906: 93–105; Christensen 1944: 386 and 487–96; Metzler 1982: 205 and Wiesehöfer 2001: 292–3.

[81] 'Assyria' refers to the core territories of the former Assyrian Empire to the west and east of the river Tigris; this comprises roughly the area of modern northern Iraq; over time the political-geographical name 'Adiabēnē' replaced the traditional name 'Assyria'. In late antique sources 'Assyria' can also refer to entire Babylonia including the southern Mesene; cf. Amm. XXIII.6.15–24; see also Sellwood 1985: 465–9 and Oelsner 1996: 112.

[82] The *Martyrology of Pusai* already mentioned royal workshops where prisoners of war were employed as skilled workers and supervised by the king.

Tabarī, Ta'rīh I 898

After a few years of his rule, when he had established his kingship and all the lands had submitted to him, he marched on Antioch, where the leading commanders of the emperor's army were stationed, and took the city. Then he ordered that a drawing be made of the city according to scale, with the number of its houses, its streets and everything that was in it, and to build him a replica city next to al-Madā'in. And the city known as 'al-Rūmiyya' was built after the image of Antioch. Then he brought the people of Antioch to settle in it, and when they entered the city-gate, the people of each house went to the building that resembled the one in which they had lived in Antioch as if they had never left it.

The accounts of Procopius and Tabarī agree on the fact that the new city was modelled upon a Western example. Whether an exact replica of Syrian Antioch or not, many public institutions were designed with the purpose of making life familiar as well as pleasant for the new inhabitants. Both authors describe a situation that must have been rather acceptable for the settlers of the new Antioch. Xusrō's attitude was not exceptional. In general, the kings guaranteed the freedom of religion, settled groups who shared ethnicity, religion or language in the same places, and awarded economic and social prestige to the skilled workers – measures and principles that compensated at least a part of the deported population to some extent for the loss of their home country.[83] Indeed, for centuries there is no attestation of any resistance of the deported population against their fate.

However, one should probably not idealise the policy of the Sasanian kings. Our sources represent the views of a privileged part of society and tend to focus on the norms, activities and achievements of the powerful, mostly of individual emperors and kings. The described 'cultural exchange' cannot have taken place without great human suffering among the captives.[84] Nevertheless, we are left to speculate about the actual circumstances of the deportations. The Byzantine historian Zonaras can probably not be trusted when he claims that on their journey from Antioch, the cities of Cilicia and Caesarea in Cappadocia those captured by Šāpūr I (240–72) received very little food and were driven to water holes like cattle in order that no water had to be carried along for them.[85] Similarly, Agathias' accusation that Šāpūr I had not been able to gain profit from his conquests because he had left nothing but mountains of corpses[86] must be judged as atrocity propaganda against the Eastern neighbour.[87] It would appear that such

[83] Wiesehöfer 1994: 258.   [84] Lieu 1986: 500.   [85] Zon. XII.23.
[86] Agath. IV.24.3–4.   [87] Metzler 1982: 216 n. 4.

comments do an injustice to Šāpūr I and other rulers, who primarily sought to use the specialised knowledge of Western workers for the benefit of their own empire.

37: Mutual cultural interest

Apart from the rather pragmatic motive to secure Western know-how, several Sasanian kings showed a 'philosophical' interest in Western civilisation and culture. Western and Eastern sources agree that in particular Xusrō I Anōšarvān (531–79), whose added title means 'the wise king', continuously strove to familiarise himself with foreign cultures. Agathias elaborately describes the king's passion for Western literature and philosophy.

Agathias II.28.1–2

(1) After saying a few words about Xusrō (I) I shall immediately return to my previous topic. For he is praised and admired excessively not only by the Persians but also by some Romans as a lover of literature and an expert on our philosophy because someone supposedly translated the Greek authors into Persian for him. (2) It is even claimed that he devoured the whole Aristotle[88] more thoroughly than Demosthenes[89] devoured Thucydides[90] and that he was full of the doctrines of Plato, the son of Ariston, that neither the *Timaeus* (although it bursts with scholarly theory and presents innumerous scientific speculations) was too demanding for him, nor the *Phaedo* or the *Gorgias*, nor any other subtle and complex dialogue, such as, for example, the *Parmenides*.

Although the author tries to be specific in his claim that Xusrō was admired unduly – he seems to doubt that the king actually knew the works of Aristotle or Plato well[91] – his words express a fundamentally critical attitude towards Eastern culture and the 'barbarians' rather than precise knowledge about Xusrō's activities.[92] In any case, the king's eagerness to get to know the works of the Greek philosophers is a remarkable testimony to his tolerance and open-mindedness as well as his desire to learn and make use of new things.[93] It is also noteworthy that – according to Agathias – the Sasanian ruler was praised not only in the East but also in the West; further on the author tells us that Xusrō welcomed numerous Western pagan

---

[88] Literally 'the one from Stagira', Aristotle's birth place.
[89] Literally 'the orator from the demos Paeania'.   [90] Literally 'the son of Olorus'.
[91] Wieschöfer 2001: 216–17 attributes the sceptical attitude of the Byzantine historian to his excessive patriotism.
[92] On these prejudices see Cameron 1969–70: 172–6 and Duneau 1966: 13–22; Pugliese-Caratelli 1971: 597–604.
[93] On Xusrō's attempts to write medical works see Sezgin 1970: 186; for further references see Shahbazi 1990: 293; in general on the efforts of late Sasanian kings to acquire knowledge on foreign cultures see Wieschöfer 2001: 216–21; on philosophy in particular see Walker 2002: 45–9.

philosophers[94] exiled after 529 when Justinian (527–65) had closed the Academy in Athens, the last institution of pagan erudition.[95] One of these, Priscianus, wrote a treatise entitled 'Answers by the philosopher Priscianus to the questions posed by the Persian king Xusrō' (*Prisciani philosophi solutiones eorum de quibus dubitavit Chosroes Persarum rex*).[96] When the Neo-Platonists were disappointed by their experience in Persia and wished to return the king actually supported them by negotiating an amnesty for them in the 'eternal peace' of 532.[97]

Eastern sources confirm Xusrō's exceptional desire for erudition as well as his open-mindedness and tolerance. The king himself composed a book of his exploits which has survived in the works of the Persian author Ibn Miskawayh, who died in the year 1043. This author's universal history was written in Arabic and among other topics covers the history of Persia from its beginnings to the end of the Sasanian Empire. In a manner that was characteristic for his time, Ibn Miskawayh attributes much significance to the Persian monarchy during the Sasanian period. He wrote during a period that saw a Persian reaction to the Arab supremacy and the beginnings of modern Persian 'national literature'.[98] The author points out that his account followed Xusrō's own book, which the king had written about his conquests and the way he ruled his empire.[99]

The Book of Deeds of Xusrō I Anōšarvān; Ibn Miskawayh, Taǧārib al-umam,
p. 206, l. 2 – p. 207, l. 7

When we had finished studying the lives of our ancestors . . . we turned to the lives of the Romans and the people from India, and we took from these what was laudable, using our intellect to select (as a standard for this) and choosing according to our discrimination (distinguishing with our cleverness). And we picked out from all of it that which embellishes our rulers turning it into a guide for exemplary behaviour and custom. (While doing so) our souls were not at variance with us about what our passions favour.

(Then) we told them about it and informed them of it and wrote to them of what we disliked of their behaviour and declared these things forbidden suggesting alternatives. We have not disliked anyone because they belonged to a different religion or a different religious community. We have not been selfish with (the knowledge) we received, yet we have also not disdained to learn what (knowledge) they possess. For acknowledging the learning of truth and knowledge and pursuing it are the most significant embellishments for a king, while their scorning of learning and

---

[94] Agath. ii.30.3.
[95] On the Greek philosophers' flight to the court of Xusrō I see Schöffler 1979: 37–41; see also Hartmann 2002a: 123–60; 2002b: 59–86.
[96] Altheim and Stiehl 1954: 22–6.   [97] Agath. ii.31.1–4.
[98] Caetani 1909: xii–xiii.   [99] Grignaschi 1966: 17.

hiding from the search for knowledge causes them the greatest harm. For whoever does not learn has no insight. When I had examined what these two peoples possessed of governmental and political cleverness and when I had combined the noble deeds of my ancestors with what I gathered through my own reasoning, what I had myself found out, and what I received from the kings who do not belong to us, I established the work from which follow success and goodness. I dismissed the other nations, for I found no insight, nor intelligence, nor cleverness in them but rather I found them to possess injustice, envy, deception, greed, avarice, maladministration, ignorance, (a tendency to) break agreements, and little reward. No government can prosper on the basis of these things, nor do they generate prosperity.

The passage attests to Xusrō's efforts in gaining all sorts of knowledge about different cultures. This aspect of Sasanian kingship, which had been ignored for a long time, has received its deserved attention by more recent scholars.[100] Admittedly, Xusrō I tries to appear in the best light,[101] but his intellectual curiosity and his willingness to learn from foreign peoples and to appreciate other cultures are as obvious as his tolerance with regard to persons of a different faith. Numerous further testimonies confirm the extent to which the king engaged in the study of philosophy and literature, theology, statecraft, law and medicine.[102] Both he and Xusrō II Parvēz (602–28) were largely responsible for the fact that Sasanian culture flourished during the late phase of the Empire.[103] F. Altheim and R. Stiehl give an accurate assessment by calling late Sasanian Iran a centre for the exchange of both religions and ideologies.[104]

Our study of the relations between Rome and Iran from the third to the seventh century has shown the following. Reducing the Sasanian–Roman confrontations to episodes of war and ignoring the role the East played in establishing close relations is inappropriate. This holds true although the Eastern power seems to have been more willing to receive Western ideas than vice versa. Both empires made intensive use of the many different ways in which they could exercise influence on the other. This influence was felt in all aspects of life, political, diplomatic, economic and cultural. As the Byzantine author and diplomat Peter the Patrician put it, 'It is obvious for all mankind that the Roman and the Persian Empires are just like two lamps; and it is necessary that, like eyes, the one is brightened by the light of the other and that they do not angrily strive for each other's destruction.'[105] Unfortunately, the hopes articulated in these words were not fulfilled.

---

[100] Garsoïan 1983: 586–92 and Shahbazi 1990: 592.
[101] On the clear 'self-praise' of the king see also Wiesehöfer 2001: 217.
[102] Cf. the references in ibid.   [103] On late Sasanian culture see Wiesehöfer 2001: 216–21.
[104] Altheim and Stiehl 1957: 275.   [105] Petrus Patricius, frg. 13; see **17**.

Lists of Sasanian Kings and Roman emperors

SASANIAN KINGS			ROMAN EMPERORS	
Ardašīr I	224–239/40; died 241/42		Alexander Severus	222–235
			Maximinus Thrax	235–238
			Gordian I	238
			Gordian II	238
			Pupienus	238
			Balbinus	238
Šāpūr I	239/40 [241/42?]– 270/72		Gordian III	238–244
			Philip the Arab	244–249
			Decius	249–251
			Trebonianus Gallus	251–253
			Aemilianus	253
			Valerian	253–260
			Gallienus	253–268
			Claudius II	268–270
			Quintillus	270
Hormizd I	270/72–273		Aurelian	270–275
Bahrām I	273–276			
			Tacitus	275–276
Bahrām II	276–293		Florianus	276
			Probus	276–282
			Carus	282–283
			Numerian	283–284
			Carinus	283–285
			Diocletian	284–286

SASANIAN KINGS		WESTERN EMPIRE		EASTERN EMPIRE	
Bahrām III	293	Maximian	286–305	Diocletian	286–305
Narsē	293–302				
Hormizd II	302–309				
		Constantius I	305–306	Galerius	305–311
Adarnarsē	309	Severus	306–307		
		Maxentius	306–312		
		Maximian	307–308	Licinius	308–324
		Constantine I	306–337	Maximinus Daia	309–313

RE-UNITED EMPIRE

Šāpūr II	309–379

Constantine II	337–340
Constans	337–350
Constantius II	337–361
Julian	361–363
Jovian	363–364

EASTERN EMPIRE

Valens	364–378
Theodosius I	379–395

Ardašīr II	379–383
Šāpūr III	383–388
Bahrām IV	388–399

Arcadius	395–408

Yazdgard I	399–420

Theodosius II	408–450

Bahrām V Gōr	420–439
Yazdgard II	439–457

Marcian	450–457
Leo I	457–474

Hormizd III	457–459
Pērōz I	459–484

Leo II	474
Zeno	474–5/476–91
Basiliscus	475–476

Balāš	484–488
Kavādh I	488–497/499–531
Ğāmāsp	497–499
Xusrō I	531–579
Anōšarvān	
Hormizd IV	579–590

Anastasius I	491–518
Justin I	518–527
Justinian I	527–565
Justin II	565–578
Tiberius II	578–582
Maurice	582–602

Bahrām VI Čōbīn	590–591
Xusrō II Parvēz	590–628

Phocas	602–610
Heraclius	610–641

Bistām	591–595
Kavādh II Šērōē	628
Ardašīr III	628–630
Šāhrbarāz	630
Xusrō III	630
Bōrān	630–631
Āzarmēduxt	631
Hormizd I	631–632
Xusrō IV	reign uncertain
Pērōz II	reign uncertain
Xusrō V	reign uncertain
Yazdgard III	633–651

Chronological table

224	The Sasanian Empire is founded
c. 226/227	Ardašīr I attacks Hatra
230–232	Ardašīr I invades Roman territory
232/233	Severus Alexander responds with counter-attacks
235/236 (?)	Ardašīr I conquers Nisibis and Carrhae
240/241	The Sasanians conquer Hatra
242–244	Gordian III marches against Persia
243	Nisibis and Carrhae are reconquered; the Romans are victorious at Rhesaina and advance into the Sasanian province of Āsūrestān
244	Šāpūr I defeats Gordian III at Mišīk and concludes peace with Philip the Arab
252	Šāpūr I conquers Armenia
253	Šāpūr I advances into Mesopotamia and Syria; the Sasanians are victorious at Barbalissos
253	The Palmyrene prince Odaenathus scores first successes against the Sasanians
253/4 or 255–257	The Sasanians advance into Cappadocia
256	Šāpūr I rejects Odaenathus' offer of alliance; rapprochement between Rome and the Palmyrene prince
260	Šāpūr I is victorious at Edessa; Valerian is captured; the Sasanians advance into Cilicia, Cappadocia, Lycaonia; a large number of inhabitants of the Roman Empire are deported into the Sasanian Empire
260	Odaenathus counter-attacks the Sasanians
262–264	Odaenathus defeats the Sasanians several times and advances to Ktēsiphōn twice (262; 264?)

267	Odaenathus is assassinated
267–272	Zenobia rules in Palmyra; the 'Palmyrene Empire' is founded (from 271/272)
272	Aurelian destroys Palmyra
276–293	The Zoroastrian priest Kartēr is at the height of his power under Bahrām II; upon Kartēr's initiative Mani is imprisoned (277)
279	The emperor Probus receives the title *Persicus maximus*
283	Carus attacks Persia and advances to Ktēsiphōn
From 286	Diocletian introduces measures to protect the Roman eastern frontier
288	Diocletian and Bahrām II conclude peace
290 (?)	Diocletian installs Tiridates III as Armenian king
295 (?)	Diocletian adopts the title *Persicus maximus*
296	Sasanian–Roman confrontations resume; Narsē invades Armenia
297	Diocletian issues an edict against the Manichaeans; Galerius is defeated in Mesopotamia
298	The Romans are victorious against Narsē in Armenia at Satala; peace of Nisibis entails considerable advantages for the Romans
before 309	Hormizd II attacks the Romans without any success
312	Maximinus Daea fights a war in Armenia
328	The Arab prince Imru'ulqais dies
22 May 337	Constantine the Great dies in the middle of preparations for a Persian war
338	Šāpūr II resumes hostilities with Rome and conquers Armenia
From 339/340	Christians are persecuted in the Persian Empire under Šāpūr II
350	Šāpūr II is unsuccessful in capturing Nisibis after besieging the city twice
359	Šāpūr II captures Amida and Singara
363	Julian attacks Persia; military catastrophe and the emperor's death; Julian's successor Jovian concludes a disadvantageous *foedus* with Šāpūr II
367	Šāpūr II has the Armenian king Arsaces assassinated
371	Šāpūr II attacks Armenia
377	Romans and Sasanians divide Armenia between them

387 (?)	A treaty confirms the partition of Armenia
408	Arcadius asks Yazdgard I to become guardian of his son Theodosius
408/409	Byzantium and the Sasanian Empire conclude a trade agreement
410	Synod of Seleucia-Ktēsiphōn; Yazdgard I allows the Christians to practise their religion in the Sasanian Empire
420	Persecutions of the Christians resume in the Sasanian Empire
421	Byzantine–Sasanian war
422	Bahrām V Gōr and Theodosius II conclude peace
439–442	Byzantine–Sasanian war; Leo I refuses to make monetary contributions for the protection of the Caucasus passes; Yazdgard II advances into Roman territory
443–450	Yazdgard II suffers defeats against the Hephthalites in the East
465	Leo receives a Sasanian embassy complaining that the Zoroastrian Magians were impeded in practising their rites in Cappadocia
After 474	During the first half of his reign the emperor Zeno makes subsidiary payments to Pērōz I towards the fortresses in the Caucasus; payments cease after Pērōz I's death in 484
484	Synod of Bēt Lāpāt; the Christians in the Sasanian Empire follow the Nestorian doctrine
484	Pērōz I dies in battle against the Hephthalites
From 494	Mazdakite movement and long lasting turmoil in the Sasanian Empire
502–532	First Sasanian–Byzantine war in the sixth century; Kavādh I starts the war when Anastasius I refuses to support him financially against the Hephthalites
503	The Sasanians conquer Amida
506	Peace is concluded
522	Kavādh I asks Justin to adopt his son Xusrō in order to secure his son's succession
526	Military confrontations resume
529	Numerous pagan philosophers seek refuge at the court of Xusrō I in Ktēsiphōn when the academy in Athens is closed by Justinian; Justinian installs the Ghassanid al-Hārit V ibn Ǧabala (Arethas) as the leader of many Arab tribes; he thereby sets up a counter weight to the Lahmids fighting on behalf of the Sasanians

532	'Eternal peace' is concluded
538	Ambassadors of the Gothic king Wittiges appeal to Xusrō I in Ktēsiphōn and try to persuade him to go to war against Byzantium
540–562	Second Sasanian–Byzantine war in the sixth century, triggered by invasions of the Lahmid Alamoundaros into Roman territory
540	Xusrō I conquers Antioch; the inhabitants of the Syrian metropolis are deported to the Sasanian Empire and resettled in the new foundation Vēh-Antiok-Xusrō
544	The Sasanians fail at their attempt to conquer Christian Edessa
545	Both sides agree on an armistice
549	Fighting continues
551	A five-year armistice is concluded, which does not include Lazika
552	Justinian tries to introduce the breeding of silk worms in Byzantium in order to gain independence from the Sasanian intermediate trade
556/557	Peace negotiations take place and a general armistice is concluded
562	Justinian and Xusrō I Anōšarvān conclude a *foedus*
From 568	Romans and Turks enter diplomatic relations
570	The Sasanians advance into the Yemen
572–590	Third Sasanian–Byzantine war in the sixth century
588/589	The end of the reign of Hormizd IV sees confrontations with the Turks along the Eastern Sasanian frontier
590/591	Maurice intervenes in rivalries over the Sasanian throne; Xusrō II Pārvēz prevails against the rebel Bahrām VI Čōbīn
602	Xusrō II has the last Lahmid ruler Numān III assassinated; Xusrō II's 'benefactor' Maurice is overthrown by Phocas; the Sasanian king begins war against the Romans and advances into Armenia and Cappadocia
604	Several Arab tribes unite and destroy a Sasanian army at Dū Kār
c. 605	The Sasanians conquer the important border cities Amida, Rhesaina, Kallinikos and Kirkesion; the Romans lose all of Mesopotamia
c. 608–610	The Sasanians advance into Asia Minor

611	Syrian Antioch is conquered
613	Tarsus and Damascus are conquered
614	Jerusalem falls and the Holy Cross is taken to Ktēsiphōn
615	The Sasanians capture Chalcedon; Roman attempts at reconciliation with the Sasanians fail
619	The Sasanians conquer Egypt
622	Heraclius embarks on a Roman counter offensive
623	The Romans free Asia Minor from Sasanian control
626	The Sasanians and Avars attack Constantinople but fail
627	The Sasanians are defeated at Niniveh
628	Kavādh II Šērōē and Heraclius conclude peace
628/629	The Sasanians return their conquests in Armenia, Mesopotamia, Syria, Palestine and Egypt to the Romans
630	The Holy Cross is restored to Jerusalem
636	The Arabs defeat the Romans at the Yarmūk river; in the following period the important Roman Eastern provinces are lost
636	The Arabs defeat the Sasanians at Qādīsīya
642	The Arabs defeat the Sasanians at Nihāvand
651	Yazdgard III, the last Sasanian king, is assassinated

Glossary

amicitia
The Latin term *amicitia* describes various personal or political aspects of friendship, i.e. it is used in the context of relations between individuals as well as states. Outside Rome *amicitia* can point to a treaty or to friendly relations between two states that existed without an official *foedus*. *Amicitia* required bilateral consent. In general, the declaration of *amicitia* was motivated by the desire for a reconciliation of interests.

breviarium
Breviaria were short histories written in a continuous narrative, in contrast to a 'chronicle', which was in general a list-type record of events and dates in chronological order. *Breviaria* intended to both entertain and teach. They primarily served to provide uneducated new elites with a necessary historical and cultural knowledge. This genre became particularly popular during the fourth century AD.

catafractarii
This was the mailed cavalry that the Romans faced for the first time in 190 BC when they fought the Seleucid king Antiochus III. The *catafractarii* contributed significantly to Crassus' defeat at Carrhae against the Parthians in 53 BC. The impact of this unit was also responsible for the military strength of the Sasanians in the third and fourth centuries AD. The *catafractarii* were armed with a heavy lance and attacked their enemies' lines frontally in a single body.

Christological controversies
After Constantine the Great had become a supporter of Christianity deep theological confrontations emerged within the Roman Empire. During the time of bishop Alexander I of Alexandria (312–28) the main dispute was

over *Arianism*. According to Arius, a cleric from Antioch, Christ was not truly divine. In contrast, Alexandrian theologians announced that God the Father and Jesus were of one substance. The controversy escalated, and Constantine the Great, concerned about the unity of the empire, convened the Council of Nicaea (325), which condemned Arius and prescribed the Alexandrian doctrine. The Council of Constantinople (381) confirmed this conclusion and ended the dispute, which was labelled 'Trinitarian' according to the three natures of the divine. Shortly after, the controversy flared up again, this time with much greater consequences. It revolved around the nature of Christ, the relationship between the human and the divine in Christ. The patriarch of Constantinople, Nestorius, refused to call the Virgin Mary 'the bearer of God' (*theotokos*) and clearly distinguished between two natures in Christ (so called extreme *dyophysitism*). In contrast, the patriarch of Alexandria, Cyril I (412–44), proclaimed that Christ was of one nature and that in him god and man had become one (*monophysitism*). Another Council took place at Ephesus in 431 and condemned Nestorius as a heretic. Under Dioscurus (444–54) the power of the patriarch of Alexandria appeared to be at its zenith. However, new Christological controversies erupted. The archimandrite Eutyches, an adherent of the Alexandrian doctrine at Constantinople, took Cyril's doctrine a step further and argued that after his incarnation the two natures of Christ became one divine nature. At the so-called Robber Synod of Ephesus (449) Dioscurus was once more able to promote *monophysitism* successfully. Under the emperor Marcian (450–7), however, a different religious policy began. The Council of Chalcedon (451) brought about a famous and final decision on the Christological dispute, by way of defining Christ as both god and man, two natures that were inconvertible but also inseparable (so called moderate *dyophysitism*). This formula repudiated both Nestorianism and *monophysitism*. All later attempts to integrate the positions failed.

clibanarii
Very similar to the *cataphractarii*, these mailed cavalry units were additionally protected by a cuirass made of small plates that covered the whole body. They are attested from the third century AD onwards.

comes
In late antiquity this was the rank of leading officials employed at the imperial court and in the provinces, in both the civil and military administration of the Roman Empire. The *comes commerciorum* was responsible for the

trade in the border provinces, the *comes foederatorum* for the supervision of the allied non-Roman units, who were mostly commanded by generals appointed from their own tribes and peoples. The *comes (sacrarum) largitionum*, who was a court official, was in charge of the imperial finances; among other things he supervised the collection of taxes and customs duties, controlled all mints and the yields of the mines and was responsible for the budgets of civil and military service. The titles and exact duties of the individual *comites* varied considerably in the course of late antiquity.

Constantinian revolution

This is an expression coined by modern scholarship to express the new relationship between the Roman state and Christianity after the reign of Constantine the Great (306–37), when the persecutions of the Christians were finally abandoned. Constantine's conversion to the Christian faith and the fact that pagan cults were increasingly undermined in state and society certainly entailed tremendous historical consequences. At the end of the fourth century Theodosius the Great declared Christianity as the only orthodox religion in the Roman Empire.

dux

Aside from the general meaning 'leader', in particular the leader of an army or a military unit, from the third century AD onwards the term also described a military rank. When Diocletian reorganised the administration of the Roman Empire he separated civil and military functions. From then on, the *dux* was in charge of the troops positioned in the border provinces. He was essentially the military official responsible for the protection of the frontiers.

foedus

Originally, the term *foedus* described an obligation under oath and therefore pertained to religious law. Later, this formal aspect gave way to the emphasis on a 'treaty' or 'alliance'. Increasingly, the term defined an official treaty between states. By concluding such a formal treaty, a *foedus*, the armed confrontations between rivalling powers were ended and precise terms of peace established. A *foedus aequum* was based on the equal status of both empires. In the case of a *foedus iniquum* one empire had to acknowledge the rule of the other. Prior to the conclusion of a *foedus* ambassadors had to be exchanged. The terms of the treaty were written down and came into effect only when the two sides had formally signed them.

imperium maius
This is the power status of a military command that superseded the authority of other officials in their sphere of command.

Incense route
This is the name of one of the most famous caravan routes in antiquity.
It commenced in southern Arabia and ran along the western coast of the
Arabian peninsula to the commercial centres in north-west Arabia (Petra,
Bostra). Via this trade route Arabia's luxury goods were transported to the
Roman East, among other things the much desired frankincense.

Istakhr
The town was a religious centre of the Sasanians in the Persis. During
the Sasanian period it was as significant as Persepolis had been during the
Achaemenid period. After the Islamic conquest of the Sasanian Empire
Istachr was destroyed.

ius Italicum
By being granted the *ius Italicum* communities outside Italy gained a privileged legal status. This entailed autonomous administration and independence from the provincial governors, but most importantly fiscal privileges
and a special legal treatment of landed property in the area, which probably enjoyed tax exemption as a rule. However, we do not know the precise
content and details of this privilege.

Kūšān
This was the name of a dynasty of central Asia that flourished particularly
during the first centuries BC and AD, when it united parts of central Asia,
Iran, Afghanistan and India to form an important empire. During the
Arsacid period these so-called 'Indoscythians' were powerful opponents of
the Parthians. At the time of the rise of the Sasanian dynasty the power of
the Kūšān, who were a possible threat at the north-eastern borders of the
Sasanian Empire, was already waning.

Lazi
This culture of Scythian origin inhabited Colchis, a region situated along
the south-eastern shore of the Black Sea, bordering Armenia and the Caucasus. The Lazi gained historical significance only in late antiquity, when
they took over power from the ancient Colchians. They were a vassal state
of Rome and subject to Sasanian influence only between 470 and 522.

Magians (*magoi*)

According to Herodotus, the *magoi* were a Median tribe. The Greeks also perceived them as a priestly caste, who were particularly knowledgeable with regard to the interpretation of dreams, as well as astrology and magic, and who served first the Median kings and later the Achaemenid rulers. In the Sasanian period the Magians were the most important religious officials within the Zoroastrian religious community.

magister

This was the rank of a variety of Roman officials who, especially in late antiquity, could be extremely powerful. The officials were always masters of one particular field of activity. The *magister equitum* was thus commander of the cavalry, and the *magister officiorum* presided over the offices, i.e. he was the head of the civil administration of the empire. The *magister militum per Orientem* was responsible for the troops stationed on the Eastern frontier, which included the recruitment of and jurisdiction over these; in contrast, the *magister militum praesentalis* commanded the soldiers stationed in the capital and therefore performed his duties in the immediate environment of the emperor.

Mani/Manichaeism

Mani (216–77) was the founder of the Persian religion that was named Manichaeism after him. Already as a child Mani was inspired by visions in which the right faith was communicated to him. He claimed to be the last prophet and saviour of mankind. Although Mani acknowledged that Zarathustra, Buddha and Jesus had preached the truth in earlier times, he wanted to correct the mistakes made by other religions since and to preserve the good aspects of these religions. As it incorporated Iranian, Babylonian, Indian and Christian elements, Manichaeism was a syncretistic religion, a factor that must have contributed to its popularity. It was comparable to the other great world religions in that it offered salvation and answers regarding fundamental questions about the origin of the world, the soul, the body and the character of evil. Mani took care that his doctrines were written down in order that they were not modified by later transmission. Manichaeism was therefore clearly a book religion. During the reign of Šāpūr I (240–72) Mani was free to travel and preach his religion, which spread quickly throughout the Sasanian Empire. After the death of Šāpūr, however, the Zoroastrian priests, who did not tolerate any other religion besides their own, urged the new king to imprison Mani. In the following period the Manichaeans were persecuted in the Sasanian Empire and many of them sought refuge in both the West and the East.

Medes

Originally the Medes were an Iranian people of horsemen who migrated to the Iranian mountain regions at the beginning of the first millennium BC and who from the eighth century BC onwards became very significant. In alliance with the Babylonians the Medes overthrew the powerful Assyrian Empire and extended their rule into Asia Minor to the river Halys (590–585). Around 550 BC the Persian Cyrus revolted against the Median king Astyages. The Persians became the successors of Median rule and were often incorrectly called 'Medes' by the Greeks.

Monophysitism
see Christological controversies

Nabataeans

The Nabataeans were a people in northern Arabia who became significant from the fourth century BC onwards. Their confrontations with the rivalling successors of Alexander the Great brought them in contact with the Greek world. Petra, the capital of the Nabataean Empire, was a major centre of the flourishing caravan trade along the Incense Route. The Nabataean Empire reached its greatest extension around 100 BC. From the middle of the first century BC it became dependent on Rome. Upon the instigation of the emperor Trajan in AD 106 it was integrated into the Roman Empire and became the province of Arabia, of which the new capital was Bostra.

Nestorians
see Christological controversies

Persis

This was the region in south-eastern Iran that became the political centre of the Achaemenid Empire and a centre of Iranism. After the conquest of Alexander the Great the impact of 'Hellenism' did not affect this area much so that the 'Iranian spirit' could develop further. Important places in the Persis were Persepolis, Pasargadai, Istachr and Naqš-i Rustam.

phylarchos

The Greek title was used for holders of both magisterial and military offices. In late antiquity the chiefs of Arabian tribes were often called phylarchs. Already Cicero used the term with this specific meaning.

Praetorian prefect
The office was created by Augustus. A *praefectus praetorio* was appointed from members of the equestrian rank and in charge of the praetorian cohorts, the elite troops of the emperor in Rome. Gradually his military duties were extended to include civil functions, and the number of office holders varied between one and three. Constantine the Great reorganised the office by assigning exclusively civil functions to the praetorian prefect. He became the most important imperial administrator, who commanded the large administrative districts of the empire, the *praefecturae* (Gallia, Italia, Illyricum, Oriens), which were in turn divided into dioceses. In late antiquity the praetorian prefect was one of the highest officials in the Roman Empire.

Saracens/*Sarakenoi*
Authors of the first three centuries AD use the name *Sarakenoi* for a nomadic Arab tribe from the Sinai desert, which was in close contact with the Roman governor of the province of Arabia. In late antiquity and during the Middle Ages Christian authors in particular used the term for all Arabs, later for the Muslims, to some extent for all non-Christians.

Satrap
This is the title of Achaemenid, later also Seleucid, Parthian and Sasanian provincial governors. Within their satrapies, the geographical regions assigned to the satraps, they were responsible for the collection of tribute; in times of war they were the military commanders of the troops within their sphere of influence. They also held diplomatic as well as judicial powers. Because of the concentration of power within the hands of individual satraps the central power of the Great king was frequently challenged by individual satraps.

Scyths
Peoples who were perceived as dangerous equestrian tribes inhabiting areas along the Black Sea, the Don and the Dnieper rivers to the lower Danube, were collectively referred to as 'Scyths' by ancient sources. The Greek historian Herodotus describes their society and customs at length in the fourth book of his *Histories*. In the seventh and sixth centuries BC they entertained close trade relations with the Greek colonies along the Black Sea coast. Some of these tribes settled in these regions whereas others at times moved deep into Western Asia. Among the most famous Scythian tribes are the Sakai, who inhabited the region east of the Caspian Sea. Later, the name

'Scyths' was used for tribes of the Iranian Sarmatae and the nomadic tribes who lived around the Black Sea.

Silk Road

The Silk Road or Silk Route was a famous ancient trading route, which was used for trading many desired luxury goods such as silk, pottery, mirrors and pigments but also facilitated the exchange between different religions and cultures. The Silk Road extended from China across the oases of the Tarim River valley to the West. It went through Samarkhand, Merv, Ekbatana (Hamadan) into Mesopotamia, from there it continued to Syria, via Palmyra to Antioch on the Orontes or Tyrus to the Eastern Mediterranean.

solidus

Because of the increase in the price of gold Constantine replaced the previous gold denomination, the *aureus*, with this slightly lighter gold coin, which during the course of late antiquity became the main Roman denomination. The *solidus* weighed 1/72 of a Roman pound of gold.

tabularius

In the Roman Empire a *tabularius* was responsible for dispatching and delivering letters or other written communications. He could be commissioned by private individuals or by public institutions. Because of their large numbers, imperial messengers (*tabularii Augusti*) were organised according to the example of the military and belonged to the respective fields of imperial administration. When they dispatched particularly important official communications they were allowed to use the *cursus publicus*, the imperial mail system.

Tetrarchy

The modern term tetrarchy refers to the simultaneous rule of four emperors, two Augusti and two Caesars, with the latter of lower status than the former. This system was introduced by Diocletian in AD 293. Each of the four tetrarchs was in charge of one of four geographic areas within the Empire. By way of adoption all four tetrarchs were closely related. The reigns of each were carefully fixed beforehand in order to secure and determine succession. Although this system was abandoned in favour of dynastic rule after Constantine had defeated Licinius in 324, the model of 'multiple rule' clearly influenced the character of imperial government in late antiquity.

Vassal kings
In Iran these were individual local princes who tried to retain their independence from the central power, the King of kings. In the Parthian Empire the claim for power of the vassal kings led to the disintegration of the empire and contributed significantly to the fall of Arsacid rule.

Zarathustra/Zoroaster – Zarathustrianism/Zoroastrianism
Zoroaster is the Greek form of the old Iranian male name Zarathustra. The Iranian religion of Zarathustrianism/Zoroastrianism was named after this religious founder or prophet. His date is as controversial as his origins. The prevalent view is that he lived around 1000 BC in central Asia/Eastern Iran. However, both a much earlier date (c. 1200 BC) and a much later lifetime in the seventh or sixth century BC, which would correspond to the ancient tradition, have been suggested.

Bibliography

Abbott, N. (1968) 'Gundi Shapur: a preliminary historical sketch', in *Ars Orientalis* 7: 71–3.

'Abd al-Husain Zarrīnkūb (1975) 'The Arab conquest of Iran and its aftermath', in *CHI* IV: 1–56.

Abka'i-Khavari, M. (2000) *Das Bild des Königs in der Sasanidenzeit. Schriftliche Überlieferungen im Vergleich und Antiquaria.* Hildesheim.

Adontz, N. (1970) *Armenia and the Period of Justinian. The Political Conditions Based on the Naxara System.* Translated with partial revisions by N. G. Garsoïan. Lisbon.

Alcock, S. E. (ed.) (1997) *The Early Roman Empire in the East.* Oxford.

Alföldi, A. (1937) 'Die Hauptereignisse der Jahre 253–261 n. Chr. im Orient im Spiegel der Münzprägung', *Berytus* 4: 62–3, reprinted in Alföldi (1967).

(1939) 'The crisis of the Empire (AD 249–270)' in *CAH* XII: 165–231.

(1967) *Studien zur Geschichte der Weltkrise des 3. Jahrhunderts nach Christus.* Darmstadt.

Alföldi A., Straub, J., and Rosen, K. (eds.) (1964–1991) *BHAC* (13 vols.). Bonn.

Alföldy, G. (1971) 'Cassius Dio und Herodian. Über die Anfänge des Neupersischen Reiches', *RhM* N. F. 114: 360–6.

(1974) 'The crisis of the third century as seen by contemporaries', *GRBS* 15: 89–111.

Algaze, G. (1989) 'A new frontier: first results of the Tigris–Euphrates Archaeological Reconnaissance Project 1988', *JNES* 48: 241–81.

Algaze, G. et al. (1991) 'The Tigris–Euphrates Reconnaissance Project. A Preliminary Report of the 1989–1990 Seasons', *Anatolica* 17: 175–240.

Alonso-Nuñez, J. M. (1988–9) 'The Roman universal historian Pompeius Trogus on India, Parthia, Bactria and Armenia', *Persica* 13: 125–55.

Alram, M. (1996) 'Die Geschichte Ostirans von den Griechenkönigen in Baktrien und Indien bis zu den iranischen Hunnen', in *Weihrauch und Seide*, ed. W. Seipel. Milan and Vienna: 119–40.

Al-Salihi, W. (1979) 'Hatra. Aspects of Hatran religion', *Sumer* 26: 187–93.

Altheim-Stiehl, R. (1982) 'Die Zeitangaben der mittelpersischen Dipinti in der einstigen Synagoge zu Dura-Europos', *Boreas* 5: 152–9.

(1985) 'Der Beginn der sāsānidischen Reichsherrschaft', in *Chronik von Arbela 1985*: 13–16.

(1992) 'The Sasanians in Egypt – Some evidence of historical interest', *BSAC* 31: 87–96.

(1998) 'Egypt IV: relations with Persia in the Sasanian Period', *EncIr* VIII: 252–4.

Altheim, F. and Stiehl, R. (1954) *Porphyrios and Empedokles*. Tübingen.

(1955–7) 'Mohammeds Geburtsjahr', *La Nouvelle Clio* 7–9: 113–22.

(1957) *Finanzgeschichte der Spätantike*. Frankfurt am Main.

(1965–7) *Die Araber in der Alten Welt*. Vol. II, 1965; vol. IV, 1967. Berlin.

Ananian, P. (1961) 'La data e le circostanze della consecrazione di S. Gregorio Illuminatore', *Le Muséon* 84: 43–73, 317–60.

Anderson, J. G. C. (1934) 'The eastern frontier from Tiberius to Nero', in *CAH* X: 743–80.

Andreotti, R. (1969) 'Su alcuni problemi del rapporto fra politica di sicurezza e controllo del commercio nell'impero romano', *RIDA* 3ᵉ série 16: 215–57.

Angeli Bertinelli, M. G. (1989) 'Al confine tra l'impero romano e la Persia in età tardoantica: la questione della Lazica', *QC* N.S. 1: 117–46.

Antoniadis-Bibicou, H. (1963) *Recherches sur les douanes à Byzance*. Paris.

Arce, J. J. (1974) 'On Festus' sources for Julian's Persian expedition', *Athenaeum* 52: 340–3.

Arnaud, P. (1987) 'Les guerres des Parthes et de l'Arménie dans la première siècle avant n. è.: problèmes de chronologie et d'extension territoriale (95 BC – 70 BC)', *Mesopotamia* 22: 129–46.

Ash, Rh. (1999) 'An exemplary conflict: Tacitus' Parthian battle narrative (Annals 6. 34–35)', *Phoenix* 53: 114–35.

Asmussen, J. P. (1983) 'Christians in Iran', *CHI* III. 2: 924–48.

Assfalg, J. (1966) 'Zur Textüberlieferung der Chronik von Arbela', *OrChr* 50: 19–36.

Atiya, A. S. (1991) *A History of Eastern Christianity*, 2nd edn. London.

Austin, N. H. (1972) 'Julian at Ctesiphon: a fresh look at Ammianus' account', *Athenaeum* 50: 301–9.

Austin, N. J. E. and Rankow, B. (1995) *Exploratio, Military and Political Intelligence in the Roman World from the Second Punic War to the Battle of Adrianople*. London.

Azarpay, G. (1981–2) 'Bishapur VI: an artistic record of an Armeno-Persian alliance in the fourth century', *Artibus Asiae* 43: 171–89.

(1982) 'The role of Mithra in the investiture and triumph of Šāpūr II', *IrAnt* 17: 181–7.

Bachrach, B. S. (1973) *A History of the Alans in the West*. Minneapolis, Minn.

Back, M. (1978) *Die sassanidischen Staatsinschriften. Studien zur Orthographie und Phonologie des Mittelpersischen der Inschriften zusammen mit einem etymologischen Index des mittelpersischen Wortgutes und einem Textcorpus der behandelten Inschriften*. ActIr 18. Troisième série. Textes et Memoires. Leiden.

Badian, E. (1971) *Roman Imperialism in the Late Republic*, 2nd edn. Ithaca and New York. (German edn. 1980)

Bagnall, R. S. (2003) *Later Roman Egypt: Society, Religion, Economy and Adminis-tration.* Aldershot, Hampshire et al.

Bailey, H. W. (1943) *Zoroastrian Problems in the Ninth-Century Books.* Oxford.

Bakhit (1987) *Proceedings of the Second Symposium on the History of Bilad al-Sham during the Early Islamic Period up to 40 AH/640 A. D.* Vol. 1. Amman.

Baldus, H. R. (1971) *Uranius Antoninus. Münzprägung und Geschichte.* Antiquitas III 11. Bonn.

Ball, W. (1989) 'Soundings of Seh Qubba, a Roman frontier station on the Tigris in Iraq', in French and Lightfoot (1989): 7–18.

(2000) *Rome in the East. Transformation of an Empire.* London et al.

(ed.) (2003) *Ancient Settlement in the Zammar Region. Excavations by the British Archaeological Expedition to Iraq in the Sadam Dam Salvage Project, 1985–86.* BAR International Series 1096. Oxford.

Balsdon, J. P. V. D. (1979) *Romans and Aliens.* London.

Bandy, A. C. (ed.) (1983a) *John Lydus, De Magistratibus Populi Romani,* ed. and tr. A. C. Bandy. Philadelphia.

(1983b) *On Powers or The Magistracies of the Roman State.* Ioannes Lydus with introduction, crit. text and translation. Philadelphia.

Barceló, P. A. (1981) *Roms auswärtige Beziehungen unter der Constantinischen Dynas-tie (306–363).* Eichstätter Beiträge 3. Regensburg.

Bardill, J. (1999) 'The great palace of the Byzantine emperors and the Walker Trust Excavations', *JRA* 12: 216–30.

Barišić, F. (1954) 'Le siège de Constantinople par les Avares et les Slaves en 626', *Byzantion* 24: 371–95.

Barnes, T. D. (1976) 'Imperial Campaigns, AD 285–311', *Phoenix* 30: 179–86.

(1980) 'Imperial chronology', *Phoenix* 34: 163.

(1981) *Constantine and Eusebius.* Cambridge.

(1982) *The New Empire of Diocletian and Constantine.* Cambridge.

(1985) 'Constantine and the Christians of Persia', *JRS* 75: 126–36.

(1998) *Ammianus Marcellinus and the Representation of Historical Reality.* New York.

Basham, A. L. (ed.) (1968) *Papers on the Date of Kanishka.* Leiden.

Baynes, N. H. (1904) 'The first campaign of Heraclios against Persia', *EHR* 19: 694–702.

(1910) 'Rome and Armenia in the fourth century', *EHR* 25: 625–43, reprinted in Baynes (1955), 186–208.

(1912) 'The restoration of the Cross at Jerusalem', *EHR* 27: 287–99.

(1955) *Rome and Armenia in the Fourth Century.* Byzantine Studies and Other Essays. London.

Bedoukian, P. Z. (1980) *Coinage of the Ataxiads of Armenia.* Royal Numismatic Society Special Publication No. 10. London.

Bellamy, J. A. (1985) 'A new reading of the Namārah Inscription', *Journal of the American Oriental Society* 105: 31–51.

Bengtson, H. (1974) *Zum Partherfeldzug des Antonius (36 v. Chr.).* Munich.

Bering-Staschewski, R. (1981) *Römische Zeitgeschichte bei Cassius Dio.* Bochum.

Bier, C. (1993) 'Piety and power', in *Official Cult and Popular Religion in the Ancient Near East*, ed. E. Matsushima. Heidelberg: 172–94.

Bird, H. W. (1986) 'Eutropius and Festus: Some reflections on the Empire and imperial policy in AD 369/370', *Florilegium* 8: 11–22.

Birley, A. R. (1971) *Septimius Severus. The African Emperor*. London. (First published in paperback 1999.)

(1976) *Lives of the Later Caesars. The First Part of the Augustan History (Hadrianus – Heliogabalus)*. London.

(1987) *Marcus Aurelius. A Biography*. London.

(1988) *The African Emperor: Septimius Severus*. London.

(1998) *Hadrian. The Restless Emperor*. 2nd edn. London et al.

Birley, E. (1956) 'Hadrianic Frontier Policy', *in Carnuntia. Ergebnisse der Forschungen über die Grenzprovinzen des römischen Reiches*, ed. E. Swoboda. Graz: 25–33.

Bivar, A. D. H. (1970) 'Trade between China and the Near East in the Sasanian and early Muslim periods', in *Pottery and Metalwork in T'ang China*, ed. W. Watson. London: 1–11.

(1972) 'Cavalry equipment and tactics on the Euphrates frontier', *DOP* 26: 271–91.

(1983a) 'The history of Eastern Iran', *CHI* III. 1: 181–231.

(1983b) 'The Political History of Iran under the Arsacids', in *CHI* III.1: 21–99.

Bivar, A. D. H. and Boyce, M. (1998) 'Eṣtaḵr I. History and Archaeology. II: As a Zoroastrian religious centre', *EncIr* VIII: 643–6.

Bleckmann, B. (1992) *Die Reichskrise des III. Jahrhunderts in der spätantiken und byzantinischen Geschichtsschreibung: Untersuchungen zu den nachdionischen Quellen der Chronik des Johannes Zonaras*. Quellen und Forschungen zur Antiken Welt. Vol. I. Munich.

Blockley, R. C. (1973) 'Festus' source on Julian's expedition', *CP* 68: 54–5.

(1980) 'Doctors and diplomats in the sixth century AD', *Florilegium* 2: 89–100.

(1981) *The Fragmentary Classicising Historians of the Later Roman Empire. Eunapius, Olympiodorus, Priscus and Malchus*. Vol. I. Liverpool.

(1983) *The Fragmentary Classicising Historians of the Later Roman Empire. Eunapius, Olympiodorus, Priscus and Malchus*. Vol. II: Text, translation and historiographical notes. Liverpool.

(1984) 'The Romano-Persian peace treaties of AD 299 and 363', *Florilegium* 6: 28–49.

(1985a) 'Subsidies and diplomacy: Rome and Persia in Late Antiquity', *Phoenix* 39: 62–74.

(1985b) *The History of Menander the Guardsman*. Liverpool.

(1987) 'The division of Armenia between the Romans and Persians at the end of the fourth century AD', *Historia* 36: 222–34.

(1989) 'Constantius II and Persia', in *Studies in Latin Literature and Roman History* V, ed. C. Deroux. Brüssel: 468–89.

(1992) *East Roman Foreign Policy. Formation and Conduct from Diocletian to Anastasius*. Leeds.

Blum, G. (1980) 'Zur religionspolitischen Situation der persischen Kirche im 3. und 4. Jahrhundert', *ZKG* 91: 11–32.

Bobzin, H. (2000) *Mohammed*. Beck Wissen vol. 2144. Munich.

Bonamente, G., Duval, N., Paschoud, F. et al. (eds.) (1991) *Historiae Augustae Colloquia (HAC)*. Bari.

Börm, H. (2006) 'Die Persericonig im Imperium Romanum. Chosroes I und der sasanidische Einfall in das Oströmische Reich 540n. Chr', *Chiron* 36: 301–28.

Bosi, F. (1994) 'The nomads of Eurasia in Strabo', in *The Archaeology of the Steppes. Methods and Strategies. Papers from the International Symposium held in Naples 9–12 November 1992*, ed. B. Genito. Naples: 109–22. (= Istituto Universitario Orientale, Series Minor XLIV).

Bosworth, A. (1976) 'Vespasian's reorganization of the north-east frontier', *Antichthon* 10: 63–78.

(1977) 'Arrian and the Alani', *Harv. St. Class. Ph.* 81: 218–29.

Bosworth, C. E. (1983) 'Iran and the Arabs before Islam', in *CHI* III. 1: 593–612.

(1985–7) 'Arabs and Iran in the pre-Islamic period', *EncIr* 1985/87: 201–3.

(1999) *The History of al-Tabari (Ta'rīkh al-rusul wa'l mūluk)*. Vol. V: *The Sasanids, the Byzantines, the Lakmids and Yemen*. New York.

Bounni, A. (ed.) (1996) *Palmyra and the Silk Road. International Colloquium*. AAAS 42. Damascus.

Bounni, A. and Al-As'ad, K. (1988) *Palmyra: History, Monuments and Museum*. Damascus.

Bowersock, G. W. (1973) 'Syria under Vespasian', *JRS* 43: 123–9.

(1983) *Roman Arabia*. Cambridge and London.

Bowersock, G. W., Brown, P., and Grabar, O. (eds.) (1999) *Late Antiquity: A Guide to the Postclassical World*. Cambridge, MA.

Bowie, E. L. (1999), 'The Greek novel', in Swain 1999: 39–59.

Boyce, M. (1957) 'The Parthian *gosan* and the Iranian minstrel tradition', *JRAS*: 10–45.

(1975) *A Reader in Manichaean Middle Persian and Parthian*. ActIr. Teheran-Liège.

(1982) *A History of Zoroastrianism*. Vol. II. Leiden.

(1984a) *Zoroastrians. Their Religious Beliefs and Practices*, 2nd edn. London, Boston, Melbourne and Harley.

(1984b) *Textual Sources for the Study of Zoroastrianism*. Manchester.

(1985) 'Ahura Mazdā', *EncIr* 1: 684–7.

(1987) 'Arsacid religion', *EncIr* II: 540–1.

(1994) 'The sedentary Arsacids', *IrAnt* 29: 241–51.

Brandt, H. (1998) *Geschichte der römischen Kaiserzeit. Von Diokletian und Konstantin bis zum Ende der Konstantinischen Dynastie (284–363)*. Berlin.

Braun, O. (1915) *Ausgewählte Aspekte persischer Märtyrer*. Mit einem Anhang: Ostsyrisches Mönchsleben (aus dem Syrischen übersetzt). BdK. Bd. 22. Kempten and Munich.

Braund, D. (1986) 'The Caucasian frontier: myth, exploration and the dynamics of imperialism', in Freeman and Kennedy (1986): 31–49.

(1989) 'Coping with the Caucasus: Roman responses to local conditions in Colchis', in French and Lightfoot (1989): 31–43.

(1991) 'Procopius on the economy of Lazica', *CQ* 41: 221–5.

(1994) *Georgia in Antiquity. A History of Colchis and Transcaucasian Iberia 550 BC – AD 562.* Oxford.

Brentjes, B. (1978) *Das alte Persien: Die iranische Welt vor Mohammed.* Vienna.

Breuer, St. (1987) *Imperien der Alten Welt.* Stuttgart et al.

Brock, S. P. (1978) 'A martyr at the Sasanid court under Vahran II: Candid', *AnalBolland* 96: 167–81.

(1982) 'Christians in the Sasanian Empire: A case of divided loyalists', in *Religion and National Identity: Papers Read at the Nineteenth Summer Meeting and the Twentieth Winter Meeting of the Ecclesiastical History Society.* Studies in Church History 18, ed. St. Mews. Oxford: 1–9.

(1984) *Syriac Perspectives on Late Antiquity.* London.

(1985) 'The christology of the Church of the East in the synods of the fifth to early seventh century', in *Aksum-Thyateira: a Festschrift for Archbishop Methodios,* ed. G. Drogas. London: 125–42.

(1992) *Studies in Syriac Christianity.* London.

(1996) 'The Church of the East in the Sasanian Empire up to the sixth century and its absence from the councils in the Roman Empire', in *Syriac Dialogue. First Non-Official Consultation on Dialogue within the Syriac Tradition,* Vienna: 69–85.

Brocker, M. and Nau, H. (eds.) (1997) *Ethnozentrismus. Möglichkeiten und Grenzen des interkulturellen Dialogs.* Darmstadt.

Brodersen, K. (1986) 'The date of the secession of Parthia from the Seleucid Kingdom', *Historia* 35: 378–81.

(1987) 'Das Steuergesetz von Palmyra', in *Palmyra. Geschichte. Kunst und Kultur der syrischen Oasenstadt.* Katalog, ed. E. Ruprechtsberger. Linz und Frankfurt: 153–61.

Brodka, D. (1998) 'Das Bild des Perserkönigs Chosros I. in den "Bella" des Prokopios von Kaisareia', in *Studies of Greek and Roman Civilization,* ed. J. Styka. Krakow: 115–24.

Brown, P. (1969) 'The diffusion of Manichaeism in the Roman Empire', *JRS* 59: 92–103.

(1971) *The World of Late Antiquity.* London.

Browning, J. (1979) *Palmyra.* London.

Burgess, R. W. (1999) 'The dates of the first siege of Nisibis and the death of James of Nisibis', *Byzantium* 69: 7–17.

Bury, J. B. (1958) *History of the Later Roman Empire from the Death of Theodosius I. to the Death of Justinian (395–565).* Vol. II. London.

(1966) *A History of the Later Roman Empire from Arcadius to Irene, 395 AD to 800 AD* (2 vols.). London. (Reprint of 1889).

Butcher, K. (2003) *Roman Syria and the Near East.* London.

Büttner-Wobst, T. (1978) 'Der Tod Kaiser Julians. Eine Quellenstudie', in Klein (1978): 24–47.

Caetani, L. (ed.) (1909) *The Tajārib al-umam or History of Ibn Miskawayh*. Faksimile der Manuskripte der Hagia Sofia. Vol. I. E. J. W. Gibb Memorial Series VIII I. Leiden.

Cameron, A. (1969–70) 'Agathias on the Sasanians', *DOP* 23–4: 67–183.

(1970) *Agathias*. Oxford.

(1985) *Procopius and the Sixth Century*. London.

(1993a) *The Later Roman Empire (AD 284–430)*. London.

(1993b) *The Mediterranean World in Late Antiquity, AD 395–600*. London.

(1995) *The Byzantine and Early Islamic Near East. States, Resources and Armies*. Studies in Late Antiquity and Early Islam. Vol. III. Princeton, New Jersey.

Cameron, A. and Garnsey, P. (eds.) (1998) *The Cambridge Ancient History, Volume XIII: The Late Empire, AD 337–425*. Cambridge.

Cameron, A. and Long, J. (1993) *Barbarians and Politics at the Court of Arcadius*. Berkeley.

Cameron, A., Ward-Perkins, B., and Whitby, M. (eds.) (2000) *The Cambridge Ancient History, Volume XIV: Late Antiquity. Empire and Successors, AD 425–600*. Cambridge.

Campbell, D. (1986) 'What happened at Hatra? The problems of the Severan siege operations', in Freeman and Kennedy (1986): 51–8.

Campbell, J. B. (1993) 'War and diplomacy: Rome and Parthia, 31 BC–AD 235', in *War and Society in the Roman World*, eds. J. Rich and G. Shipley. London: 213–40.

(1999) 'Kataphraktoi', *DNP* 6: 339.

Capizzi, C. (1969) *L'imperatore Anastasio I (491–518)*. Studio sulla sua vita, la sua opera e la sua personalità. Orientalia Christiana Analecta 184. Rome.

Carney, T. F. (1971) *John the Lydian, De Magistratibus*. Lawrence, Kansas.

Carson, R. A. G. (1982) 'The date of the capture of Valerian I', in *Actes du 9ième Congrès International de Numismatique. Berne 1979*. Vol. I. Louvain: 461–5.

Casey, P. J. (1996) 'Justinian, the limitanei, and Arab-Byzantine relations in the sixth century', *JRA* 9: 214–22.

Casey, R. P. (1998) 'Armenien I. im Altertum', in *RGG* I⁴: 763–6.

Castritius, H. (1968/9) 'Der Armenierkrieg des Maximinus Daia', *JbAC* 11/12: 94–103.

Charlesworth, M. P. (1970) *Trade-Routes and Commerce of the Roman Empire*. 2nd edn. New York

Chaumont, M.-L. (1960) 'L'inscription de Kartir à la "Ka'bah de Zoroastre". Texte, Traduction, Commentaire', *JA* 248: 339–80.

(1969) *Recherches sur l'histoire d'Arménie de l'avènement des sassanides à la conversion du royaume*. Paris.

(1976) 'L'Arménie entre Rome et l'Iran. De l'avènement d'Auguste à l'avènement de Dioclétian', *ANRW* II 9.1: 71–194.

(1979) 'A propos de la chute de Hatra et du couronnement de Shapur Ier', *AAntHung* 27: 207–37.

(1984) 'Etudes d'histoire parthe. v. La route royale des Parthes de Zeugma à Séleucie du Tigre d'après l'Itinéraire d'Isidore de Charax', *Syria* 61: 63–107.

(1986a) 'Argbed', *EncIr* II: 400–1.

(1986b) 'Les grands rois sassanides d'Arménie', *Ir Ant* 8: 81–93.

(1987a) 'Armenia and Iran II', *EncIr* II: 418–38.

(1987b) 'Antioch', *EncIr* II: 119–25.

(1990) 'A propos des premières interventions parthes en Arménie et des circonstances de l'avènement de Tigrane le Grand', in *From Alexander the Great to Kül Tegin*, ed. J. Harmatta. Budapest: 19–31.

Christensen, A. (1944) *L'Iran sous les Sassanides*. 2nd edn. Copenhagen. (Reprint Osnabrück 1971.)

Christensen, A. S. (1980) *Lactantius the Historian. An Analysis of the 'De Mortibus Persecutorum'*. Copenhagen.

Christian, D. (1998) *A History of Russia, Central Asia and Mongolia*. Vol. I: *Inner Eurasia from Prehistory to the Mongol Empire*. Oxford et al.

Chronik von Arbela (1985) *Die Chronik von Arbela*. Translated by P. Kawerau. CSCO. Vol. 468. Scriptores Syri. Tom. 200. Louvain.

Chrysos, E. K. (1976) 'Some aspects of Roman–Persian legal relations', *KΛHRONOMIA* 8: 1–60.

(1978) 'The title BAΣIΛEYΣ in early Byzantine international relations', *DOP* 32: 29–75.

(1993) 'Räumung und Aufgabe von Reichsterritorien. Der Vertrag von 363', *BJb* 193: 165–202.

Clauss, M. (1981) 'Der magister officiorum in der Spätantike (4.–6. Jahrhundert). Das Amt und sein Einfluß auf die kaiserliche Politik', *Vestigia* 32: 147.

Clermont-Ganneau, C. (1898) 'The Taking of Jerusalem by the Persians AD 614', *Palestine Exploration Fund*, Quarterly Statement: 36–54.

Colledge, M. A. R. (1967) *The Parthians*. London.

Colvin, I. (2003) *Procopius and Agathias on Roman and Sasanian Intervention in Lazika in the Sixth Century*. D. Phil. thesis. Oxford.

Compareti, M. (2002) 'The Sasanians in Africa', *Transoxania* 4: 1–6.

Conduché, D. (1978) 'Ammianus Marcellinus und der Tod Julians', in Klein (1978): 355–80.

Coulston, J. C. (1986) 'Roman, Parthian and Sassanid tactical developments', in Freeman and Kennedy (1986): 59–75.

(1990) 'Later Roman armour, 3rd–6th centuries AD', *Journal of Roman Military Equipment Studies* 1: 139–60.

Cowe, S. P. (1991) 'The significance of the Persian War (571–91) in the Narratio de rebus Armeniae', *Muséon* 104: 265–76.

Craven, L. (1920) 'Antony's oriental policy until the defeat of the Parthian expedition', *Social Science Series* v 3.2, University of Missouri. Missouri.

Crawford, M. H. and Reynolds, J. M. (1977) 'The Aezani copy of the Prices Edict, *ZPE* 26: 125–51.

(1979) 'The Aezani copy of the Prices Edict' *ZPE* 34: 163–210.

Creed, J. L. (1984) *Lactantius. De Mortibus Persecutorum. Edited and Translated*. Oxford.

Crees, J. H. E. (1965) *The Reign of the Emperor Probus*. Rome.

Croke, B. (1984) 'Marcellinus and Dara: a fragment of his lost *de temporum quali-tatibus et positionibus locorum*', *Phoenix* 38: 86–8.

(1992) *Christian Chronicles and Byzantine History – Fifth–Sixth Centuries*. Aldershot.

(1995) *The Chronicle of Marcellinus: Translation and Commentary*. Sydney.

(2001) *Comes Marcellinus and his Chronicle*. Oxford.

Croke, B. and Crow, J. (1983) 'Procopius and Dārā', *JRS* 73: 143–59.

Crone, P. (1991) 'Kavad's heresy and Mazdak's revolt', *Iran* 29: 21–42.

Crow, J. (1981) 'Dara, a late Roman fortress in Mesopotamia', *Yayla* 4: 12–20.

Crump, G. A. (1975) *Ammianus Marcellinus as a Military Historian*. Historia Einzelschriften 27. Wiesbaden.

Dabrowa, E. (1980) 'Les limes anatoliens et la frontière caucasienne au temps des Flavians', *Klio* 62: 382–8.

(1981) 'Les rapports entre Rome et les parthes sous Vespasien', *Syria* 58: 187–204.

(1983) *La politique de l'état parthe à l'égard de Rome*. Krakow.

(1984) Le programme de la politique en Occident des derniers Arsacides, *IrAnt* 19: 149–65.

(1989) 'Roman policy in Transcaucasia from Pompey to Domitian', in French and Lightfoot (1989): 77–111.

(ed.) (1994) *The Roman and Byzantine Army in the East*. Krakow.

Daim, F., Kaus, K., and Tomka, P. (eds.) (1996) *Reitervölker aus dem Osten. Hunnen und Awaren*. Burgenländische Landesausstellung 1996. Begleitbuch und Katalog. Eisenstadt.

Dani, A. H., Litvinsky, B. A., and Zimmer Zafi, M. H. (1996) 'Eastern Kushans, Kidarites in Gandhara and Kashmir, and later Hephthalites', in *History of Civilizations of Central Asia*, vol. III: *The Crossroads of civilizations: AD 250 to 750.*, ed. B. Litvinsky. Delhi: 163–83.

Daryaee, T. (1999) 'The coinage of Queen Boran and its significance for late Sasanian imperial ideology', *Bulletin of the Asia Institute* 13: 77–82.

(2001–2) 'Memory and history: the construction of the past in late antique Persia', *Nāme-ye Irān-e Bāstan* 1–2: 1–14.

(2002) 'The collapse of the Sasanian power in Fars (Persis)', *Nāme-ye Irān-e Bāstan* 2,1: 3–18.

(2003) 'The Persian gulf trade in late antiquity', *Journal of World History* 14, 1: 1–6.

Deberoise, N.C. (1938) *A Political History of Parthia*. Chicago.

De Blois, L. (1975) 'Odaenathus and the Roman–Persian War of 252–264 AD', *TALANTA* 6: 7–23.

(1978–9) 'The reign of the emperor Philip the Arabian', *TALANTA* 10–11: 11–43.

Decret, F. (1979) 'Les conséquences sur le christianisme en Perse de l'affrontement des empires romain et sassanide. De Shāpūr Ier à Yazdgard Ier', *Recherches Augustiennes* 14: 91–152.

De Decker. D. (1979) 'Sur le destinataire de la lettre au roi des Perses et la conversion de l'Arménie à la religion chrétienne', *Persica* 8: 99–116.

de Jong, A. (1997) *Traditions of the Magi: Zoroastrianism in Greek and Latin Literature*. Leiden.

De Laet, S. J. (1949) *Portorium*. Brügge.

De Ligt, L. (1993) *Fairs and Markets in the Roman Empire. Economic and Social Aspects of Periodic Trade in a Pre-Industrial Society.* Amsterdam.

Demandt, A. (1968) 'Studien zur Kaaba-i-Zardoscht', *AA* 83: 520–40.

    (1989) *Die Spätantike. Römische Geschichte von Diocletian bis Justinian 284–565 n. Chr.* HAW III 6. Munich.

    (1995) *Antike Staatsformen. Eine vergleichende Verfassungsgeschichte der Alten Welt.* Berlin.

DeMenasce, J. P. (1983) 'Zoroastrian Pahlavi writings', *CHI* III. 2: 1187–8.

Den Boer, W. (1972) *Some Minor Roman Historians*. Leiden.

Dennis, G. T. (1981) *Maurice, Strategikon*. Vienna.

    (1985) *Three Byzantine Military Treatises*: Text, Translation and Notes. Washington, D.C.

Dennis, G. T. and Gamillscheg, E. (1981) *Das Strategikon des Maurikios.* CFHB 17. Vienna.

Derakhshani, J. (1995) *Die Zeit Zarathustras. Rekonstruktion der altiranischen Chronologie.* Geschichte und Kultur des Alten Ostiran I 1. Teheran.

De Ste. Croix, G. E. M. (1991) *The Class Struggle in the Ancient World.* 2nd edn. London.

Devos, P. (1966) 'Les Martyrs persans à traveurs leurs actes syriaques', in *Atti de Convegno sul tema: La Persia e il mondo graeco-romano* (Roma 11–14 aprile 1965). Rome: 213–42.

Devreesse, R. (1943) 'Arabes-Perses et Arabes-Romains. Lakhmides et Ghassanides', *RevBibl* 51: 263–307.

Diebler, S. (1995) 'Les hommes du roi: sur la representátion souveraine dans les relations diplomatiques entre Byzance et les Sassanides d'après les historiens byzantines du sixième siècle', *StIr* 24: 187–217.

Dihle, A. (1994) *Die Griechen und die Fremden*. Munich.

Dijkstra, K. (1990) 'State and steppe. The socio-political implications of Hatra Inscription 79', *Journal of Semitic Studies* 35: 81–98.

Dillemann, L. (1961) 'Ammien Marcellin et les pays de l'Èuphrate et du Tigre', *Syria* 38: 87–157.

    (1962), *Haute Mésopotamie orientale et pays adjacents.* Paris.

Dixon, K. R. and Southern, P. (1992) *The Roman Cavalry.* 2nd edn. London.

Dobbins, K. W. (1974) 'Mithridates II and his successors: A study of the Parthian crisis 90–70 BC', *Antichthon* 8: 63–79.

Doblhofer, E. (1955) *Byzantinische Diplomaten und östliche Barbaren. Aus den Excerpta de legationibus des Konstantinos Porphyrogennetos ausgewählte Abschnitte des Priskos und Menander Protektor.* Übersetzt, eingeleitet und erklärt von E. Doblhofer, 2nd edn. Graz.

Dodgeon, M. H. and Lieu, S. N. C. (eds.) (1991) *The Roman Eastern Frontier and the Persian Wars (AD 226–363). A Documentary History.* London – New York. (Reprint 2002.)

Doise, J. (1945) 'Le partage de l'Arménie sous Théodose Ier', *REA* 47: 274–7.

Dölger, F. (1964) 'Die "Familie der Könige" im Mittelalter', in *Byzanz und die europäische Staatenwelt. Ausgewählte Vorträge und Aufsätze*, ed. F. Dölger. Darmstadt: 34–69.

Donner, F. M. (1981) *The Early Islamic Conquests.* Princeton.

(1995) 'Centralized authority and military autonomy in the early Islamic conquests', in Cameron (1995): 337–60.

(2005) 'The background to Islam', in Maas (2005): 510–533.

Dörries, H. (1954) *Das Selbstzeugnis Kaiser Konstantins.* Abhandlung der Akademie der Wissenschaften Göttingen. Philologisch-Historische Klasse, 3. Folge, Nr. 34. Göttingen.

Downey, G. (1950) 'Aurelian's victory over Zenobia at Immae, AD 272', *TAPhA* 81: 57–68.

(1953) 'The Persian campaign in Syria in AD 540', *Speculum* 28: 340–8.

(1961) *A History of Antioch in Syria. From Seleucus to the Arab Conquest.* Princeton, New Jersey. (3rd edn. Princeton 1974.)

(1963) *Ancient Antioch.* Princeton, New Jersey.

Dreher, M. (1996) 'Pompeius und die kaukasischen Völker', *Historia* 45: 188–207.

Dressel, H. (1973) *Die römischen Medaillone des Münzkabinetts der staatlichen Museen zu Berlin.* Bearbeitet von K. Regling, Textband. Zürich.

Drexhage, R. (1982) 'Der Handel Palmyras in römischer Zeit', *MBAH* 1: 17–34.

(1983) Die 'Expositio totius mundi et gentium'. Eine Handelsgeographie aus dem 4. Jahrhundert n. Chr., eingeleitet, übersetzt und mit einführender Literatur (Kap. XXII–LXVII) versehen. *MBAH* 2.1: 3–41.

(1988) *Untersuchungen zum römischen Osthandel.* Bonn.

Drijvers, J. W. (1976) *The Religion of Palmyra.* Leiden.

(1977) 'Hatra, Palmyra, Edessa. Die Städte der syrisch-mesopotamischen Wüste in politischer, kulturgeschichtlicher und religionsgeschichtlicher Beleuchtung', *ANRW* II 8: 799–906.

(1980) *Cults and Beliefs at Edessa.* EPRO Tome 82. Leiden.

(1994) 'The Syriac romance of Julian. Its function, place of origin and original language', in *VI. Symposium Syriacum 1992*, ed. R. Lavenant. Rome: 201–14.

(1998) 'Strabo on Parthia and the Parthians', in Wiesehöfer (1998a): 279–93.

(1999) 'Ammianus Marcellinus' image of Arsaces and early Parthian History' in Drijvers and Hunt (1999): 193–206.

Drijvers, J. W. and Hunt, D. (eds.) (1999) *The Late Roman World and its Historian. Interpreting Ammianus Marcellinus.* London and New York.

Driven, L. (1999) *The Palmyrenes of Dura Europos. A Study of Religious Interaction in Roman Syria.* Leiden.

Duchesne-Guillemin, J. (1964) *La religion de l'Iran ancien.* Paris.

(1983) 'Zoroastrian Religion', *CHI* III. 2: 866–908.

Duneau, J. F. (1966) 'Quelques aspects de la pénétration de l'hellénisme dans l'empire perse sassanide (IVᵉ–VIIᵉ siècles)', in *Mélanges offerts à R. Grozet*, Poitiers: 13–22.

Eadie, J. W. (1967a) *The Breviarium of Festus. A Critical Edition with Historical Commentary.* London.

(1967b) 'The development of Roman mailed cavalry', *JRS* 57: 161–73.

(1985) 'Artifacts of annexation: Trajan's grand strategy and Arabia', in *The Craft of the Ancient Historian: Essays in Honour of Ch. G. Starr*, eds. J. W. Eadie and J. Obers. Lanham, Md.: 407–23.

(1989) 'Strategies of economic development in the Roman East: The Red Sea trade revisited', in French and Lightfoot (1989): 113–20.

(1996) 'The transformation of the eastern frontier 260–305', in *Shifting Frontiers in Late Antiquity*, eds. R. W. Mathisen and H. S. Sivan. Aldershot and Hampshire: 72–82.

Eggermont, P. H. L. (1968) 'The Historia Philippica of Pompeius Trogus and the foundation of the Scythian empire', in Basham (1968): 97–102.

Ehling, K. (1996) 'Der Ausgang des Perserfeldzuges in der Münzpropaganda des Jovian', *Klio* 78: 186–91.

Ehrhardt, N. (1998) 'Parther und parthische Geschichte bei Tacitus', in Wiesehöfer (1998a): 295–307.

Enderlein, V. and Sundermann, W. (eds.) (1988) *Schahname. Das Persische Königsbuch. Miniaturen und Texte der Berliner Handschrift von 1605.* Leipzig und Weimar.

Endreß, G. (1997) *Der Islam. Eine Einführung in seine Geschichte.* 3rd edn. Munich.

Enoki, K. (1955) 'The origin of the White Huns or Hephtalites', *E & W* VI. I: 231–7.

Ensslin, W. (1936) 'Zu dem vermuteten Perserfeldzug des rex Hannibalianus', *Klio* 29: 102–10.

(1939) 'Sassanid Persia: (VI) The wars with Rome', *CAH* XII: 126–37.

(1942) *Zur Ostpolitik des Kaisers Diokletian. SBAW. Ph.-h. Kl. 1942/1.* Munich.

Equini Schneider, E. (1993) *Septimia Zenobia Sebaste.* Rome.

Erdmann, K. (1941) *Das iranische Feuerheiligtum.* Leipzig.

Evans, J. A. S. (1996) *The Age of Justinian: Circumstances of Imperial Power.* London and New York.

Ezov, A. (2000) 'Reconnaissance and intelligence in the Roman art of war writing in the imperial period', in *Studies in Latin Literature and Roman History.* Coll. Latomus 254, ed. C. Deroux. Brussels: 299–317.

Felix, W. (1985) *Antike literarische Quellen zur Außenpolitik des Sāsānidenstaates.* Vol. I. Veröffentlichung der Iranischen Komission Nr. 18. Sb. der Österr. Ak. d. Wiss. Ph.-h. Kl. Bd. 456. Vienna: 224–309.

Février, J. G. (1931) *Essai sur l'histoire politique et économique de Palmyre.* Paris.

Fiey, J. M. (1987) 'The last Byzantine campaign into Persia and its influence on the attitude of the local populations towards the Muslim conquerors 7–16 H./628–636 AD', in Bakhit (1987): 96–103.

Fiorani Piacentini, V. (1985) 'Ardashīr i Pāpakān and the wars against the Arabs: a working hypothesis on the Sasanian hold of the Gulf', *PSAS* 15: 57–77.

Flusin, B. (1992) *Saint Anastase le Perse et l'histoire de la Palestine au début du VII siècle.* Vol. II. Paris.

Fornara, C. W. (1991) 'Julian's Persian expedition in Ammianus and Zosimos', *JHS* III: 1–15.

Foss, C. (1975) 'The Persians in Asia Minor and the end of Antiquity', *EHR* 90: 721–47, reprinted in Foss (1990).

(1990) *History and Archaeology of Byzantine Asia Minor*. Aldershot.

(1997) 'Syria in Transition, AD 550–750: An archaeological approach', *DOP* 51: 189–269.

(2003) 'The Persians in the Roman Near East', *JRAS* 13: 149–70.

Fowden, G. (1993) *Empire to Commonwealth. Consequences of Monotheism in Late Antiquity*. Princeton, New Jersey.

(1994) 'The last days of Constantine: oppositional versions and their influence', *JRS* 84: 146–70.

Frank, T. (ed.) (1940) *An Economic Survey of Ancient Rome IV. Roman Africa, Roman Syria, Roman Greece, Roman Asia*. Baltimore.

Freeman, P. (1994) 'Pompey's eastern settlement: a matter of presentation?', in *Studies in Latin Literature and Roman History VII*. Collection Latomus 227, ed. C. Deroux. Brussels: 143–79.

Freeman, P. and Kennedy, D. (eds.) (1986) *The Defense of the Roman and Byzantine East*. BAR International Series 297. Oxford.

Freis, H. (1994) *Historische Inschriften zur römischen Kaiserzeit von Augustus bis Konstantin*. 2nd edn. Darmstadt.

French, D. H. and Lightfoot, C. S. (eds.) (1989) *The Eastern Frontier of the Roman Empire. Proceedings of a Colloquium Held at Ankara in September 1988*. BAR International Series 553. Oxford.

Frend, W. H. C. (1979) *The Rise of the Monophysite Movement*. Cambridge.

Frendo, J. D. (1975) *Agathias. The Histories. Translated with an Introduction and Short Explanatory Notes*. CFHB II A. Berlin and New York.

(1985) 'The territorial ambitions of Chosroes II: an Armenian view?', *Florilegium* 7: 30–6.

(1989) 'Theophylact Simocatta on the revolt of Bahram Cobin and the early career of Khusrau II', *Bulletin of the Iranian Institute*, N.S. 3: 77–88.

(1992) 'Sasanian irredentism and foundation of Constantinople: historical truth and historical reality', *Bulletin of the Asia Institute* 6: 59–68.

(1995) 'The early exploits and final overthrow of Khusrau II (591–628): panegyric and vilification in the last Byzantine Iranian conflict', *Bulletin of the Asia Institute* 9: 209–14.

Frézouls, E. (ed.) (1976) *Palmyre. Bilan et perspectives. Colloque de Strasbourg 1973*. Strasbourg.

Frézouls, E. and Jacquemin, A. (eds.) (1995) *Les relations internationales. Actes du Colloque de Strasbourg 15.–17.6.1993*. Paris.

Frye, R. N. (1972) 'Byzantine and Sasanian trade relations with northeastern Russia', *DOP* 26: 265–96.

(1977) 'The Sassanian system of walls for defense', in *Studies in Memory of Gaston Wiet*, ed. M. Rosen-Ayalon. Jerusalem: 7–15.

(1983a) 'The political history of Iran under the Sasanians', *CHI* III. 1: 116–80.

(1983b) 'Bahrain under the Sasanians', in *Dilmun: New Studies in the Archaeology and Early History of Bahrain*, ed. D. T. Potts. Berlin: 167–70.

(1983c) 'Achaemenid echoes in Sasanian times', in *Kunst, Kultur und Geschichte der Achämenidenzeit und ihr Fortleben*. Archäologische Mitteilungen aus Iran. Erg. Band 19, eds. H. Koch and D. N. Mackenzie. Berlin: 247–52.

(1984) *The History of Ancient Iran*. HAW III 7. Munich.

(2000) 'Parthian and Sasanian history of Iran', in *Mesopotamia and Iran in the Parthian and Sasanian Periods: Rejection and Revival c. 238 BC–AD 642. Proceedings of a Seminar in Memory of V. G. Lukanin*, ed. J. Curtis. London: 17–22.

Fuchs, H. (1964) *Der geistige Widerstand gegen Rom in der antiken Welt*. 2nd edn. Berlin.

Fuhrmann, M. (1977) 'Die Mönchsgeschichte des Hieronymus', *Entretiens sur L'antiquité classique* 23. Geneva: 41–89.

Fukai, S. (1972) *Taq-i-Bustan IV: Text*. The Tokyo University Iraq-Iran Archaeological Expedition, Report 20. Tokyo.

Fukai, S. and Horiuchi, K. (1962–72) *Taq-i-Bustan I–II: Plates*. The Tokyo University Iraq-Iran Archaeological Expedition, Report 10. 13. Tokyo.

Funke, P. (1996) 'Die syrisch-mesopotamische Staatenwelt in vorislamischer Zeit. Zu den arabischen Macht- und Staatenbildungen an der Peripherie der antiken Großmächte im Hellenismus und in der römischen Kaiserzeit', in *Beiträge zur Erforschung von Akkulturation und politischer Ordnung in den Staaten des hellenistischen Zeitalters. Akten des Internationalen Hellenismus-Kolloquiums 9.–14. März 1994 in Berlin*, ed. B. Funck. Tübingen: 217–38.

Gajé, J. (1965) 'Comment Sapor a-t-il "triomphé" de Valérien?', *Syria* 42: 343–88.

Gall, H. v. (1980) 'Relieffragment eines elymäischen Königs aus Masğed-e Soleiman', *IrAnt* 15: 241–50.

(1990) *Das Reiterkampfbild in der iranischen und iranisch beeinflußten Kunst parthischer und sāsānidischer Zeit*. Teheraner Forschungen. Berlin.

Garsoïan, N. G. (1967) 'Politique ou orthodoxie? L'Arménie au IVe siècle', *REtArm* 4: 297–320, reprinted in Garsoïan (1985): 297–320.

(1971) 'Armenia in the fourth century. An attempt to redefine the concepts "Armenia" and "loyalty"', *REtArm* 8: 342–52.

(1973–4) 'Le rôle de l'hiérarchie chrétienne dans les rapports diplomatiques entre Byzance et les Sassanides', *REtArm* 10: 119–37.

(1983) 'Byzantium and the Sasanians', *CHI* III. 1: 568–92.

(1985) *Armenia between Byzantium and Sasanians*. London.

(1989) *The Epic Histories attributed to P'awastos Bazandac'i*. Cambridge.

(1997a) 'The Aršakuni dynasty (AD 12–428)', in Hovannisian (1997) 63–94 (revised edition New York 2004).

(1997b) 'The Marzparnate (428–652)', in Hovannisian (1997): 95–116 (revised edn. New York 2004).

Garucci, R. (1870) 'Brass medallion, representing the Persian victory of Maximianus Galerius', *NC* 10: 112–18.

Gaube, H. (1982) 'Mazdak: historical reality or invention?', *StIr* 11:111–22.

Gaudemet, J. (1970) 'Le concept d'imperium dans l'Histoire Auguste', *BHAC* 1968/69. Antiquitas IV 7. Bonn: 91–7.

Gauger, J.-D. (1998) *Sibyllinische Weissagungen.* Griechisch-Deutsch. Neu übersetzt und herausgegeben. Düsseldorf et al.

Gawlikowski, M. (1973) *Le temple palmyrénien. Étude d'épigraphie et de topographie historique.* Palmyre VI. Warsaw.

(1985) 'Les princes de Palmyre', *Syria* 62: 251–61.

(1990) 'Les dieux de Palmyre', *ANRW* II 18.4: 2605–77.

(1994) 'A fortress in Mesopotamia: Hatra', in Dabrowa (1994): 47–56.

Gero, S. (1981) *Barsauma of Nisibis and Persian Christianity in the Fifth Century.* CSCO 426. Louvain.

Ghirshman, R. (1948) *Les Chionites-Hephtalites. Mémoires de la délégation archéologique française en Afghanistan.* Vol. XIII. Cairo.

(1954) *Iran from the Earliest Times to the Islamic Conquest.* Harmondsworth.

(1956–71) *Bichapour* I–II. Paris.

(1962) *Iran: Parthians and Sassanians.* London.

(1965) 'A propos l'écriture cunéiforme vieux-perse', *JNES* 24: 248–9.

Gignoux, Ph. (1983) 'Die religiöse Administration in sasanidischer Zeit: Ein Überblick', in *Kunst, Kultur und Geschichte der Achämenidenzeit und ihr Fortleben.* AMI. Erg. Bd. 10, eds. H. Koch and D. N. MacKenzie. Berlin: 253–66.

(1984a) 'Church–state relations in the Sasanian Period', *Bulletin of the Middle Eastern Culture Centre in Japan* 1: 72–80.

(1984b) 'L'organisation administrative sasanide: Le cas du marzbān', *JSAI* 4: 1–29.

(1987) 'Anerān', *EncIr* II: 30–1.

(1991a) 'D'Abnūn à Māhān. Étude de deux inscriptions sassanides', *StIr* 20: 9–22.

(1991b) *Les quatres inscriptions du mage Kirder. Textes et concordances.* Cahier de Studia Iranica 9. Leuven.

Gilliam, J. F. (1941) 'The Dux Ripae at Dura', *TAPhA* 72:157–75.

Girardet, K. M. (1998) 'Die Konstantinische Wende und ihre Bedeutung für das Reich. Althistorische Überlegungen zu den geistigen Grundlagen der Religionspolitik Konstantins d. Gr.', in *Die Konstantinische Wende*, ed. E. Mühlenberg. Gütersloh: 9–122.

Gnoli, Gh. (1985) 'The Quadripartition of the Sassanian Empire', *E. & W.* N. S. 35: 265–70.

(1987) 'Basileus basileôn Arianôn', in *Orientali I. Tucci Memoriae Dicata.* Vol. II. Serie Orientale Roma LVI 2, eds. Gh. Gnoli and L. Lanciotti. Rome: 509–32.

(1989) *The Idea of Iran. An Essay on its Origin.* Serie Orientale Roma LXII. Rome.

(1991) 'L'inscription de Šābūr à la Ka'be-ye Zardošt et la propaganda sassanide', in *Histoire et cultes de l'Asie Centrale préislamique*, eds. P. Bernard and F. Grenet. Paris: 57–63.

(1993) *Iran als religiöser Begriff im Mazdaismus.* Rheinisch-Westfälische Akademie der Wissenschaften: Geisteswissenschaften; G 320. Opladen.

Göbl, R. (1974) *Der Triumph des Sāsāniden Šāpuhr über die Kaiser Gordianus, Philippus und Valerianus. Die ikonographische Interpretation der Felsreliefs.* Vienna.

Golden, P. B. (1990) 'The peoples of the South Russian steppes', in *The Cambridge Ancient History of Early Inner Asia*, ed. D. Sinor. Cambridge: 256–84.

(1992) *An Introduction to the History of the Turkic People. Ethnogenesis and State-Formation in Medieval and early Modern Eurasia and the Middle East.* Turcologica vol. IX. Wiesbaden.

Goldman, B. (1989) 'The imperial jewel at Taq-i Bustan', *Archaeologia Iranica et Orientalis. Miscellanea in honorem L. Vanden Berghe*, eds. E. Meyer and E. Haerinck. Gent: 831–46.

Goubert, P. (1949) 'Les rapports de Khosrau II, roi des rois sassanide, avec l'empereur Maurice', *Byzantion* 19: 81–98.

(1951) *Byzance avant l'Islam. Vol. I: Byzance et l'orient sous les successeurs de Justinien, l'empereur Maurice.* Paris.

Graf, D. F. (1978) 'The Saracens and the defense of the Arab frontier', *BASOR* 229: 1–26.

(1989) 'Rome and the Saracens: Reassessing the nomadic Menace', in *L'Arabie préislamique et son environment historique et culturel*, ed. T. Fahd. Leiden: 341–400.

Grancsay, S. V. (1963) 'A Sasanian chieftain's helmet', *The Metropolitan Museum of Art Bulletin* 21: 253–62.

Gray, E. W. (1973) 'The Roman eastern limes from Constantine to Justinian – perspectives and problems', *Proc. African Class. Ass.* 12: 24–40.

Greatrex, G. (1984) *Procopius and the Persian Wars.* Oxford.

(1993) 'The two fifth-century wars between Rome and Persia', *Florilegium* 12: 1–14.

(1998) *Rome and Persia at War: 502–532.* Leeds.

(2000) 'The background and aftermath of the partition of Armenia in AD 387', *AHB* 14.1–2: 35–48.

(2005) 'Byzantium and the East in the sixth century', in Maas (2005): 477–509.

Greatrex, G. and Bardill, J. (1996) 'Antiochos the Praepositus: a Persian eunuch at the court of Theodosius II', in *DOP* 50: 171–97.

Greatrex, G. and Lieu, S. N. C. (2002) *The Roman Eastern Frontier and the Persian Wars. Part II AD 363 – 630. A Narrative Sourcebook.* London and New York.

Greenwood, T. (forthcoming) 'Armenian neighbours (600–1045)', in *The Cambridge History of the Byzantine Empire*, ed. J. Shepherd. Cambridge, in press.

Gregory, S. E. (1997) *Roman Military Architecture on the Eastern Frontier.* 3 vols. Amsterdam.

Grenet, F. (1990) 'Observations sur les titres de Kirdir', *StIr* 19: 87–94.

Gricourt, J. (1965) 'Alexandre Sévère "Parthicus Maximus"?', in *Congresso Internationale di Numismatica 11.–16. Settembre 1961.* Vol. II. Rome: 319–26.

Grignaschi, M. (1966) 'Quelques spécimens de la littérature sassanide conservés dans les bibliothèques d'Istanbul', *JA* 254: 1–142.

(1971) 'La riforma tributaria di Hosrō I e il feudalismo Sassanide', in Persia (1971): 87–147.

Gropp, G. (1977) 'Die Festung Derbent zwischen Hunnen und Sasaniden', *ZDMG Suppl.* III. 19. Dt. Orientalistentag 1975: 1619–25.

Gruen, E. S. (1984) *The Hellenistic World and the Coming of Rome.* 2 vols. Berkeley.

Grumel, V. (1967) 'La reposition de la Vraie Croix à Jerusalem par Héraclius: Le jour et l'année', in *Polychordia: Festschrift Franz Dölger. ByzF* 2: 139–49.

Guey, J. (1961) 'Autour des Res Gestae Divi Saporis. 1. Deniers (d'or) et deniers d'or (decompte) anciens', *Syria* 38: 261–75.

Guidi, I. (ed. and trans.) (1903) *Chronicum Anonymum, CSCO* Scr. Syr. 1–2. Leipzig.

Guillaumont, A. (1969–70) 'Justinien et l'église de Perse', *DOP* 24–5: 41–66.

Güterbock, K. (1906) *Byzanz und Persien in ihren diplomatisch-völkerrechtlichen Beziehungen im Zeitalter Iustinians. Ein Beitrag zur Geschichte des Völkerrechts.* Berlin.

Gutmann, B. (1991) *Studien zur römischen Außenpolitik in der Spätantike (264–395 n. Chr.).* Bonn.

Guyot, P. and Klein, R. (1994) *Das frühe Christentum bis zum Ende der Verfolgung.* Vol. II: *Die Christen in der heidnischen Gesellschaft.* Darmstadt.

Hage, W. (1973) 'Die oströmische Staatskirche und die Christenheit des Perser-reiches', *ZKG* 84: 174–87.

Halfmann, H. (1986) 'Die Alanen und die römische Ostpolitik unter Vespasian', *EA* 8: 39–50.

Hall, E. (1989) *Inventing the Barbarian. Greek Self-Definition through Tragedy.* Oxford.

Hamblin, W. (1986) 'Sasanian military science and its transmission to the Arabs', in *British Society for Middle Eastern Studies, Proceedings of the 1986 International Conference on Middle Eastern Studies.* Oxford: 99–106.

Hamilton, F. J. and Brooks, E. W. (trans.) (1899) *The Syriac Chronicle Known as that of Zachariah of Mytilene.* London. Reprinted 1979.

Hardy, E. R. (1929) 'New light on the Persian occupation of Egypt', *Journal of the Society of Oriental Research* 13: 185–9.

Harmatta, J. (1974) *The Struggle for the Possession of South Arabia between Aksum and the Sasanians. Actes du IVe congrès international des études éthiopiennes (Rome 1972).* Rome.

(1975) 'Der östliche Hintergrund der Partherkriege unter Marcus Aurelius', in *Eirene: Actes de la XIIe conférence internationale d'études classiques 1972.* Amsterdam: 445–7.

(1979) *Studies in the Sources on the History of Pre-Islamic Central Asia.* Budapest.

(1997) 'The origin of the Huns', *Acta Classica Universitatis Scientiarum Debrece-niensis* 33: 159–73.

(2000) 'The struggle for the "silk route" between Iran, Byzantium and the Türk Empire from 560 to 630 AD', in *Kontakte zwischen Iran, Byzanz und der Steppe im 6.–7. Jh.*, ed. C. S. Balint. Budapest: 249–52.

Harper, P. (1983) 'Sasanian silver', *CHI* III.2: 1113–29.

Harris, W. V. (1979) *War and Imperialism in Republican Rome 327–70 BC.* Oxford (reprinted 1991 with a new preface and updated bibliography).

Hartmann, U. (2001) *Das palmyrenische Teilreich.* Berlin.

(2002a) 'Geist im Exil. Römische Philosophen am Hof der Sasaniden', in *Grenzüberschreitungen. Formen des Kontakts zwischen Orient und Okzident im Altertum*, eds. M. Schuol, U. Hartmann, and A. Luther. Stuttgart: 123–60.

(2002b) 'Griechische Philosophen in der Verbannung', in *Gelehrte in der Antike. A. Demandt zum 65. Geburtstag*, eds. A. Goltz, A. Luther and H. Schlange-Schöningen. Cologne et al.: 58–86.

Hauser, St. R. (1998) 'Hatra und das Königreich der Araber', in Wiesehöfer (1998a): 493–528.

(2000) 'Ecological limits and political frontiers, The "Kingdom of the Arabs" in the eastern Jazira in the Arsacid period', in *Landscapes, Territories, Frontiers and Horizons in the Ancient Near East*. Vol. II: *Geography and Cultural Landscapes*, eds. L. Milano et al. Padova: 187–200.

(2001a) 'Orientalism', *DNP* 15/1: 1233–43.

(2001b) 'Greek in subject and style, but a little distorted. Zum Verhältnis von Orient und Okzident in der Altertumswissenschaft', in *Posthumanistische klassische Archäologie. Historizität der Wissenschaftlichkeit von Interessen und Methoden*, eds. S. Altekamp et al. Munich: 83–104.

Haussig, H.-W. (1959) *Kulturgeschichte von Byzanz*. Stuttgart (published in English (1971) *A History of Byzantine Civilization*. London).

(1966) 'Awaren, Shuan-Shuan und Hephtaliten', in *Geschichte Mittelasiens*. HdOr 1,5,5, eds. K. Jettmar et al. Leiden: 106–22.

(1983) *Die Geschichte Zentralasiens und der Seidenstraße in vorislamischer Zeit*. Darmstadt.

Heather, J. P. (1998) 'Jaths and Huns, c. 320–425', in *CAH* XIII: 487–515.

Heichelheim, F. M. (1944) 'Supply bases for Caracalla's Parthian campaign', *CP* 39.2: 113–15.

Heiler, F. (1971) *Die Ostkirchen*. Munich et al.

Helm, R. (1932) 'Untersuchungen über den auswärtigen diplomatischen Verkehr des römischen Reiches im Zeitalter der Spätantike', *Archiv für Urkundenforschung* 12: 375–436. (Now Olshausen, E. (ed.) (1979) *Antike Diplomatie*. Darmstadt: 321–408.)

Henning, W. B. (1958) 'Mitteliranisch', in *HdO* I 4.1: 96.

Herrmann, A. (1966) *A Historical Atlas of China*. Amsterdam.

Herrmann, A. and von Soden, W. (1959) 'Dolmetscher', *RAC* 4: 24–49.

Herrmann, G. (1980) *The Sasanian Rock Reliefs at Bishapur I: Bishapur III, Triumph attributed to Shapur I*. Iranische Denkmäler. Reihe III. Lieferung 9. Berlin.

(2000) 'The rock reliefs of Sasanian Iran', in *Mesopotamia and Iran in the Parthian and Sasanian Periods: Rejection and Revival c. 238 BC–AD 642. Proceedings of a Seminar in Memory of V. G. Lukanin*, ed. J. Curtis. London: 35–45.

Herrmann, G., MacKenzie, D. N., and Howell, R. (eds.) (1989) *The Sasanian Rock Reliefs at Naqsh-i Rustam 6. The Triumph of Shapur*. Representation of Kerdir and Inscription. Iranische Denkmäler. Reihe II. Lieferung 13. Berlin.

Hersh, C. A. (1980) 'The coinage of Quintus Labienus Parthicus', *Schweiz. Numismat. Rundschau* 59: 41–5.

Herzfeld, E. (1948) *Geschichte der Stadt Samara*. Hamburg.

Hewsen, R. H. (1978–79) 'The successors of Tiridates the Great: a contribution to the history of Armenia in the fourth century', *REtArm* 13: 99–126.

(1992) *The Geography of Ananias of Sirak* (AŠXARHAC'OYC'). *The Long and the short Recensions. Introduction, Translation and Commentary.* Wiesbaden.

(2001) *Armenia. A Historical Atlas.* London.

Higgins, M. J. (1939) *The Persian War of the Emperor Maurice* (582–602). Part 1: *The Chronology, with a Brief History of the Persian Calendar.* Washington, D.C.

(1941) 'International relations at the close of the sixth century', *CHR* 27: 279–315.

(1955) 'Chosroes II's votive offerings at Sergiopolis', *ByzZ* 48: 89–102.

Hillman, T. P. (1996) 'Pompeius ad Parthos?', *Klio* 78: 380–99.

Hinds, M. (1984) 'The first Arab conquests in Fārs', *Iran* 22: 39–55.

Hinz, W. (1969) *Altiranische Funde und Forschungen.* Berlin: pl. 76–7. 97.

(1971) 'Mani and Karder', in Persia (1971): 485–99.

Hoffmann, J. G. E. (1880) *Iulianos der Abtrünnige. Syrische Erzählungen.* Leiden.

Hohl, E. (ed.) (1976–85) *Historia Augusta. Römische Herrschergestalten.* 2 vols. Stuttgart.

Holt, F. L. (1999). *Thundering Zeus. The Making of Hellenistic Bactria.* Los Angeles and London.

Holum, K. G. (1982) *Theodosian Empresses: Women and Imperial Dominion in Late Antiquity.* Berkeley, Los Angeles and London.

(1992) 'Archaeological evidence for the fall of Byzantine Caesarea', *BASOR* 286: 73–85.

Honigmann, E. (1935) *Die Ostgrenze des Byzantinischen Reiches von 363 bis 1071 nach griechischen, arabischen, syrischen und armenischen Quellen.* Brussels.

Hovannisian, R. G. (ed.) (1997) *The Armenian People from Ancient to Modern Times.* Vol. 1. *The Dynastic Periods: From Antiquity to the Fourteenth Century.* Basingstoke, London and New York (revised edn. New York 2004).

Howard-Johnston, J. J. (1989) 'Procopius. Roman defences north of the Taurus and the new fortress of Citharizon', in French and Lightfoot (1989): 203–28.

(1994) 'The official history of Heraclius' Persian campaigns', in Dabrowa (1994): 57–87.

(1995a) 'The siege of Constantinople in 626', in *Constantinople and its Hinterland*, eds. C. Mango and G. Dagron. Aldershot: 131–42.

(1995b) 'The two great powers in late antiquity. A comparison', in Cameron (1995): 157–226.

(1999) 'Heraclius' Persian campaigns and the revival of the Eastern Roman Empire 622–630', *War in History* 6: 1–44.

(2006) *East Rome, Sasanian Persia and the End of Antiquity: Historiographical and Historical Studies.* Aldershot.

Howard-Johnston, J. J. and Thomson, R. W. (1999) *The Armenian History attributed to Sebeos.* Liverpool.

Hoyland, R. (1997) *Seeing Islam as Others Saw It. A Survey and Evaluation of Christian, Jewish and Zoroastrian Writings on Early Islam.* Princeton.

Humbach, H. (1984) 'A Western approach to Zarathustra', *Journal of the K. R. Cama Oriental Institute* 51: 15–32.

Humbach, H. and Skjaervo, P. O. (1983) *The Sassanian Inscription of Paikuli*. Part 3.1: restored text and translation. Wiesbaden.

Humphrey, J. H. (1995–9) *The Roman and Byzantine Near East*. 2 vols. Portsmouth, RI.

Hunger, H. (1978) *Die hochsprachliche profane Literatur der Byzantiner*. HAW 12.5. 2 vols. Munich.

Hunt, D. (1998) 'The Successors of Constantine', *CAH* XIII: 11–14, 39–43, 73–7.

Hunter, R. (ed.) (1998) *Studies in Heliodorus*. Cambridge.

Huskinson, J. and Sandwell, I. (eds.) (2004) *Culture and Society in Later Antioch. Papers from a Colloquium, London, 15th December 2001*. Oxford.

Hutter, M. (1988) *Mani und die Sasaniden*. Innsbruck.

(1992) 'Manichäismus oder Zoroastrismus. Das Ringen zwischen Mani und Kirdir um die Staatsreligion', in *Akten des Melzer-Symposiums 1991*, eds. W. Slaje and C. Zinko. Graz: 152–69.

Huyse, Ph. (1998) 'Kerdīr and the first Sasanians', in *Proceedings of the Third European Conference of Iranian Studies* (*Cambridge, 11th to 15th September 1995*), ed. N. Sims-Williams. Wiesbaden: 109–20.

(1999) *Die dreisprachige Inschrift Šābuhrs I. an der Ka'ba-i Zardušt (ŠKZ)*. 2 vols. Corpus Inscriptionum Iranicarum III 1. London.

(2002) 'La revendication de territoires achéménides par les Sassanides: Une réalité historique?', in *Iran: Questions et connaissances. Actes du IVe congrès européen des études iraniennes, organisé par la Societas Iranologica Europaea, Paris, 6–10 Septembre 1999*, vol. 1: *La période ancienne. Textes réunis par Ph. Huyse*. StIr 25. Paris: 297–311.

Inostrancev; C. A. (1926) 'The Sasanian military theory. Translated by L. Bogdonov', *Journal of the K. R. Cama Oriental Institute* 7: 7–25.

Isaac, B. (1989) 'Luttwak's "Grand Strategy" and the eastern frontier of the Roman Empire', in French and Lightfoot (1989): 231–4.

(1992) *The Limits of Empire. The Roman Army in the East*. 2nd edn. Oxford.

(1993) 'An open frontier', in *Frontières d'empire. Nature et signification des frontières romaines*, eds. P. Brun, S. van der Heeuw, Ch. R. Whittaker. Nemours: 105–14 (now in B. Isaac, *The Near East Under Roman Rule. Selected Papers*. Mnemosyne Suppl. 177, 1998: 403–26).

(1995) 'The army in the late Roman East: the Persian Wars and the defence of the Byzantine provinces', in Cameron (1995): 125–55.

James, S. (1985) 'Dura-Europos and the chronology of Syria in the 250s AD', *Chiron* 15: 111–24.

Jandora, J. W. (1986) 'Developments in Islamic warfare: the early Islamic conquests', *Studia Islamica* 64: 101–13.

Jeffreys, E. et al. (eds.) (1986) *The Chronicle of John Malalas*. Byzantina Australiensia 4. Melbourne.

Jeffreys, E., Croke, B., and Scott, R. (eds.) (1990) *Studies in John Malalas*. Sydney.

Johne, K.-P. (1998) 'Historia Augusta', in *DNP* v: 639–40.

Jones, A. H. M. (1964) *The Later Roman Empire 284–602. A Social, Economic and Administrative Survey*. Vol. II. Oxford.

Kaegi, W. E. (1981a) 'Constantine's and Julian's strategies of strategic surprise against the Persians', *Athenaeum* 69: 209–13.

(1981b) *Byzantine Military Unrest 471–483. An Interpretation.* Amsterdam.

(1982) *Army, Society and Religion in Byzantium.* London.

(1992) *Byzantium and the Early Islamic Conquest.* Cambridge.

(2003) *Heraclius: Emperor of Byzantium.* Cambridge et al.

Kaim, B. (2004) 'Ancient fire temples in the light of the discovery at Mele Hairam', *IrAnt* 39: 323–37.

Kaizer, T. (2000) 'Some remarks about the religious life of Hatra', *Topoi* 10: 229–52.

(2002) *The Religious Life of Palmyra.* Oriens et Occidens vol. IV. Stuttgart.

Karayannopulos, J. (1958) *Das Finanzwesen des frühbyzantinischen Staates.* Munich.

Karras-Klapproth, M. (1988) *Prosopographische Studien zur Geschichte des Partherreiches auf der Grundlage antiker literarischer Überlieferung.* Bonn.

Kawar, I. (1956) 'The Arabs in the peace treaty of AD 561', *Arabica* 3: 181–213.

(1957–8) 'Ghassān and Byzantium: A new terminus a quo', *Der Islam* 33: 232–55.

(1959) 'The Patriciate of Arethas', *ByzZ* 52: 321–43.

Keaveney, A. (1981) 'Roman treaties with Parthia, circa 95 – circa 64 BC', *AJPh* 102: 196–212.

(1982) 'The king and the war-lords: Roman–Parthian relations circa 64–53 BC', *AJPh* 103: 412–28.

Keitel, E. (1978) 'The role of Parthia and Armenia in Tacitus' Annals 11 and 12', *AJPh* 99: 462–73.

Kennedy, D. and Northedge, A. (1988) 'The history of 'Ana, classical sources', in *Excavations at 'Ana*, ed. A. Northedge. Warminster: 6–8.

Kennedy, D. and Riley, D. (1990) *Rome's Desert Frontier from the Air.* London.

Kennedy, D. L. (1982) *Archaeological Explorations on the Roman Frontier in North-East Jordan.* Oxford.

(1983) 'The frontier policy of Septimius Severus. New evidence from Arabia', in Mitchell (1983): 876–88.

(1986) ' "European soldiers" and the Severan siege of Hatra', in Freeman and Kennedy (1986): 397–410.

(1987) 'The garrisoning of Mesopotamia in the Late Antonine and Early Severan period', *Antichthon* 21: 57–66.

(1989) 'The military contribution of Syria to the Roman imperial army', in French and Lightfoot (1989): 235–46.

(1990) 'The East', in *The Roman World*, ed. J. Wacher. London: 266–308.

(1996a) 'Parthia and Rome: eastern perspectives', in Kennedy (1996c): 67–90.

(1996b) 'Syria', in *CAH* x. 2: 703–36.

(1996c) *The Roman Army in the East.* Ann Arbor (JRA Suppl. Ser.).

Kennedy, H. (1992) 'Antioch: from Byzantium to Islam and back again', in *The City in Late Antiquity*, ed. J. Rich. London: 181–98.

Kent, R. G. (1953) *Old Persian Grammar Texts Lexicon.* 2nd edn. New Haven.

Kerler, G. (1970) *Die Aussenpolitik in der Historia Augusta.* Bonn.

Kessler, K. (1980) *Untersuchungen zur historischen Topographie Nordmesopotamiens.* Wiesbaden.

Kettenhofen, E. (1982) *Die römisch-persischen Kriege des 3. Jahrhunderts n. Chr. Nach der Inschrift Šāhpurs I. an der Kaʿbe-ye Zartošt [ŠKZ].* Beiheft TAVO B 55. Wiesbaden.

(1983) 'The Persian campaign of Gordian III and the inscription of Sapuhr I at the 'Kaʾ be-ye Zartošt', in Mitchell (1983): 151–71.

(1984) 'Die Einordnung des Achämenidenerbes durch Ardašīr. Eine interpretatio romana', *OLP* 15: 177–90.

(1986) 'Zur Siegestitulatur Kaiser Aurelians', *Tyche* 1: 138–46.

(1994a) 'Einige Überlegungen zur sasanidischen Politik gegenüber Rom im 3. Jh. n. Chr.', in Dabrowa (1994): 99–108.

(1994b) 'Deportations II. In the Parthian and Sasanian period', *EncIr* 7: 297–308.

(1995a) 'Die Eroberung von Nisibis und Karrhai durch die Sāsāniden in der Zeit Kaiser Maximins (235/36 n. Chr.)', *IrAnt* 30: 159–77.

(1995b) 'Die Chronik von Arbela in der Sicht der Althistorie', *Simblos* 1: 287–319.

(1995c) *Tirdād und die Inschrift von Paikuli. Kritik der Quellen zur Geschichte Armeniens im späten 3. und frühen 4. Jh. n. Chr.* Wiesbaden.

(1996a) 'Dvin', *EncIr* 7: 616–19.

(1996b) 'Darband', *EncIr* 7: 13–19.

(1998) 'Die Arsakiden in armenischen Quellen', in Wiesehöfer (1998): 325–53.

Kienast, D. (1990) *Römische Kaisertabelle. Grundzüge einer römischen Kaiserchronologie.* Darmstadt.

Kirsten, E. (1959) 'Edessa', *RAC* 4: 552–98.

(1963) 'Edessa. Eine römische Grenzstadt des 4. bis 6. Jahrhunderts im Orient', *JbAC* 6: 144–72.

Kissel, Th. (1998) 'Konstanten der Infrastruktur – Historische Wegekontinuität im nordsyrisch-obermesopotamischen Kulturraum am Beispiel der Flußübergänge am Mittleren Euphrat', in *Religion – Wirtschaft – Technik. Althistorische Beiträge zur Entstehung neuer kultureller Strukturmuster im historischen Raum. Nordafrika/Kleinasien/Syrien.* Mainzer Althistorische Studien vol. 1, ed. L. Schuhmacher. St. Katharinen: 147–78.

Klein, R. (1977) *Constantius II. und die christliche Kirche.* Darmstadt.

(ed.) (1978) *Julian Apostata.* WdF vol. 509. Darmstadt.

(1997) 'Galerius', in *Die römischen Kaiser. 55 historische Porträts von Caesar bis Iustinian,* ed. M. Clauss. Munich: 278–82.

Klima, O. (1957) *Mazdak. Geschichte einer sozialen Bewegung im sassanidischen Persien.* Prague.

(1977) *Beiträge zur Geschichte des Mazdakismus.* Prague.

Klimkeit, H.-J. (1990) *Die Seidenstraße,* 2nd edn. Cologne.

Koch, H. (1992) *Es kündet Dareios der König . . . Vom Leben im persischen Großreich.* Mainz am Rhein.

Koder, J. (1997) 'Thema', *LMA* 8: 615–16.

Kolb, F. (1987a) *Diocletian und die erste Tetrarchie.* Untersuchungen zur antiken Literatur und Geschichte 27. Berlin.

(1987b) *Untersuchungen zur Historia Augusta.* Antiquitas 4, 20. Bonn.

(1988) 'L'ideologia tetrarchica e la politica religiosa di Diocleziano', in *I Christiani e l'impero nel IV secolo.* Colloquio sul Christianesimo nel mondo antico, eds. G. Bonamente and A. Nestori. Macerata: 17–44.

(1995) 'Chronologie und Ideologie der Tetrarchie', *Ant Tard* 3: 27–31.

Kollautz, A. (1985) 'Das militärwissenschaftliche Werk des sog. Maurikios', *Byzantiaka* 5: 87–136.

Kondoleon, Ch. (ed.) (2000) *Antioch. The Lost Ancient City.* Princeton.

Konrad, M. (1999) 'Research on the Roman and early Byzantine frontier in North Syria', *JRA* 12: 392–410.

Kornemann, E. (1947) *Große Frauen des Altertums.* 3rd edn. Wiesbaden.

Körner, Ch. (2002) *Philippus Arabs. Ein Soldatenkaiser in der Tradition des antoninisch-severischen Prinzipats.* Untersuchungen zur antiken Literatur und Geschichte vol. 61. Berlin.

Kramers, J. H. (1935–7) 'The military colonization of the Caucasus and Armenia under the Sassanids', *BSOS* 8: 613–18.

Kraus, Th. (1967) *Propyläen Kunstgeschichte.* Vol. ii: *Das römische Weltreich. Mit Beiträgen von Andreae et. al.* Berlin.

Kreucher, G. (2003) *Der Kaiser Marcus Aurelius Probus und seine Zeit.* Historia Einzelschriften 174. Wiesbaden.

Kuhnen, H.-P. (1999) 'Limes VII', *DNP* 7. Südlicher Vorderer Orient: 220–3.

Kulesza, R. (1994) 'Persian deportations – Greeks in Persia', *EOS* 82: 221–50.

Lang, D. M. (1962) *A Modern History of Georgia.* London.

(1966) *The Georgians.* London.

(1983) 'Iran, Armenia und Georgia', *CHI* iii. 1: 505–36.

Laubscher, H. P. (1975) *Der Reliefschmuck des Galeriusbogens in Thessaloniki.* Berlin.

Lee, A. D. (1986) 'Embassies as evidence for the movement of military intelligence between the Roman and Sasanian Empire', in Freeman and Kennedy (1986): 455–461.

(1987) 'Dating a fifth century war in Theodoret', *Byzantion* 57: 188–91.

(1989) 'Campaign preparations in late Roman-Persian warfare', in French and Lightfoot (1989): 257–65.

(1991) 'The role of hostages in Roman diplomacy with Sasanian Persia', *Historia* 40: 366–74.

(1993a) *Informations and Frontiers. Roman Foreign Relations in Late Antiquity.* Cambridge.

(1993b) 'Evagrius, Paul of Nisibis and the problem of loyalties in the mid-sixth century', in *Journal of Ecclesiastical History* 44: 569–85.

Lenssen, J. (1999) 'The Persian invasion of 359: presentation by suppression in Ammianus Marcellinus' Res Gestae 18.4.1 – 18.6.7', in Drijvers and Hunt (1999): 40–50.

Lepper, F. A. (1948) *Trajan's Parthian War.* Oxford.

Leppin, H. (1996) *Von Constantin dem Großen zu Theodosius II.: Das christliche Kaisertum bei den Kirchenhistorikern Socrates, Sozomenus und Theodoret.* Hypomnemata 110. Göttingen.

Lerner, J. D. (1996) 'Seleucid decline over the eastern Iranian plateau', *Berytus* 42: 103–12.

(1999) *The Impact of Seleucid Decline on the Eastern Plateau. The Foundations of Arsacid Parthia and Graeco-Bactria.* Historia Einzelschriften 123. Stuttgart.

Levy, R. (1996) *The Epic of the Kings: Shahnama, the National Epic of Persia/Ferdowsi.* 2nd edn. Costa Mesa, Calif.

Lewis, N. and Reinhold, M. (1955) *Roman Civilization. Selected Readings Edited with an Introduction.* 2 vols. New York.

Liebeschütz, J. H. W. G. (1972) *Antioch. City and Administration in the Later Roman Empire.* Oxford.

(1977) 'The defense of Syria in the sixth century', in *Studien zu den Militärgrenzen Roms II,* ed. C. B. Ruger. Cologne: 487–99.

(1990) *Barbarians and Bishops.* Oxford.

Liebmann-Frankfort, Th. (1969a) *La frontière orientale dans la politique extérieure de la république Romaine depuis la traité d' Apamée jusqu'à la fin des conquêtes asiatiques de Pompée (189/8–63).* Académie royale de Belgique. Classe des lettres et sciences morales et politiques. Mém. 59. Brussels.

(1969b) 'L'histoire des Parthes dans le livre XLI de Trogue Pompée: Essai d'identification de ses sources', *Latomus* 28: 894–922.

Lieu, S. N. C. (1986) 'Captives, refugees and exiles: A study of cross-frontier civilian movements and contacts between Rome and Persia from Valerian to Jovian', in Freeman and Kennedy (1986): 475–505.

(1992) *Manichaeism in the Later Roman Empire and Medieval China.* 2nd edn. Manchester and Tübingen.

(1994) *Manichaeism in Mesopotamia and the Roman East.* Leiden.

Lightfoot, C. S. (1983) 'The site of Roman Bezabde', in *Armies and Frontiers in Roman and Byzantine Anatolia,* ed. St. Mitchell. Oxford: 189–204.

(1986) 'Tille – A late Roman equites fort on the Tigris', in Freeman and Kennedy (1986): 509–29.

(1988) 'Facts and fiction – The third siege of Nisibis', *Historia* 37.1: 105–25.

(1989) 'Sapor before the walls of Amida', in French and Lightfoot (1989): 285–94.

(1990) 'Trajan's Parthian war and the fourth-century perspective', *JRS* 80: 115–26.

Lippold, A. (1974) 'Hephthalitai', *RE* S 14: 127–37.

Litvinsky, B. A. (1996) 'The Hephthalite Empire', in *History of Civilizations of Central Asia.* Vol. III: *The Crossroads of Civilizations: AD 250 to 750,* ed. B. A. Litvinsky. Paris: 135–62.

Loewe, M. (1971) 'Spices and silk. Aspects of world trade in the first seven centuries of the Christian era', *JRAS:* 166–79.

Lopez, R. S. (1945) 'Silk industry in the Byzantine Empire', *Speculum* 20: 1–42.

Lordkipanidse, O. and Brakmann, H. (1994) 'Iberia II', *RAC* 129: 12–106.

Luther, A. (1997) *Die Syrische Chronik des Josua Stylites.* Untersuchungen zur antiken Literatur und Geschichte. Vol. 49. Berlin.

(2004) 'Der politische Status der Region am mittleren Euphrat im 2. Jh. n. Chr. und die Organisation des palmyrenischen Fernhandels', in *Commerce*

and Monetary System in the Ancient World: Means of Transmission and Cultural Interaction, eds. R. Rollinger and Chr. Ulf. Stuttgart: 327–51.

Luttwak, E. N. (1976) *The Grand Strategy of the Roman Empire from the First Century A. D. to the Third.* Baltimore.

Maas, M. (ed.) (2005) *The Cambridge Companion to the Age of Justinian.* Cambridge.

MacDermot, B. C. (1954) 'Roman emperors in the Sassanian reliefs', *JRS* 44: 76–80.

MacDonald, D. J. (1979) 'The genesis of the res gestae Saporis', *Berytus* 27. 77–83.

(1981) 'The death of Gordian III – another tradition', *Historia* 30: 502–8.

(1986) 'Dating the fall of Dura-Europos', *Historia* 35: 45–68.

MacKenzie, D. N. (1979) 'Mani's Sabuhragan', *BSOAS* 42: 500–34.

(1982) 'Rezension zu M. Back (1978)', *IF* 87: 285.

(1989) 'Kerdir's inscription: synoptic text in transliteration, transcription, translation and commentary', in Herrmann, MacKenzie and Howell (1989): 35–72.

Mackintosh, M. C. (1973) 'Roman influences on the victory-relief of Shapur I of Persia', *California Studies in Classical Antiquity* 6: 181–203.

MacMullen, R. (1976) *Roman Government's Response to Crisis A.D. 235–337.* New Haven.

(1980) 'How big was the Roman army?', *Klio* 62: 451–60.

Macomber, W. (1968) 'The authority of the catholikos patriarch of Seleucia-Ctesiphon', in *I patriarcati orientali nel primo millennio. Relazioni del congresso tenutosi al Pontificio Istituto Orientale nei giorni 27–30 Dicembre 1967.* Orientalia Christiana Analecta 181. Rome: 179–200.

Maenchen-Helfen, O. J. (1973) *The World of the Huns: Studies in their History and Culture*, ed. M. Knight. Berkeley.

(1978) *Die Welt der Hunnen.* Vienna.

Magie, D. (1919) 'Roman policy in Armenia and Transcaucasia and its significance', *Annual Report of the American Historical Association*: 297–304.

(1921–32) *The Scriptores Historiae Augustae vol. I–III.* London and Cambridge, Mass.

Mahé, A. and Mahé, J.-P. (1993) *Moïse de Khorène. Histoire de L'Arménie. Nouvelle traduction de L'arménien classique par A. et J.-P. Mahé (d'après Victoire Langlois) avec une introduction et des notes.* Paris.

Mahét, J.-P. and Thomson, R. W. (eds.) (1997) *From Byzantium to Iran: Armenian Studies in Honour of N. G. Garsoïan.* Atlanta.

Malitz, J. (1984) 'Caesars Partherkrieg', *Historia* 33: 21–59.

Manandian, H. A. (1965) *The Trade and Cities of Armenia in Relation to Ancient World Trade.* Translated by N. G. Garsoïan. Lisbon.

Mango, C. (1985) 'Deux études sur Byzance et la Perse sassanide', *TravMem* 9: 91–117.

(1990) *Nikephoros, Patriarch of Constantinople: Short History, Text, Translation, and Commentary.* Dumbarton Oaks Papers x. CFHB xiii. Washington D.C.

Mango, C. and Scott, R. (1997) *The Chronicle of Theophanes Confessor. Byzantine and Near Eastern History AD 284–813. Translated with Introduction and Commentary.* With the assistance of G. Greatrex. Oxford.

Maricq, A. (1955) 'Hatra de Sanatrouq', *Syria* 32: 273–88.

Maricq, A. and Honigmann, E. (1953) *Recherches sur les Res Gestae Divi Saporis. Académie royale de Belgique. Classe de lettres et des sciences morales et politiques* 47.4. Bulletin épigraphique 1953 [254]. Brussels.

Maróth, M. (1979) 'Le siège de Nisibe en 350 ap. J.-Chr. d'après des sources syriennes', *AAS* 27: 239–43.

Marquart, J. (1901) *Eranshahr nach der Geographie des Ps. Moses Xorenac'i*. Berlin.

Marshall, B. A. (1976) *Crassus. A Political Biography*. Amsterdam.

Masia, K. (2000) 'The evolution of swords and daggers in the Sasanian Empire', *Iranica Antiqua* 35: 185–9.

Matthews, J. F. (1984) 'The tax law of Palmyra: evidence for economic history in a city of the Roman East', *JRS* 74: 157–80.

(1986) 'Ammianus and the eastern frontier in the fourth century: a participant's view', in Freemann and Kennedy (1986): 549–64.

(1989a) *The Roman Empire of Ammianus*. London.

(1989b) 'Hostages, philosophers, pilgrims, and the diffusion of ideas in the late Roman Mediterranean and Near East', in *Tradition and Innovation in Late Antiquity*, eds. F. M. Clover and R. S. Humphreys, Madison: 29–49.

Mattingly, H. (1936) 'The Palmyrene Princes and the Mints of Antioch and Alexandria'. *NC* 16: 95. 102. 109.

Mayerson, P. (1989) 'Saracens and Romans: micro-macro relationship', *BASOR* 274: 71–9.

Mazzarino, S. (1971) 'L'Anonymus post Dionem e la "topica" delle guerre romanopersiane 242/4 d. C. – 283/(4?) d. C.', in Persia (1971): 655–78.

McCullough, W. S. (1982) *A Short History of Syriac Christianity to the Rise of Islam*. Chico, CA.

McGeer, E. (1995) *Showing the Dragon's Teeth: Byzantine Warfare in the Tenth Century*. Washington, D.C.

Meier, M. (2003) *Das andere Zeitalter Justinians: Kontigenzerfahrung und Kontigenzbewältigung im 6. Jahrhundert n. Chr*. Hypomnemata 147. Göttingen.

Merten, E. W. (1968) *Zwei Herrscherfeste in der Historia Augusta. Untersuchungen zu den pompae der Kaiser Gallienus und Aurelianus*. Antiquitas IV 5. Bonn.

Metzler, D. (1982) *Ziele und Formen königlicher Innenpolitik im vorislamischen Iran*. Münster.

(1991) 'Kommagene von Osten her gesehen', in *Studien zum antiken Kleinasien. F. K. Dörner zum 80. Geburtstag gewidmet*. Asia Minor Studien 3. Bonn: 21–7. (reprinted in J. Wagner (ed.) (2000) *Gottkönige am Euphrat. Neue Ausgrabungen und Forschungen in Kommagene*. Mainz am Rhein: 51–5).

(1992/3) 'Rezension von E. Hall, Inventing the barbarian. Greek self-definition through tragedy', *Hephaistos* 11/12: 215–23.

Meyer, H. (1980) 'Die Frieszyklen am sogenannten Triumphbogen des Galerius in Thessaloniki. Kriegschronik und Ankündigung der zweiten Tetrarchie', *JDAI* 95: 374–444.

Meyer, M. (1990) 'Die Felsbilder Shapurs I', *JDAI* 105: 237–302.

Michalak, M. (1987) 'The origins and development of Sassanian heavy cavalry', *Folia Orientalia* 24: 73–86.

Michalowski, K. and Gawlikowski, M. (1966–85) *Études Palmyréniennes* 1–8. Warsaw.

Mielczarek, M. (1993) *Cataphractari and Clibanarii. Studies in the Heavy Armoured Cavalry of the Ancient World*. Lodz.

Millar, F. (1971) 'Paul of Samosata, Zenobia and Aurelian: the church culture and political allegiance in third century Syria', *JRS* 61: 1–17.

(1993) *The Roman Near East*. Cambridge.

(1996) *The Roman Near East 31 B.C. – A.D. 337*. 3rd edn. Cambridge and London.

(1998a) 'Caravan cities: the Roman Near East and long-distance trade by land', in *Modus Operandi: Essays in Honour of G. Rickman*, eds. M. Austin et al. London: 119–37.

(1998b) 'Dura-Europos under Parthian rule', in Wiesehöfer (1998a): 473–92.

(2006) *Rome, the Greek World and the East*. Vol. III: *The Greek World, the Jews and the East*. Eds. H. M. Colton and G. H. Rogers. Chapel Hill.

Miller, D. A. (1971) 'Byzantine treaties and treaty-making 500–1025 AD', *Byzantinoslavica* 32: 56–76.

Miller, J. I. (1969) *The Spice Trade of the Roman Empire 29 B.C. to A.D. 641*. Oxford.

Minorsky, V. (1943–6) 'Roman and Byzantine campaigns in Atropatene', *BSOAS* 11: 243–65.

Mitchell, S. (2006) *A History of the Later Roman Empire AD 284–641. The Transformation of the Ancient World*. Blackwell.

Mitchell, St. (ed.) (1983) *Armies and Frontiers in Roman and Byzantine Anatolia: Proceedings of a Colloquium Held at University College Swansea 1981*. BAR International Series 156. Oxford.

(1993) *Anatolia. Land, Men and Gods in Asia Minor*. Vol. I *The Celts in Anatolia and the Impact of Roman Rule*. Oxford.

Mohl, J. (1838–55) *Le livre des Rois I–VII*. Paris.

Morony, M. G. (1984) *Iraq after the Muslim Conquest*, Princeton, NJ.

(1987) 'Syria under the Persians, 610–629', in Bakhit (1987): 87–95.

(1990) 'Bēt Lapaṭ', *EncIr* IV: 187–8.

(1997) 'Sāsānids', *EI* IX: 70–83.

(2001–2) 'The late Sasanian economic impact on the Arabian Peninsula', *Nāme-ye Irān-e Bāstān/The International Journal of Ancient Iranian Studies* I: 25–37.

(2004) 'Economic Boundaries? Late Antiquity and Early Islam', *Journal of the Economic and Social History of the Orient* 47.2: 184–8.

Mosig-Walburg, K. (1982) *Die frühen sāsānidischen Könige als Vertreter und Förderer der zarathustrischen Religion*. Frankfurt am Main.

(1999) 'Zur Schlacht bei Singara', *Historia* 48: 330–84.

(2002) 'Zur Westpolitik Shāpūrs II', in *Iran: Question et connaissance*. Vol. I: *La periode ancienne. Textes réunnis par Ph. Huyse. StIr*. Cahier 25. Paris: 329–47.

Mukherjee, B. N. (1969) 'Ta-hsia and the problem concerning the advent of nomadic peoples in Greek Bactria', *E & W* 19: 395–400.

Müller, C. D. G. (1969) 'Stellung und Bedeutung des Katholikos-Patriarchen von Seleukeia-Ktesiphon im Altertum', *OrChr* 53: 227–45.

(1981) *Geschichte der orientalischen Nationalkirchen. Die Kirche in ihrer Geschichte. Ein Handbuch. Bd. 1, Lieferung D2.* Göttingen.

Müller, F. L. (1996) *Herodian. Geschichte des Kaisertums nach Marc Aurel. Griechisch und deutsch mit Einleitung, Anmerkungen und Namenindex versehen.* Stuttgart.

Müller, W. W. (1991) 'Himyar', *RAC* 15: 303–31.

Munro-Hay, S. C. (1991) *Aksum. An African Civilisation of Late Antiquity.* Edinburgh.

Nakamura, B. (1993) 'Palmyra and the Roman East', *GRBS* 34: 133–50.

Narain, A. K. (1987) 'The Saka Haumavarga and the Amyrgoi: The problem of their identity', *Bulletin of the Asia Institute*, New Series 1: 27–31.

(1990) 'Indo-Europeans in Inner Asia', in *The Cambridge History of Early Inner Asia*, ed. D. Sinor. Cambridge: 151–76.

Negin, A. N. (1995) 'Sarmatian cataphracts as prototypes for Roman equites cataphractarii', *Journal of Roman Military Equipment Studies* 6: 65–75.

Neusner, J. (1965–70) *A History of the Jews in Babylonia.* Vols. I–V. Leiden.

Nicholson, O. (1983) 'Taq-i Bostan, Mithras and Julian Apostate: An irony', *IrAnt* 18: 177–85.

Nicolle, D. (1996) *Sassanian Armies. The Iranian Empire, early 3rd to mid 7th Centuries AD.* Stockport.

Nigosian, S. (1978) 'Zoroastrianism in 5th century Armenia', *Studies in Religion* 7: 425–34.

Nöldeke, Th. (1874) 'Über den syrischen Roman von Kaiser Iulian', *ZDMG* 28: 262–92.

(1878) 'Geschichte des Ardachsir i Papakan, aus dem Pehlewi übersetzt, mit Erläuterungen und einer Einleitung versehen', in *Beiträge zur Kunde der indogermanischen Sprachen* 4: 22–69.

(1879) *Geschichte der Perser und Araber zur Zeit der Sasaniden. Aus der arabischen Chronik des Tabari übersetzt und mit ausführlichen Erläuterungen versehen.* Leiden.

(1887a) *Aufsätze zur persischen Geschichte.* Leipzig.

(1887b) *Die ghāssanischen Fürsten aus dem Hause Gafna's.* Abh. der Kgl. Akad. der Wissenschaften. Ph.-h. Kl. 2. Berlin.

(1892) *Persische Studien II.* Sitzungsberichte der Kaiserlichen Akademie der Wissenschaften. Ph.-h. Kl. Vol. 126. Abh. 12. Vienna.

(1920) *Das Iranische Nationalepos.* 2nd edn. Berlin and Leipzig.

North, J. A. (1981) 'The development of Roman imperialism', *JRS* 71: 1–9.

Nyberg, H. S. (1959) 'Die sassanidische Westgrenze und ihre Verteidigung', in *Septentrionalia et Orientalia. FS B. Kargren.* Stockholm: 316–26.

Oates, D. (1955) 'A note on the three inscriptions from Hatra', *Sumer* 11: 39–44.

(1968) *Studies in the Ancient History of Northern Iraq.* London.

O'Connor, C. (1993) *Roman Bridges.* Cambridge.

Oded, B. (1979) *Mass Deportations and Deportees in the Neo-Assyrian Empire.* Wiesbaden.

Oelsner, J. (1996) 'Adiabene', *DNP* 1: 112.

Oikonomidès, N. (1971) 'Correspondence between Heraclius and Kavādh-Široe in the Paschale Chronicle (628)', *Byzantion* 41: 269–81.

(1976) 'A chronological note on the first Persian campaign of Heraclius (622)', *BMGS* 2: 1–9.

Olbrycht, M. J. (1998) *Parthia et ultiores gentes. Die politischen Beziehungen zwischen dem arsakidischen Iran und den Nomaden der eurasischen Steppen.* Munich.

(2003) 'Parthia and nomads of Central Asia. Elements of steppe origin in the social and military developments of Arsacid Iran', in *Militär und Staatlichkeit. Mitteilungen des SFB 'Differenz und Integration'* 5, ed. I. Schneider. Orient-wissenschaftliche Hefte 12. Halle: 69–103.

Olshausen, E. (1997) 'Deportationen zu Anfang der Auseinandersetzungen zwischen Griechen und Persern', *Orbis Terrarum* 3: 101–7.

Oost, S. I. (1958) 'The death of the Emperor Gordian III', *CP* 53: 106–7.

Ostrogorsky, G. (1963) 'Geschichte des Byzantinischen Staates'. *HAW* XII 1.2. Munich.

(1965) *Geschichte des byzantinischen Staates.* Munich.

Overlaet, B. J. (1982) 'Contribution to Sasanian armament in connection with a decorated helmet', *IrAnt* 17: 189–206.

(1989) 'Swords of the Sasanians, notes on scabbard tips', in *Archaeologia Iranica et Orientalis. Miscellanea in honorem L. Vanden Berghe,* eds. L. De Meyer and E. Haerinck. Ghent: 741–55.

Palmer, A., Brock, S., and Hoyland, R. (1993) *The Seventh Century in West-Syrian Chronicles.* Liverpool.

Panitschek, P. (1990) 'Zur Darstellung der Alexander- und Achaemenidennach-folge als politisches Programm in kaiserzeitlichen Quellen', *Klio* 72: 457–72.

Parker, S. T. (1986a) 'Retrospective on the Arabian frontier after a decade of research', in Freeman and Kennedy (1986): 633–60.

(1986b) *Romans and Saracens. A History of the Arabian Frontier.* Winona Lake, MN.

(1997) 'Geography and strategy on the southeastern frontier in the late Roman period', in *Roman Frontier Studies 1995. Proceedings of the XVII. International Congress of Roman Frontier Studies,* ed. W. Groenman-Wateringe. Oxford: 115–19.

Paschoud, F. (1971–89) *Zosime. Histoire nouvelle.* Tom. I–III. Texte établi et traduit par F. Paschoud. Paris.

Paterson, W. F. (1969) 'The Sassanids', *Journal of the Society of Archer-Antiquaries* 12: 29–32.

Pattenden, P. (1983) 'The Byzantine early warning system', *Byzantion* 53: 258–99.

Paul, K. (1983) *Von Nero bis Konstantin dem Grossen. Politische und soziale Aspekte einer kirchengeschichtlichen Wende.* Frankfurt.

Peacock, D. P. S. (1994) 'Rome and India', *JRA* 7: 457–8.

Peck, E. H. (1969) 'The representations of costumes in the reliefs of Taq-i Bustan', *Artibus Asiae* 31: 101–46.

Peeters, P. (1924) 'Démétrianus éveque d'Antioche?', *AnalBolland* 42: 288–314.

(1925) 'Le Passionaire d'Adiabène', *AnalBolland* 43: 261–304.

(1931) 'L'intervention politique de Constance II dans la Grande Arménie en 338', *BAB* 5.17: 10–47 (reprinted in *Subsidia Hagiographica* 27, 1951, 222–50).

(1947) 'Les ex-voto de Khosrau Aparwez à Sergiopolis', *AnalBolland* 65:5–56.

Pekáry, Th. (1961) 'Autour des Res Gestae Divi Saporis. 2. Le "tribut" aux Perses et les finances de Philippe l'Arabe', *Syria* 38: 275–83.

Pellat, Ch. (1971) 'Amr ibn 'Adī, *EI* III²: 450.

Persia (1971) = *Atti del convegno internazionale sul tema: La Persia nel medioevo (Roma 31 marzo- 5 aprile 1970)*. Academia Nazional dei Lincei. Quaderno N. 160. Rome.

Pieler, P. (1972) 'L'aspect politique et juridique de l'adoption de Chosroès proposée par les Perses à Justin', *RIDA* 3,19: 399–433.

Pigulevskaja, N. (1969) *Byzanz auf den Wegen nach Indien. Aus der Geschichte des byzantinischen Handels mit dem Orient vom 4. bis 6. Jahrhundert*. Revised German edition. Berlin.

Pink, K. (1931) 'Die Goldprägung des Diocletianus und seiner Mitregenten (284 bis 305)', *NZ* 64. N. F. 24: 3. 47. 50.

Pohl, W. (1988) *Die Awaren. Ein Steppenvolk in Mitteleuropa 567–822 n. Chr.* Munich.

Pohlsander, H. A. (1980) 'Philip the Arab and Christianity', *Historia* 29: 464–5.

Pollard, N. (2000) *Soldiers, Cities and Civilians in Roman Syria*. Ann Arbor.

(2004) 'Roman material culture across imperial frontiers? Three case-studies from Parthian Dura-Europos', in *The Greco-Roman East. Politics, Culture, Society*, ed. S. Colvin. Cambridge: 119–44 (= Yale Classical Studies 31).

Pond, M. Sh. (1970) *The Arch of Fabius: a Sculptural Record of the Age of the Tetrarchies*. Ann Arbor.

Porada, E. (1980) *Alt Iran. Die Kunst in vorislamischer Zeit*. Baden-Baden (reprint of the revised edition of 1979).

Portmann, W. (1989) 'Rede des Libanios und das Datum der Schlacht von Singara', *ByzZ* 82: 1–18.

Potter, D. S. (1987) 'Alexander Severus and Ardashir', *Mesopotamia* 22: 147–57.

(1990) *Prophecy and History in the Crisis of the Roman Empire. A Historical Commentary on the Thirteenth Sibylline Oracle*. Oxford.

(1991) 'The inscription of the bronze Herakles from Mesene: Vologeses IV's war with Rome and the date of Tacitus' Annals', *ZPE* 88: 277–90.

(1996a) 'Palmyra and Rome: Odaenathus' titulature and the use of the imperium maius', *ZPE* 113: 271–85.

(1996b) 'Gaining information on Rome's neighbours', *JRA* 9: 528–32.

(2004) *The Roman Empire at Bay, AD 180–395*. London and New York.

Potts, D. T. (1989) 'Gundeshapur and the Gondeisos', *IrAnt* 24: 323–35.

(1990) *The Arabian Gulf in Antiquity*. 2 vols. Oxford.

(1997) 'The Roman relationship with the Persicus Sinus from the rise of Spasinou Charax (127 BC) to the reign of Shapur II (AD 309–79)', in *The Early Roman Empire in the East*, ed. S. E. Alcock. Oxford: 89–107.

Preißler, H. (1975) 'Arabien zwischen Byzanz und Persien', in *Geschichte der Araber. Von den Anfängen bis zur Gegenwart.* Vol. I: *Vorraussetzungen, Blüte und Verfall des arabisch-islamischen Feudalreiches*, eds. L. Rathmann et al. 2nd edn. Berlin: 36–56.

Preusser, C. (1911) *Nordmesopotamische Baudenkmäler altchristlicher und islamischer Zeit.* Leipzig, Reprint Osnabrück 1984.

Pugliese Caratelli, G. (1971) 'La Persia dei sasanidi nella storiografia romana da Ammiana a Procopio', in *Convegna internazionale sul tema: La Persia nel medioevo, Roma, 31. marzo–5 aprile 1970*, Roma. (= Academia Nazional dei Lincei. Quaderno n. 160).

Raaflaub, K. A. (1996) 'Born to be wolves? Origins of Roman imperialism', in *Transitions to Empire. Essays in Greco-Roman History, 360–146 B.C. in Honour of E. Badian*, eds. R. W. Wallace and E. Harris. Norman: 273–314.

Rahimi-Laridjani, F. (1988) *Die Entwicklung der Bewässerungslandwirtschaft im Iran bis in sasanidisch-frühislamische Zeit.* Wiesbaden.

Rajak, T. (1998) 'The Parthians in Josephus', in Wiesehöfer (1998a): 309–24.

Raschke, M. G. (1978) 'New studies in Roman commerce with the East', *ANRW* II 9.2: 604–1378.

Rawlinson, G. (1875) *The Seven Great Monarchies of the Ancient Eastern World or the History, Geography, and Antiquities of Chaldaea, Assyria, Babylon, Media, Persia, Parthia, and Sassanian or New Empire.* Vol. III. New York.

Reade, J. (ed.) (1996) *The Indian Ocean in Antiquity.* London.

Redgate, A. E. (1998) *The Armenians.* Oxford and Malden, Mass. Reprint 1999.

Reining, G. J. and Stolte, B. (eds.) (2002) *The Reign of Heraclius (610–41). Crisis and Confrontation.* Leiden.

Richter-Bernburg, L. (1993) 'Mani's Dodecads and Sasanian Chronology', *ZPE* 95: 71–80.

(2002) 'Gondesapur II: History and Medical School', *EncIr* XI 2: 131–3.

Ridley, R.-T. (1973) 'Three notes on Julian's expedition (363)', *Historia* 22: 317–30.

(1984) *Zosimos. New History. A Translation with Commentary* (Byzantina Australiensia 2). Canberra.

Riedlberger, P. (1998) 'Die Restauration von Chosroes II', in *Electrum Vol. II: Ancient Iran and the Mediterranean World*, ed. E. Dabrowa. Cracow: 161–75.

Rist, J. (1996) 'Die Verfolgung der Christen im spätantiken Sasanidenreich. Ursachen, Verlauf und Folgen', *OrChr* 80: 17–42.

Roaf, M. (1998) 'Persepolitan echoes in Sasanian architecture. Did the Sasanians attempt to re-create the Achaemenid Empire?', in *The Art and Archaeology of Ancient Persia. New Light on the Parthian and Sasanian Empires*, eds. V. S. Curtis, R. Hillebrandt, and J. M. Rogers. London, and New York: 1–7.

Rodenwaldt, G. (1940) 'Ein lykisches Motiv', *JDAI* 55: 55–6.

Rose Gräser, E. (1940) 'The edict of Diocletian on maximum prices', in *An Economic Survey of Ancient Rome V*, ed. T. Frank. Baltimore: 307–421.

Rösger, A. (1978) 'Die Darstellung des Perserfeldzuges des Severus Alexander in der Historia Augusta', in *BHAC* 1975/76: 167–74.

Ross, S. K. (2001) *Roman Edessa. Politics and Culture on the Eastern Fringes of the Roman Empire (114–242 C.E.)*. London.

Rostovtzeff, M. I. (1932) *Caravan Cities*. Translated by D. and T. Rice. New York.

(1943) 'The Parthian shot', *AJA* 47: 174–87.

(1943/4) 'Res Gestae Divi Saporis and Dura', *Berytus* 8: 17–60.

Rothstein, G. (1968) *Die Dynastie der Lahmiden in al-Ḥīra. Ein Versuch zur arabisch-persischen Geschichte zur Zeit der Sasaniden*. Berlin. (First edition 1899).

Rougé, J. (1966) *Expositio totius mundi et gentium. Introduction, texte critique, traduction, notes et commentaire*. Paris.

Rubin, B. (1960–95) *Das Zeitalter Iustinians*. Vol. i, 1960; Vol. ii *Aus dem Nachlass* ed. by C. Capizzi. Berlin.

Rubin, Z. (1975) 'Dio, Herodian and Severus' second Parthian War', *Chiron* 5: 419–41.

(1986) 'Diplomacy and war in the relations between Byzantium and the Sassanids in the fifth century AD', in Freemann and Kennedy (1986): 677–95.

(1995) 'The reforms of Khusro Anūshirwān', in *The Byzantine and Early Islamic Near East. States, Resources, Armies. Studies in Late Antiquity and Early Islam*. Vol. iii, ed. A. Cameron. Princeton: 227–97.

(1998) 'The Roman Empire in the res gestae divi Saporis – the Mediterranean world in Sasanian propaganda', in *Ancient Iran and the Mediterranean World. Proceedings of an International Conference in Honour of J. Wolski held at the Jagiellonian University, Crakow, in September 1996*, ed. E. Dabrowa. Crakow: 177–85.

Ruffing, K. (1999) 'Wege in den Osten. Die Routen des römischen Süd- und Osthandels (1. bis 2. Jahrhundert n. Chr.)', in *Stuttgarter Kolloquium zur Historischen Geographie des Altertums 7, 1999: Zu Wasser und zu Land. Handelswege in der antiken Welt*, eds. E. Olshausen and H. Sonnabend. Stuttgart: 360–75.

Russell, J. R. (1990) 'Kartīr and Mānī: A Shamanistic model of their conflict', in *Iranica Varia. Papers in Honor of E. Yarshater*. ActIr 30. Leiden: 180–93.

(2001) 'The Persian invasion of Syria/Palestine and Asia Minor in the reign of Heraclius: archaeological and numismatic evidence', in *The Dark Centuries of Byzantium (7th–9th c.)*, ed. E. Kontoura-Galake. Athens: 41–71.

Sachau, E. (1907) 'Von den rechtlichen Verhältnissen der Christen im Sasanidenreich', *Mitteilungen des Seminars für orientalische Sprachen zu Berlin* 10, 2: 69–95.

Said, E. W. (1978) *Orientalism*. London.

Sako, L. (1986) *Le rôle de la hiérarchie syriaque orientale dans les rapports diplomatiques entre la Perse et Byzance aux Ve–VIIe siècles*. Paris.

Samolin, W. (1957–8) 'Some notes on the Avar problem', *Central Asiatic Journal* 3: 62–5.

Sancisi-Weerdenburg. H. (1983) *The Zedan and the Ka'bah*. AMI. Erg.Bd. 10. Berlin.

Sayılı, A. (1965) 'Gondeshapur', *EI* ii²: 1119–20.

Schenk Graf von Stauffenberg, A. (1931) *Die römische Kaisergeschichte bei Malalas*. Griechischer Text der Bücher ix–xii und Untersuchungen. Stuttgart.

Schieber, A. S. (1979) 'Antony and Parthia', *RstorAnt* 9: 105–24.

Schippmann, K. (1971) *Die iranischen Feuerheiligtümer*. Berlin.

(1980) *Grundzüge der parthischen Geschichte*. Darmstadt.

(1990) *Grundzüge der Geschichte des sasanidischen Reiches*. Darmstadt.

Schlumberger, D. (1935) Le dévelopment urbain de Palmyre, *Berytus* 2: 149–67.

(1939) 'Bornes frontières de la Palmyrène', *Syria* 20: 43–73; Nr. 13.

Schlumberger, J. (1974) *Die Epitome de Caesaribus. Untersuchungen zur heidnischen Geschichtsschreibung des 4. Jahrhunderts n. Chr*. Munich.

Schmidt, K. (2002) *Friede durch Vertrag. Der Friedensvertrag von Kadesch von 1270 v. Chr., der Friede des Antalkidas von 386 v. Chr. und der Friedensvertrag zwischen Byzanz und Persien von 562 v. Chr*. Frankfurt am Main.

Schmitt, R. (2000) *Die iranischen Sprachen in Geschichte und Gegenwart*. Wiesbaden.

Schneider, R. M. (1998) 'Die Faszination des Feindes. Bilder der Parther und des Orients in Rom', in Wiesehöfer (1998a): 95–147.

Schöffler, H. H. (1979) *Die Akademie von Gondischapur. Aristoteles auf dem Weg in den Orient*. Stuttgart.

Schönebeck, H. v. (1937) 'Die zyklische Ordnung der Triumphreliefs am Galeriusbogen in Saloniki', *ByzZ* 37: 361–71.

Schottky, M. (1989) *Media Atropatene und Gross-Armenien in hellenistischer Zeit*. Bonn.

(1991) 'Parther, Meder und Hyrkanier. Eine Untersuchung der dynastischen und geographischen Verflechtungen im Iran des 1. Jhs. n. Chr.', *AMI* 24: 61–134.

(1994) Dunkle Punkte in der armenischen Königsliste, *AMI* 27: 223–35.

Schreiner, P. (1983) 'Theophylaktos Simokates und das Perserbild der Byzantiner im 6. und 7. Jahrhundert', *ZDMG* Suppl. 5: 301–6.

(1985) *Theophylaktos Simokates. Geschichte*. Übersetzt und erläutert. Stuttgart.

Schrier, O. J. (1992) 'Syriac evidence for the Romano-Persian War of 421–422', *GBRS* 33: 75–86.

Schuol, M. (2000) *Die Charakene. Ein mesopotamisches Königreich in hellenistisch-parthischer Zeit*. Oriens et Occidens Bd. 1. Stuttgart.

Schwaigert, W. (1989) *Das Christentum in Hūzistān im Rahmen der frühen Kirchengeschichte Persiens bis zur Synode von Seleukeia-Ktesiphon im Jahre 410*. Marburg.

Schwarte, K.-H. (1994) 'Diokletians Christengesetz', in *E fontibus haurire. FS H. Chantraine,* ed. R. Günther and S. Rebenich. Paderborn: 203–40.

Scott, R. (1992) 'Diplomacy in the sixth century, the evidence of John Malalas', in *Byzantine Diplomacy: Papers from the Twenty-Fourth Spring Symposium of Byzantine Studies,* eds. S. Franklin and J. Shepard. Aldershot: 159–66.

Seager, R. (1996) 'Ammianus and the status of Armenia in the peace of 363', *Chiron* 26: 275–84.

(1997) 'Perceptions of eastern frontier policy in Ammianus, Libanius and Julian (337–363)', *CQ* 47: 253–68.

Segal, J. B. (1955) 'Mesopotamian communities from Julian to the rise of Islam', *PBA* 41: 127.

(1970) *Edessa. 'The Blessed City'*. Oxford.

Sellheim, R. (1994) 'Taq i-Bustan und Kaiser Julian (361–363)', *Oriens* 34: 354–66.

Sellwood, C. D. (1985) 'Adiabene', *EncIr* I: 459–65.

Seston, W. (1939) 'Le roi sassanide Narsès, les Arabes et le Manichéisme', in *Mélanges syriens offerts à R. Dussaud*. T.I. Paris: 227–34. (German tr. in Widengren (1977): 362–73.)

(1940) 'De l'authenticité et de la date de l'édit de Dioclétien contre les Manichéens', in *Mélanges de philologie, de littérature et d'histoire anciennes offerts à A. Ernout*. Paris: 345–54 (reprinted in Widengren (1977): 374–84).

(1946) *Dioclétien et la tétrarchie. I: guerres et réformes (284–300)*. Paris.

Sevcenko, I. (1992) 'Re-reading Constantine Porphyrogenitus', in *Byzantine Diplomacy: Papers from the Twenty-Fourth Spring Symposium of Byzantine Studies*, eds. J. Shepard and S. Franklin. Aldershot: 167–95.

Sezgin, F. (1967) *Geschichte des arabischen Schrifttums*. Vol. I. Leiden.

(1990) *Geschichte des arabischen Schrifttums*. Vol. III. Leiden.

Shahbazi, A. Sh. (1986) 'Army. 5. The Sasanian period', *EncIr* II: 496–99.

(1989) 'Bahram VI Cobin', *EncIr* III: 519–22.

(1990) 'Byzantine-Iranian relations', *EncIr* IV: 588–99.

(1991) *Ferdowsī*. Costa Mesa.

(1992) 'Carrhae', *EncIr* 5: 9–13.

(2002a) 'Gondēšāpūr I: The city', *EncIr* XII 2: 131–3.

(2002b) 'Recent speculations on the "traditional date of Zoroaster"', *StIr* 31.1: 7–45.

(2002c) 'Early Sasanian's claim to Achaemenid heritage', *Nāme-ye Irān Bāstān* 1/1 (2001) [2002]: 61–73.

Shahîd, I. (1965) 'Ghassān', *EI* II²: 1020–1.

(1971a) 'Al-Hīra', *EI* III²: 462–3.

(1971b) *The Martyrs of Najran: New Documents*. Subsidia Hagigraphica 49. Brussels.

(1984a) *Rome and the Arabs. A Prolegomenon to the Study of Byzantium and the Arabs*. Washington, D.C.

(1984b) *Byzantium and the Arabs in the Fourth Century*. Washington, D.C.

(1986) 'Lakhmids', *EI* v²: 632–4.

(1988) *Byzantium and the Semitic Orient before the Rise of Islam*. London.

(1995a) *Byzantium and the Arabs in the Sixth Century*. Vol. I, part 1: *Political and Military History*; part 2: *Ecclesiastical History*. Washington, D.C.

(1995b) 'Al-Numān (III) B. Al-Mundhir', *EI* VIII: 119–20.

(2000) 'Byzantium and the Arabs in the sixth century: à propos of a recent review', *ByzF* 26: 125–60.

(2002) *Byzantium and the Arabs in the Sixth Century*. Vol. II, part 1: *Toponyms, Monuments*. Washington, D.C.

Shaked, Sh. (1990) 'Administrative functions of priests in the Sasanian period', in *Proceedings of the First European Conference of Iranian Studies I*, eds. Gh. Gnoli and A. Panaino. Rome: 262–74.

Shaki, M. (1978) 'The social doctrine of Mazdak in the light of Middle Persian evidence', *ArOr* 46: 289–306.

Shepherd, D. (1983) 'Sasanian art', *CHI* III. 2: 1055–1112.

Sherwin-White, A. N. (1977) 'Ariobarzanes, Mithridates and Sulla', *CQ* 27: 173–83.

(1984) *Roman Foreign Policy in the East 168 B.C. to A.D. 1.* London.

Sidebotham, S. E. (1986a) 'Ports of the Red Sea and the Arabia-India trade', *MBAH* 5.2: 16–36.

(1986b) *Roman Economic Policy in the Erythra Thalassa.* Mnemosyne Suppl. 91. Leiden.

(1989) 'Ports of the Red Sea and the Arabia-India trade', in French and Lightfoot (1989): 485–509.

(1996) 'Roman interests in the Red Sea and the Indian Ocean', in Reade (1996): 287–308.

Simpson, St. J. (2000) 'Mesopotamia in the Sasanian period: Settlement patterns, arts and crafts', in *Mesopotamia and Iran in the Parthian and Sasanian Periods*, ed. J. Curtis. London: 57–66.

Sinor, D. (1990a) 'The establishment and dissolution of the Türk Empire', in *The Cambridge History of Early Inner Asia*, ed. D. Sinor. Cambridge: 285–316.

(1990b) 'The Hun period', in *The Cambridge History of Early Inner Asia*, ed. D. Sinor. Cambridge: 177–205.

Skjaervo, P. O. (1983) *The Sassanian Inscription of Paikuli.* Part 3.2: Commentary. Wiesbaden.

Smith, R. (1999) 'Telling tales. Ammianus' narrative of the Persian expedition of Julian', in Drijvers and Hunt (1999): 89–104.

Smith, S. (1954) 'Events in Arabia in the sixth century', *BSOAS* 16: 425–68.

Sommer, M. (2003a) *Hatra. Geschichte und Kultur einer Karawanenstadt im römisch-parthischen Mesopotamien.* Sonderband AW. Mainz am Rhein.

(2003b) 'Hatra – imperiale und regionale Herrschaft an der Steppengrenze', *Klio* 85: 384–98.

(2004) *Die Soldatenkaiser.* Darmstadt.

Sonnabend, H. (1986) *Fremdenbild und Politik. Vorstellung der Römer von Ägypten und dem Partherreich in der späten Republik und frühen Kaiserzeit.* Frankfurt am Main, Bern and New York.

Speck, P. (1988) *Das geteilte Dossier. Beobachtungen zu den Nachrichten über die Regierung des Kaisers Herakleios und die seiner Söhne bei Theophanes und Nikephoros.* ΠΟΙΚΙΛΑ BYZANTINA 9. Bonn.

(1990) 'Review of Mango (1990)', *ByzZ* 83: 471–8.

(2000) *Varia III: Beiträge von P. Speck mit zwei Nachträgen von A. Berger und O. Kresten.* ΠΟΙΚΙΛΑ BYZANTINA 18. Bonn.

Speidel, M. P. (1980) 'The Caucasus frontier. Second century garrisons at Asparus, Petra and Phasis', *Roman Frontier Studies 1979*: 657–60.

(1984) 'Cataphractii, clibanarii and the rise of the later Roman mailed cavalry', *EA* 4: 151–6.

(1985) 'Valerius Valerianus in charge of Septimius Severus' Mesopotamian campaign', *CP* 80: 321–6.

Speyer, W. (1992) 'Barbar I', *RAC Suppl. I* 5/6: 811–95.

Sprengling, M. (1940a) 'Kartir, Founder of Sasanian Zoroastrianism', *American Journal of Semitic Languages and Literatures* 57: 197–228.

(1940b) 'Shapuhr I, the Great on the Kaabah of Zoroaster (KZ)', *American Journal of Semitic Languages and Literatures* 57: 360–71.

(1953) *Third Century Iran. Sapor und Kartir.* Chicago.

Springberg-Hinsen, M. (1989) *Die Zeit vor dem Islam in arabischen Universalgeschichten des 9. bis 12. Jahrhunderts.* Religionswissenschaftliche Studien 13. Würzburg.

Spuler, B. (1952) *Iran in früh-islamischer Zeit.* Wiesbaden.

(ed.) (1961) *Religionsgeschichte des Orients in der Zeit der Weltreligionen.* HdO I 8.2. Leiden.

Standish, J. F. (1970) 'The Caspian Gates', *G&R* 178: 17–24.

Stausberg, M. (2002) *Die Religion Zarathustras. Geschichte – Gegenwart – Rituale.* Stuttgart, Berlin and Cologne.

Stein, A. (1941) 'The ancient trade route past Hatra and the Roman posts', *JRAS* 9: 299–316.

Stein, E. (1949) *Histoire du Bas-Empire.* Vol. II. *De la disparation de l'empire d'occident à la mort de Justinien (476–565)*, ed. J.-R. Palanque. Paris.

Stewart, J. (1928) *Nestorian Missionary Enterprise.* Edinburgh.

Stock, K. (1978a) 'Yazdan-Friy-Sapur. Ein Grossgesandter Sapurs III. Ein Beitrag zur persisch-römischen Diplomatie und Diplomatik', *StIr* 7: 165–82.

(1978b) 'Comes Commerciorum. Ein Beitrag zur spätantiken Verwaltungsgeschichte', *Francia* 6: 599–609.

Stoll, O. (1998) 'Römische Militärarchitekten und ihre Bedeutung für den Technologietransfer', in *Religion – Wirtschaft – Technik. Althistorische Beiträge zur Entstehung neuer Strukturmuster im historischen Raum Nordafrika/ Kleinasien/Syrien.* Mainzer Althistorische Studien vol. I, ed. L. Schumacher. St. Katharinen: 254–70.

Stolte, B. H. (1971a) 'The death of the emperor Gordian III and the reliability of the Res Gestae Divi Saporis', in *Acta of the Fifth International Congress of Greek and Latin Epigraphy Cambridge 1967.* Oxford: 385–6.

(1971b) 'The Roman Emperor Valerian and Sapor I, King of Persia', *RstorAnt* 1: 157–62.

Stoneman, R. (1992) *Palmyra and its Empire. Zenobia's Revolt against Rome.* Ann Arbor.

Stratos, A. N. (1967) 'The Avars' attack on Byzantium in the year 626', in *Polychordia: Festschrift Franz Dölger.* BF 2 (1967): 370–6.

(1968–72) *Byzantium in the Seventh Century.* Vol. I: 602–34. Translated by M. Ogilvie-Grant; vol. II: 634–41. Translated by H. T. Hionides. Amsterdam.

Straub, J. (1980) Scurra barbarus, *BHAC* 1977/78. Antiquitas IV 14: 233–53.

(1985) 'Die Sassaniden als aemuli imperii im Urteil des Ammianus Marcellinus', in *From Late Antiquity to the Early Byzantium. Proceedings of the Byzantological Symposium in the 16th International Eirene Conference.* Prag: 37–40 (reprinted in J. Straub (1986): 218–22).

(1986) (ed.), *Regeneratio imperii II. Aufsätze über Roms Kaisertum und Reich im Spiegel der heidnischen und christlichen Publizistik.* Darmstadt.

Streck, M. (1997) 'Istakhr', *EI²* iv: 219–22.

Strobel, K. (1989) 'Jüdisches Patriarchat, Rabbinentum und Priesterdynastie von Emesa: Historische Phänomene innerhalb des Imperium Romanum der Kaiserzeit', *Ktema* 14: 39–77.

(1993) *Das Imperium Romanum im 3. Jahrhundert. Modell einer historischen Krise? Zur Frage der Strukturen breiterer Bevölkerungsschichten in der Zeit von Marc Aurel bis zum Ausgang des 3. Jhs. n. Chr.* Stuttgart.

(2001) 'Das Imperium Romanum 180–284/85 n. Chr. – Kontinuitäten, langfristiger Wandel und historische Brüche', in *Das Altertum. Vom Alten Orient zur Spätantike*, eds. E. Erdmann and K. Uffelmann. Idstein: 239–78.

Sundermann, W. (1963) *Die sasanidische Herrscherlegitimation und ihre Bedingungen.* Berlin.

(1986) 'Mani, India and the Manichaean religion', *South Asian Studies* 2: 11–19.

(1990) 'Shapur's coronation', *Bulletin of the Asia Institute N. S.* 4: 295–9.

Suolathi, J. (1947) *On the Persian Sources Used by the Byzantine Historian Agathias.* Studia Orientalia. Helsinki.

Swain, S. (1993) 'Greek into Palmyrene. Odaenath as corrector totius orientis?', *ZPE* 99: 157–64.

(1999) *Oxford Readings in the Greek Novel.* Oxford.

Sykes, P. (1921) *A History of Persia.* Vol. 1. 2nd edn. London.

Syme, R. (1968) *Ammianus and the Historia Augusta.* Oxford.

Synelli, K. (1986) Οι διπλοματικές σχέσεις Βυζαντίον και Περσίαςέως τον στ'αιώνα. Athens.

Szádeczky-Kardoss, S. (1979) 'Bemerkungen zur Geschichte (Chronologie und Topographie) der sassanidisch-byzantinischen Kriege', in *Studies in the Sources on the History of Pre-Islamic Central Asia*, ed. J. Harmatta. Budapest: 113–18.

Szepessy, T. (1984) 'Die Aithiopika des Heliodoros und der griechische sophistische Liebesroman', in *Beiträge zum griechischen Liebesroman*, ed. H. Gärtner. Hildesheim et al.: 432–50.

Tafazzoli, A. (2000) *Sasanian Society. I. Warriors. II. Scribes. III. Dehqans*, New York.

Tanabe, K. (1981) 'An identification of the chain-armoured equestrian image at the larger grotto, Taq-i Bustan', *Orient* 17: 105–18.

(1991) 'Bahrām III. Sakanshah und shakanshak?', *Bulletin of Ancient Orient Museum* 12: 7–39.

Tardieu, M. (1990) *Les paysages reliques. Routes et haltes syriennes d'Isidore à Simplicius.* Paris.

Täubler, E. (1964) *Imperium Romanum. Studien zur Entwicklungsgeschichte des römischen Reiches.* Vol. 1: *Die Staatsverträge und Vertragsverhältnisse.* Rome.

Teitler, H. (1999) 'Viva vel lecta? Ammianus on Persia and the Persians', in Drijvers and Hunt (1999): 216–23.

Teixidor, J. (1979) *The Pantheon of Palmyra.* Leiden.

(1984) *Un port romain du désert: Palmyre.* Paris.

(1995) 'Conséquences politiques et culturelles de la victoire sassanide à Nisibe', in Frézouls and Jacquemin (1995): 499–510.

Thompson, E. A. (1950) 'The foreign policies of Theodosius II and Marcian', *Hermathena* 76: 58–75.

(1996) *The Huns* (rev. P. J. Heather). Oxford.

Thomson, R. W. (1976) *Agathangelos. History of the Armenians.* Albany.

(1980) *Moses Khorenats'i. History of the Armenians. Translation and Commentary on the Literary Sources.* 2nd edn. Cambridge, Mass. and London.

(1982) *Elishe, History of Vardan and the Armenian War. Translation and Commentary by R. W. Thomson.* Cambridge.

(1991) *The History of Lazar P'arpec'i.* Atlanta.

(1999) *The Armenian History attributed to Sebeos.* Translated, with notes, by R. W. Thomson. Historical Commentary by J. Howard-Johnston. Assistance from T. Greenwood. Part 1. Liverpool.

(2000) 'Armenia in the fifth and sixth century', in *CAH* xiv: 662–77.

(2001) *The Armenian Adaptation of the Ecclesiastical History of Socrates Scholasticus (commonly known as 'The Shorter Socrates'). Translation of the Armenian Text and Commentary.* Leuven, Paris and Sterling, VA.

Thorley, J. (1969) 'The development of trade between the Roman Empire and the East under Augustus', *G&R* N. S. 16: 209–23.

Timpe, D. (1962) 'Die Bedeutung der Schlacht von Carrhae', *MH* 19: 104–29.

(1975) 'Zur augusteischen Partherpolitik zwischen 30 und 20 v. Chr.', *WJA* N. F. 1: 155–69.

Tinnefeld, F. (1971) *Kategorien der Kaiserkritik in der byzantinischen Historiographie von Prokop bis Niketas Choniates.* Munich.

(1993) 'Ceremonies for foreign ambassadors at the court of Byzantium and their political background', *ByzF* 19: 193–213.

Toumanoff, C. (1954) 'Christian Caucasia between Byzantium and Iran', *Traditio* 10: 109–90.

(1963) *Studies in Christian Caucasian History.* Georgetown.

(1969) 'The third century Armenian Arsacids – a chronological and genealogical commentary', *REtArm* 6: 233–81.

(1971) 'Caucasia and Byzantium', *Traditio* 27: 111–58.

Toynbee, A. (1973) *Constantine Porphyrogenitus and his World.* Oxford.

Treadgold, W. (1997) *A History of the Byzantine State and Society.* Stanford, CA.

(2001) *A Concise History of Byzantium.* New York.

Trombley, F. (1999) 'Ammianus Marcellinus and fourth-century warfare: a protector's approach to historical narrative', in Drijvers and Hunt (1999): 17–28.

(2005) 'The late Roman practice of war on the Syrian frontier (AD 502–641)', in *Krieg – Gesellschaft – Institution. Beiträge zu einer vergleichenden Kriegsgeschichte,* eds. B. Meißner, O. Schmitt, and M. Sommer. Berlin: 387–416.

Trümpelmann, L. (1975) 'Triumph über Julian Apostata', *JNG* 25: 107–11.

(1992) *Zwischen Persepolis und Firuzabad. Gräber, Paläste und Felsreliefs im Alten Persien.* Mainz am Rhein.

(1994) *Iranische Denkmäler.* Lieferung 6. Reihe II: Iranische Felsreliefs. B. Das sasanidische Felsrelief von Dārāb. Berlin.

Tucci, M. J. (1992) *The Battle of Carrhae: The Effects of a Military Disaster on the Roman Empire.* Columbia, Miss.

Turcan, R. (1966) 'L'abandon de Nisibe et l'opinion publique (363 ap. J. C.)', in *Mélanges d'archéologie et d'histoire offerts à André Piganiol.* Vol. II, ed. R. Chevalier. Paris: 875–90.

Turtledove, H. (1977) *The Immediate Successors of Justinian. A Study in the Persian Problem.* Los Angeles.

(1983) 'Justin II's observance of Justinian's Persian treaty of 562', *ByzZ* 76: 292–301.

Tyler, P. (1975) *The Persian War of the Third Century AD and Roman Imperial Monetary Policy AD 253–263.* Historia Einzelschriften 23. Wiesbaden.

Tyler-Smith, S. (2000) 'Coinage in the name of Yazdgird III (AD 632–651) and the Arab conquest of Iran', *NC* 160: 135–70.

Vanden Berghe, L. (1984) *Reliefs rupestres de l'Iran ancien.* Brussels.

van de Mierop, M. (1997) 'On writing a history of the ancient Near East', *Bibliotheca Orientalis* 54: 285–306.

Van der Vin, J. P. A. (1981) 'The return of Roman ensigns from Parthia', *Bulletin Antieke Beshaving* 56: 117–39.

van der Walk, M. (1941) 'Remarques sur la date des Éthiopiques', *Mnemosyne* 9: 97–100.

van Rompay, L. (1995) 'Impetuous martyrs? The situation of the Persian Christians in the last years of Yazdgard I (419–420)', in *Martyrium in Multidisciplinary Perspective. Memorial Louis Reekmans,* eds. M. Lamboigts and P. van Deun. Louvain: 363–75.

van Wickevoort Crommelin, B. (1998) 'Die Parther und die parthische Geschichte bei Pompeius Trogus – Iustin', in Wiesehöfer (1998a): 259–77.

Vasiliev, A. A. (1935–50) *Byzance et les arabes,* tr. H. Grégoire and M. Canard. 2 vols. Brussels.

(1950) *Justin the First. An Introduction to the Epoch of Iustinian the Great.* Dumbarton Oaks Studies 1. Cambridge.

Veh, O. (ed.) (1970) *Prokop. Perserkriege. Griechisch-Deutsch.* Munich.

(1978) *Prokop. Gotenkrieg. Griechisch-Deutsch.* 2nd edn. Munich.

(1990) *Zosimos. Neue Geschichte. Übersetzt und eingeleitet von O. Veh, durchgesehen und erläutert von St. Rebenich.* Munich.

Verosta, S. (1964) 'International law in Europe and Western Asia between 100 and 650 AD', *Recueil de cours. Académie de droit international* 113. Leiden.

(1965) 'Die oströmisch-persischen Verträge von 562 n. Chr. und ihre Bedeutung für das Völkerrecht', *AAWW* 102: 153–6.

Vivian, M. R. (1987) *A Letter to Shapur: The Effect of Constantine's Conversion on Roman-Persian Relations.* Ann Arbor.

von Schönebeck, H. (1937) 'Die zyklische Ordnung der Triumphreliefs am Galeriusbogen in Saloniki', *ByzZ* 37: 361–71.

von Wickevoort-Crommelin, B. (1994) 'Euphratgrenze (römisch)', *DNP* 4: 272–3.

von Wissmann, H. (1964) 'Himyar. Ancient history', *Le Muséon* 77: 429–99.

Wada, H. (1970) *Prokops Rätselwort Serinda und die Verpflanzung des Seidenbaus von China nach dem oströmischen Reich.* Cologne.

Wagner, J. (1983) 'Provincia Osrhoenae. New archaeological finds illustrating the military organization under the Severan Dynasty', in Mitchell (1983): 103–30.

    (1985) *Die Römer an Euphrat und Tigris.* Sondernummer AW 16. Mainz am Rhein.

Walker, J. Th. (2002) 'The limits of late antiquity: philosophy between Rome and Iran', *The Ancient World* 33.1: 45–9.

Walser, G. (1984) *Hellas und Iran. Studien zu den griechisch-persischen Beziehungen vor Alexander.* Darmstadt.

Warmington, B. H. (1977) 'Objectives and strategy in the Persian War of Constantius II', in *Limes. Acts of the XI Limes Congress 1976*, ed. J. Fitz. Budapest: 509–20.

    (1986) 'The source of some Constantinian documents in Eusebius' Ecclesiastical History and Life of Constantine', *Studia Patristica* 18.1: 93–8.

Watt, J. W. (2000) *The Chronicle of Pseudo-Joshua the Stylite*, translated by J. W. Watt and F. Trombley. Liverpool.

Wheeler, B.-M. (1991) 'Imagining the Sasanian capture of Jerusalem', *OCP* 57: 69–85.

Whitby, L. M. (1983) 'Arzanene in the late sixth century', in Mitchell (1983): 205–18.

    (1986a) 'Procopius and the development of defences in Upper Mesopotamia', in Freeman and Kennedy (1986): 717–35.

    (1986b) 'Procopius' description of Dara (Buildings II, 1–3)', in Freeman and Kennedy (1986): 737–83.

    (1988) *The Emperor Maurice and his Historian: Theophylact Simocatta in Persian and Balkan Warfare.* Oxford.

Whitby, L. M. and Whitby, M. (1986) *The History of Theophylact Simocatta. An English Translation with Introduction and Notes.* Oxford.

    (1989) *Chronicon Paschale 284–628. Translated with Notes and Introduction.* Liverpool.

Whitby, M. (1995) 'Recruitment in Roman armies from Justinian to Heraclius (c. 565–615)', in Cameron (1995): 61–124.

    (1998) 'Defender of the cross: Georgia of Pisidia on the Emperor Heraclius and his deputees, in *Propaganda and Power. The Role of Panegyric in Late Antiquity*, ed. M. Whitby. Leiden: 247–73.

    (2000) *The Ecclesiastical History of Euagrius Scholasticus.* Translated Texts for Historians 33. Liverpool.

Whitehouse, D. (1996) 'Sasanian Maritime Activity', in Reade (1996): 339–49.

Whitehouse, D. and Williamson, A. (1973) 'Sasanian maritime trade', *Iran* 11: 29–49.

Whittaker, C. R. (1994) *Frontiers of the Roman Empire.* Baltimore and London.

Whittow, M. (1995/9) 'Rome and the Jafnids: writing the history of a sixth-century tribal dynasty', in *The Roman and Byzantine Near East*. 2 vols., ed. J. H. Humphrey. Portsmouth: Vol. II, 207–24.

Widengren, G. (1952) 'Xosrau Anōšurvān, les Hephthalites et les peuples turcs. Ètudes préliminaires des sources', *Orientalia Suecana* 1: 69–94.

(1961) *Mani und der Manichäismus*. Stuttgart.

(1965) *Die Religion Irans*. Stuttgart.

(1971) 'The establishment of the Sasanian Dynasty in the light of new evidence', in Persia (1971): 711–82.

(1976) 'Iran, der grosse Gegner Roms: Königsgewalt, Feudalismus, Militärwesen', *ANRW* II 9.1: 219–306.

(ed.) (1977) *Der Manichäismus*. WdF 168. Darmstadt.

(1983) 'Sources of Parthian and Sasanian history', *CHI* III. 2: 1261–83.

Wiesehöfer, J. (1982) 'Die Anfänge sassanidischer Westpolitik und der Untergang Hatras', *Klio* 64: 437–47.

(1986a) 'Ardašīr I – History', *EncIr* 4: 371–6.

(1986b) 'Iranische Ansprüche an Rom auf ehemals achaimenidische Territorien', *AMI N. F.* 19: 177–85.

(1989) 'l-yṭlb ṯr 'byh. Hormizd II. und Rom', in *Migratio et Commutatio. FS Th. Pekáry*, eds. H.-J. Drexhage and J. Sünskes. St. Katharinen: 68–71.

(1993) 'Geteilte Loyalitäten. Religiöse Minderheiten des 3. und 4. Jahrhunderts n. Chr. im Spannungsfeld zwischen Rom und dem sāsānidischen Iran', *Klio* 75: 362–82.

(1994) 'Zum Nachleben von Achaimeniden und Alexander in Iran', in *AchHist* VII: 389–97.

(1996) ' "King of kings" and "philhellên": kingship in Arsacid Iran', in *Aspects of Hellenistic Kingship*, eds. P. Bilde et al. Aarhus: 55–66.

(ed.) (1998a) *Das Partherreich und seine Zeugnisse. Beiträge des internationalen Colloquiums Eutin (27.– 30. Juni 1996)*. Historia Einzelschriften 12. Stuttgart.

(1998b) 'Mare Erythraeum, Sinus Persicus und Fines Indiae. Der Indische Ozean in hellenistischer und römischer Zeit', in *Der indische Ozean in historischer Perspektive*, ed. St. Conermann. Hamburg: 10–36.

(1998c) 'Istachr', *DNP* v: 1145–6.

(1998d) 'Gundeshapur', *DNP* v: 10.

(2001) *Ancient Persia from 550 BC to 650 AD*. Translated by A. Azodi. 2nd edn. London and New York. (German ed. of 1994, *Das antike Persien. Von 550 v. Chr. bis 650 n. Chr.* Zurich and Munich.)

(2005) 'Rome as enemy of Iran', in *Cultural Borrowings and Ethnic Appropriations in Antiquity*, ed. E. S. Gruen. (Oriens et Occidens 8) Stuttgart: 105–20.

Wiesehöfer, J. and Huyse, Ph. (eds.) (2006) *Īrān und Anīrān. Studien zu den Beziehungen zwischen dem Sasanidenreich und der Mittelmeerwelt. Beiträge des Internationalen Colloquiums in Euien, 8–9 Juni 2000*. Stuttgart.

Wiessner, G. (1967) *Untersuchungen zur syrischen Literaturgeschichte I: Zur Märtyrerüberlieferung aus der Christenverfolgung Schapurs II*. AAG. Ph.-h. Kl. 3. Folge Nr. 67. Göttingen.

Wiita, J. E. (1977) 'The ethnika in Byzantine military treatises', Ph. D. diss. University of Minnesota.

Wilcox, P. and McBride, A. (1986) *Rome's Enemies (3): Parthians and Sasanid Persians.* London.

Will, E. (1983) 'Le développement urbain de Palmyre', *Syria* 60: 69–81.

(1992) *Les Palmyréniens. La venise des sables.* Paris.

Williams, A. (1972) 'Persian Gulf commerce in the Sassanian period and the first two centuries of Islam', *BCHI* 9/10: 97–109.

Winkelmann, F. (1991) *Euseb von Kaisareia. Der Vater der Kirchengeschichte.* Berlin.

Winkler, J. J. (1982) 'The mendacity of Kalasiris and the narrative strategy of Heliodoros' *Aithiopika*', *YCS* 27: 93–158.

Winter, E. (1987) 'Handel und Wirtschaft in sāsānidisch – (ost-)römischen Verträgen und Abkommen', *MBAH* VI 2: 46–74.

(1988) *Die sāsānidisch-römischen Friedensverträge des 3. Jahrhunderts n. Chr. – Ein Beitrag zum Verständnis der außenpolitischen Beziehungen zwischen den beiden Großmächten.* Frankfurt.

(1989a) 'Legitimität als Herrschaftsprinzip: Kaiser und "König der Könige" im wechselseitigen Verkehr', in *Migratio et Commutatio. FS Th. Pekáry*, eds. H.-J. Drexhage and J. Sünskes. St. Katharinen: 72–92.

(1989b) 'On the regulation of the Eastern frontier of the Roman Empire in 298 AD', in French and Lightfoot (1989): 555–71.

(1994) 'Die Bedeutung des Grenzraumes für den diplomatischen Verkehr: Das Imperium Romanum und seine östlichen Nachbarn', in *Stuttgarter Kolloquium zur Historischen Geographie des Altertums* 4. Geographica Historica 7, eds. E. Olshausen and H. Sonnabend. Bonn: 589–607.

(1996) *Staatliche Baupolitik und Baufürsorge in den römischen Provinzen des kaiserzeitlichen Kleinasien.* Asia Minor Studien 20. Bonn.

(1998) 'Römischer Ethnozentrismus in der späten Republik. Das Griechenbild Ciceros', *LAVERNA* 9: 46–65.

Winter, E. and Dignas, B. (2001) *Rom und das Perserreich. Zwei Weltmächte zwischen Konfrontation und Koexistenz.* Studienbücher Geschichte und Kultur der Alten Welt. Berlin.

Wirth, G. (1978) 'Julians Perserkrieg. Kriterien einer Katastrophe', in Klein (1978): 455–507.

(1980/1) 'Rom, Parther und Sassaniden. Erwägungen zu den Hintergründen eines historischen Wechselverhältnisses', *AncSoc* 11/12: 305–47.

Wirth, P. (ed.) (1967) *Byzantinische Forschungen 1. Polychordia. Festschrift für F. Dölger.* Amsterdam.

Wissemann, M. (1982) *Die Parther in der augusteischen Dichtung.* Frankfurt and Bern.

(1984) 'Rom und das Kaspische Meer', *RhM N. F.* 127: 166–73.

Witschel, Ch. (1999) *Krise – Rezession – Stagnation? Der Westen des römischen Reiches im 3. Jahrhundert n. Chr.* Frankfurter Althistorische Beiträge Bd. 4. Frankfurt.

Wolski, J. (1957) 'The decay of the Iranian Empire of the Seleucids and the chronology of the Parthian beginnings', *Berytus* 12: 35–52.

(1966) 'Les Achéménides et les Arsacides. Contribution à l'histoire de la formation des traditions iraniennes', *Syria* 43: 65–89.

(1969) 'Der Zusammenbruch der Seleukidenherrschaft in Iran im 3. Jh. v. Chr.', in *Der Hellenismus in Mittelasien*. WdF. Vol. 91, eds. F. Altheim and J. Rehork. Darmstadt: 188–254.

(1976) 'Iran und Rom. Versuch einer historischen Wertung der gegenseitigen Beziehungen', *ANRW* II 9.1: 195–214.

(1983a) 'Les rapports romano-parthes et la question de l'Arménie', *Ktema* 8: 269–77.

(1983b) 'Die Parther und ihre Beziehungen zur griechisch-römischen Kultur', *Klio* 65: 137–49.

(1983c) 'Sur le "philhellénisme" des Arsacides', *Gerion* 1: 145–56.

(1985) 'Dans l'attente d'une nouvelle histoire de l'Iran arsacide', *IrAnt* 20: 163–73.

(1992) 'Sur l'authenticité des traités romano-perses', *IrAnt* 27: 169–87.

(1993) *L'Empire des Arsacides*. AcIr 3, 32. Leiden.

(2003) *Seleucid and Arsacid Studies: A Progress Report on Developments in Source Research*. Crakow.

Woods, D. (1996) 'The Saracen defenders of Constantinople', *GRBS* 37: 259–79.

Wright, W. (1872) *Catalogue of Syriac Manuscripts in the British Museum III*. London.

Wylie, G. (1990) 'How did Trajan succeed in subduing Parthia where Marc Anthony failed?', *AHB* 4, 2: 37–43.

Yarshater, E. (1971) 'Were the Sasanians heirs to the Achaemenids?', in Persia (1971): 517–31.

(1983a) 'Mazdakism', in *CHI* III. 2: 991–1024.

(1983b) 'Iranian national history', in *CHI* III. 1: 359–480.

York, J. M. (1972) 'The image of Philip the Arab', *Historia* 21: 320–32.

Young, F. (1983) *From Nicaea to Chalcedon*. London.

Young, G. K. (2001) *Rome's Eastern Trade. International Commerce and Imperial Policy 31 BC–AD 305*. London and New York.

Yusuf, S. M. (1945) 'The battle of al-Qadisiyya', *Islamic Culture* 19: 1–28.

Yuzbashian, K. N. (1986) 'The chronology of the Armeno-Georgian insurrection against the Sassanians at the end of the vth century', *Palestinskij Sbornik* 28: 51–5.

(1996) 'Le Caucase et les Sassanides', in *Il Caucaso. Cerniera fra culture dal Mediterraneo alla Persia*, ed. Centro Italiano di Studi Sull' alto medioevo. 2 vols. Spoleto: 143–64.

Zaehner, R. C. (1975 [1956]) *The Teachings of the Magi. A Compendium of Zoroastrian Beliefs*. 2nd edn. London.

(1961) *Dawn and Twilight of Zoroastrianism*. London.

Zahrnt, M. (1986) 'Zum Fiskalgesetz von Palmyra', *ZPE* 62: 279–93.

Zakythinos, D. A. (1979) *Byzantinische Geschichte 324–1071*. Vienna, Cologne and Graz.

Zanker, P. (1987) *Augustus und die Macht der Bilder*. Munich.

Zeimal, E. V. (1993) 'The political history of Transoxania', *CHI* III.1: 232–62. (Reprint from 1983.)

Ziegler, K. H. (1964) *Die Beziehungen zwischen Rom und dem Partherreich.* Wiesbaden.

(1972) 'Die Chimäre des internationalen Schiedsgerichts im römisch-persischen Friedensvertrag vom Jahre 562 n. Chr.', *Index* 3: 427–42.

Zimmermann, M. (1999a) *Kaiser und Ereignis. Studien zum Geschichtswerk Herodians.* Vestigia. Vol. 52. Munich.

(1999b) 'Herodians Konstruktion der Geschichte und sein Blick auf das stadtrömische Volk', in *Geschichtsschreibung und politischer Wandel im 3. Jh. n. Chr. Kolloquium zu Ehren K.-E. Petzolds anläßlich seines 80. Geburtstags.* Historia Einzelschriften 127, ed. M. Zimmermann. Stuttgart: 119–43.

Zuckerman, C. (2002) 'Heraclius in 625', *REB* 60: 189–97.

Zyromski, M. (1998) 'The relations between Sassanian Persia and the Roman Empire during the principate: part of the Roman "grand strategy" or only response to crisis?', *EOS* 85: 107–19.

Index of sources

Index of translated sources

Index of names

Index of place names

339

General index